AN INTIMATE AFFAIR

The publisher gratefully acknowledges the generous contribution to this book provided by the General Endowment Fund of the University of California Press Foundation.

An Intimate Affair

WOMEN, LINGERIE, AND SEXUALITY

JILL FIELDS

UNIVERSITY OF CALIFORNIA PRESS
Berkeley Los Angeles London

University of California Press, one of the most distinguished university presses in the United States, enriches lives around the world by advancing scholarship in the humanities, social sciences, and natural sciences. Its activities are supported by the UC Press Foundation and by philanthropic contributions from individuals and institutions. For more information, visit www.ucpress.edu.

The following chapters were previously published in different form and appear here courtesy of their original publishers: chapter 1 as "Erotic Modesty: [Ad]dressing Female Sexuality and Propriety in Open and Closed Drawers, 1800–1930," *Gender & History* 14, no. 3 (November 2002): 492–515; and also in Carole Turbin and Barbara Burman, eds., *Material Strategies: Dress & Gender in Historical Perspectives* (London: Blackwells, 2003); chapter 2 as " 'Fighting the Corsetless Evil': Shaping Corsets & Culture, 1900–1930," *Journal of Social History* 33, no. 2 (Winter 1999): 355–84; and in *Beauty & Business: Commerce, Gender, and Culture in Modern America,* ed. Philip Scranton (New York: Routledge, 2001), 109–41; and chapter 4 as "From Black Venus to Blonde Venus: The Meaning of Black Lingerie," *Women's History Review* 15, no. 4 (September 2006): 611–23, www.tandf.co.uk/journals.

University of California Press
Berkeley and Los Angeles, California

University of California Press, Ltd.
London, England

Library of Congress Cataloging-in-Publication Data
Fields, Jill.
   An intimate affair : women, lingerie, and sexuality / Jill Fields.
     p.   cm.
   Includes bibliographical references and index.
   ISBN 978-0-520-22369-1 (cloth : alk. paper)
   ISBN 978-0-520-25261-5 (pbk. : alk. paper)
   1. Lingerie—History.   2. Women's clothing—History.   3. Clothing and dress—Symbolic aspects.   4. Clothing and dress—Erotic aspects.
5. Advertising—Fashion.   I. Title.
GT2073.F54   2007
391.4′209—dc22   2006021747

Manufactured in the United States of America
16 15 14 13 12 11 10 09 08 07
10 9 8 7 6 5 4 3 2 1

The paper used in this publication meets the minimum requirements of ANSI/NISO Z39.48–1992 (R 1997) *(Permanence of Paper).*

Contents

Illustrations

Acknowledgments

Recognition is a feminist issue, and thus I'm happy to thank the following people whose assistance—intellectual, emotional, and material—contributed to the completion of my book. Of course, any errors remain mine. I also wish to thank everyone who contributed to making the book's illustrations possible. I made every possible effort to determine and give proper credit for each one and will gladly correct any errors or omissions in future editions.

My work on this topic began as a seminar paper while I was a graduate student at the University of Southern California. Its further evolution as a doctoral thesis would not have occurred without the encouragement of my generous and exceptional professors Lois Banner, Steve Ross, and Tania Modleski. Although I did not enter graduate school with the subject of this book in mind, I could not have had a dissertation committee better suited to its fullest development. I am especially grateful to Lois Banner, who, on several occasions when I showed up at her office with a new chapter, immediately sat down to read it, even while serving as department chair. These sessions became impromptu master classes in the art of historical writing and helped me immeasurably. I have also been very fortunate that our research interests have continued to dovetail, for long after my degree was granted, Lois e-mailed or called whenever she came across sources that might be helpful. (They always were.) Steve Ross was also an excellent role model for solid and inventive research, professional integrity, and clear expression of complex ideas. He was a warm and welcoming presence in the history department when I was just beginning my graduate studies, initially in another field. He also became a supportive family friend. Studying feminist and cultural theory with Tania Modleski greatly enriched my ability to identify and make sense of the source materials I found, and the process was so inspiring I wrote a song about it. The research grants I received through the University of Southern California, the Haynes Foundation Fellowship, McVicar Dissertation Fellowship, and Sharon Tedesco Fellowship were an enormous help in completing my dissertation. I also received the Woodrow Wilson Dissertation Grant in Women's Studies, which brought my work to the attention of University of California Press editor Naomi Schneider. Naomi's early interest in publishing this book, and her unflagging support and patience ever since, has been critical to getting it into print. Also at UC Press, Laura Harger was ever-efficient and wonderfully responsive during the production process; Adrienne Harris's enthusiasm and expert copy-editing skills were enormously helpful.

My first extensive foray into the costume archives came after I received the Royal Ontario Museum's (ROM's) Veronika Gervers Research Fellowship in Costume and Textile History. Adrienne Hood, then director of the costume and textile department and now at the University of Toronto, kindly shared with me her extensive expertise in material culture analysis and generally made my stay in Toronto very enjoyable, as did the extended Ann Shteir family. The ROM staff and curators, especially Shannon Elliot, were all extremely helpful and patient, even though I asked to see almost every piece of underwear in their collection. The Stella Blum Research Grant from the Costume Society of America funded research at the Costume Institute at the Metropolitan Museum of Art in New York City. When I arrived there, I was quite surprised that the institute's then-director, the late, wonderful, and prolific Richard Martin, and the institute's current head, Harold Koda, wished to meet this ingenue in costume studies to hear more about my research. Our conversation was a great way to begin my work in New York. In that city, the curators and special collections library staff at the Met and the Fashion Institute of Technology graciously granted my every request to view their artifacts and texts. My travel to Washington, D.C., was supported by the Marshall Fishwick Travel to Popular Culture Collection Grant awarded by the Popular Culture Association and American Culture Association Endowment Fund Program. Historian and Smithsonian costume curator Claudia Brush-Kidwell was extremely helpful, from literally lending a hand while we navigated wooden drawers filled with undergarments around narrow corners in the archives to consulting closely with me once we got them out. At Cornell University, I was able to pore through the fascinating ILGWU materials in a very collegial setting, thanks to Richard Strassberg and the fine staff of the Kheel Center for Labor-Management Documentation. I was very lucky as well to be able to talk with retired undergarment workers at their ILGWU meetings in New

York City and Bayonne, New Jersey, from whom I learned much. Fernanda Perrone at the Rutgers Special Collections Library was an outstanding guide to the feminist art materials there. In addition, the research assistance I received at the Southern California Research Library, the Los Angeles County Museum of Art costume collection, and the Margaret Herrick Library was always the best. I must also thank all the people I stayed with during my many research trips: in New York, Sue Graff, Tom Huhn and Nancy Steele, and the Steinmans; in Washington, D.C., my wonderful cousins Lori Fields and Marlin Risinger and their friends Anne Hollander and Roger McCreery; and in Los Angeles, the always elegant hosts Stephanie Barish and Scott Chamberlin and my ever-lovin' brother, Bill Fields, and his partner, Dan Saunders. Special thanks to Bob Huppert and Bill Rangel, who kept Winston Rodney company while I was away.

I am grateful for insightful comments I received on sections of this book that appeared as chapters, conference papers, and journal articles. I thank scholars R. Ruth Linden, Adrienne Hood, Peter Stearns, Tom Zakim, Patricia Cunningham, Jackson Lears, Stephen Norwood, Pat Seed, Carole Turbin, Barbara Burman, Jessica Weiss, Margaret Finnegan, Tony Michels, Tressa Berman, the editors and anonymous reviewers of the *Journal of Social History* and *Gender and History*, and the exceptional community of historians who form the annual UCLA Teaching Workshop on U.S. Women's History. Eileen Boris, Regina Sanchez-Morantz, and Vicki Ruiz closely read the entire manuscript and provided many thoughtful, smart, and useful suggestions that I did my best to incorporate.

Friends who were always interested in hearing about my ideas, research experiences, and progress include Andrea Scott, Stephanie Barish, Dorrit Vered, Mary Jean, Meryl Geffner, Marty Bridges, Sylvia Savala, Mary Coomes, Dorothy Brinckerhoff, Paul Gilmore, Robert Lloyd, Jim Blechman, and title maestro Glenn Silber. Early on, Emily Feigenson helped me realize during a critical phone conversation that I had already worked out the chapter structure for my dissertation. I began to think of Constance Young as my own personal 1-800 editorial service because she was always willing to draw upon her impeccable understanding of the English language to help me get something right. Colleagues at California State University, Fresno, who have been especially supportive include Loretta Kensinger, Malik Simba, Michelle DenBeste, Jan Slagter, Kathryn Forbes, and Lynn Jacobssen. My conversations with CSU Fresno's greatest treasure, Lillian Faderman, were always enlightening and energizing. In addition, the research assistance I received from my very able graduate students Margaret Wilkins and Cieja Montgomery and by the efficient staff of the Interlibrary Loan Department of the Henry Madden Library was invaluable. I am also very grateful for the support I received in the form of research grants and much-appreciated course releases by CSU Fresno's dean of the College of Social Sciences (formerly Ellen Gruenbaum and currently Luz Gonzalez) and university provost (formerly Michael Ortiz and currently Jeri Echeverria).

I have enjoyed the trust of my sisters, Linda and Jana, and my entire family in the worthiness of this project, and I dedicate this book to my parents, Valerie and Jerry Fields, whose intellectual curiosity and passion for education infuse my own. I also dedicate this book to the memory of my favorite sources. My paternal grandmothers, Tillie Marder Boxbaum and Helen Pollock Fields, wore with aplomb the garments detailed here. In addition, my maternal grandmother, Mildred Rosenstein Schwartz, had an incredible memory for the details of everyday life in the past century. She loved sharing her stories with me as much as I loved hearing them and was always "tickled silly" when her steel-boned girdle set off airport metal detectors. Dedicated ILGWU Local 62 officer Mabel Durham Fuller invited me to stay at her house in upstate New York so that we could talk in depth because, as she put it, "You're helping my union!" I hope I have in some way fulfilled her wish. Finally, I happily thank Ken Mate for his fine editing skills and for providing me a beautiful place to work during semester breaks and weekends in Los Angeles, as well as just the right amount of unbeatable distractions so that I could clear my head while walking with Hercules in Silver Lake, hiking in the Sierras, or exploring the streets of Paris. His intellectual perspectives on lingerie surely enriched my own.

Introduction

Sexual Foundations

Clothes are but a symbol of something hid deep beneath.
Virginia Woolf, *Orlando,* 1928

I didn't get much sleep last night
thinking about underwear.
Lawrence Ferlinghetti, "Underwear," 1961

In February 2005, the Virginia House of Delegates voted 60–34 to ban the intentional display of "below-waist undergarments, intended to cover a person's intimate parts, in a lewd or indecent manner," with violators subject to a fifty-dollar fine. Though the bill's sponsor believed the law was "a vote for character" that would "do something good not only for the state of Virginia, but for this entire country," the proposal instead attracted widespread ridicule, and within a week, the bill quietly died by unanimous bipartisan vote in a state senate committee. In the interim, opponents to the bill, including representatives of the American Civil Liberties Union, pointed out the unconstitutionality of legislating a "state dress code" and also the likelihood of unequal enforcement of a law that seemed to target the baggy-trouser, boxer-short–revealing fashions of young black men, a group already subjected unfairly to greater police scrutiny. However, news reports such as "Show Me Your Thong, Show Me the Money" implied that the bill was also an effort to control the popular fashion among young women of displaying thong underwear worn beneath low-rise jeans. This was certainly the case for a similarly thwarted 2004 Louisiana bill, mocked on *The Daily Show* as "Thong of the South." This bill was likely inspired by a 1998 statute passed in the former Louisiana Confederate state capital of Opelousas, where, the police chief claimed, "You won't find sagging pants." One state legislator's aims went further. He hoped that "if we pull up their pants, we can lift their minds while we're at it."[1]

These recent proposals were not the first efforts to institute state-sponsored fashion police, or to identify clothing as a signifier of morality and mental state. From the sumptuary laws of the early modern era in

Western history to present-day legal enforcement of dress codes in public, at school, and at work, there have been repeated attempts to regulate what people wear. The association of clothing with character and propriety, and the expression through fashion of class status, gender identity, and cultural affiliation, supports such regulatory efforts, as do less formal rules such as the familiar fashion "dos and don'ts" presented in the mass media. In that apparel both symbolizes and constructs individual and group relationships to institutions of power, laws and dress codes that dictate fashions in dress also symbolize and construct means of social control. Yet the widespread attempts throughout history to establish legal and less formal rules of dressing point to an equally long history of challenges to the authority of lawmakers, officials, and tastemakers to determine the fashion of others. In other words, enforcement mechanisms have often failed to prevent people from wearing clothing that authorities considered improper. Clearly, fashion, both as a set of regulatory practices and as a system of signification, has been an arena of social struggle not only about what can be worn but also about what that attire means.

The division between male and female dress has been and remains fundamental to clothing design, and this distinctive apparel has played a central role in constructing gender difference. Clothing thus provides a rich arena in which to explore how masculine and feminine identities take shape and change over time. Yet because the formation of gendered identities takes place within a social order of gender-based inequalities, women's and men's experiences of getting dressed differ in more ways than just which clothes they put on. Dress codes, for example, affect both male and female clothing choices, but because historically there has been greater concern about controlling the sexuality of female bodies, there has been correspondingly greater interest in controlling the dress of women and girls. As one Missouri female high school student said recently in a *St. Louis Post-Dispatch* report on high school dress codes designed to curb "provocative" clothing, "I think they're much stricter on the girls." Such bias was certainly evident in a widely reported 2004 San Diego, California, incident in which a high school assistant principal demanded that female students tell her which kind of underwear they had on before she would permit them to enter a school dance. If a girl admitted to wearing a thong, she was sent home, but if she said otherwise, the vice principal lifted up the student's skirt in front of the other students in line to see if she were telling the truth. The administrator was later demoted and reassigned to another school after outraged parents demanded her removal.[2]

Underwear, although worn next to the body and thus ostensibly hidden from outside view, is a crucial part of the gendered fashion system. Private and sexualized, yet essential to the shaping of the publicly viewed silhouette, intimate apparel—a term in use by 1921—is critical to making bodies feminine. Undergarments are especially significant to feminization of the body because they are associated with sexual anatomy often perceived as vessels of essential femininity. As such, undergarments are broadly understood as powerfully erotic fetish objects. Yet intimate apparel also places the body in ambiguity. Adorned in undergarments, the body is clothed but not dressed. And, as the first layer of clothing, they are also the last barrier to full disclosure of the body. Moreover, intimate apparel's varied construction, from the delicate lace of lingerie to the armor of boned corsetry, provides a range of symbolic and real restraints. The uncertainty, transitory status, body-shaping ability, and multiple forms of intimate apparel heighten the power of underwear and foundation garments to represent the sexualized female body, in whole and in parts, and to signal changing ideals of femininity.[3]

Alterations of undergarment design and function, in dynamic relationship with shifts in outerwear, provide material evidence of larger social changes taking place in women's lives. The history of these garments' evolving shape and purpose thus reveals how women's struggles for self-definition interact with resistant social forces to reconfigure gender distinctions. The decline of the rigid nineteenth-century Victorian corset, for example, was a key factor in the transition to twentieth-century fashion and modern moral codes; the "corsetless" dresses designed by French couturier Paul Poiret in 1908 both drew on and furthered public disenchantment with the rigid corset, which was already under attack by the aesthetic, feminist, and health and hygiene movements. And although most American women had some form of foundation garment in their wardrobes throughout the first half of the twentieth century, the revival of fashionable corsetry after World War II, which was especially vigorous in the 1950s, paralleled the renewed emphasis on domestic femininity in that era. The New Look, presented by Christian Dior in 1947, sparked the corset's return to fashion. Warner's consolidated the trend with its successful introduction of the Merry Widow corset in 1952, timed to the release of a similarly named Hollywood film that included a lengthy scene with Lana Turner costumed in a gleaming white long-line corset and high heels. Such fashionable corsetry manifested nostalgia for an imagined prewar past of more starkly defined gender differentiation when women were more clearly subordinated, while also providing a means for modern middle-class women to embody the twentieth-century ideal—already popular in the 1920s—of being both respectably nice and desirably naughty.[4]

This twentieth-century period also marked the emergence of under-garment workers unions, from the 1909 chartering of the first undergarment local of the International Ladies Garment Workers Union (ILGWU) to the era of the organization's greatest strength in the 1950s. The parallels between the narratives of fashion and those of labor are not coincidental. Twentieth-century undergarments developed not only in relation to the abandonment of the nineteenth-century corset but also within the context of increasing mass production of garments. Throughout this era, undergarment manufacture was the third-largest branch of the women's wear industry. In 1913, 13,517 undergarment workers labored in 375 shops in New York City, and these shops accounted for about two-thirds of the $70 million to $80 million value of such production in the United States. After a general strike in the trade that year, just over half these workers became members of the ILGWU. By the early 1950s, the New York metropolitan area was still the largest center of undergarment production. But although New York–based companies in 1954 accounted for over 60 percent of the more than $828 million in intimate apparel sales nationally, only 35 percent of the 112,234 undergarment workers in the United States were employed there. Many companies maintained their headquarters in New York City but moved production facilities to areas like the South where the labor movement was weaker. Still, about 60 percent of New York City's 39,210 undergarment workers belonged to the ILGWU throughout the 1950s, though the geographic dispersal of production away from New York City caused a decline in union strength in the intimate apparel trade nationally. Moreover, the distancing of apparel manufacture from the cultural production of fashion in New York City, which remained a leading locale for the fashion press and for design and merchandising activities, had additional consequences for both undergarment workers and consumers.[5]

The ability of New York City workers to found an undergarment local in 1909 not only marked the garments' transition to industrialized production but also signaled their entry into mass consumption and mass culture. Representations of intimate apparel proliferated as manufacturers and retailers sought to sell the output of factory production: Myriad intimate apparel texts and depictions increasingly appeared in trade journals, women's magazines, mail-order catalogs, and shop-window displays to describe new designs and promote brand- and style-named products, explain fashion trends, and offer shopping, fitting, and care guides. As a result, knowledge and information about these garments, including the ideas they conveyed about women's bodies, became abundantly available. The mass production of objects thus provided an opportunity for the production of words and images that ascribed meanings to and created structures for using and interpreting these commodities.[6]

. . . . .

Though previous costume studies, such as those by Elizabeth Ewing and C. Willett and Phillis Cunnington, have outlined the history of twentieth-century undergarments, no body of work exists for the twentieth century that equals the examination of the nineteenth-century corset by scholars such as Lois Banner, David Kunzle, Helene Roberts, and Valerie Steele. This book explores the history of undergarments in modern America both as manufactured objects and cultural icons, intertwining their fabrication and distribution as mass-produced goods and objects of material culture with their construction and circulation as representations of the female body and producers of meanings. A comprehensive approach is especially useful because, as Douglas Kellner notes, the "political economy and production of culture is an important component in cultural studies that has been downplayed and even ignored in the recent boom in cultural studies." Moreover, the history of undergarments, whether cotton underwear, silk lingerie, or foundation garments with elastic straps and metal hooks, needs to be understood in relationship to social and economic changes such as the increasing rationalization of work and leisure and transformations in the shaping, conceptualization, and representation of female bodies. For although fashion magazines, department store displays, and Hollywood films generated important cultural meanings about clothing, sexuality, and femininity in the twentieth century, we need to also reckon with the experiences of women who made and sold intimate apparel, and the broader social conditions in which women actively participated as workers and consumers, if we are to fully understand the history of the production and consumption of intimate apparel in the United States.[7]

The interpretive frameworks and historical understandings I present in this book draw upon a range of methodologies and disciplines, including costume and art history, literary and film criticism, and social science analysis. Studies in these fields have highlighted the relationships between fashion and eroticism, fetishism, seduction, modernity, and identity, all of which are important components of the trajectory and interpretation of intimate apparel's history. Works from a variety of historical areas and academic fields that are not initially identifiable with costume history have incorporated consideration of dress. For example, social historians Christine Stansell and Kathy Peiss have analyzed the uses and meanings of working-class women's

Figure 1. Illustrating the centrality of female display within the emerging consumer culture of the early twentieth century, two fashionable women attract the attention of the male onlooker within the ad—and the gaze of magazine readers—by lifting their skirts and exposing colorful silk petticoats. *Women's & Infants' Furnisher,* July 1906. Courtesy of Special Collections, Gladys Marcus Library, Fashion Institute of Technology.

fashions, whereas Susan Porter Benson has brought new meaning to the understanding of "shop floor culture" by looking at department stores as places of both work and consumption. In addition, feminist film theorists have developed and brought critical attention to the concept of the "male gaze" as a controlling force in the creation and presentation of popular culture, and other scholars have examined the importance of Hollywood films as popularizers of lingerie and fashion generally.[8] Cultural preoccupation with larger-than-life cinematic spectacles and offscreen star personas in fan magazines and mainstream press also fostered fascination with glamour, a quality commonly ascribed to lingerie, in the twentieth century.[9] Glamour, which Lois Banner refers to as the "hallmark" of fashion and Jackson Lears sees as pervading "the world of fashion," has long been associated with the "enchantment, illusion, [and] witchery" described in the first issue of *Glamour*

11.62 to 16.50

Left: Lace Dressing™ underwire demi-bra #1095 in black, white
or shell, 34 to 36 A,B,C, reg. 18.00,
13.50. Right: Lace Royale push-up
underwire bra #1510 in white or
ivory, 34 to 36 A,B,C, reg. 22.00,
16.50. The End® Lacy Control™
hi-cut brief #386 in white or beige,
S-M-L, reg. 15.50, **11.62.** Body
Fashions, 7373.

Save 25%

Figure 2. By the late twentieth century, undergarment advertising in major newspapers legitimated the placement of photographs of undressed women adjacent to
serious news reports. *Los Angeles Times*,
1991. Courtesy, Federated.

in 1939. The magazine further defined glamour as "a quality each of us sees
in some other human—and wishes she possessed." Yet, the editors pointed
out, "everyone has potential glamour," which she can bring out with the
right combination of cosmetics, clothing, accessories, hairstyle, and deportment. The magical power of glamour thus had a material dimension that all
women could access in the theoretically democratic marketplace.[9]

A number of cultural studies, particularly those exploring the history of
sexuality, have critically assessed the contested nature of gendered consumption. Research in popular culture, particularly studies of feminine artifacts like
cosmetics and romance novels and procedures like plastic surgery, points to
the contradictions inherent in purchasing such commodities. Scholars suggest, for example, that such purchases raise questions about women's acceptance of, possible resistance to, and potential reuse of consumer culture's

profit-driven products and services. Many scholars interested in these questions have made fruitful use of Antonio Gramsci's concept of cultural hegemony because it explains culture as a dynamic terrain in which competing social groups struggle for representation. The segmentation of culture into elite, popular, mass, and subcultural groups defined by ethnicity, sexuality, age, immigrant status, or physical ability is thus a vigorous process of exchange in which overall cultural change may come from several directions. Gramsci's project—to determine the role of culture in maintaining and challenging capitalist-based hierarchies—was further developed by the important critical theorists, such as Walter Benjamin and Theodor Adorno, known collectively as the Frankfurt School. Despite the Frankfurt School's general dismay at the overwhelming power of commodified culture to limit alternatives and inhibit resistance, a process they saw unfolding with the rise of fascism in Europe, Adorno and other Frankfurt theorists' probing analysis of dominant cultural forms is useful in understanding how that power exerts itself.[10]

In modern America, relationships of domination and subordination are formed by force, acquiescence, accommodation, innovation, appropriation, and resistance, and historically these processes have taken place in a context of inequitable power distribution among contending classes and social groups. According to Gramsci, the cultural hegemony that emerges within this context results from "the 'spontaneous' consent given by the great masses of the population to the general direction imposed on social life by the dominant fundamental group; this consent is 'historically' caused by the prestige (and consequent confidence) which the dominant group enjoys because of its position and function in the world of production." Gramsci's analysis of the daily enforcement of laws and cultural standards, crucial for maintaining "spontaneous consent," implies that consent to domination occurs in part through daily actions that legitimate and enforce it. Raymond Williams has extended this idea in his analysis of "the relations of domination and subordination, in their form as practical consciousness, as in effect a saturation of the whole process of living." Though consent occurs within all spheres of social interaction, including the political and economic, this type of hegemony is usually associated with the cultural sphere. Cultural institutions and practices, including religious, moral, educational, artistic, athletic, and entertainment and leisure activities, nurture and reproduce ideologies and structures of consent, as well as those of resistance. Culture is thus an important location for the contestation of power.[11]

Fashions in dress are especially useful for analyzing culture as contested terrain because a central defining element of fashion is change. However, controlling the direction and pace of change is difficult, not only because of the fashion industry's dependence on innovation but also because of the simple fact that everyone wears clothes. As a result, mechanisms for monitoring dressing practices, such as written and unwritten dress codes and their enforcement by myriad fashion police, are widely dispersed and frequently undermined. As one exasperated high school principal put it, "This is a daily battle."[12] Moreover, the accepted power of clothing to express multiple aspects of personal identity and social status heightens the stakes of how fashion changes over time.

Feminist scholarship explains the gendered nature of social relations and their effects. Feminist theorists and women's historians, such as Judith Butler and Joan Scott, have enriched cultural analysis by asking scholars to document how contested categories, particularly the category of gender crucial to this book, are constructed. Scholars have drawn upon the groundbreaking work of historical sociologist Michel Foucault, whose reexamination of Victorian morality looked beyond conventional understandings of sexuality that posed questions in terms of repression and liberation. By analyzing how Victorians' preoccupation with sexual matters produced, rather than suppressed, particular notions about sexuality, gender, and class, Foucault opened up new fields and sources to investigation. These sources include medical, juridical, legislative, and scientific discourses that document the expanding deployment of power in regard to the body by professional experts and technicians as well as by economic and social elites. Scholars who perform close textual analysis of such documents often employ the methodologies of literary criticism and semiotics in the manner expertly demonstrated by Roland Barthes. Barthes closely analyzes fashion magazine copy as "written clothing" (in *The Fashion System*) not only to reveal how the language of fashion operates internally as a system of signification but also (in his essays in *Mythologies*) to "account *in detail* for the mystification which transforms [mass] culture into a universal nature." Thus, despite differences in approach and interpretation among the theorists and scholars I discuss here, their work shares an intensive focus on the nature of power in society: who wields it, how it is maintained, why shifts in power occur, and what the experience of living with and through cultural struggles can tell us about the lives of people in the past and about our own lives in the present.[13]

· · · · ·

More than a century ago, when the expanding industrialization of ready-to-wear clothing made fashionable garments more widely available, concerns about how to dress also proliferated. Commercial interests within the emerging "fashion-industrial complex" formed powerful new sources of authority and influence that were highly invested in shaping the direction and speed of fashion changes. Though globalization of the garment and fashion industries is a hallmark of today's transnational clothing production, both in creating the latest styles and in spreading sweatshop conditions, even in the earlier era, the gendered social relations and culture of industrialization and class formation crossed national boundaries. Historians of nineteenth-century U.S. culture regularly borrow the English term *Victorian* to underscore the parallel moral concerns, social responses, political and economic structures, and class, race, and gender identities taking shape in the United States and England. Similar transformations took place in France with the expanding influence of the bourgeoisie. Although national distinctions and regional variations were clearly significant, similarities in women's fashions in these countries provide material and visual evidence of comparable cultural concerns.[14]

Fashion commerce among these nations also stimulated similarities in modes of dress. In the United States, greater circulation of fashion publications, especially after the Civil War, provided readers with access to French and English style innovations more quickly than had been possible before. Women's magazines like *Godey's Lady's Book,* launched in 1830, included fashion images and text in each issue and regularly referred to and deferred to France as the ultimate fashion authority. By 1867, the first issue of the new U.S. weekly fashion magazine *Harper's Bazar* apprised its female readers that they could "be sure of obtaining the genuine Paris fashions simultaneously with Parisians themselves" and promoted New York as "the Paris of America" to affirm the currency of styles originating there.[15] That same year, a number of American businessmen and their families attended an international exhibition in Paris. Wives and daughters returned home with Parisian gowns, heightening U.S. women's interest in French fashion and in the magazines that publicized them.[16]

The enormously influential fashion designer Charles Frederick Worth embodies the intertwining of national narratives at the time: He was British, yet founded haute couture in midcentury Paris and by the 1870s relied heavily on a wealthy American clientele. Worth's sense of style, tailoring skills, marketing ability, prestigious clientele, and financial success were instrumental in establishing Paris as the Western fashion capital, and his links to England and the United States made him a model for high-fashion entrepreneurs in London and New York. Yet Worth was not the only transnational trendsetter. The 1860 visit to the United States by the stylish

Prince of Wales (later Edward VII) sparked American interest in his, and later his wife's, fashion choices and London trends generally. Moreover, Oscar Wilde's 1881–82 U.S. tour promoting aesthetic dress alternatives showed the full extent of cultural exchange. During his stay in the West, Wilde abandoned his necktie for the tied scarf of Colorado miners, thereby bringing a new element to European men's style some twenty-five years before the similar "ascot" adorned elite men at the fashionable English racetrack. Consequently, to obtain a full history of fashion in England, France, and the United States since the nineteenth century, we need to consider couturiers; the dressing practices of the European elite and American nouveau riches; the innovations of European and American rebel, reformers, demimondaines, artists, and workers; the growing influence of American popular culture; and the taste and decisions of local seamstresses and home sewers.[17]

Secondary sources on the history of undergarments, even those with a primary focus on one country's history, reflect the transnational character of modern fashion by incorporating evidence from England, France, and the United States, though typically without full recognition of the larger meaning of doing so. These studies also reflect the fragmentary nature of evidence on nineteenth-century undergarments, which stems partly from their status as "unmentionables" or *inexpressibles*, Victorian terms for undergarments in England and France, respectively. I have drawn primarily upon American sources and at times upon English and French sources where appropriate. My interpretation of that evidence speaks most specifically to transformations within the United States, though with cognizance of how trends in France and England affected changing fashions in America.[18]

. . . . .

Undergarments serve as sexual foundations both in conforming women's bodies to a fashionable form that conveys particular ideas of feminine attractiveness and in creating a shaped base over which outerwear styles can be properly fitted. The strong association of lingerie, corsetry, and other forms of underwear with eroticism imbues these articles of dress with a sexual life and history of their own, detached from the female bodies they are meant to adorn. One explanation for their status as sexual and commodity fetish objects within American culture, especially since World War II, is the still-persuasive traditional psychoanalytic accounts that attribute deep male anxiety to men's fear of anatomical difference, particularly the view that women lack penises and are therefore castrated. Yet the transformation of undergarments into widely enjoyed sources of erotic pleasure was made possible by the mass production and promotion of intimate apparel that emphasized binding restriction as well as ephemeral decoration of female breasts, torsos, and genitals as sexually stimulating modes of feminine attractiveness. When Freud stated that "All women . . . are clothes fetishists," he was expressing his understanding of the internal workings of the female psyche, not analyzing the effectiveness of fashion promotion in consumer society. Nonetheless, undergarments surely carry a charged erotic significance, for women as well as men, that is distinct from their seemingly neutral functions of covering sensitive flesh and protecting outerwear from body dirt and secretions.[19]

Tracing the history of undergarments both by analyzing them as artifacts and by examining their appearance in a wide variety of historical texts provides a means to materialize the less tangible significations of intimate apparel and discern their meanings for the lives of American women. My investigation of the increasing sales, changing designs, and growing importance of intimate apparel in American culture prompted a search for a broad range of evidence, as well as a willingness to employ interdisciplinary methods in assessing their importance. My analysis of fashion magazines, mail-order catalogs, advertisements, trade journals, Hollywood films, costume artifacts, oral histories, and the records of organized labor provides a narrative of changes in the construction and significance of intimate apparel over time and tracks its expanding presence in modern America. Yet as I explored these source materials to determine the history and meanings of the garments I selected for closest appraisal—drawers, corsets and girdles, brassieres, and black lingerie—I found that particular, though related stories explained each garment's past. Rather like the individual process of getting dressed, each piece has meaning on its own and as part of an ensemble. Similarly, distinctive motifs and different emphases emerged from research and analysis of intimate apparel advertisements and the records of business and organized labor. In this book, the story and larger historical context of intimate apparel's design, manufacture, purchase, display, cultural representation, and significance brings to consideration a wide range of issues, while remaining focused on the material world, events, and individuals that are linked by these garments.

Most studies of women's apparel focus either on changes in fashion designs and their meaning or on changes in the ways garments are produced. This distinction parallels the tendency to view production as a material process that takes place within the garment industry, and cultural production and consumption as the domain of the fashion industry. As I show in this book, the division between these spheres of clothing manufacture and meaning stems from the way in which the material conditions of twentieth-century apparel production developed in the United States. Increasing specialization of clothing production not only created separate manufacturing branches, like the undergarment trade itself, but also spurred development of the distinct business of fashion promotion and merchandising.

The material separation between a garment industry focused on apparel production and a fashion industry centered on clothing consumption manifested geographically in the movement of production facilities away from the elegant showrooms of New York–based undergarment firms. Yet distinctions between the garment industry and the fashion industry have had ideological effects as well. The conceptual division between the two spheres has heightened the pleasures of intimate apparel consumption by distancing ready-to-wear clothing from its suspect origins in the dingy workplaces where poorly paid immigrant women perform the unappealing manual labor of apparel production. The work of fashion promotion connects the purchase and display of new clothing to a glamorous world of wealth, creativity, and beauty where fashion designers, supermodels, and photographers are celebrities. In this manner, fashion consumption becomes divorced from the comparatively unsavory conditions of apparel production, thus denigrating the sensibilities of garment workers. Ideological separation of production and consumption is thus central to fashion promotion and to the degraded status and claims of garment workers. The growing attention paid in the twentieth and twenty-first centuries to the fashion industry's glamorous allure is due in part to its function of concealing the prosaic and often deplorable conditions of garment production. This trend, and its larger effects, certainly has benefited from the intensified removal of apparel manufacture from the United States since the 1950s. By 2002, only 134 undergarment shops, employing 11,856 workers, existed nationwide; the over $12 billion in retail sales generated by the industry that year resulted largely from production in facilities based outside the United States.[20]

·   ·   ·   ·   ·

The material shape and meaning of intimate apparel changed over time and location. Style trends; transformations in gendered, class-based, and racialized understandings of female sexuality and sexual identity; and the full development of mass production and consumption of women's clothing all contributed to the multiple and sometimes conflicting meanings of undergarments. Thong underwear, for example, is seen as highly sexual, as when it was famously flashed by 1990s White House intern Monica Lewinsky, though this underwear design also provides wearers a measure of desired propriety, if not modesty, by eliminating the visible panty line produced by more expansive styles. Thus, by writing an inclusive history sensitive to the contested, and at times contradictory, nature of cultural meanings and to the multiple participants who make and act upon them, I seek to show how women's efforts to shape their lives and their bodies according to their own desires and designs have in turn shaped the production and consumption of intimate apparel.

The first four chapters of *An Intimate Affair* focus on the histories of specific undergarments and describe changes over time in their design and style. Yet these chapters, and those that follow, also explore the relationship between these garments' histories and larger transformations in the lives of American women. Of particular consequence were efforts at redefining respectable femininity that offered women more, though still gendered, opportunities for pleasure and autonomy in the United States. Bringing multiple sources of evidence and perspectives together in considering the linked histories of American women and intimate apparel suggests possibilities for rethinking historical understandings of gendered culture, sexuality, and power in the twentieth century.

Chapter 1, "Drawers" (the term for underpants from the nineteenth through the early twentieth century), explores the relationship between pants and power by looking at the Western cultural prohibition against women wearing divided garments (trousers). The association of masculinity with trousers and femininity with dresses, and the importance of separating men and women through this distinction in attire, extended the prohibition against divided garments even to women's underwear. When middle-class women did begin to wear underpants in the early nineteenth century, their drawers were constructed with an open crotch in part, I argue, to distinguish women's drawers from men's. This function became especially clear during the startling transition from open- to closed-crotch drawers in the 1910s, a period of feminist agitation for suffrage, birth control, and better jobs and wages. The implication, and reality, of sexual access implied and permitted by open drawers coexisted with Victorian propriety and its ideology of female passionlessness and masculine domination. However, the meanings of the open crotch shifted when women began asserting group and individual claims to political power, economic independence, and sexual pleasure. By 1930, a reversal in the meaning of open-crotch drawers had occurred; when sexual access became coupled with modern female desire for skimpier fashionable attire and satisfying erotic experiences, open-crotch drawers became associated with immodesty and lasciviousness.

Who decides how and when fashion changes? I explore this central question of fashion analysis in chapter 2 by analyzing the decline of the nineteenth-century corset and its replacement by the twentieth-century girdle. Tracking this transition in corset industry trade journals reveals that corset industrialists insistently defended the need for women to wear corsets, attacked women who thought otherwise, and instructed retailers and saleswomen in innovative sales strategies and marketing techniques that borrowed from the ideologies of eugenics, scientific management, and modern conceptions of beauty and sexual attractiveness. The fact that manufacturers and retailers mounted such aggressive efforts to keep women in corsets implies that women were attempting to determine the course of fashion changes for themselves. For, if women were merely the fashion slaves they were often characterized to be, manufacturers would not have worked so hard to shape and maintain consumer demand for their products. The history of the transition from corsets to girdles reveals fashion changes as negotiated interactions among designers, manufacturers, retailers, saleswomen, dress reformers, and a wide range of consumers and provides a case study of culture as contested terrain.

Chapter 3 focuses on the twentieth-century brassiere, which came into use as a companion garment to longer turn-of-the-century corsets that sat lower on the torso in order to extend down the hips. The brassiere's cultural meaning intensified as female breasts became the most important bodily sign of gender distinction in modern America. From the breast binding in the 1920s to the uplift and separation of the breasts and their fetishization in 1940s sweater girls and pinups, brassiere design and marketing profitably deployed twentieth-century mechanisms that objectified female embodiment. Cup sizes, invented in 1935, encouraged objectification of the female body through the new practice of measuring the breast's width and depth, as well as through classification of women's bodies by standardized brassiere sizes. The glamorous and transformative power ascribed to large, firm, and uplifted breasts explains their enduring popularity among women from the late 1930s to the present.

"The Meaning of Black Lingerie," chapter 4, explores the multifaceted development of black lingerie's specialized erotic meaning by examining the interrelated histories of three topics: racialized sexuality, sex and death, and black clothing. That blackness and black bodies have for several centuries in Western culture have been linked to deviant and particularly lascivious sexuality, while whiteness and white bodies have been associated with sexual purity raises questions about the dynamics of race and sexuality. Yet black lingerie's history is also entwined with other cultural phenomena: the striking importance of widows' dressing in black within Victorian society; widespread fascination with links between sex and death, evidenced in representations of dead women as beautiful and sexualized women as deadly; and the growing embrace of black as fashionable dress for modern women in the twentieth century. This chapter also considers both production and consumption in regard to the signification of fashion, as oral histories of retired African American undergarment workers reveal that black lingerie carried far different meanings on the shop floor than in the locations and practices of consumer culture.

In chapter 5, I analyze the images and readers of a half century of intimate apparel advertisements. As feminist film theorists have shown, female spectatorship can create a dual position for women as both objects and subjects of a male gaze. In other words, to conform to conventional femininity, women construct themselves in dress and deportment as "to-be-looked-at," which requires them to look through the male gaze to see whether their bodies are attractive objects on display. However, because women may view themselves in this manner when looking at intimate apparel advertisements that evoke eroticism to promote sales, a "danger" exists that the ads will evoke homoeroticism as well. Magazine and mail-order–catalog advertisements deflect this danger by using graphic devices such as models with averted eyes and the "invisible woman," in which intimate apparel is worn around a body that is not visible. Building upon this central concept, this chapter examines related advertising themes, such as voyeurism, narcissism, differing class constructions of beauty and glamour, and attempts to resolve the "pretty-or-practical" dilemma within fashion discourse.

Chapter 6 investigates how the industrial manufacture of intimate apparel shapes the meaning of undergarments in American culture. The fashion sensibilities of garment workers at work, at leisure, and on the picket line, and the cultural activities of the ILGWU—including *Pins and Needles,* the musical staged by the union in the late 1930s that became an unexpected hit on Broadway—stood at the fault line between fashion production and consumption. The dressing practices of undergarment workers and their active participation in union activities reveal that the seemingly stark division between the glamorous fashion industry and the unglamorous garment industry results from cultural institutions and ideologies that construct social distinctions between those who sew and those who shop. Defining these groups as opposites provides an illusory coherence that makes this division seem logical, if not natural. Glamour, particularly as expressed in fashion, thus has been a powerful mechanism for mediating tensions and upholding inequity in modern America, whereas redefining or reclaiming glamour has held the potential for challenging the status quo.

In the concluding chapter, I explore the repercussions of French designer Christian Dior's 1947 New Look designs that stimulated corsetry's return to fashion prominence. Supported by a French fashion industry anxious to reassert its dominance in the disarray of postwar Europe, the New Look quickly spread to England and the United States. Opposition to the highly feminized New Look, composed of a soft shoulder, cinched waist, rounded hips and long skirt, came from such varied sources as the British government, small groups of women who organized in the United States, and prominent Hollywood designer Gilbert Adrian. Supporters of the New Look included the textile and corset industries, as well as interests concerned with firmly restoring the gender division of labor that had been undermined by national mobilization for war. Although corset industry profits surged during this period, profits also increased for the expanding sportswear trade, which promoted informality and comfort in dress. In addition, although the cinched waist prevailed, women tended to wear the most extreme versions only on special occasions, such as debutante balls and proms. This specialized use intensified the fetishized quality of corsetry, which remains highly visible today.

Costume history is commonly positioned within the discipline of art history. Costume archives and exhibitions most often are found in art museums, and costume historians frequently use paintings as source material because the representation of clothing is often central to the image. For the same reason, the appearance of clothing in art is an important topic for art historians. "Bra vs. Bra," this book's epilogue, briefly considers changes in intimate apparel from the 1960s to the present by analyzing feminist works of art that represent undergarments. Exhibited works such as *Steel Wool Peignoir* (Mimi Smith, 1966), *Lingerie Pillows* (*Womanhouse* installation, Sherry Brody, 1972) and *Bra vs. Bra* (Leslie Sharpe, 1989) vividly demonstrate the considerable range of uses and meanings of intimate apparel and raise challenging questions about gender, power, and cultural representation. They also document and comment on more recent undergarment styles. The ways in which artists and consumers utilize mass-produced goods can transform intended, dominant perceptions of these gendered objects and provide alternative or oppositional views of femininity and its expression by the female body. Artists who use intimate apparel in this manner thus provide further evidence of the significant and lasting symbolic power of intimate apparel texts, representations, and artifacts within American culture.

1 Drawers

Have you ever stopped to think that the serious subject of woman's progress and the frivolous subject of woman's clothes are very closely connected?

Woman's Home Companion, 1914

The 1928 silent film *Our Dancing Daughters* opens with a shot of a nude female metal figurine shaped to capture a dramatic moment mid-dance. The shot dissolves as a pair of bowed white satin dress shoes, sitting in front of a three-sided mirror, fade in to replace the figurine. White-stockinged legs visible from midknee down slowly materialize and fill the shoes. The legs launch into a frenetic dance, their kicking feet turning to face the mirror. The dancing ceases briefly as hands lower into view a white pair of short silk closed-crotch drawers with a leg ruffle.

These modern underpants are donned leg by leg. After focusing on a few more kicks of the heels, the scene abruptly cuts to a shot from the waist down. Now we see that the drawers are worn underneath a swinging fringed skirt. The dancing continues as a silk wraparound underskirt is placed between the fringe and the drawers to complete the ensemble, but not before hands deftly move the fringe aside to allow an unhindered look at the underwear and the legs beneath them. The final dissolve in this mirror scene reveals the full figure of Diana (top-billed actress Joan Crawford) in lavish surroundings. Now fully dressed, Diana makes some final adjustments to her clothing and hair, practices a sultry look, and deeply admires her reflected image.[1]

The cinematic focus on legs in this opening scene of *Our Dancing Daughters* is visual evidence of the notorious 1920s fascination with the newly unfettered legs of women. However, the cultural preoccupation with women's legs also extends to what does or does not lie between them. This interest in legs and crotch is surely erotically fueled. But it is also shaped, as is the erotic content itself, by social constructions of gender that proscribe distinct behaviors for men and women and regulate access to power. These gendered distinctions are entirely apparent in the arena of dress where, in

Western culture since the late Middle Ages, men have worn trousers and women, dresses.

This gendered division of clothing extended to underwear until the nineteenth century, when women began to wear drawers, an undergarment constructed of two leg tubes attached to a waistband. Previously worn only by men for warmth and to protect outer garments from the wearing effects of direct contact with the body, the name derived from the act of "drawing" them on. For women to engage in this masculine act, and to appropriate their new garment's name from the lexicon of menswear, blurred what had been a clearly marked gender boundary. Materially distinguishing female from male drawers kept that reworked boundary from shifting further. Thus, the long-held association of divided garments or trousers with masculinity and undivided garments or skirts with femininity influenced the design, use, and implications of women's drawers. Feminized by their fabric, ornamentation, and open-crotch construction, the virtually separate leg sections of nineteenth-century women's drawers were joined only at the waistband. The open seam extended below the waistband, front to back, creating the potential for exposure of the inner thighs as well as the genital area. Such distinctions from men's drawers, and the contention that drawers advanced female modesty by adding another layer of covering to women's bodies, ameliorated the problematic cross-dressing implications of drawers for women.[2]

Responding to a range of constraints and desires, the new female garment's design upheld gender distinctions that a divided garment for women challenged, and by midcentury, open drawers had become a required component of respectable middle-class women's dress in the United States and industrializing western Europe. Yet despite drawers' integration into properly modest Victorian female dress, open-crotch drawers also held erotic meanings for men and women in the nineteenth century. As the Victorian ideological framework crumbled in the twentieth century, the crotch configuration of drawers became one location in the struggle to establish the modern boundaries of women's sexual propriety.

In *Our Dancing Daughters*, the short, closed-crotch drawers worn by Diana establish the modernity of her character. Two decades earlier, bulkier drawers reached to the knees and had an open crotch. Yet the film, like many others in the 1920s, explores the redefinition of appropriate feminine behavior and dress then taking place.[3] Diana is one of three female characters who illustrate the pitfalls facing young women. In the same way that the film introduces Diana, it separately introduces Diana's best friend, Bea, and her romantic rival, Ann, with shots of their legs. As Ann finishes dressing in a sheath

Figure 3. Open-crotch drawers were worn from the early nineteenth century to the early twentieth century. With permission of the Royal Ontario Museum © ROM.

slip covered by a flouncy net party frock, she recites the central tenets of the formula for snatching a rich husband: "beauty and purity." The working-class Ann shows how a woman can easily feign these seemingly old-fashioned values through dress and the pretense of fidelity to Victorian codes of feminine behavior. In contrast, Bea demarcates the limits of permissible sexual freedom. Bea's upper-class life will be forever marred by her premarital loss of virginity, which, in the service of modern honesty, she confesses to her fiancé. The two wed, but the marriage is troubled by the inability of Bea's husband to forget her past transgressions.[4]

The object of Ann and Diana's affection is the wealthy Ben, a man of Victorian sensibilities. His concern for outward appearances and his confusion about the meaning of Diana's party-girl antics, such as when she rips off her skirt to kick her legs higher during a wild Charleston, motivates his disastrous decision to marry Ann instead. However, his inability to sense either woman's true character provokes not only heartache for Diana but also a redemptive chastisement for her excesses. In the final party scene, it's the amoral Ann who wears the flapper fringe, whereas the sobered Diana wears less revealing dress, no longer interested in exhibitionist dancing. After the party, Ann's drunken tumble down a flight of stairs leads to her ironic death at the feet of scrubwomen. The triumph of pure love between the sadder-

Figure 4. Joan Crawford dances the Charleston wearing modern short, closed-crotch drawers and little else in *Our Dancing Daughters* (1928). Courtesy of the Academy of Motion Picture Arts and Sciences.

but-wiser Diana and Ben is now possible, not only because Ann dies but also because Diana's behavior and dress no longer challenge the boundaries of propriety she earlier flaunted. A newspaper society page reports that Diana and Ben's marriage takes place two years later, confirming their strict adherence to moral guidelines. Thus, "beauty and purity" still prove to be the essential ingredients of a blissful marriage.[5]

The transition from open- to closed-crotch drawers, which was completed by the end of the 1920s, reveals how modesty and eroticism, usually paired as opposites, work together in a shifting dialectic responsive to and productive of changes in understandings about gender difference and sexuality. Costume historians, who primarily document changes in apparel through analysis of costume artifacts' design, construction, and visual culture, generally hold two related premises about open drawers: open design facilitated elimination of bodily waste made difficult by binding corsets and the lack of indoor plumbing, and changes in outerwear prompted the shift to closed drawers. Yet the long history of regulating women's ability to wear drawers and trousers in Western culture reveals the powerful forces embedded in this key distinction between male and female dress.[6] One must consider the effect of this power dynamic upon drawers' changing construction and function to understand why, even as closed-crotch drawers became increasingly available in the 1870s, open-crotch drawers predominated for another forty years. Certainly, drawers became shorter and narrower, in line with changes in skirt length and width, after World War I. Yet modifications in volume and length, while important, were similar to alterations in style that had occurred during the nineteenth century, when drawer length and volume rose and fell several times. Thus, although changes in outerwear are linked to the transition to the closed crotch, they do not fully explain it.[7]

Significantly, costume historians have left the sexual meanings of open drawers unexamined, despite the psychoanalytic theories of fashion advocated by scholars such as J. C. Flugel as early as 1930, and more recently by Valerie Steele, that explain changes in dress styles as the result of women's desires to be sexually attractive to men.[8] Nor has the topic appeared in the work of historians who explore the history of gender and sexuality through analysis of diaries, letters, advice books, medical and legal discourses, and popular culture texts. Their studies have revealed distinctions between nineteenth-century discourses that constructed white, middle-class women as sexually passionless and the actual practices of men and women. As moral concerns shifted and Victorian structures of behavior became less compelling, an increasing number of women claimed the right to sexual desire, pleasure, *and* respectability. However, at the same time, the rising consumer culture was increasingly commercializing female sexual expression, and select medical and psychoanalytic frameworks that pathologized female sexuality were gaining legitimacy. Yet women's sexual identities still varied by class and race. Discourse, public policy, and private censure set boundaries of middle-class female sexual propriety by attributing erotic proclivities to female bodies that were neither white nor middle class, and by insisting that women with an unseemly interest in sexuality were unworthy of the respect, status, and social support accorded to white, middle-class women.[9]

Combining elements of these two sets of historical methodologies and literatures reveals drawers' critical role in constructing a feminine sexuality both erotic and modest. Without disputing the practicality of open- or closed-crotch drawers, I argue that erotic meanings of open drawers, particularly the ready sexual access to female bodies they provide, also served social functions. For the functions of dress, despite clothing's attachment to the body, are neither "natural" nor removed from human intervention and social structures. Indeed, the careful consideration of social understandings *about* the functions of dress related to the body reveals the unquestioned biological explanations underlying culturally constructed gender differences, and thus how culture operates to reinforce seemingly irrefutable proof of essential, biologically based, and "natural" gender difference. The apparently functional aspects of open drawers do not negate the significance of the open crotch as the principal way of differentiating male and female drawers; rather they underscore these meanings. Serving as a material means of constructing women's bodies as different, open drawers referenced women's biological difference on a daily basis.[10]

.   .   .   .   .

Divided undergarments became part of women's fashionable dress during a period of heightening gender differentiation in the early nineteenth century, when bourgeois society and values replaced those of deposed aristocracies and undermined communal preindustrial customs throughout the West. Distinctive male and female dress represented and enacted the increasingly disparate daily lives of middle-class men and women, as capricious or extravagant fashion became gendered as feminine and keyed to the newly privatized woman's sphere.[11] This was especially appealing to the middle class, which sought legitimacy by distinguishing itself through manners and morals from those above and below.[12] Moreover, these gendered social relations and the culture of industrialization and class formation crossed national boundaries. U.S. historians borrow the English term *Victorian* to underscore the parallel moral concerns, social responses, political and economic structures, and class, race, and gender identities taking shape in the United States and England, as well as in France. Although national distinctions and regional variations remain significant in these countries, similarities in women's fashions provide material and visual evidence of comparable cultural concerns.[13]

Differences between girls' and women's dress in the nineteenth century supply evidence of the sexual meanings of crotch construction in women's drawers. Young girls were among the earliest members of the middle class to wear drawers in the late eighteenth century, a time of changing attitudes toward childhood and the construction of new age-based distinctions. As childhood became a specialized age category within the middle-class life span, specialized activities for children gained favor, and the style of children's dress became more distinct from that of adults. The previous custom of dressing young children in smaller versions of adult clothes, maintained among working-class and poor families who required their children's labor for survival, was superseded in middle- and upper-class families by the custom of dressing girls and boys in similar clothing until they were five years old. Although some subtle differences in boys' and girls' dress remained, such as the use of particular plaid fabrics for boys but not girls, both small boys and girls wore dresses. As with girls' dress, changing fashions in the ornamentation and line of boys' clothing corresponded with changes in their mothers' clothing, not their fathers'. Instead, the distinction of age group took precedence over the distinction of gender in early childhood in families that could afford to do so. Gender distinction in dress was instituted as children grew. Drawers for older boys and girls transformed into short breeches and pantalettes, respectively. A boy's rite of passage in the transition to adulthood was to don long trousers; a girl's was to abandon pantalettes.[14]

The visible drawers that most girls wore under short dresses had a closed crotch, distinguishing them from the drawers their mothers and elder sisters were just beginning to wear in the early decades of the nineteenth century. This distinctive clothing encouraged girls' active play and thus also clarified the message inherent in young women's shift to wearing open drawers, corsets, and many other layers of underclothing. However, even as a striking example of regulating female behavior through attire, the adoption of adult female apparel had implications beyond the actual physical restriction that inhibited freer movement. A central meaning of coming-of-age rituals in many cultures is that of assuming the status of potential sexual partner. A young woman's sudden donning of open-crotch drawers would make this meaning most evident to her, as well as to the men in her community. Wearing open drawers created a signal, if not the daily reality, of a woman's sexual availability.[15]

Drawers worn by young women during the first decades of the nineteenth century extended below the dress hem in order to display their lace trim.[16] Although the exposure of girls' drawers below dress hems was condoned, this practice among young women proved controversial for moral reasons, and by 1820, drawer length receded so that the undergarment could not be seen when a woman was fully dressed.[17] By the 1840s, most middle-class women wore open-crotch drawers made of lightweight fabrics such as muslins and lawns.[18] Several factors coalesced to enable women to wear drawers, and subsequently to require them to, during this period of heightening gender differentiation, including fashion's imperative of continually seizing upon innovative elements. As many costume historians note, innovations in middle-class women's fashions often derive from sports, the stage, children's wear, menswear, and working-class communities. The widespread acceptance of drawers as fashionable attire seems all too inevitable in that drawers or a divided garment were worn within all these arenas.[19]

When drawers first appeared, they were critiqued for both concealing and revealing the charms of women's legs and ankles; they were thus initially characterized as both modest and immodest. Some male commentators welcomed the erotic feelings aroused by drawers' exposure of previously hidden lower limbs, whereas others mourned the glimpse of naked flesh they had previously enjoyed when women raised their long skirts to avoid a dangerous step. This ambiguity suggests that the playful, decorative, and erotic suggestion of drawers served as an "inoculation" against the new regime of rigidly enforced gender and sex differences. In other words, women could wear a divided garment if it were feminized and sexualized, and this feminization of the garment assured that "real" trousers would still be worn only by "real" men.[20]

The outrage fomented when drawers briefly extended below dress hemlines in the 1850s points to the social forces intent on perpetuating the gendered bifurcation of dress that a divided garment for women blurred. A series of changes in the fashionable silhouette in the 1840s led to this controversy. In that decade, skirts took on an increasingly broad bell shape, achieved by suspending many heavy layers of petticoats from a tightly corseted waist.[21] A variety of social critics noted the discomfort and potential health risks of this attire. Those concerned primarily with the perceived dangers of women's preoccupation with fashion, which ranged from financial bankruptcy and disruption of the family to descent into prostitution and decay of the nation's moral fabric, sought to curb women's appetites with appeals to modesty and simplicity. Less conservative health reformers suggested slight modifications in dress, such as a shorter skirt length to avoid the gathering of dirt and dampness against the skin, and admonished against wearing tight-lacing corsets. Indeed, wearing open-crotch drawers was also considered a preventive health measure, because it exposed the genitals to the wholesome benefits of air.[22]

The most radical midcentury proposal for women's dress reform promoted the innovative design that came to be known as the Bloomer Costume, a midcalf-length dress worn with trousers that covered the legs to the ankles. Though few women actually advocated and bravely wore the Bloomer Costume, and its public use proved short-lived, the outfit generated an enormous amount of published debate, ridicule, and fear after it first appeared in 1851 in *The Lily*, Amelia Bloomer's newspaper dedicated to women's issues. The degree of opposition makes clear how dress serves as a powerful regulator of gender difference. Much of the negative attention focused on the trousers and on the costume's links with the woman's rights movement. Woman's rights activists were prominent wearers of the Bloomer Costume and often donned it for movement events.[23]

An 1851 editorial in the *New York Times* used explicitly political rhetoric to articulate the fear of women in trousers and to affirm that the right to wear them was constitutionally guaranteed, as with political rights, only to men.

> We regret to see how obstinately our American women are bent on appropriating more than their fair share of Constitutional privileges. Not that the efforts ever amount to anything more than the re-affirmation of certain arrant heresies . . . [as] the propriety of endowing their delicate forms with the apparel, appurtenances, and insignia of "manhood." But there is an obvious tendency to encroach upon masculine manners manifested ever in trifles, which cannot be too severely rebuked or too speedily repressed. . . . Anti-masculine agitation must be stayed by some means.[24]

The editorial characterizes women wearing trousers as "antimasculine" and sees the practice as a rejection of femininity, and as an attack on masculinity and on gender difference itself. Numerous cartoons appeared in magazines caricaturing women in Bloomer Costumes smoking cigars, wielding canes, and engaging in outrageous activities like proposing marriage to timid men who assume the household duties the women now refuse to perform.[25]

Critics of the Bloomer Costume also charged that revealing the ankles was immodest and improperly erotic. A report in San Francisco that prostitutes and dance-hall girls favored the outfit meant that women of proper morals should not. Similarly, complaints were made that applying the descriptive term *Turkish* to the trousers rendered the outfit dangerously heathen. Such condemnation occurred even though Turkish objects and motifs were in vogue at the time, demonstrating the multiple meanings evoked by orientalist descriptors. Indeed, some female reformers found inspiration in linking bifurcated dress with the stronger property-right protections accorded Turkish women.[26] The strategy of discursively linking transgressive groups, such as cross-dressers, prostitutes, colonized others, and feminists, undermined challenges to dominant authority. A middle-class woman's sexual reputation was often her only source of power in negotiating her material well-being and social standing through marriage. Thus, identifying certain acts as damaging to a woman's reputation was an important and persuasive means of regulating her behavior, such as constraining her from wearing the Bloomer Costume and articulating the woman's rights claims it symbolized.

Despite such criticism, organized dress reform continued to be an important component of the woman's rights movement throughout the remainder of the nineteenth century. The National Dress Reform Association published *The Sibyl: A Review of Taste, Errors, and Fashions of Society* from the time the organization formed in 1856 until 1865, and in its pages renamed a modified Bloomer costume the "American Dress." A few adherents of dress reform wore this costume, but did so primarily at home.[27] However, the subversive potential of women's determining their own style of public dress for expanded participation in education, sports, and the workforce did not escape notice. An 1870s *New York Times* editorial attack on dress reform fed upon a new strategy that characterized dress reform as a "nervous disorder" that manifests in "an abnormal and unconquerable thirst for trousers." The disease, reported the editorial, strikes "women of exceptional muscular strength, and upon those of extraordinary conversational powers" and is suggested to be a form of "hysteria." The regulation of women in trousers was essential to defusing the political claims of subjugated persons through their pathological categorization as "hysterical," "deviant," or "criminal."[28]

The fashion industry's response to the cry for reform came in the shape of the cage crinoline or hoop skirt introduced in the mid-1850s. Wearing the metal-frame crinoline obviated the need for the many heavy petticoats worn in order to produce the broadly extended bell-shaped skirt. An 1858 *Godey's Lady's Book* advertisement for Douglas & Sherwood's New Expansion Skirt noted the product's many advantages: "The steel springs . . . can be wound around the finger like a piece of tape, and will immediately resume their place upon being dropped. . . . The expansion is all in front, so that the wearer can contract or expand the skirt, without disrobing, at pleasure. . . . Their lightness recommends them." Women of all social classes, including agricultural and factory workers, desired to dress fashionably while lightening their load, and they widely adopted the crinoline. Deborah Gray White reports that young enslaved women wore hoops made from grape vines under their special-occasion and Sunday dresses. However, some female homesteaders in the West conceded to the arduous physical demands of isolated rural life and abandoned hoop skirts. Freed from fashionable requirements, some of these women took the step of wearing a form of the American Dress to ease the accomplishment of their many daily tasks.[29]

Women who wore hoops no longer had to drag around pounds of clothing, but their attention was now directed to the constant adjustments that the awkward crinoline demanded. Despite subsequent innovations, like the collapsible cage, which permitted a woman to sit in or board a coach, the crinoline's stiff swinging movement regularly exposed the legs. This phenomenon solidified the consensus that drawers had become a compulsory undergarment, worn to protect modesty rather than to encourage eroticism. Yet because drawers had an open crotch, a woman who lost her balance completely might find that though her lower legs remained covered, her upper thighs and genitals had not. Despite this much-remarked-upon potential exposure—whether of naked flesh or of legs and crotch shielded by fabric— a woman dressed in open drawers and crinoline conformed to contemporary notions of propriety and modesty.[30]

The growing volume of the bell-shaped skirt silhouette from the 1840s to the 1860s perhaps stimulated further male interest in viewing the lower female body region concealed within the increasing amount of space created by layers of petticoats and hoops. The changing fashions in drawers encouraged such interest, though drawers also protected bare legs from the direct gaze of men as long as the wearer remained upright. Two images, both titled "A Street View" and published in the New York City newspaper *The Weekly Rake* in the 1840s, illustrate men's fascination with viewing the nether regions hidden beneath women's long and full skirts. One of the illustrations shows a woman on a street who has just fallen backward and landed on her bottom, exposing her legs spread apart above her in the air. She wears both stockings and drawers, but a well-dressed man standing above her gapes directly between her legs in horror. The second image shows a woman pausing to tie her shoelace on a sidewalk. She perches her leg on a doorway step, unaware that a man hides below a sidewalk grating and is peering up her skirt. The folds in her skirt mimic the shape of her thigh and buttocks, alluding to the presence of a powerful male gaze—held even by men not so advantageously located—that penetrates clothing's concealment of female flesh.[31]

In the 1850s and 1860s, men's newspapers and magazines published similar images of upended women in crinolines exposed to overt male gazes.[32] Changes in drawers reflected the growing potential for such exposure, whether it was an opportunity to elicit male interest or an unwelcome event. Characterized as "severely plain" in the 1840s, drawers became more ornamental under the swinging crinolines of the next decades.[33] By the end of the 1860s, when a fashion magazine advised "drawers should be trimmed with frills and insertions," such decoration was becoming a defining feature of fine undergarments.[34] Chemical dyes for undergarments introduced in the 1860s promoted the novelty of colored drawers, beginning with hues of

Figure 5. "A Street View" in *The Weekly Rake* (1842) humorously illustrates the intense interest of male spectators in the crotch construction of nineteenth-century women's drawers. Courtesy, American Antiquarian Society.

solferino red and magenta. After the midcentury invention of the sewing machine, frilly and colored drawers became more widely available.[35]

These decorative drawers—designed, constructed, sold, and worn with the understanding that they were meant to be seen—clarify the relationship between concealment and display, an essential element of the interplay between modesty and eroticism. Modesty produces eroticism not only through concealment that attracts attention to the cloaked area of the body but also through the tension generated by adhering to both the discourse of modest concealment and the practice of elaborate decorative display.

· · · · ·

After the collapse of the crinoline, the fashionable silhouette of the next two decades became progressively slimmer and straighter, except for the bulges produced by the changing placement and shape of the bustle. The notorious tight lacing of 1870s and 1880s corsets may have resulted in part from the straighter skirt shape, because wide skirts foster the illusion of a smaller waistline. In this period, finer drawers began to be made of silk and trimmed with lace and hand embroidery, though the burgeoning movement of health and hygiene enthusiasts concurrently vaunted the merits of wool undergarments. The English firm Jaeger, still in business today, began producing undergarments inspired by German Dr. Gustav Jaeger's 1884 "sanitary woollen system." Wearing woolen undergarments year-round became a critical component of the "hygienic" dress popular with Americans who participated in reform health movements of this era. Drawers generally maintained their voluminous size through this period, contributing to the bulky appearance of skirts. Dress reformers also continued to press for what they termed "rational" dress.[36]

In the nineteenth century's final decades, women's increased opportunities for education, waged work, and public activities refigured the expression and performance of modesty and eroticism in dress. The mass production of bicycles gave women greater spatial mobility and profoundly altered women's relationship to divided garments. Women's magazine fiction documented anxieties about men's possible loss of control as a result of this mobility, whereas the special construction and promotion of bicycle seats for women testifies to concern about the bicycle's autoerotic possibilities. Yet women were permitted to wear trousers while cycling, and in what can be seen as an extraordinary, though long-in-coming, victory for dress reform, cycling trousers were called bloomers. Perhaps more surprising, the caption of an 1894 cover illustration for *Harper's Bazar* refers to them as "Turkish trousers." Yet *Harper's* also names the ensemble a "bicycle dress," noting that the "Turkish trousers, long and ample, are made of such fulness that when standing upright the division is obliterated." Clearly, concern about the meaning of divided garments for women influenced design and discourse.[37]

Though cycling bloomers did not reveal the shape of the legs underneath them, they still inspired stares, taunts, and suggestive magazine drawings. One *Police Gazette* drawing purported to depict a Chicago man who "lashes female bicyclists who happen to wear bifurcated skirts." The magazine also illustrated a reported incident in 1895 when Miss Coleman, a church organist in Mason, Ohio, caused a "sensation" because she arrived late to church services in "red bicycle clothes," an event that might "result in breaking up the congregation." Later that year, the *Police Gazette* noted the possibilities for financial exploitation of such sensational displays of women. A San Francisco entrepreneur achieved "a howling success" after opening the Bloomer Café with "four of the handsomest and best shaped women he could find." A drawing portrays the bustling restaurant filled with men whose eyes happily inspect the legs and buttocks of the comely "waiter girls" dressed in bloomers. However, although the café story demonstrates how bloomers could serve male interests, the magazine also reported an 1895 "Emancipation Tea" that took place in a Mechanicsburg, Ohio, home. The twenty-five guests "were all arrayed in bloomers" and "adjourned to the spacious lawn and engaged in athletic sports." An illustration captioned "Lovely Women's Bloomers" puts female bodies on display, but the adjoining text indicates that doing so does not fully undermine the larger emancipatory implications of the athletic event.[38]

While the practice of wearing cycling bloomers declined because of public pressure, girls and young women wore bloomers in the growing number of physical education classes offered at women's colleges and educational institutions.[39] These new athletic and intellectual opportunities for women coincided with the full flowering of luxurious, elaborate, and self-consciously erotic undergarments. The decorative ruffles, lace, and flounces that appeared on women's underclothes between the late 1890s and about 1908 are associated with the reign of King Edward VII, known at home and abroad for his interest in fashion and his love of sensual pleasures. His ascension to the throne in 1901 and nine-year reign marked the formal end of Victorian rule and coincided with the first decade of the new century. Previous fashions in dress and morality would soon seem archaic, and the Victorian aesthetic gave way to the embrace of frivolity in fashion, dubbed the "cult of chiffon" by an English fashion advice author in 1902. As Alma Whitaker humorously recalled in 1923 Los Angeles, "Not until the Edwardian era was our moral backsliding complete. . . . 'Twas then that we admitted the decollete nightie into the bosom of our family, and the peek-a-boo shirtwaist followed swiftly upon its improper heels. 'Twas then that 'bloomers,' that unwomanly bifurcated garment, first received general support in the 'underworld.' "[40]

The image of women in frilly, frivolous, erotic, and expensive Edwardian lingerie contrasted sharply with the serious and purposeful Progressive-era New Woman reformer and the athletic Gibson Girl. The contrasts between these concurrent iconic images mark the origins of a split in twentieth-century women's clothing between the "pretty" and the "practical," two words that pop up frequently in lingerie advertisements of the twentieth century. Such advertisements attempted to resolve this contradictory choice by acknowledging the difficulties women experienced when selecting garments according to a system of meaning that defined femininity in clothing in opposition to the functional. Yet women retained—and manufacturers promoted—the possibility of wearing erotic undergarments beneath serious, businesslike, or practical clothing, a trend that surged in popularity during the 1980s boom of "sexy" lingerie and "power" suits for professional career women.[41] One can interpret this mix in a number of ways. In that underwear is the most immediate layer of clothing worn next to the naked flesh and, too, because it covers the parts of the body often associated with sexual difference, it functions in a cultural sense to represent the body's sexualized self-awareness of gender distinctions. Highly feminized underwear can reassure a woman or her intimates that underneath it all, a "real" woman exists at her core. However, the sensation of wearing such garments also holds some autoerotic potential. As a mid-1910s issue of *Vogue* observed, "Nothing caresses her to the same purring delight as a soft, silken peignoir or a fluffy matinée."[42]

During this period of greater mobility and growing opportunities for women, closed-crotch drawers became more widely available. However, most women still wore open drawers until the 1910s. For example, a Butterick guide for dressmakers printed in 1911 and 1916 assumes a preference for open drawers by providing only brief instructions for closed drawers at the end. *Knickers,* a term first used around 1880, were initially distinguished from drawers by their closed crotch, though by the 1890s, the term also referred to open drawers. *Knickers* is a diminutive of *knickerbockers,* drawers with either an elastic or tape back-buttoning waistband and legs gathered at the knee. Despite the term's popular use in Great Britain to refer to women's underpants, which continues to the present, it originated in the United States. In 1809, Washington Irving published his *History of New York* under the name Diedrich Knickerbocker, a surname he took from a friend who lived in Albany. In 1831, *knickerbocker* became a popular term for a New Yorker, especially a descendant of early Dutch settlers. Illustrations in Irving's book of Dutch settlers in knee breeches are the link between this text and the article of clothing.[43]

Nineteenth-century women's knickers were usually less decorative than drawers, because their primary function was to provide warmth and protection. Yet their status as "functional" garments requires deconstruction. Open drawers' practical benefits may have included greater comfort, because the closed crotch was often constructed by a wide fabric insert or gusset that contributed to the bulk of material between the legs. This aspect would especially come into play around 1910, when the corset extended down the legs, pressing them together. Nevertheless, despite such potential discomfort, closed-crotch drawers increasingly became an option during the Edwardian period.[44]

Because dress is both sensual and visual, deeper understanding of costume changes and their significance requires close textual analysis of garments as material artifacts, as well as their two-dimensional representation. A 1901 mail-order catalog from Eaton's, Canada's leading retailer, demurely indicates the closed-crotch status of nineteen drawers for sale only by a subtle visual cue: a row of short dashes that designate a closed seam. The next page hawks corset covers, garments increasingly also known by the term *camisoles* and worn over the corset to cover the upper torso. Corset covers were drawers' complements, made of similar fabric and trim. They were available in a variety of necklines, denoted through descriptions of shapes such as round or square and attributes such as high, low, or décolleté. Though this page describes only five of twenty corset covers and chemises as having low or décolleté necklines, the two female half-figures in the illustration both wear this type, perhaps revealing Eaton's acknowledgment of the style more likely to catch the reader's attention. By exposing more of the body, particularly the breasts, the lower neckline emphasizes this undergarment's erotic aspects.[45]

Though drawers and camisoles were sold separately, sets of undergarments, an innovation of this period related to the development of the twentieth-century bridal trousseau, were also available. Analysis of illustrations in catalogs and undergarment sets in costume collections suggests that the dual and competing meanings of drawers as both erotic and modest was further articulated at this time by splitting sets into open- and closed-crotch types. Extant undergarment sets and catalog illustrations link the low neckline to the open crotch and the high neckline to the closed. One catalog page of sets reveals ambivalence about a set's potential for titillation. A sleeve detail awkwardly overlays the deepest plunge of the décolleté neckline of a garment in a bridal set, allowing the viewer to see the sleeve trim but also avoiding a full view of the low, revealing neckline.[46]

Open-drawer sets, including those handmade for bridal trousseaux, further foreground the erotic aspect. Made with extremely delicate, lightweight, and translucent fabrics, the low-neck camisoles in the sets close (or open) at the front with a single wisp of ribbon threaded through lace trim.[47] Camisoles in closed-drawer sets, which often open at the center back or front with a series of small buttons, are also often longer than those in open-crotch sets.[48] Closed-drawer sets with high-neckline camisoles frequently have less decoration and are made of heavier and stiffer fabric. When present, ornamentation is often symmetrical and orderly, unlike the flounces and ribbons of open-drawer sets. The movement of these embellishments attracts attention to the body, especially when the set is worn without an additional layer of clothing. Flounces hint at disarray, a long-noted heightener of erotic suggestion.[49]

The central implication of the open-drawer, low-neckline sets is sexual access. These garments are flimsier and easier to remove, though sexual intercourse is possible while wearing any pair of open drawers. Lisa See surmises that this expediency explained the appeal of the open drawers her great-grandfather sold to Chinese immigrant women who worked as prostitutes in late-nineteenth-century California.[50] The open design is overtly erotic, conveying a sense of desire kindled by the implication that sexual activity could commence at any moment. Whether a working girl or wife, a woman might wear such undergarments because they make her feel sexually attractive, because she feels valued only for such attraction, or because she finds that they stimulate her own erotic feelings and seductive intentions. She might enjoy the "caress" of the fabric or the active declaration of sexual arousal the garments convey. She might, however, also be bound to notions of femininity, and perhaps to circumstances, that define the female body in exclusively sexual or reproductive terms that in turn tie her to a submissive role in other areas of life.

An 1883 Frenchwoman's advice about the importance of the "conjugal chemise" makes clear the erotic implications and purpose of the similarly designed open-drawer, low-neckline camisole sets:

> Do not describe it to young girls . . . but it must be placed in their bridal trousseau. They will not wear it immediately; but after a while they will understand the value of this oriental silk or batiste, with large lace inserts, all aquiver with valenciennes flounces that embellish it at the

Figure 6. This
1904 open-crotch
drawers and
camisole set for a
bridal trousseau is
made of light,
translucent fabric
trimmed with a
"transparent net-
work" of lace and
ribbon inserts.
With permission
of the Royal
Ontario Museum
© ROM.

hem. They will become accustomed to this transparent network, which in front—from the beginning of the bosom to the belt—reveals the charming graces of a young and supple bust.

Roland Barthes's concept of "appearance-as-disappearance" also figures here. His critical question, "Is not the most erotic portion of a body *where the garment gapes* . . . the intermittence of skin flashing between . . . articles of clothing?" explains not only the effects of such trousseau articles' design but also the sexual appeal and eroticizing effects of open drawers generally.[51]

Closed-drawer sets, however, provide greater modesty, both in clothing a greater area of the body and in designs that attract less attention to the body. Their fabric lends a sense of the ordinary, of the everyday, as these undergarments maintain their protective function of shielding outerwear from flesh and adding a layer for warmth. Modesty does not necessarily inhibit sexual pleasure, but these garments convey a sense of a properly restrained sexuality. The choice of modest undergarments might express discomfort with open display of sexual excitement or might instead reveal a pragmatic need for undergarments that last longer and serve a wider range of purposes. A woman who wears them might not put sexual expressiveness at the forefront of her identity or might in fact identify modesty as her chief allure.

The interplay of modesty and eroticism clearly generates both contradictory and consonant meanings. Yet this central dialectic of fashion sets up a framework for understanding female bodies in particular ways—a gendered embodiment—that ultimately dissolves such distinctions and resolves their contradictions. Identifying particular practices in dress as modest forms a complement to those defined as erotic, marking female bodies as sexual whichever set of practices a woman engages in. The open or closed option furthers the distinction of meaning that each garment transfers to the body and the psyche of the woman who wears it. Modesty, which the influential Flugel considered to be one of three basic functions of clothing, is thus an inherently gendered, critical component of a Western fashion system that constructs different meanings for men and women.[52]

· · · · ·

In the early twentieth century, the practice of linking modesty with concealment and eroticism with display was challenged in new ways. The emerging world of consumerism and commercialized leisure exposed undergarments in public spaces by daylight and on theater screens by the flickering lights of movie projectors, heightening tensions about the presumed opposition of modesty and eroticism. The traditional practice of exhibiting the bridal trousseau to wedding guests became "indecent," at the same time that advertising, department store displays, and film images widely disseminated knowledge of what lay beneath women's outer clothing. These new sites of display altered fashion practices. Most of the hundreds of thousands of women visitors to the new amusement parks, for example, experienced firsthand the entertainment value of the public exposure of their drawers when surprise blasts of air from beneath the ground blew up their skirts on certain attractions. In one Coney Island attraction, this event occurred while women unknowingly walked in a darkened room across a stage in front of an unseen audience. The erotic tension generated by concealment and display was thus destabilized in the new contexts that legitimized open display of undergarments while attempting to retain their sexual meanings.[53]

By 1908, Eaton's and Sears catalogs allowed for the explicit choice of open or closed drawers in many of the styles it advertised. Costume historians Phillis and C. Willett Cunnington also note that "closed knickers acquired more colour" and began sharing the same variety of fabrics as open drawers, including cotton, linen, silk, flannel, flannelette, natural and knitted wool, and silk. In addition, an option introduced in the mid-1880s, the "divided skirt," became more widely available at this time. The split reality of this undergarment remained hidden behind the folds of its skirtlike exterior. Some versions had a button-fastening gusset crotch, which allowed the wearer to open or close the crotch at appropriate moments. Thus, divided skirts mediated the skirt/trouser and open-/closed-crotch dyads.[54]

After 1909, the fashionable silhouette and the undergarments required to produce it changed. Skirts narrowed, some to such an extreme degree that they were termed "hobble skirts." Some women wore a fetter, or "hobble garter," around their calves to prevent their skirts from splitting open when they walked.[55] In line with these changes, the volume in drawers decreased, as did the number of layers of undergarments generally.[56] The slimmer line of the 1910s began to give way to the 1920s "boyish" silhouette. Indeed, the "flapper" emerged as early as 1913 as the bohemian version of the prevalent working-class pleasure seeker, although the style would not become mainstream until the next decade.[57] The freer movement women needed for dancing and amusement-park attractions stimulated innovations in underwear, such as the "tango knickers" that appeared in 1914.[58] The terms *drawers* and *knickers* were becoming interchangeable in this transitional period, although drawers kept their association with the older open-crotch style of underwear whereas knickers continued to refer to more modern modes through the 1920s in the United States and England.[59]

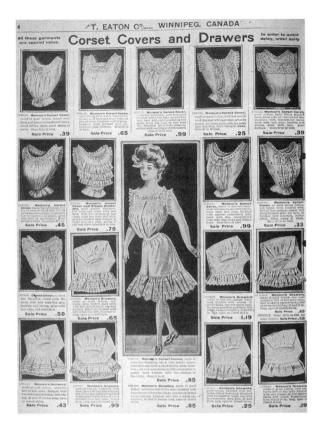

Figure 7. Eaton's, Canada's largest department store, offered "open or closed" drawers in its 1908 mail-order catalog. Courtesy, University of Toronto Press.

According to *Women's Wear Daily*, the use of closed drawers superseded that of open drawers by 1917.[60] Thus, the growing acceptance of closed drawers occurred in the 1910s' context of intensive public discussion of women's sexuality and women's rights.[61] The active and controversial campaigns for suffrage and birth control not only brought forward these issues but also brought women into the streets and newspapers to contest prevailing attitudes and statutes and to express their own views. Women won access to the vote and to birth control by agitation, organization, and persuasion, means that in themselves helped change views of women's proper sphere and behavior and generated public power for women. Both campaigns also provided a forum for people opposed to women's equal political status and reproductive self-determination. These issues spoke directly to the subject of power, given that access to birth control might make women men's sexual equals just as suffrage made them equal citizens. Women's activism in the birth control and suffrage movements was comparable to their increasing partnership in the public culture of commercial amusements and their growing presence in higher education, professional and white-collar occupations, and the labor movement. In a range of arenas, women defied long-held notions of female propriety to pursue political aims, professional achievement, economic goals, and pleasurable experiences.[62]

The closing of the crotch during this contentious period had cultural ramifications, including a reversal in the meanings of the open and closed crotch. The modesty associated with open-crotch drawers converted to wantonness, whereas transgressive connotations of closed-crotch drawers as trousers became muted. Several core issues of the suffrage movement are relevant to the latter connotations because of the link between trousers and power. Because the ultimately successful campaign to decriminalize birth control involved the detachment of sexual activity from procreation, women's public activism on this issue suggested an overturning of the Victorian ideology of passionlessness, and thus also of open drawers' connotation of modesty.

Increased agitation for birth control came on the heels of heightened fears of "race suicide," a white middle-class response to higher birthrates of immigrants, nonwhites, and the working class. Articulating opposition to women's waged work and higher education in terms of race suicide was an attempt to justify maintaining limited opportunities for women. Placing maternal obligations in terms of national, race, and class duty does, however, draw on a notion of voluntarism. Thus, the proponents of race-suicide theories also propelled, however unwittingly, the acceptance of maternity and sexual pleasure as a choice for women.[63]

The movement of closed drawers from the dominant choice to virtually the only option continued with the entry of the United States into World War I. The war gave women opportunities to work in a variety of traditionally male occupations, some of which necessitated wearing trousers. Thus, once again, a divided garment emerged from beneath the skirt and became acceptable women's wear. The donning of trousers was not without controversy, and both opponents and proponents of women's entry into new occupations used trousers as a symbol. One-piece outfits long known as overalls were called "womanalls" in some areas to soften the impact of women's capable assumption of "manly" tasks that involved risk, strength, stamina, and dirt. Women's work trousers were also called bloomers to clearly demark and identify them as feminine. Ironically, a name that once caused shock waves now became a tool for assuaging anxieties.[64]

The experiences of women during World War I were an important step toward the later twentieth-century acceptance of women's practice of wearing a divided garment as outerwear on a daily basis. The potential for permitting women to wear trousers during the war years is revealed in the surprisingly flexible attitude of Chicago garment manufacturer Matt Rae, who stated in 1917, "A woman will wear overalls or any kind of bloomers only so long as she absolutely has to. Of course, if they prefer to wear bloomers we can make them as easily as we can skirts." Bloomers and overalls were being sold for gardening and housework but were considered "too new" or improper to be worn for other purposes. Rae and other skirt manufacturers agreed that overalls would not affect the skirt business at that time.[65]

The common sight of working-class women wearing divided garments while engaged in war work set in motion the legitimization of women in trousers. Upper-class women's contribution followed, when the elegant lounging-pajama sets they wore at home or at beach resorts in the 1920s later became acceptable street wear.[66] The appearance of a "pajama-clad chorus" in the 1924 Broadway play *Be Yourself* also contributed to changing perceptions. *Women's Wear Daily* found the chorus costumes a sign that "pajamas are becoming dignified by use elsewhere than in the boudoir." The work of avant-garde American women designers, such as sartorial and political radical Elizabeth Hawes, further expanded the presence of women in pants. Hawes, reportedly the first woman to wear men's jeans in New York City, not only offered women's trousers in the 1930s but also photographed models wearing them with legs boldly astride. Thus, the ultimate acceptance of trousers for women emerged from the confluence of working-class women's successful intrusion on the gender division of labor, upper-class women's leisure pursuits, the creative vision of designers, and the great popularizing impact of stage and screen.[67]

The acceptance of work trousers and pajamas for women, whether begrudging or enthusiastic, likely contributed to the growing use of closed drawers in the late 1910s and 1920s. The declining use of the rigid nineteenth-century corset, considered by most historians to be virtually obsolete after the war, implies as well the declining need to wear open drawers to simplify the passage of bodily waste. Yet the continuing use of twentieth-century styled corsets and the new girdles could present similar difficulties. Of undeniable importance were the hem hikes and skimpier dresses of the postwar period, which threatened to expose the crotch. However, this latter reasoning follows the logic of modesty, ignoring the logic of eroticism.

The design of combinations, one-piece undergarments that served as both drawer and chemise, complicates analysis. Combinations, made of silk and chamois leather, first appeared in the 1870s, though originally they were not worn next to the skin. Dr. Jaeger's 1880s woolen combinations marked the origin of the garment still known as the union suit.[68] Their use was promoted by rational dress advocates who believed in the healthful qualities, particularly greater warmth and comfort, of wool or cotton bifurcated undergarments.[69] Nineteenth-century combinations of both the decorative and practical types predominantly had open crotches, following the trends in drawers and knickers. In the twentieth century, variations on the combinations concept proliferated because the garments allowed for fewer layers of undergarments, helping women achieve the slimmer silhouette of the day.[70] By the 1910s, some combinations with open crotches were referred to as "envelope chemises" because of an attached overskirt that gave the effect of a chemise. Combinations with "teddy-bear drawers," known as teddies after the mid-1920s, had a closed crotch and open slash at the outer thigh seams.[71] The 1917 English term *cami-knickers* described combinations made of delicate fabrics rather than wools or cottons, whereas 1920s "step-ins," though made of similar fabrics, were associated with comfort and modernity.[72] Their popularity led to use of the term *separate step-ins* to refer to contemporary short drawers.[73]

Several 1920s variations of combinations addressed the transition taking place in crotch treatment. Some combinations had crotch pieces with buttons that, like divided skirts, allowed either an open or a closed crotch.[74] Others had a narrow piece of fabric attached to the inside center front and back of the combination, which hung several inches below the crotch and had buttons at midpoint between the legs.[75] A more extreme version replaced this button tab with a thin ribbon. These combinations looked similar to slips but were shorter than the slips of that period. The addition of the narrow tab or ribbon is puzzling in that it served no apparent purpose. Though this addition may have kept the combination from riding up if the wearer raised her arms or performed some other vigorous movement, it was more likely an archaic vestige of the sort that occasionally remains with the design of clothing even after it has lost its function. Military uniforms, for example, often retain once-useful aspects as residual embellishments.[76] Given that combinations were considered to be half drawers, the tab or ribbon gave the wearer a semblance of propriety that a slip worn without drawers could not. Worn during the last years of open-crotch drawers, these combinations provided the final opportunity for a woman to retain modesty while remaining free of closed fabric between her legs.

In 1925, according to Mary Louise Roberts, French journalist René Bizet concluded that "every aspect of female dress had not only changed but become the mirror opposite of what it had been in 1900." Six years later, Alabama observer Matilda Kitchens concluded that "modesty was eventually the force that closed the door on open-seat drawers' dominance."[77] These writers suggest that the disappearance of the tab and ribbon crotch was the result of a reversal in the prevailing meanings of open- and closed-crotch drawers. The open-crotch design's earlier connotations of modesty and propriety transformed into those of eroticism and lascivious intent. The closed crotch, previously thought improper, unhealthful, or conducive to cross-dressing, came to signify modesty and propriety. These newer meanings, which hold to the present day, make clear that the crotch closed as notions about and public expressions of women's sexuality changed in the first decades of the twentieth century.

Proof of the reversal that Bizet identified also lies with the last garment to retain the open crotch, the union suit. In that the design of the union suit is so similar for men and women, the suit approached gender neutrality and thus was desexualized. Union suits could retain an open crotch longer because, unlike most other women's undergarments, their erotic potential was muted rather than amplified. The sexual access open drawers provided could coexist with women's propriety only in the context of an ideology of female passionlessness and social structures of masculine domination. When women publicly asserted their own claims to sexual pleasure, political power, and economic independence, an open crotch was no longer respectable.[78]

The history of women's divided undergarments is as enmeshed in controversy as the wearing of trousers which were not hidden from public view. Continuing restrictions on women's freedom to wear closed, divided garments worn previously only by men ensured that these garments remained associated with masculine power and privilege. Thus, the switch to closed drawers could be seen as a sign of women's growing economic opportunities and increased control over sexual access to their bodies. A 1924 *Women's Wear Daily* advertisement for the McLoughlin's Fitz-U Bloomer suggests the unfolding possibilities for greater freedom of movement and control. An ice-skating young woman in her flapper hat, sleeveless fur-trimmed sports shirt, and Fitz-U Bloomer stretches one arm in front of her, leading her gaze and body forward, while her other arm reaches back to hold her raised bent leg at the ankle. The patented "seamless"-crotch bloomer, available in double or single reinforcement, sells, according to the ad copy, because it is "stretchable and non-breakable even to the stitch. It gives every comfort and longer wear, because there is no Tension or Binding Crotch Seams. Nothing to Pull, Split or Break, as it is all Give; still the Bloomer clings beautifully to the form." Though not meant as outerwear, the bloomer, thanks to the wide gusset in the crotch, allows the skater to arch her leg in the air and enjoy the full capabilities of her body without fearing unexpected revelation of her flesh or a penetrating male gaze.[79]

The skater is a young woman, however, and the closed-crotch drawers that contributed to the construction of the adolescent silhouette of the 1920s flapper evoke the drawers that girls had worn since the nineteenth century, which allowed greater freedom of movement but within a restricted range of activity. Women's closed-crotch, divided undergarments, which became known as step-ins rather than drawers as the terminology for such garments became gender specific in this decade, reassured anxieties through their association with the virginal. However, their presexual status did not entirely negate the erotic appeal of the flapper's step-ins, not only because step-ins revealed more of the legs but also because of the seductive quality that idealized virginity holds for some individuals. In addition, as a required component of postwar women's fashionable dress, step-ins were associated with the pleasures accorded by freer courtship relations and recreational marital sex. Most important, these recently condoned practices and the clothing women wore to engage in them were codified as modern in the 1920s by identifying Victorianism with prudery—an outdated sexual ideology exemplified by the now-ridiculed abundance and weight of that era's women's clothing. This view helped construct the "myth of Victorian repression" which, as historian Christina Simmons points out, "represented a cultural adjustment of male power to women's departure from the Victorian order. It constituted a strategic modification rather than a decline of male dominance."[80]

The commercially successful 1937 comedy *Topper*, based on the popular 1926 novel by Thorne Smith, interprets this transformation. Closed-crotch step-in drawers are key to the film's (and novel's) narrative resolution. The casting of top-billed Cary Grant and Constance Bennett focuses viewers' attention on the Kerbys, a live fast/die young couple. Yet at the heart of this picture is the endangered marriage of Cosmo and Mrs. Topper (Roland Young and Billie Burke). Mrs. Topper's old-fashioned sensibilities, which influence her fashion choices and demand of her husband a boring, routinized, alcohol-free existence, endanger her marriage. A pair of lacy, closed-crotch step-ins come to symbolize the sexual excitement and fun that are new requirements for the modern woman who wishes to keep her husband from straying and to find acceptance among her social peers. When at the film's end Mrs. Topper dons the step-ins, which she previously associated with women of dubious reputation, she shows that she has made the needed transition from Victorianism. What is also apparent is that Cosmo Topper will now rule the roost as well as the office, as the film shows that when Mrs.

Figure 8. Cosmo Topper (Roland Young) shows his proper wife (Billie Burke) a pair of sexy modern underpants in the hilarious 1937 film *Topper*. Courtesy of the Academy of Motion Picture Arts and Sciences.

Topper conforms to the new fashion in underpants, she also relinquishes her power to regulate home life and social morality.[81]

Topper makes clear that excessive indulgence in sensual pleasures is a fatal mistake, but lack of such pleasures leads to unhappiness and divorce. Fortunately, however, the lingerie shop is a stop on the road to marital bliss that is accessible to all. Wearing step-in drawers signifies women's adherence to the new codes of middle-class marital sexuality, which allow women sexual passion, but in the service of pleasing their husbands and keeping them from straying. Moreover, women must relinquish the domestic power they achieved in the Victorian era through their status as the passionless, moral superiors of men in order to conform to the redefined contours of modern, sexualized femininity.[82]

. . . . .

The contradictory meanings of nineteenth-century open drawers as both modest and erotic allowed white, middle-class female bodies simultaneously to conform to and defy the ideals of the cult of true white womanhood, and thus be construed both as sexually accessible to male prerogative and also as sexually desirous subjects. Nonetheless, unequal access to social power and the strikingly divergent understandings of male and female sexuality that dominated in this period meant that men and women experienced the sexual aspects of open drawers differently. Open drawers provide material evidence that female submission to gendered codes of respectability was eroticized. The dynamic interplay of modesty and eroticism not only afforded middle-class women space to maneuver within the strictures of propriety but also maintained cultural codes that constructed women in terms of sexual attractiveness and availability to men, ensuring that they demonstrated adherence to the tenets of true womanhood.

Open drawers also tell us something about white, middle-class men's desires. Certainly, defining their female peers as sexually passionless and thus morally superior was a key cultural tool for keeping women of their class economically dependent and politically disenfranchised, and for marginalizing women of lower classes. However, the acceptance of open drawers included an unspoken acknowledgment that men did not dispense completely with respectable women's erotic capacities. Working through a complex set of needs and desires, men could find heightened sexual pleasure in open drawers' eroticization of the very modesty necessary for women to maintain social respectability in their eyes.

By 1930, short, closed-crotch drawers like those worn by modern Diana in *Our Dancing Daughters* and the reformed Mrs. Topper became the norm. The larger, longer, and open drawers worn by proper middle-class women until the early twentieth century were viewed as hopelessly old-fashioned, prudish, and ridiculous. Yet open-crotch drawers in our own era hold an entirely different meaning, with their strong evocation of eroticism. Turn-of-the-century changes in crotch design and meanings of women's drawers reveal how new constructions of female sexuality took shape in a critical transitional period. Open drawers remained in vogue throughout the nineteenth century, when Victorian modesty for women was supposedly the predominant cultural code. Wearing these drawers marked a female body as conforming to the dictates of respectable femininity, including the unspoken provision of sexual accessibility. In contrast, a woman wearing a divided, closed-crotch under- or outer garment in that period would be engaging in the sexually charged and unrespectable transgression of cross-dressing. In the early twentieth century, women increasingly wore shorter, closed-crotch drawers as they struggled and won the right to vote, and sought to share public space with men, assert their sexual desires, and engage in waged labor. Significantly, the accepted sexual and moral meanings of open- and closed-crotch undergarments reversed along with women's preference in crotch construction. By the 1920s, the reworked requirements of modern sexual propriety meant that reputable women, who successfully incorporated claims to sexual pleasure into a new definition of respectability, would don only closed-crotch step-ins. As a result, in the twentieth century, open-crotch undergarments primarily signified eroticism. Yet the reversal only went so far. New requirements of sexually seductive dress replaced older modes. Women's new freedoms would not come unchecked, for as women leveled the playing field of sexual pleasure, they no longer could commandeer men on the basis of moral superiority. The transition from open to closed drawers not only reveals the power of clothing as a medium of signification but also shows how women's struggles for autonomy interact with resistant social forces to reconfigure gender distinctions. The abandonment of Victorian feminine ideals and conceptions of modesty ironically both accompanied the shift to closed-crotch drawers and prompted open drawers' reinscription in American culture with a high erotic charge.

2 Corsets and Girdles

Loosen your girdle and let 'er fly!

Athlete Babe Didrikson Zaharias

During the nineteenth century, virtually all free-born women in the United States wore corsets. Yet from midcentury onward, the purpose and meaning of the corset generated heated debate among physicians, ministers, couturiers, feminist dress reformers, health and hygiene activists, and advocates of tight-lacing. Their lengthy argument suggests that keeping women in corsets was an ongoing project.

In the early twentieth century, these corset debates intensified. Turn-of-the-century corset styles became even more constricting, and thus protests against their use gained ground. In addition, young women in the 1910s began to reject the Victorian moral sensibilities—and the fashions inspired by them—that symbolically and literally restricted women's mobility in both private and public spheres. Women's claims to wage work, academic and physical education, public protest over access to suffrage and birth control, and pleasurable leisure activities such as dancing at tango parties all brought daily corset wear into question. Arguments supporting corset use changed as a result. And, though most women continued to wear corsets, demands for more comfort in clothing and the rising appeal of "modernity" as a sales tool changed their shape.

G. B. Pulfer, treasurer and general manager of the Kalamazoo Corset Company, explained in the trade journal *Corsets & Lingerie* why women wore corsets in 1921: "Fear! Fear of ill health, fear of sagging bodies, fear of lost figure, fear of shiftless appearance in the nicest of clothing, fear of sallow complexion. Fear sends them to the corsetiere, trembling; the same corsetiere from whom they fled mockingly a couple of years back, at the beck of a mad style authority who decreed 'zat ze body must be free of ze restrictions, in order zat ze new styles shall hang so freely.' "[1]

Pulfer addressed these comments to the journal's national readership of corset manufacturers, retailers, department store buyers, and saleswomen. His article was one of a series addressing industry concerns about women's continued consent to wearing corsets and was part of an intensive coordinated effort by manufacturers to revitalize and revamp pro-corset argumentation. Thus, Pulfer's article also addressed the fear of corset manufacturers. Their fear, which exploded on the panicked pages of *Corsets & Lingerie* throughout the early 1920s, was of losing control over how and when women changed the way they dressed.[2]

Scholarship on nineteenth-century women's history and dress explores the power of corsets to regulate women's behavior as well as to signify women's subordinate status. Studies by Helene Roberts, David Kunzle, Lois Banner, and Valerie Steele demonstrate the well-established and lasting iconic power of the corset as a conveyor of social meaning. Just as these scholars disagree about what corsets meant to female corset wearers as well as to corset defenders and opponents of both genders, their studies also make abundantly clear that the corset became a locus for a number of competing significations. To move beyond previous corset controversies, we thus need to ask not only how dressing practices function as structures of domination or resources of resistance but also how these functions are instituted and why these practices generate both contested and contradictory meanings. These questions address not only the history of the corset as an enduring and pervasive article of women's clothing but also the history of how the interpretations of the corset affected women's lives as they struggled to alter the shape of femininity and gender relations.[3]

Building on earlier works, this chapter begins at the turn of the century, when use of the rigid nineteenth-century corset declined, and continues through the first decades of the twentieth century, when challenges to the corset intensified. Significantly, this time frame also encompasses an era of heightened agitation for women's political, sexual, economic, and social equality. Yet we know that achievements in one period do not prevent backlashes in succeeding decades. Analysis of how the commercialized practice and ideology of corsetry shaped the way women viewed, imagined, and experienced their own bodies can help us understand both the persistence and the reshaping of problematic gender structures and identities.

Corset manufacturers' coordinated response to women's new widespread defiance of older fashion standards, which enlisted corset saleswomen to deploy a merchandising campaign against the "corsetless evil," emphasized youthful standards of beauty, developed scientific discourse that viewed the female body as inherently flawed, and connected ideologies of racial purity, national security, and heterosexual privilege to corset use. Examining the marketing strategies developed to keep women in corsets, as well as efforts to corral oppositional practices, reveals how the corset's instrumentality changed in the twentieth century. Nineteenth-century efforts to keep women corseted drew upon, legitimated, and constructed particular notions about femininity, propriety, and the female body. In the twentieth century, corset discourses also incorporated ideas about race, nation, and the importance of science and modernity to everyday life. Thus, the meanings that corsetry impressed upon women's bodies shifted with industrialization; women's fears of aging, imperfect, inferior, unfashionable, and unscientific bodies replaced earlier fears of moral turpitude and questionable respectability. Most significantly, industrialists' fear of diminishing profits played and preyed upon the long-standing cultural fear of unrestrained women.

·   ·   ·   ·   ·

After 1900, corsets became progressively longer on the hips, and the top of the corset moved down the torso toward the waistline. The popularity of the uncomfortable S-curve corsets favored by Gibson Girls of this era, which threw the bust forward and the buttocks back, declined after 1905 with wider use of straight-front corsets. The S curve blunted the athleticism and mobility of the Gibson Girl, and the obvious manipulation of the body necessary to create the S-curve silhouette was an easy target for anticorset agitation, which defended the "natural" body. However, the necessity of wearing a corset was also vigorously defended throughout this period, and, once the straight-front corsets succeeded the S-curve corsets, anatomical reasons were cited as the basis for the corset's necessity.[4]

Havelock Ellis was among the experts cited in the popular press who claimed that females of the human species required corseting because the evolution from "horizontality to verticality" was more difficult for females than for males. "Woman might be physiologically truer to herself," Havelock Ellis insists, "if she went always on all fours. It is because the fall of the viscera in woman when she imitated man by standing erect induced such profound physiological displacements . . . that the corset is morphologically essential."[5] A supporting argument claimed that recent archaeological finds in Crete and Greece, in addition to the discovery of cave paintings in Spain and France, proved that women had cinched their waists for the past 40,000 years due to anatomical necessity. Thus, corseting continued to be an evolutionary requirement. Demonstrating the extent to which present concerns colored the interpretation of ancient representations, one commentator detected the "debutante slouch," a hunched posture popularized by young women in the 1910s, in the cave paintings.[6]

Straight-front corsets remained quite long over the thighs to conform the body to the slimmer line of skirts. These longer corsets could be extremely confining, and women who wore them had difficulty bending their legs enough to sit down. The binding of the legs persisted with the notorious "hobble skirt," introduced in 1908, which had an extremely narrow hemline around the ankles that inhibited walking. French couturier Paul Poiret claimed that he invented the hobble skirt as part of his successful "war upon [the corset]." Poiret states in his autobiography, "Like all great revolutions, that one had been made in the name of Liberty—to give free play to the abdomen: it was equally in the name of Liberty that I proclaimed the fall of the corset. . . . Yes, I freed the bust but I shackled the legs."[7]

Women in the United States did not toss away their corsets *en masse* after Poiret's introduction of dresses designed to be worn without corsets. Indeed, to achieve the fashionable line, most women still had to be corseted. In fact, Poiret's corsetless fashions were in part an appropriation of design ideas from the cultural fringe which he marketed to the middle class. Since the nineteenth century, the idea of abandoning the corset had been floating in the margins of feminist dress reform and the aesthetic and communitarian movements. In addition, turn-of-the-century health and hygiene movements, as well as the availability of bicycles, encouraged active play for adult urban dwellers. Furthermore, a growing number of women experienced the benefits of organized sports in women's colleges. Women's access to sports and physical exercise in this period heightened their desire for less restrictive garments and prompted the development and marketing of sports corsets made of lighter and more flexible materials. Embedded in the sports corset was thus a measure of give and take between women's demands for greater comfort and freedom of movement and manufacturers' needs for profits from continued corset sales.[8]

By 1914, another popular phenomenon, the tango, also affected corset use among active American women. Women began removing their stiff corsets at parties in order to dance, and corset manufacturers responded once again by marketing dance corsets. But, like the flapper, who appeared in the mid-1910s but did not gain mainstream attention until the next decade, corsetlessness remained the domain of a daring minority of mostly young and slim women at this time. Yet although *Vogue* conceded in 1914 that "the mode of the corsetless figure is an established one—for a season, at least," it also noted that "the point has been reached where women do not have to be dictated to, as formerly, in the matter of corsets." Rather than doing away with corsets entirely, *Vogue* argued that because many corset models were now available, "the present mode is not a uniform one. . . . A

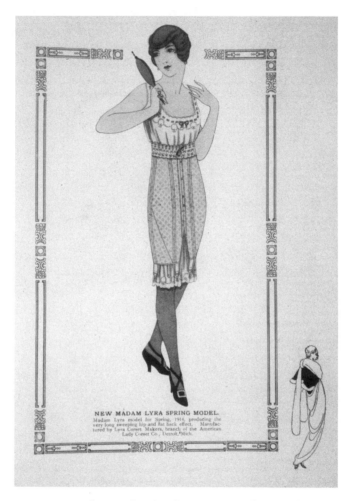

NEW MADAM LYRA SPRING MODEL.
Madam Lyra model for Spring, 1914, producing the
very long sweeping hip and flat back effect. Manufactured by Lyra Corset Makers, branch of the American
Lady Corset Co., Detroit, Mich.

Figure 9. "Producing the very long sweeping hip and flat back effect," corsets in the early 1910s conformed women's bodies to the narrow skirt silhouette then fashionable. *Women's & Infants' Furnisher,* January 1914. Courtesy of Special Collections, Gladys Marcus Library, Fashion Institute of Technology.

Figure 10. This ad for an early sports corset appeared in the April 1918 issue of *Women's & Infants' Furnisher*. Courtesy of Special Collections, Gladys Marcus Library, Fashion Institute of Technology.

year ago where one or two corsets would answer, it is now not a luxury, but a necessity, to have a greater number, and each of a different sort." Thus, corset manufacturers' decision to supply women with lighter and more flexible corsets was not mere concession but also a means to increase the number of corsets sold. Nonetheless, increasing the number of corset styles began to dissolve monolithic fashion standards, and women gained greater power to determine their own shapes within fashionability.[9]

Vogue duly noted the dangers of women's expanded power in a 1917 article entitled "Woman Decides to Support Herself." The article gave the sportswoman credit for the initial blow toward "undermining the power of fashion" while castigating her "absurd willingness to support her figure without external aid." It then analyzed "the fatal mistake of couturiers" that had caused this turn of events. Couturiers, *Vogue* explained, did not foresee the ramifications of their recent designs for the so-called natural figure. Significantly, shaping a woman's body into the "natural figure" required looser corsets than women had worn before. When couturiers attempted to reimpose a more constricted waist, "the unexpected, the unprecedented, happened. Women refused to wear them; they actually did that unheard-of thing." Eventually, according to *Vogue,* fashionable women and couturiers reached a compromise: waists would be taken in, but not much.[10]

Women's desires for self-sufficiency, alluded to in the article's title, were not, of course, limited to the sphere of dress. Agitation for suffrage and birth control was in full swing by 1917, including daily picketing in front of the White House until the passage of women's suffrage in 1919. In addition, once World War I ended, some of the mid-1910s subcultural trends hit the mainstream. Shorter skirt lengths, which shockingly revealed women's bare legs, became a focus of controversy. While ministers admonished from their pulpits, college deans instituted dress codes, and women formed short skirt defense leagues, debates raged in the popular press about what was seen as either the new immodesty or the new freedom in women's dress and behavior.[11]

Debates about the redefinition of women's propriety took place amid the uncertainty of postwar reconstruction. In 1919, an unprecedented four million workers participated in more than three thousand strikes to consolidate wartime gains and achieve further improvements in working conditions. Employers saw in this labor unrest the influence of the Bolshevik revolution and viewed both as merely the first stage in the undoing of the current world order. In 1920, the U.S. Department of Justice responded to this fear by arresting thousands of radicals and deporting hundreds of immigrants to quell opposition. Known as the Red Scare, this state suppression of dissent disrupted many lives and raised troubling questions about the government's role in maintaining power at the expense of constitutional freedoms.[12]

The construction of corsetlessness as a dangerous evil drew upon moral language similar to that employed in the domestic suppression of radicalism. Corsetlessness had, after all, long been identified with radical feminist and utopian movements. Confusion also persisted about which postwar changes were American and modern and which were foreign and menacing. For example, when New York City resident Mildred Rosenstein, whose lifelong anticommunism probably began in those years, bobbed her waist-length hair in the late 1910s, her brother called her a Bolshevik. As late as 1925, a report on corset manufacturers' efforts to "reestablish a vogue for their wares" related the "query, 'are corsets only another obsolete tradition to be cast aside'" to "the unchartered freedom of the Bolshevist figure."[13]

· · · · ·

Concerns about whether women would continue to wear corsets took place at a time when women challenged other conventions of propriety in dress.

The expanded availability of ready-to-wear clothing in the early twentieth century increased the possibilities for fashioning one's own style, and thus for committing "fashion don'ts." Mass production also facilitated quicker translation of individual choices into widespread fashion trends. The growing availability of wage work for women enabled a wide range of shoppers to buy a variety of less expensive articles of clothing and put them together as they pleased. Some cities passed laws to suppress fashion changes they deemed indecent. This legislative means of regulating dress drew on the long-standing tradition of sumptuary laws. Such statutes first appeared in Europe in the late thirteenth century to exclude all but the aristocracy from wearing particular garments, colors, and fabrics. Though enforcement proved difficult, sumptuary laws continued to flourish throughout the next several centuries. By the late eighteenth century, when the ascendant bourgeoisie established its right to display acquired wealth, such statutes had become irrelevant.[14]

Legal statutes governing clothing in the nineteenth and twentieth centuries regulated gender rather than class status. Some laws, for example, forbade cross-dressing and women's wearing of trousers. Male transvestites were subject to arrest and imprisonment, whereas prohibitions against female cross-dressing meant that a woman had to wear a minimum of three identifiably female articles of clothing to avoid arrest. In the early twentieth century, the state also defined and controlled standards of female modesty through laws mandating appropriate street wear. The Illinois state legislature, for example, considered a bill in 1911 to prohibit both hobble skirts and bifurcated "harem" skirts.[15] As in previous eras, such attempts at state sartorial control did not always succeed. In Traverse City, Michigan, Mayor Swanton's order banning knickerbockers for women prompted a protest parade by "club women, shop workers, clerks, stenographers and high school girls." Moreover, the women were backed by chamber of commerce claims that the ban would "seriously interfere with tourist and resort business." Sensitivity to fashion trends could be an important component in maintaining a city's financial solvency.[16]

School and workplace dress codes in the early twentieth century provided additional means of restricting what women could wear. At Vassar College in 1922, pressure from "staid Poughkeepsie" led Miss Palmer, head warden at Vassar, to believe that students should not be "the first to introduce the garment [knickerbockers] to Poughkeepsie" and to ban it outside of sport wear on campus. Though the newspaper account of this incident expresses certainty that students would observe the ruling, dissent among students persisted. Protestors insisted that women at Vassar should have the same freedom as students at Smith, Barnard, and Cornell, where knicker-bockers were not regulated.[17]

Whereas women like the Vassar students sought greater mobility in dress, they also wanted to dress in up-to-date, "modern" clothing. The heightened emphasis on currency, and the diminished influence of moral imperatives as ready-to-wear options increased, fueled the fashion system itself because it encouraged women to consult fashion experts about the latest styles. The proliferation of women's fashion magazines and fashion columns in daily newspapers kept the female public informed about the current mode and ways to achieve it. *Good Housekeeping* even touted its fashion savvy to promote the magazine's circulation among its modest middle-class readership.

> Walk down almost any street. You will see three or four—or perhaps five—different "styles." Which one is correct; which one reflects the taste and discrimination and quality of design that *are* the accepted mode? How can you distinguish? . . . Those who want the outré, the garish, the vulgar, will find nothing to interest them in *Good House-keeping*'s fashion department. But those of you who want the newest fashions, authenticated and certain, those who want to avoid costly mistakes, those who want to dress well and with distinction on a modest income will utilize the many fashion services provided by *Good House-keeping*.[18]

Good Housekeeping also explained the importance of attention to clothes and fashion trends, commenting that "the care of [women's] appearance has much to do with . . . success in life." However, the magazine also acknowledged the need to limit such attention: "Follow the fashions wisely but not too well. This means, judge for yourself the style which is smart—perhaps even a trifle extreme—but which has no tinge of vulgarity and which, above all things, is one that will be becoming to you. . . . It is better to err on the side of conservatism than to follow too blindly the vagaries, and often vulgarities of fashion."[19]

Apparel and retail trade journals also outlined strategies to influence customers' fashion sensibilities. *Women's & Infants' Furnisher* advised retailers to exploit saleswomen's potential for fashion guidance.

> Many times women select their clothes because of similar styles noted on others, whereas, such garments may not be at all suited to their own individual appearance or contour. For this reason a campaign of education is always wise in retail stores to teach women what to buy and the tactful salesgirl can easily sway the prospective purchaser. . . . The folk who sell women's wear at retail may not always know more about the

subject of proper selection than their patrons, but . . . in the majority of cases the shoppers are willing to be guided by expert advice, real or alleged, if the guiding is done diplomatically.[20]

Not all women in the early 1920s were willing to accept the authority of such fashion arbiters to determine the look of modernity. The No Longer Skirt League was formed by "twenty of Montreal's smartest and prettiest girls rebelling against fashion designers' attempt to reimpose long skirts on women." Members pledged to continue wearing short skirts and to "do all they can to induce other young women to keep their skirts short." Women widely supported this point of view. Even Mrs. Frederick G. Smith, president of the Massachusetts State Federation of Women's Clubs, saw "nothing objectionable in the dress of the present-day woman." Short skirt supporters prevailed, and shorter lengths remained fashionable throughout the 1920s.[21]

The vast and probing apparatus of fashion policing meant that women's "spontaneous consent" to corset use or other predominant styles of dress required force as well. Individual resistance could spread, and group-sponsored revolt within the highly charged symbolic sphere of attire occurred, even if infrequently. Yet fashion's critical dependence on innovation calls for ongoing modifications in dress. Furthermore, style dissent as well as the style of dissent can be incorporated into the fashion system as raw material for the next fad. Corset manufacturers and retailers responded to their customers' potential rejection of corsets in this era of greater fashion choice and rebellion by reformulating their product as an essential component of modern dress. In their efforts to maintain control, they used fashion institutions as a policing apparatus.

· · · · ·

Trade journals were an industry mechanism for disseminating pro-corset arguments. In 1921, *Corsets & Lingerie* identified corsetlessness as a dangerous and evil fad. According to subsequent trade accounts, this fad began after the end of World War I. However, as we have seen, corsetlessness had been a twentieth-century look since Poiret's introduction of corsetless dresses in 1908. *Vogue* magazine acknowledged this fashion trend in a 1914 pro-corset article entitled "Corseting the Corsetless Figure." That same year, *Corsets & Lingerie* noted "the popularity . . . of the corsetless figure," and a 1915 ad for foundations advertised its product in a similar way. Yet six years later, this trade journal expressed a decided panic about corsetlessness.

Moreover, it continued to refer to the specter of the evil corsetless fad throughout the 1920s.[22]

In his 1921 *Corsets & Lingerie* article, "Fighting the Corsetless Evil," G. B. Pulfer described industry strategies for stifling corsetlessness:

> The same publicity media which spread this first corsetless fad story . . . is now being utilized to spread the story of danger, the warning that has aroused our sane women to righteous fear, the warning that's sending them back to the corset shop . . . in droves. . . . When it was announced that no corset shall now be the rule, it was expected that the American corset manufacturer and the merchant would gasp, then bow their heads in gentle and piteous submission to the commands of the Parisian boulevardier. But did they? They did not. . . . The publicity campaign that sprang into life immediately could not have been more ably managed if it had been under one directing general. . . . The corset manufacturers have flooded the trade with literature and advice on how to spread the true story of the corsetless fad. The newspapers have helped considerably.[23]

Pulfer concludes by exhorting readers to "keep your literature going out, Mr. Corset Maker; keep your customers informed, Mr. Dealer."

Trade journal articles, such as "Evils of the No-Corset Fad," "Flappers Are Responsible for Corsetless Craze," and "Eminent Surgeons Endorse the Corset," indicted corsetlessness as a threatening menace. The articles enumerated horrors such as dissipation of muscular strength, injury to internal organs, corruption of standards of beauty, damage to moral fiber, contamination of race pride and purity, and destruction of American sovereignty. Some of these contentions, particularly the medical and hygienic, had been articulated previously in nineteenth-century debates about the corset. Other claims, like the patriotic and racial, were more recent concerns.[24]

The identification and explication of corsetlessness as an evil fad not only bolstered support among those whose livelihoods depended upon the continuing use of the corset but also armed the industry with the weapon of ideology. As G. B. Pulfer quite openly pointed out, the industry could disseminate this ideology in a range of tactical discourses, from public advertisements in mass-circulation print media to private conversations with women customers in the intimacy of corset fitting rooms. Through this deployment of pro-corset ideologies—culled from the discourses of professionalized medicine, the eugenics movement, and Victorian constructions of femininity and circulated through mass media and the marketplace—manufacturers constructed the corset as an instrument of cultural hegemony.

Extreme assertions in the trade journals about the wide-ranging detrimental effects of corsetlessness convey manufacturers' panic about the potential for women to stop wearing corsets. Panic is also evident in their many contradictory statements, at one moment expressing relief over the fad's demise, at the next moment citing the continuing need to exhort against it, and finally bemoaning the fad's ongoing effect on sales and profits. In addition, one can sense panic in confused comments about manufacturers' continuing ability to manipulate women's fickle fashion sensibilities. Moreover, the trade journal articles seem to emanate more from emotion than fact, in that the authors produce no data to support their fears about declining corset sales. As one popular magazine said, "Naturally these groups of elders are in a panic—'Are corsets doomed?'"[25]

The postwar economic depression of 1920 to 1922 also contributed to the climate of anxiety. The clothing industry was one of the first to decline, in April 1920. Prior to this time, production had finally reestablished levels close to those in force before the 1914–1915 depression. In other words, 1919, a year of "general prosperity and expansion" in the industry, was followed by yet another slump. The garment industry reached its lowest level of employment in June 1921, when employment was 35 percent below June 1914 levels. Figures for the underwear industry, which do not include corsets, show a dramatic 50 percent drop in sales between 1920 and 1921. Profitability in that sector of the trade returned in 1922, though sales remained below 1920 levels for several years.[26]

Census statistics for the corset industry, however, indicate insignificant change in the value of products manufactured between 1919 and 1921 and show a 3.2 percent increase between 1921 and 1923. Therefore, no evidence exists to substantiate trade journal reports of a frightening drop in corset sales, especially considering the depression in the garment industry and in the U.S. economy generally. In fact, the corset industry managed very ably through this short but sharp economic decline. Thus, the ideological nature of the corset panic, spawned by wider circumstances of social transition and economic upheaval, seems clear.[27]

The three tactics of the corset-panic articles—denial, attack, and incorporation—relied on assertions drawn from medicine, politics, and the culture of beauty and fashion, but not economics. Corset manufacturers and department store buyers, often the authors of these articles, drew on proscriptive discourses to infuse corset use with ideologies of domination. As a result, corset manufacturers as well as the more powerful social classes as a whole benefited because these discourses circulated in new ways, including the further commodified probing of female flesh. The successful imposition of controlling ideologies via the corset thus worked to reinscribe women's subordination generally. Corset manufacturers eased their panic about losing control of their female market by invoking, and thus reinforcing, broader structures of control.

Denial of the fad's existence helped mitigate the fears of people in the trade. It also reproduced the deflating idea that corsetlessness was not popular, and therefore not fashionable. In a July 1921 interview entitled "Corsets Still in Vogue," Miss O'Neill, a department store corset buyer, said that "while the fad for the corsetless effect is still raging, it is more a matter of 'effect' than of actuality." Manufacturers accommodated modern sensibilities by offering a new lighter and more flexible girdle as the up-to-date alternative to the corset. Though girdles initially were considered appropriate only for smaller women, the Elastowear Manufacturing Company opened up the girdle market by producing Elasto girdles for "stout women." Trade journals also discussed the importance of renaming corsets as girdles to shake off the notion that corsets were passé. In addition, the older corset itself was cited as the cause of current figure problems, which required newer corsets and girdles for correction.[28]

However, assigning blame for the instigation and spread of the corsetless fad was problematic for manufacturers. Laying the blame on Paris had its appeal but was a double-edged strategy. Ultimately, this argument undermined manufacturers' desires to keep women under the sway of elite style makers as much as possible. The idea of a top-down fashion regime appealed to manufacturers because it provided a more controlled progression of fashion changes. Questioning the importance of Paris as an arbiter of fashionability could be dangerous.

The August 1921 article "Parisian Women Wear Corsets" illustrates one way in which the trade tried to avoid this dilemma. This article claimed within the same paragraph that Parisian women had gone without corsets in past years, that U.S. readers' idea in 1920 that these women weren't wearing corsets was erroneous, that the corsetless trend in France was exaggerated in the American press, and that in any event, all French women, including couturier mannequins, were wearing corsets once again. Three months later, "Paris on the Corset Question" reasserted Parisian hegemony. "The question of corsets or no corsets as raised by the recent styles put forward by the foremost Parisian couturiers is being answered by Parisian couturiers in a characteristically Parisian fashion. The new corsets are more like the corsetless figure than the corsetless figure itself. . . . That is Parisian

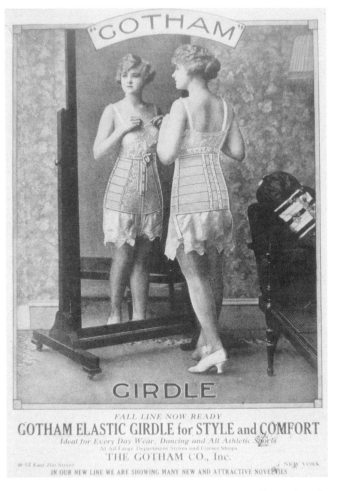

Figure 11. Manufacturers renamed corsets as girdles and made them with modern elastic. *Women's & Infants' Furnisher,* August 1921. Courtesy of Special Collections, Gladys Marcus Library, Fashion Institute of Technology.

cleverness all over. They have made a figure more natural than the natural figure and far more beautiful."[29]

Other arguments suggested that American women's body types were different from European women's and thus still required corseting. In a curious *Corset and Underwear Review* article called "The American Woman and Her Corset," columnist Gertrude Nickerson claimed that the American woman must wear restrictive garments because she

> has no definite type. We are a composite race of women . . . [who] must acknowledge our mixed blood and, while we are very proud of it, let us not forget just what it means where our figure is concerned. As we develop and approach maturity some "wayback" foreign grandmother, or several at once, may and most likely will make her hereditary attack upon us. . . . We now realize that we have indeed a handicap which we must accept as a result of our mixed races. We can understand now why the real American woman requires her corset or confining foundation for figure training more than her sisters overseas.[30]

Sisters closer to home unfortunately bore the brunt of racial arguments. Leonard Florsheim, Corset and Brassiere Association vice president and head of Kabo Corset Company, constructed the specter of the "grotesque" Indian squaw to safely position white middle-class American women between overly sophisticated French women and uncivilized indigenous American women. In his November 1921 *Corsets & Lingerie* interview, "The Evils of the No-Corset Fad," Florsheim first preyed upon fears of corsetlessness as a cause of premature aging and a thickened waistline before launching his racial attack.

> The Indian girls are known for shapely body lines in their youth, despite the fact that they never get a chance to enjoy the protection of corset or brassiere. They grow and develop "wildly." But at the age when they acquire the sobriquet of squaw, what a transformation! Squaws, especially those who have become mothers, are well known for their grotesque bodies. Nature has given them in youth well developed, shapely lines, muscles that withstand the first score and ten, but then nature changes her course and begins to add weight that gradually rounds out and converts form into the well known "mattress-tied-in-the-middle" proportions.[31]

Florsheim's depiction allowed white women both to identify with and to reject the impact of "nature" upon American Indian women.

Dutch surgeon Dr. Jan Schoemaker broadened the scope of racial concerns in an interview the following month.

Firmly-muscled women are vital, charming, full of that potential race
force which must be coined into American supremacy among men to-
morrow. But we are not trying to breed Amazons, nor are we trying to
raise a race of Oriental dancers. Your corsetless girl has naturally to fall
into one class or the other. The moment you begin to get too much of
the Amazon variation, you begin to get fuzzy upper-lips with them, and
a frothy type of male, a sort of listless love-bird, sufficiently spineless
to be able to mate and marry the domineering female of the Amazon
type.[32]

According to the doctor, corsetlessness promoted dangerous transformations in male as well as female character and anatomy and thus had disastrous consequences for the white American "race" and its global prospects
in the political and economic realignments of the postwar era.

Dr. Schoemaker embellished his homophobic hint about "fuzzy upper-
lips" in his discussion of the exercise regime required of a corsetless woman
if she were to maintain muscular health. "There is in Holland a Mrs. Dr.
Mensendieck who undertakes this sort of work for women who have ambitions in that direction. She compels them to go through their exercises absolutely nude, and on each individual of a class . . . she keeps her eye. When
a certain set of muscles sag down, as of course they will, she cries out at the
woman, 'Keep that stomach in. Hold up there in the rear.' And so on."[33] By
renouncing the corset, women thus invited a new sort of subjugation to
bodily discipline. Moreover, they now had to submit to the critical and intrusive gaze of a harsh and clearly unfeminine female authority.

Schoemaker expounded further on the dangers of women's new claims
to authority in spheres outside of fashion and health. Although the doctor
conceded that women of a certain natural build might go without corsets,
he disparaged these active and politically engaged New Women by sug-
gesting that they failed to be either men or women. "The woman with a
tight-muscled tense abdominal wall, flat hips, mannish chest, is usually to
be pitied. She is unfortunate. If she has been produced and admired in quantities in England . . . it is not because the English are producing any health-
ier race, but because the number of biological mistakes among females are
[sic] increasing." He also linked this type of woman to feminists who favored corsetlessness. "There is a certain strident type of woman publican
abroad in the land today who welcomes any move toward freedom appearing to register new approximation to sex equality." However, the race will
survive such women because "women who imitate men are not the kind
that Nature selects to mother the next generation." Connecting corsetlessness with a dismissive portrayal of radical politics and ideas about racial de-

generacy, Schoemaker attacks all three in his effort to stifle women's desires to control their bodies and their destinies in the postsuffrage era.[34]

In November 1922, the Royal Worcester Corset Company announced the "retreat to the perfect figure," a shape achievable only with the aid of a corset. Although census figures indicate an increase in corset manufacturers' profits the following year, the trade journals, perhaps as a measure of their lingering anxiety, continued to proclaim the end of corsetlessness throughout the decade. The "renaissance of the corset" and the declining popularity of the corsetless figure were noted as late as 1930, and Lily of France president Joel Alexander was still assuring buyers of the long-awaited return of "real corsets" in January 1935.[35]

. . . . .

A 1921 series of articles on specialized fitting procedures discusses the importance of corseting young girls because they are the "future mothers of our race." When the time arrives, maternity corsets will protect not only her health but also her child's. Utilizing the strategy of incorporation, the new 1920s emphasis on the science and art of corset fitting acknowledged past discomfort but laid the blame on the fit of the corset, not on the garment itself. The science of corset fitting, often taught at special sessions organized by corset companies, singled out a young girl's first experience in the corset shop as critically important in making her into a lifelong corset customer.[36]

Linking corsets with "science" dated back to the nineteenth century, when medical arguments were used to promote corset wearing and to combat the health claims of corset opponents. Nineteenth-century doctors like brothers I. DeVer and Lucius C. Warner, founders of the Warner Brothers Company in Bridgeport, Connecticut, named their late-1870s designs the "Sanitary Corset" and "Health Corset" to highlight their benefits. In the 1920s, manufacturers' reliance on scientific arguments intensified, as they expanded marketing strategies beyond the focus on corset design to include corset fitting.[37]

Corset fitting became a part of corset selling and marketing after the introduction of the straight-front corset, which needed "to be fitted in nearly every case." As a result, most corset departments installed corset fitting rooms. In a 1925 publication entitled *The Principles of Scientific Corset Fitting*, Bertha A. Strickler, supervisor of instruction at the Modart Corset Company, explained that recent changes in corsetry compelled a greater level of specialized training for corset fitters. The past practice of buying corsets over the counter was possible when corsets served the singular purpose of suppressing the waist. She claimed that fitting contemporary corsetry required more than waist measurement because "today corsets are scientifically designed and must be scientifically fitted." However, an earlier account provided an alternative viewpoint, explaining that "these advantages are not altogether new in the modern corset except in so far as they are now universal whereas they were formerly restricted to the made-to-order corset or the ready-made one of exorbitant price." The wide availability of ready-to-wear corsets through their mass production and marketing changed consumption patterns considerably.[38]

Recasting corset fitting as a science in the 1920s relied on the widespread knowledge of and faith in the practices of scientific management. The transformation of industrial work in the early twentieth century to emphasize efficiency and rationalization, as well as the turn to technology for problem solving, required fewer skills of workers, which in turn reduced their power in the workplace. By adopting the ideologies of scientific management, corset manufacturers transformed the consumption experiences of saleswomen and their customers when they bought, sold, and wore corsets. Though this strategy sought to keep women customers bound in corsets, it did, at least temporarily, give corset saleswomen a measure of new status and prestige. However, women's bodies were literally the vehicle for shifting scientific management ideologies from the workplace to the marketplace and the home.[39]

Many major corset manufacturers sponsored special courses in "scientific corsetry," "scientific reduction," or "scientific corset fitting." Most courses took place in New York City, where many corset companies had their showrooms and factories, though companies also sponsored courses in regional commercial centers like Chicago, Dallas, and Atlanta. These courses offered a new way for companies to distinguish their products from others that were on the market. They also demonstrated companies' concerns about women's health and their reliance on scientific methods to insure it.[40]

Some corset school curriculums emphasized the importance of medical knowledge in corset fitting. The International School of Scientific Corsetry, sponsored by the International Corset Company, included the subjects of anatomy and medical fitting in its 1921 curriculum, which also covered modern merchandising, retail advertising, and "scientific salesmanship." Kleinart's School of Scientific Reduction employed Dr. Harriet Von Buren Peckham in 1925 to deliver a series of lectures on "the proper way to reduce every part of the body, together with practical suggestions for fitting every type of figure." For the latter part of the course, Dr. Peckham was "assisted by expert fitters, competent models and an experienced sales woman." Attendees would also have the opportunity to "fit the reducers on a live model."[41]

The Modart Company's course included the section "The Anatomical Requirements of a Corset," which explained the medical condition of "ptosis." Modart claimed that most women suffered from ptosis, "a loss in muscles of the power to contract." However, although improperly fitted corsets caused ptosis, properly fitted corsets were needed to arrest its development. Ptosis was linked to the stress of "modern city life to which women are not yet adjusted. . . . Constipation, debility, headaches, backaches, sallow complexion, appendicitis, general weakness are some of the ailments associated with this condition."[42]

Department store retailers nationwide became persuaded of the value of sending their employees to corset fitting schools as the profit margins of corset departments rose. In 1917, *Women's Wear Daily* credited the presence of trained corsetieres in department stores with increasing the sales of higher priced, and thus more profitable, corsets. Departments with trained corsetieres also had fewer returns and less need for alterations, the bane of retailers. Moreover, from the 1920s through the 1940s, corset departments usually had the highest profit margins of all departments within a store.[43]

The Warner Brothers Company noted the profitability of corset departments in a 1921 trade-journal advertisement, citing a National Retail Dry Goods Association report. Warner argued that merchants would see even better profits if they carried fewer corset lines. The company's seven-point plan for improving retail profits included the admonition to "educate your salesgirls that they can ably assist the customer in her selection. It is the worst possible mistake to sell a woman a corset that is not designed for her figure."[44]

Corset schools primarily sought to educate retailers and saleswomen in the finer points of selling the sponsor's particular brand. With the proliferation of types and styles of corsets by the early 1920s, many major companies produced several lines of corsets for "stout," "average," and "slender" figures.[45] Within these figure types, companies might offer additional styles for bodies heavier on the top or the bottom, for long- or short-waisted figures, or for maternity and postsurgical wear. Companies also differentiated style lines by price. As *Good Housekeeping* noted in 1921, "Nowadays a single corset company will have almost one hundred models, each one made up in a variety of sizes." Retail buyers and saleswomen thus needed to know quite a bit about each company's product line to determine which corset would best fit each customer. Companies depended on saleswomen's mastery of this information to sell their products. Warner Brothers, for example, sent out pamphlets in 1921 to corset departments throughout the United States to explain its figure-type classifications and the corsets appropriate for each type, with the expectation that having an illustrated guide on hand would direct saleswomen to show and sell Warner's corsets. *Corsets & Lingerie* also endorsed collaboration between manufacturers and retailers in a 1925 editorial, stating that "the lines which were going best were the lines in which the manufacturer cooperated with the store in teaching the girls how to sell corsets."[46]

Corset companies' creation of figure-classification schemes also bolstered their claims to scientific validation of their products and to the need for professional fitters. Each company's classification scheme corresponded to a line of corsets. Selling retail buyers on a figure-classification scheme thus helped sell retailers on the corresponding line of corsets. Given this marketing focus, companies' schemes seldom concurred on the "scientific" classifications of women's bodies. Gossard's early twentieth-century chart defined nine figure types, Warner's 1921 classification had eight, and Berlei's 1926 study of Australian women found five.[47]

Figure-typing schemes allowed corset companies to standardize product lines and formed an organizing principle for merchandising. In 1929, the Bon Ton company explained that its chart of nine figure types, "What Figure Type Are You?" was "the basis of our entire merchandising plan . . . and makes possible for the first time real scientific control of fit, balanced model stocks, smaller inventories, fast turnover and more sustained profits." Yet an unstated but critical element of this plan was persuading women to identify with the figure types. Once a woman identified herself in terms of "her" type, she would more readily buy the corset deemed appropriate, if not necessary, for her body. Though scientific references assured women of the medical necessity of corseting, and of the rational character of corset design and fit, manufacturers made figure-type appeals on aesthetic grounds as well. A later typology by the Flexees Company, for example, evoked more elegant figure identities than Bon Ton's "Type A through J," offering the Renaissance (full-hip), Grecian (average), Parisienne (full-bust), Debutante (junior), and Egyptian (full-bust, straight-hip) models.[48]

A survey conducted in New Jersey by the U.S. Department of Agriculture in the 1930s, funded by the Works Progress Administration, provides a measure of corset manufacturers' and retailers' success in persuading Americans of the importance and legitimacy of figure types. According to *Time* magazine, this "gynemetric survey" measured "each subject—matron, maid, scrubwoman, show girl . . ." in "59 different places, [with] special recordings made to check the 'sitting spread.' " The survey produced the unintentionally ironic determination that "only two million out of forty million women have ideal proportions." However, at least the ideally pro-portioned figure still occurred more often than the "tall hip-heavy" and the "tall top-heavy," the two rarest of the nine types. The highly publicized con-clusion that only a small percentage of women had perfect figures under-scored the necessity for most women to conform to ideal standards of beauty by transforming the appearance of their flawed bodies with figure-shaping undergarments.[49]

Commercial classification of figure types intensified both the notion of the "problem figure" and the identification of "figure faults." Late-nine-teenth-century corsets had constructed the hourglass figure by remolding women's bodies into a general curved shape with a nipped-in waistline. Dress design and strap-on garments like bustles provided additional shaping. Twentieth-century outerwear was less elaborate and involved fewer layers of clothing. Foundation garments assumed the entire burden of molding the body into the fashionable silhouette. The identification of figure faults thus came about as women's bodies became more publicly visible.

The greater public presence and freedom in body display and movement that women achieved in the 1920s were attenuated by this reformulated and internalized emphasis on female imperfection. Marketing corsets on their ability to solve "figure faults" meant that identification of faults assumed greater importance in persuading women to buy corsets, focusing them on the effort to disguise their defects. Corset saleswomen, for example, were in-structed first to identify a customer's figure type and then to determine her particular figure problems. However, companies recognized that pointing out figure flaws to customers was not necessarily good form. One sales-woman's guide suggested that "the salesgirls should be cautioned never to point out figure faults to a customer. If she had a roll at the waistline and a long girdle is selected to minimize this, the salesgirl should not say, 'That terrible roll will not look as bad with this corset.' Instead she should remark, 'What a lovely, smooth waistline this girdle gives you. Your silhouette looks so well in it.' " Another guide admonished, "Never tell the stout customer she is stout. Emphasize the fact that she has good proportions. . . . Remem-ber you are selling the joy of possession as well as comfort and fit."[50]

Saleswomen's tactfulness about figure faults relied upon women's mag-azines explicit attention to such matters. *Good Housekeeping*'s 1921 series "How to Choose the Right Corset" advised consultation with a trained corsetiere but also advocated education about corset fitting for all women, as an informed customer would be better able to "make an intelligent selection of a corset," especially if a competent corsetiere were not available in her area. The articles describe the intricacies of measuring procedures, such as where to measure the bust and hips, when to take a breath to allow for "diaphragm and rib expansion," and which measurements to take while sitting. Beyond these standard measurements, one had to make allowance for "irregularities" such as "one hip higher than the other, a curved spine, an excessively large, heavy abdomen, unusually full bust, etc." Illustrations show how the correct corset could resolve common figure problems, such as a "deep back curve," "protruding abdomen and sunken chest," and "too much flesh . . . below hips." Tips in "Adjustment and Care of the Corset" recommend removing and relacing corsets in the evening and suggest that "if there is a surplus of flesh over the abdomen, place the hand inside the corset and smooth the flesh back toward the sides, not up in the front." Such magazine articles prepared women for their shopping experience by familiarizing them with terminology, fitting methods, and ways of understanding their bodies. The articles could also reassure corset customers once they returned home with their purchases.[51]

Figure-classification schemes and the identification of figure faults objectified and commodified women's bodies in new ways. Manufacturers and retailers colluded in subjecting women's bodies to the scrutiny and discipline of scientific rationalization. Corset saleswomen were on the front lines of enacting the regulation of women's bodies through corsetry and helped articulate strategies to sell corsets. Ethel Allen, supervisor of instruction at the Kabo School of Corsetry, acknowledged this function, stating that "with every sale by an expert corsetiere goes the all-important and invaluable message to her customer of the proper selection of a model and the proper method of adjustment. They get the many 'dos and don'ts' of our profession, and the assurance that a properly fitted corset can be a thing of beauty, of comfort and of great self-respect."[52]

The relationship between corset saleswomen and customers both worked against and assisted the rationalization process. Exposing intimate figure problems to a corsetiere and granting her the probing access to the body necessary for measurement created a special relationship between customer and corsetiere. As *Women's Wear Daily* noted, "A corset fitter gets much closer to her customers than the average salesperson can. Customers talk much more freely to their corset fitters than they do the girl who sells gloves, and they are willing to confide, in a manner of speaking, to the fitter, because usually the corset fitter has her own clientele, who insist on coming to that particular fitter each time they purchase a new corset." Charlotte Drebing, a corset buyer for the Crosby Brothers Mercantile Company of Kansas, agreed. "Corset customers . . . are the most appreciative people in the world. Because a good foundation garment can do such a vital job for a woman, she is eternally grateful to anyone who helps her find one—and that's why any service you can give her is worth while."[53]

A corsetiere especially benefited from customers with identifiable figure faults, because women's desires for rectification promoted dependence on the corset fitter's expertise. Ethel Allen, referring to the problematic full-proportioned figure type, knew "no other class of customers who are more appreciative and loyal" and reported that the top-heavy figure type "is willing to pay almost any price for a garment which will give her comfort and at the same time give her the easy graceful figure she so much desires." The top-heavy figure "will not only give to the corsetiere her patronage but will become a loyal booster among all her friends and acquaintances." Another sales manual noted that "the larger woman knows she is difficult to fit, and is willing to pay more than the slender woman. Juniors and slender women can buy garments any place at any price, but the larger woman, when correctly fitted, is everlastingly grateful and becomes a loyal repeat customer." Large women customers also augmented job prospects for large women as corsetieres, because "Mrs. Larger Woman feels more comfortable when a larger woman fits her." This customer also provided a source of job satisfaction. "Larger women are important to your business because properly corseted she looks 'smart' and gives you the feeling of having accomplished something."[54]

The relationship between corsetiere and customer was not without tension. One guide for saleswomen noted that "the worst faux pas of all is to say: 'I wear this girdle myself for my own roll.' No woman wants to be identified in any way with the salesgirl.'"[55] However, Ethel Allen avoided the potential for a subservient relationship to customers by positing an alternative metaphor.

> As corsetieres we must never lose sight of the fact that we stand in the relation of a hostess to our guest, the customer, while she is in our shop or department. Were we serving afternoon coffee and one of our guests refused coffee we would immediately say, "Let me make you a cup of tea." Even so with our business guests. If they are prejudiced against either front-laced or back-laced corsets, show them first what you consider correct. Call their attention to the corrective points of the garment for their particular needs. Then if you cannot convince them that your judgement is correct, without argument simply give them what they want and give with it a sweet smile and willing service.[56]

The professionalization of corset fitting through specialized training and assumption of the title "corsetiere" also bolstered saleswomen's status with both customers and department store managers. Corset schools thus enhanced manufacturers' promotional needs, retailer's profit margins, and corset saleswomen's power as workers, while heightening the presence of "scientific" epistemologies and fostering specialization in women's daily lives. Corset-fitting manuals, usually written by experienced corsetieres who taught in corset schools, consistently stressed the professional aspects of this work. Positioning the corsetiere as "physician to her customer's body," a role fostered by instruction in anatomy and the work of fitting maternity and postoperative corsets, helped give the corsetiere professional status. Jean Gordon, author of *The Good Corsetiere*, published by the Strouse, Adler Company explained, "When one is ill, the patient wants the family doctor who comes to the bedside with a friendly, gracious attitude. . . . When a customer enters the corset department with a sick figure, she too, wants kindness."[57]

Another professionalization strategy was to characterize corset fitting as an art. "A new salesgirl must be taught to consider her job as one of beautifying women. Instead of working with cosmetics she works with garments. Instead of beautifying the face and head she must improve the entire body of her customer. It is in some cases a tall order. She may be called upon to achieve the impossible. But whatever she can accomplish helps to increase beauty and in this respect is a work of art." Ethel Allen noted that women seek "the services of a thoroughly competent and trained professional corsetiere, one who understands all the alluring intricacies of the human form divine."[58]

. . . . .

Figure-type classification included the bodies of girls and younger women in the category of problem figures. However, the "young girl figure," described as slim and "undeveloped," was a problem for manufacturers because it did not conform to the usual description of figure types that required corseting. The 1920s corset panic heightened manufacturers' attention to the young-girl figure not only because younger women were most likely to achieve the corsetless look without a corset but also because the fashionable 1920s silhouette was based on the young-girl figure. By targeting this figure and convincing women that it required a corset, manufacturers convinced all fashion-conscious women that corsets remained a necessity.[59]

The special corsets developed for the young-girl figure were part of the garment industry's growing interest in the youthful market (termed "junior" by the late 1920s) as a means of increasing sales. Corset manufacturers were especially interested in exploiting the growing distinction between clothing for younger women and that for older women because "the junior customer has no set habits or buying tendencies which must be overcome" and thus seemed "to be a new hope for the corset industry." Lucien T. Warner noted "the necessity of courting this trade, for upon the younger generation of women the future of the corset industry depends."[60]

Manufacturers were still concerned that younger women in the 1920s might never wear corsets if they did not undergo the initiation into corset wearing that women in previous generations had. They looked closely at the circumstances of a young girl's first corset fitting to find ways of luring young women to a corsetiere. Once at a corset fitting, a young woman, and perhaps her mother, could also be drawn into corset discourses that would convince her of a lifelong need of corsetry. "Even the young girls who have never before ventured into a corset department find a new delight in looking at the attractive garments, and convincing sales talk . . . soon brings them into the fitting rooms." Concerns about initiating young girls into corsetry persisted into the 1940s, when *Corsets & Brassiere* advised, "It may take urging to get her into her first girdle, but your efforts will be rewarded as she blossoms into a model customer. . . . It's up to you to win her confidence and build her into a life-long customer."[61]

Since the early twentieth century, the "college girl" had been identified as a customer with special needs because of her age and lifestyle rather than because of her figure type per se. The college-girl category also included the white-collar worker, or "business girl," whose corset needs presumably differed from those of older women who did not work outside the home. A 1910 advertisement for H&W Sheathlyne Corset Waists aimed toward college girls noted that "by encouraging deep breathing, it [the corset waist] quickly develops the chest and bust." In 1915, Wanamakers, a large department store, created the first special corset fitting room for young women who wore "misses" sizes. *Women's & Infants' Furnisher* stated that this innovation was "one of the most striking that has come out in some time," especially because of the "undeveloped possibilities" of "catering particularly to young girls."

One of the principal reasons that very few retail stores have the business that should come to them in misses' corsets is the failure of stores to take into consideration the natural reticence of girls to enter into any discussion of . . . individual corset problems with matrons and dowagers about. By providing a special demonstration and fitting room for misses, it is safe to say that any store so doing will reap the benefit of an

Figure 12. Manufacturers in the 1940s continued to target the young girl to "build her into a life-long customer." *Corsets & Brassieres,* August 1946. Courtesy of Special Collections, Gladys Marcus Library, Fashion Institute of Technology.

immediate appreciation of this delicacy. And, since appreciation expresses itself in terms of dollars and cents, it can hardly be other than a profitable investment.[62]

Manufacturers indeed developed this profitable concept, and by 1929, *Corsets & Brassieres* included a monthly "Junior Department" in each issue. Juniors were girls between twelve and eighteen years of age, and the column often dealt with the special care required for their commercial rite of passage. "Each child is fitted as her individual need requires and for this work there are special fitters trained to care for the children. . . . The younger girls do not like being disrobed and fitted, but now that the new silhouette is so apparent even the 12-year-olds are offering much less resistance."[63]

Miss Mildred Tucker, head of a corset department in Denver, discussed the importance of "tactfulness" in dealing with the "little girls and even college girls [who] are not quite used to the return of youth to corsets, which the new Princess line in dress styles has necessitated." She explained that "tact . . . usually consists of compliments and direct conversation to the child." Another column noted, "Buyers who are wise will put their best foot forward to encourage and capture this class of customers." By March 1930, Lucien T. Warner reported that "a large number of smaller sizes are being called for by the younger girl."[64]

In July 1930, the Corset and Brassiere Manufacturers Association laid plans for the first National Junior Corset Week the following September.[65] This event was a specialized version of the earlier National Corset Week, a coordinated national advertising campaign by merchants, retailers, and trade journals to boost corset sales. *Corsets & Lingerie* explained the need for such a cooperative effort in a 1924 editorial.

Why A Week? . . . Most people found out they could do a lot in a week if they all started to talk at once and talked long enough and loud enough. . . . If the corset industry wants to put corsets on every woman and keep them there; all they've got to do is talk a language that most American women understand—English. Talk to each age-group of women about their particular corset problems and if the industry is smart, and economical as well, they'll also get about 10,000 merchants to do a lot of talking for them.[66]

The editorial also encouraged manufacturers to imitate other branches of the garment industry in their use of "the principle" of style. Style played an especially important role in the younger market, as the editorial noted: "If corsets were as crazy as some of the shoes we see, the flapper would buy a pair of corsets with every new dress."[67]

The National Junior Corset Week's purpose was clear. "Insistent propaganda has really aroused an interest on the part of the young girl, and buyers realizing that they have succeeded in luring the girl into the department are tireless in these efforts to keep her interest." Lauding the junior department at Gimbel's Department Store in New York City, *Corsets & Brassieres* reported that "every possible kind of restraining garment that is manufactured for the young figure is found here . . . made to appeal to the eye of the discriminating youngster. . . . There are many girls, not only the debutantes and society girls but even working girls who are willing to pay for better class merchandise, just as these girls have always been fastidious in the matter of their lingerie." Following Junior Week, *Corsets & Brassieres* reported "increased sales among the younger women in all the larger retail centers. Girls who never before wore a foundation garment came in to buy some type of fashion-forming garment and college girls stocked up generously for the season's needs." Three years later, the trade journal stated that "nearly all the stores now have special sections in their corset departments devoted to garments for the young figure."[68]

Making lighter and more flexible girdles in junior sizes was one means of keeping young women in foundation garments. Girdles were available in increasing numbers as the means of producing elastic stretch fabrics improved. In the 1910s, elastic insets in corsets offered a way to improve the garments' flexibility. The number of elastic and rubber sections in corsets increased into the 1920s. However, the primarily elastic girdles available in 1921 were still considered novelty items. Several years later, when the youth appeal of elastic girdles was more apparent, manufacturers' and retailers' resistance to them ended. By 1924, elastic step-in girdles were on sale in corset departments nationwide.[69]

As use of elastic girdles spread, rubber reducing corsets became extremely popular novelty items for several years. One of the best-known national brands was the Madame X. These controversial all-rubber corsets were marketed not only on their ability to slim the wearer's appearance but also as a device to help the wearer actually lose weight. Manufacturers and retail buyers debated the staying power of rubber girdles on the market but acknowledged that their presence raised the price of foundations generally. The ability to sell great quantities of the more expensive rubber corsets let manufacturers and retailers know that women were willing to pay more for corsets.[70]

. . . . .

The decline of the chest-flattening "boyshform" silhouette in the late 1920s (see chapter 3), and the return to the "womanly" figure in the 1930s, created a strong market for corsetry, even during the worst years of the Depression.[71] The industry had responded on many fronts to the 1920s threat of the corsetless look. Profitability continued as the foundation market broadened to include young girls, juniors, and college coeds, as well as the numerous figure types of older women. Identifying a variety of types allowed manufacturers to produce, and retailers to market, corsets for particular groups of women. This strategy of segmentation also produced and marketed new understandings of the female body, which personalized and intensified the scientific discourse in women's intimate everyday lives.

The new perceptions about the female body that the industry deployed also encouraged most women to identify themselves in terms of flaws and to thus construct their subjectivity in self-deprecating terms. However, the industry was unable to completely suppress skepticism about at least some aspects of figure faults. Corset-fitting advice from the early 1920s to the late 1930s, for example, frequently addressed the special need for "diaphragm control" because of the accumulation of "excess" flesh over the lowered waistlines of corsets, noting which corsets provided the necessary control and how they did so. However, all this attention eventually exasperated at least one trade journalist, who confessed, "The diaphragm, for some unknown reason, is still an important consideration, and this thing and that thing are being used to take care of diaphragms, some of which can certainly be trusted to take care of themselves." Moreover, manufacturers and retailers could not dismiss women's desires for greater comfort and freedom of movement. Although the corsetless fad did not free women from the obligation to be corseted, some women could at least wear the more flexible and lightweight stretch girdles. Yet the popularity of even the light pantie girdle in the 1930s did not mitigate widespread use of more binding foundations. "All-in-one" garments, for example, which first appeared in the 1920s, firmly shaped and controlled the entire torso from bust to hips.[72]

The well-organized corset industry continued to benefit from its persistent interventions in fashion changes and its construction of women's desires for "ideal figures." It reaped the results when accentuated waistlines returned in the 1930s but at this point was too close to the corset panic years to rest on its laurels. Its ongoing machinations reaped even greater rewards after the end of World War II, when fashionable corsetry returned with pinching vengeance and fetishized glory in new structured forms, such as waist cinchers or "waspies," that supported the popular, and contested, New Look of 1947.[73]

Corsets' fading fashionability and their replacement by the new restrictive girdles in this period occurred amid contestation and negotiation among women who purchased and wore these garments, manufacturers and retailers who produced and sold them, and fashion experts like department store saleswomen and fashion writers. As moral imperatives lessened in women's fashions, women sought, and in some measure achieved, greater freedom of choice and mobility in dress. However, fashion industrialists worked hard to maintain control over the shape of women's bodies and over women's fashion choices. Drawing on modernist ideologies, they refuted claims about the damaging health effects of corset use by repositioning corsets within contemporary scientific discourses, and they countered young women's rejection of corsets as old-fashioned by designing lighter and more flexible foundation garments and marketing them as contemporary girdles. Using existing fashion institutions, including popular magazines, trade journals, and department stores, and creating new ones, such as corset fitting schools, corset manufacturers and retailers actively interceded to influence fashion change. Women's demands for more comfortable attire, and their demonstrated willingness to defy conventional notions of feminine propriety, prompted manufacturers' organized opposition to the "corsetless fad" and their subsequent development of policing strategies aimed at women of all ages. Their efforts sustained figure-shaping garments as essential elements in women's wardrobes. Although wearing these garments would no longer be a measure of a woman's moral propriety, it could attest to her knowledge of modern techniques of constructing a fashionable body and show that she valued an up-to-date appearance. Women's "spontaneous consent" to wearing these garments was an ongoing and contested process that served fashion industry needs for steady sales. Innovations in dress that supported women's desires for comfort would continue because industrialists sought not to end women's desires for fashion change but to contain them.

Throughout the early twentieth century and in succeeding decades, the high profit margins of departments selling corsets, girdles, and other foundation garments in stores nationwide provide one measure of the success of manufacturers' and retailers' marketing strategies. American women's continuing preoccupation with conforming to particular notions of beauty in regard to body size and shape is another. The late-twentieth-century interest in diet drugs and programs, women's willingness to undergo liposuction surgery to reduce and reshape their abdomens and hips, and the strong sales

Figure 13. The 1930s return to the "womanly" figure did not end requirements for a smooth silhouette and slim "e-fect." *Corsets & Brassieres,* August 1930. Courtesy of Special Collections, Gladys Marcus Library, Fashion Institute of Technology.

of "body shapers" (the current term for flexible foundation garments) all demonstrate that women's struggles getting in and out of corsets have not entirely ended. For the meaning of these methods of reshaping female bodies goes beyond their immediate physical effect. As Michel Foucault notes, "The endlessly repeated play of dominations . . . is fixed, throughout its history, in rituals, in meticulous procedures that impose rights and obligations. It establishes marks of its power and engraves memories on things and even within bodies."[74] Imbuing 1920s corsetry with essentialist notions about flawed female bodies, racial hierarchies, nationalist imperatives, dubious sexual identities, and suspect political standpoints inscribed dominant ideologies upon women's bodies. Persuasive because of their power in other spheres, these mediations of women's relationship with their own bodies long outlasted the corsets and girdles women wore in the early decades of the twentieth century.

3 Brassieres

Miss Turner, we are students of Alhambra High. We have a sort of club. We want a picture of you in a glamorous pose. You know what we mean. . . .

Life, December 23, 1940

In 1937, Hollywood film director Mervyn LeRoy was looking for a young actress to play a small but pivotal role in his next film, *They Won't Forget.* This social drama drew on a 1915 incident in which Leo Frank, a northern Jewish man, was lynched in a southern town after his questionable conviction for the murder of a local girl. He was later proven to be innocent. In the film, a white northern teacher suffers a similar fate after a sensational trial for the rape and murder of his female student. LeRoy's dilemma in this restricted era of mainstream filmmaking was how to make clear the sexual nature of the crime without explicit verbal or visual reference to it. He found his solution in the body and costuming of Hollywood High School student Lana Turner.[1]

Turner's casting meeting with LeRoy came about as a result of her much-mythologized "discovery" at a Hollywood malt shop, later erroneously identified as Schwab's Drug Store. LeRoy, who had already interviewed thirty young women for the part, found the combination of "sex appeal and innocence" in the seventeen-year-old Turner more than sufficient compensation for her lack of acting experience or training. However, the director augmented Turner's dramatic potential by costuming her in a tight belted sweater and skirt as she walked briskly down the town's main street. LeRoy explained his inspiration for the outfit by noting, "I figured that a tight sweater on a beautiful young girl would convey to the audience everything we couldn't say outright."[2]

Turner later described her shocked reaction to her cinematic presence, which she first viewed at a public preview screening.

> Out of the darkness and hush of the big theatre, a girl came on the screen. . . . She wore a tight sweater and her breasts bounced as she walked. . . . Someone in the audience whistled. There were also some

gasps. Then The Thing was gone. I understood later why this girl was there and why she was a Thing. She was the motive for the entire picture. . . . She had to look like a girl men would like to rape. . . . But she certainly did not seem to be me. Mother and I crept out of the theater and stumbled into a cab. . . . I held myself very self-consciously, trying not to bounce. . . . For quite a while I was ashamed to face people.[3]

The vocal reaction to her screen body by young men in the audience undoubtedly contributed to Turner's self-consciousness. To be sure, the import of their whistles and yells was not lost on studio press agents in attendance, who quickly released Turner publicity stills from the film, dubbing her "America's Sweater Girl." Public response was such that Turner's star began to climb even before the film's debut.[4]

Fan interest in Turner remained high over the next two years, in which she played lead or second lead in six films. More than a dozen college fraternities chose her as their "sweetheart," prompting columnist Walter Winchell to call her "America's Sweater Girl Sweetheart." The studio compared her to both 1920s "It" girl Clara Bow and 1930s "bombshell" Jean Harlow. As with these earlier screen stars, Turner's beauty and expressive sexuality contributed to her success. However, although "It" encompassed Bow's entire person and personality and Harlow's slinky bias-cut gowns and explosive personality made her a "bombshell," Turner's initial notoriety stemmed largely from one physical feature—her large, uplifted breasts tightly covered in fuzzy wool—as well as from her apparent innocence of their visual effect. And, despite Turner's refusal to appear onscreen or pose in a sweater again, the Sweater Girl moniker was one she could never shake, as her 1995 obituaries clearly demonstrate.[5]

From the vantage point of the late-twentieth-century obsession with large firm breasts, evident in the vogue for padded uplift brassieres and the continuing popularity of hazardous implant operations into the twenty-first century, the response to Turner's silhouette may seem unremarkable. Yet public perceptions of Bow's and Harlow's sensuality had not focused on chest size. Although both stars' fashion sensibilities contributed to their popularity, Bow's included a flattened bustline and Harlow's took form in a looser, often unstructured bust of ordinary dimensions. Questions remain, then, about how and why the fashionable shape of American women's breasts changed by the end of the 1930s and what this process tells us about the enduring popularity of large, uplifted breasts into the present day. Moreover, these changes in breast dimension compel analysis of the cultural meanings they produced, which not only affected women's everyday experience of their bodies but also transformed the construction of feminine identity in the United States.

. . . . .

The brassiere is a twentieth-century garment. Worn today by virtually every woman in the United States from about the age of twelve, the brassiere first emerged in the early 1900s and became a standard item of dress within the next thirty years. This garment now fuels a $2.5 billion industry. It also played a critical part in the history of twentieth-century American women's clothing, because the shaping of women's breasts was an important element in changing the fashionable silhouette. Moreover, the growing cultural preoccupation with women's breasts during the twentieth century *itself* contributed to the shaping of this silhouette and the meanings it produced. The brassiere was thus a critical site of gender differentiation, as well as a source of pleasure and power, in twentieth-century American culture and continues to be so today.[6]

Before widespread adoption of the brassiere, the breasts were encased in structured garments called "bust improvers." These garments, similar to corsets in their use of flexible boning and lacing, produced the turn-of-the-century pouter-pigeon-breast effect known as the monobosom. Fashions did not treat breasts as a separate entity at this time but rather as part of the chest or bosom area of the female body. This construction of the bosom therefore did not recognize women's breasts as divided into two parts. In addition, though the bust was thrown forward by the tightly laced, popular straight-front corsets, the bosom was "worn low." Thus, although elegant evening dresses might include décolleté necklines not permissible in day wear, creation of cleavage through pressing the breasts upward and together was not a feature of this period.[7]

One measure of the brassiere's significance in the transition from nineteenth- to twentieth-century dress is that so many people claim its invention. French corsetiere Herminie Cadolle's late-nineteenth-century design, the "Well-Being," is said to be the first modern garment to support the bosom without constricting the diaphragm. English designer Lady Duff Gordon brought the luxurious fabrics and decoration of Edwardian outerwear to her designs of undergarments in the early twentieth century and asserts in her autobiography, "I brought in the brassiere in opposition to the hideous corset of the time." However, French couturier Paul Poiret maintained that his 1908 designs of corsetless fashions precipitated the demise of the corset and the subsequent need for the brassiere.[8] And American socialite Caresse Crosby, who patented her 1913 design of two handkerchiefs

Figure 14. The monobosom dominated at the turn of the century. With permission of the Royal Ontario Museum © ROM.

sewn together with straps of pink ribbon and later sold the patent to the Warner Brothers Corset Company for $1,500, claims in her autobiography, "I can't say the brassiere will ever take as great a place in history as the steamboat, but I did invent it." Crosby's innovation was the briefer length and soft construction, which slightly separated the breasts.[9] Adding to the confusion, even the origin of the term *brassiere* is unclear. Though the word is French, which seems to imply adoption of the French term for this garment into English, the dictionary meaning of *brassière* is "shoulder strap." However, costume historian Elizabeth Ewing finds that the more common definition of this word in France is "infant's under-bodice." In French, the term for the garment we know in English as a brassiere is *soutien-gorge*, literally "breast (or bosom) supporter."[10]

As Duff Gordon and Poiret indicate, the invention and adoption of brassieres were directly related to changes in corsetry. Nineteenth-century corsets reached above the ribs and supported the breasts. Women wore a chemise underneath the corset and then donned a corset cover or camisole to further clothe the upper torso. As skirt widths narrowed, corsets lengthened to conform the hips to this shape. As a result, the top of corsets moved down the body toward the waistline, leaving the breasts without support. Early appraisal of these new "topless" corsets identified the brassiere as the "top" to these new garments. As one 1914 commentator explained, "When low-top corsets became fashionable, the good lady remembered the breast, then leading a quiet life of steady though restricted popularity, and bringing it into instant favor, bedecked it with trimming." In addition, the growing popularity of shirtwaists led to the new perception of the "brassiere . . . as a practical necessity." Unlike earlier boned dress waists, shirtwaists were soft blouses, often made at this time of sheer fabrics. Brassieres essentially took "the place of lining."[11]

Mass production of brassieres began very early in the twentieth century. Growing sales undoubtedly provoked Warner's interest in purchasing Crosby's patent and fueled competing claims to the brassiere's invention. Early brassieres were quite similar in shape and size to corset covers or camisoles, but they differed in function because they clothed a newly unbound, rather than a corseted, upper torso. The earliest brassiere advertisement I found in the *Women's & Infants' Furnisher* dates from 1905 and touts the "points of superiority" of the De Bevoise brassieres manufactured in Newark, New Jersey, since 1904. Within one year, Chas. R. De Bevoise & Co. had offices in Los Angeles, Chicago, and Boston. This company established such a strong early presence in the trade that the garment was known for a time as a "De Bevoise."[12]

The Benjamin & Johnes company, founded in 1884 as makers of bustles and children's waists, also claimed 1904 as the year it began manufacturing brassieres.[13] However, the H&W Company slogan, "Originators of the Brassiere," signals another claim to the first commercial production of brassieres in the United States. This company's self-authenticated story is that it added brassieres to its line of corset waists in 1900 in response to a request from a New York department store buyer who brought one back from France.[14]

J. L. Alberts of the Charma Brassiere Company claimed that his firm was the third manufacturer to enter the field, and, whatever the actual order, many additional American companies, including Ovida, Cain, Venus, and

Figure 15. This company's position in the industry was so strong, a brassiere was known for a time as "a De Bevoise." These styles show brassieres in transition from the corset covers and camisoles they replaced. *Women's & Infants' Furnisher,* February 1914. Courtesy of Special Collections, Gladys Marcus Library, Fashion Institute of Technology.

Model, were soon making brassieres. In 1914, *Women's & Infants' Furnisher* boldly declared, "No one, in these days of low corset tops, asks if brassieres will sell, but rather which brassiere will sell best." Five years later, *Women's Wear Daily* advised retailers on how to cope with a predicted "shortage in brassieres" as orders exceeded production in "all the standard brassiere houses." By 1921, approximately one hundred American companies were producing brassieres, with between $40 million and $50 million of retail business annually. Many of these companies were established corset manufacturers that diversified their product lines with this growing and lucrative market.[15]

In the mid-1910s, the brassiere began its transformation into the garment we would recognize today. Initially, the brassieres were sleeveless—or occasionally short-sleeved—waist-length garments with a front garter that attached to the corset to maintain a smooth line from torso to hips. Its design began to change with the ebbing of the pouter-pigeon monobosom shape, at which point the bust silhouette became softer, more flattened, and slightly compressed. As use of the chemise, worn underneath the corset since the Middle Ages, declined, women for the first time wore both brassieres and corsets or girdles next to their skin. As slimmer silhouettes became fashionable in the 1910s, new brassiere designs merged functions that had previously required multiple articles of clothing to further reduce the size and number of undergarments. The H&W Sheathlyn model "combined bust formers and corset waists," which the company promoted as a "boon to slender women," whereas De Bevoise advertised "models . . . specifically designed to be worn without any corset cover under sheer lingerie waists" and to overcome "a common objection . . . that [brassieres] were too plain and unsightly to expose under sheer waists, and hence required a corset cover worn under them."[16]

Over the next several decades, the primary challenge in brassiere design was to combine figure shaping and stylish ornamentation. The delicate and lightweight brassieres of this era provided covering for the breasts but did not support them, though wearing the garment tightly pressed against the skin provided some restraint. The new slim line brought forward the ornamental aspects of brassiere design, in numerous soft and highly decorative brassieres, and reduced women's interest, albeit temporarily, in bust enhancement. Instead, the freed upper torso of 1910s fashions became another problematic body part for larger women, and thus a site for profitable exploitation by the fashion industry. Rubber and fabric bust reducers, aimed at the fashion needs of large-breasted women, furthered the mechanics of breast shaping. As one trade journal explained in 1914,

Fashion never long neglects the most lucrative class of her followers—those too lavishly endowed by Nature with a silhouette that must be controlled to the desired shape and size. This is always a difficult problem, but in this day of low corsets it is simply doubled, for where the corset used to cover and control the entire figure, it now leaves that most elusive and often disproportionate part above the waistline entirely out of the running, and so Fashion has been most eager in her calls for bust controls or reduction brassieres.[17]

This mid-1910s trend set the stage for the extreme breast compression of the 1920s flapper era.[18]

One variation of decorative brassieres, bandeaux, became popular in the mid-1910s because some styles provided both support and ornamentation. Circling the torso with a band of fabric and suspended from the shoulders by narrow self-fabric or ribbon straps, bandeaux closed in front or back with a row of hook and eyes or with a ribbon tie. A style known as the ribbon bandeau was made entirely of strips of ribbon sewn together. Worn at times with decorative ribbon corsets, the extremely unstructured ribbon bandeaux might also be part of wedding ensembles or trousseaux. Other short bandeaux approximated the Crosby design, and, unlike other 1910s styles, resembled today's brassieres. Bandeaux were available in waist-length styles, often with an attached corset garter, or in a shorter midriff length. The short bandeau "which makes no attempt at all to go down over the corset, confining itself entirely to holding the bust" was still deemed a "novelty" by *Women's Wear Daily* in 1919.[19]

In addition to options in length, the greatest difference between turn-of-the-century brassieres and 1910s bandeaux was the "drop shoulder." The term was initially used to describe the bandeaux' innovative lack of structured armholes. Previously, reinforced armholes had been a featured selling point of some brassieres, because this area was often the first part of the garments to wear out, due to rubbing against the corset top. The drop shoulder also put forward "the real principle of brassiere success, namely, support of the bust and under-arm from the back, and not, as the original name and design taught, from the arm and shoulder."[20]

Two further important innovations from this period were strapless and sports brassieres. Strapless brassieres would not become a dominant style until the 1950s, but they were introduced in small numbers for wear with "the fashionable filmy blouse and under evening frocks." These relatively simple strapless models had a "string of tape which comes from the sides of the back and ties firmly in front." Others had "scientific boning of the back which keeps the garment up, preventing slipping of any sort," and may have worked better.[21] Women wore narrow, back-tying bandeaux with elastic across the front under bathing and other sports costumes as early as 1916. The fifth anniversary of the Lucile Somarco Sport Brassiere was marked in 1921 by an advertisement with a woman wearing the brassiere while holding a tennis racket. However, sport brassieres virtually disappeared in the 1930s, though retailers sold brassieres made from certain fabrics like batiste on that basis, as part of a "brassiere wardrobe."[22]

One significant innovation of the late 1910s was not in design but in marketing. Boyshform began in 1919 and immediately began nationwide advertising to establish its trade name as synonymous with the "flat boy-like" silhouette. Company president W. E. Pruzan attributed his success to intensive advertising, complemented by the expertise and contacts of long-time national brassiere saleswoman Dorothy Bickum, whom Pruzan wooed from rival Vogue Brassiere Company. Boyshform advertised itself in trade journals as "the Name That Made Brassieres Popular" and took credit as well for inventing the flattened-breast look. Brassiere manufacturers ran national advertising in women's magazines as early as 1916, when the De Bevoise company advertised in *Ladies' Home Journal* and *Vogue.* But the striking aspect of the Boyshform campaign was Pruzan's decision to launch the company itself with an intensive advertising plan at a time when the transition to "name brand" identification was just unfolding. In addition, Boyshform based its success on a name and product aimed at the newly emerging junior figure, a strategy that linked the company to the leading edge of fashionability. Moreover, Boyshform's trade-journal advertisements, which touted their nationwide advertising efforts and described their "sales plan" for "dealer co-operation," are an early example of the strategy of promoting sales to retailers by convincing wholesale buyers that a national advertising plan would move merchandise in their stores. Among Boyshform's techniques were in-store displays, electric signs, "wall placards," and a fashion show and giveaway contest at the Million Dollar pier in Atlantic City during the second annual Miss America pageant.[23]

· · · · ·

As the early 1920s success of the Boyshform trade name suggests, although the reduction of the bust had been a feature of pre–World War I close-fitting fashions, the flattened bust became more extreme and self-conscious in the postwar period. After World War II, many established brassiere companies also began producing flattening styles. In 1921, the Model Brassiere Company

Flattening effect bandeau of unusually beautiful flesh color Satin Brocade. This garment truly exemplifies the Model art of perfecting a type demanded by Fashion.

Courtesy of Model Brassiere Co.

Figure 16. An elegant setting glamorizes bandeaux that achieve the potentially painful "flattening effect." *Women's & Infants' Furnisher,* February 1921. Courtesy of Special Collections, Gladys Marcus Library, Fashion Institute of Technology.

advertised thirty styles of "flattening effect bandeaus," and H&W listed 112 styles of "bandeaus and bust confiners." The 1920 Montgomery Ward mail-order catalog offered several styles of reducing brassieres and "bust confiners," and the 1922 catalog also featured a bandeau "designed to give flattening effect."[24]

Brassieres engineered to bind the breasts tightly against the body confirmed their shaping and "corrective" functions, which worked in the same manner as the corset. This development was a significant change from the brassiere's original incarnation as an alternative to the camisole. As with some corsets, the beautiful fabrics and ornamentation of binding brassieres initially averted attention from their potential to cause pain and injury. Yet actually putting one on and wearing it must not have been pleasant, especially for large-breasted women. Breast binders were often long-line bandeaux of firm fabric, with one or more garters that attached to the corset. The corset and bandeau thus together produced a straight line from chest to hips. Long-line binding brassieres with attached stocking garters gave slim women both fashionable corsetlessness and constriction.[25]

Though medically minded fashion critics had assailed corsets over the previous seventy years, costume historian Elizabeth Ewing notes, "There were no protests against the flattening of the figure on health grounds." Perhaps the uproar over "corsetlessness," in which corset defenders conceded that older corsets were unhealthy and newer ones were healthful, overshadowed the potential dangers of constrictive brassieres, as they too were seen as modern. Binding may also have appeared to be nothing more than silly fashion business as usual, given that discomfort was an accepted element in female fashion. Yet when the trend died out a few years later, health concerns and recognition of the damaging effects of binding became features of brassiere promotion.[26]

Since the 1920s, the association of the slim straight line with "boyishness" has influenced popular thought about the reason for and meaning of breast compression. Commentators often posit a connection between the early twentieth-century movement toward gender equality in suffrage, work, and leisure, with women's desires to suppress gender distinction through an androgynous look. A psychoanalytic interpretation reads the 1920s straight silhouette and cropped hair as means of denying or assuaging collective and individual grief for millions of young male war casualties by putting simulations of male adolescent figures on city streets.[27] More critical analysis sees promotion of the boyish look as an infantilization of women's bodies timed to temper their burgeoning social and cultural power. Yet the possibility also exists of viewing the straight silhouette as an approximation of not male but female adolescence. The adoption of closed drawers at this time supports that view, as does the promotion of breast-confining brassieres, which create an impression of youthful slimness. This interpretation of the "boyishness" central to 1920s fashion produces a view of 1920s flappers as prevoting and protosexual females who did not compete with adult males for political power, sexual satisfaction, jobs, or other opportunities. Moreover, this analysis provides an important historical anchor for discerning the power issues embedded in the "thinning" of the ideal American women that began in this era. The construction of a Girlish Form by wearing the Look Slim Brassiere, the names of two lesser-known 1920s brassiere companies, thus had long-term implications, signaling the limitations to be imposed on women's bodies as youthful proportions became the standard by which they would be judged throughout their lives.[28]

Analyzing the straight silhouette as a feminization rather than a masculinization of women's fashion makes sense for another reason: the flattened bust was produced by restraining and molding the female body. Along with ornamentation, restraint and molding are key components in defining clothing as feminine. In addition, discomfort itself, even to the point of injury, was a well-established building block of femininity in fashion by the 1920s. By this time as well, the eroticism of dressing female bodies in a respectable form of bondage was inseparably linked with femininity. Together, these factors indicate that breast binding was a means of feminizing fashion, equal to the breast projection and uplift that brassieres provided in later decades.

The popularity of fashionable dress that required flattening brassieres to fit properly encouraged the growing perception that brassieres were essential components of modern underclothes. But because brassieres' function and design changed so radically within a short period of time, it was uncertain whether they should be deemed underwear or corsetry. This question was important to department store managers eager to arrange merchandise in the most profitable manner possible. Brassiere manufacturers preferred that their products remain in corset departments, especially because many of them manufactured both types of garments. Some companies continued to put boning in various brassiere styles solely to legitimate the garments' classification as corsetry. This decision proved to be pivotal because, in the early 1920s, trade journals reported that brassieres were "the big stimulators of the corset department." One manufacturer advised that "in order to increase corset sales, brassiere and corsets should be sold together and not in separate sections."[29]

Ideological, emotional, and psychological concerns also helped keep brassieres and corsets together. Montgomery Ward's catalog asserted that women's need of "smooth unbroken lines" and the need to avoid "a break at the waistline" stemmed solely from the demands of fashion. However, dividing the female body into upper and lower parts by designing the separate topless corset and brassiere apparently disturbed many women for other reasons. As the buyer at Saks Fifth Avenue in New York City explained, "The brassiere saleswomen . . . work closely with those of the corset, and consequently the customer doesn't go away feeling as if she were divided into two parts. Rather there is a feeling of unity between corset and brassiere. They seek out, here, brassieres that bring about this feeling of oneness."[30]

Women may have sought this feeling of oneness in reaction to the rationalization of the body dictated by separate garments for top and bottom. Like the de-skilling of labor processes based on "scientific management" theories employed at that time, more precise measurements of the body and more detailed shaping via the specialized brassiere and low corset conceptually detached body parts from each other and from the body as a whole. Reconstructing the body as separate parts mediated by scientific understandings, and creating commodities to clothe each part, undermined women's experience of their bodies as cohesive physiological and subjective entities. Thus, the widespread embrace of scientific management had serious effects on the consumption as well as on the production of commodities and bodies. The uneasiness of women purchasers of brassieres and corsets may have reflected their resistance to the rationalization and commodification of their bodies in the workplace, in medicine, and in dressing practices.[31]

Combination garments, known colloquially by the Warner's style name Corselette, also addressed the desire for a "feeling of oneness." In practical terms, corselettes eliminated the bulge of flesh often created between the bottom of the brassiere and the top of the corset. This bulge was antithetical to the smooth straight silhouette. Although corselettes were promoted as a "solution to the corset problem . . . which can scarcely be recognized as belonging to the same family as the tortuous affairs of the departed wasp-waisted era," the garments also proved antithetical to the new body freedom promised by outerwear dress designs. For although the newly visible legs of corselette wearers remained free, these binding garments encased the body from armpits to thighs. Nonetheless, corselettes' ability to resolve women's desires for "oneness" boosted sales, outpacing those of brassieres in 1926. The trade viewed the rising popularity of combinations as ultimately helpful to brassiere sales. "The advent of the combination . . . has also brought women to the realization that the brassiere is a necessary part of their dress, for while they have accepted the corset, this combination garment has taught them that the brassiere is just as important for the proper moulding and holding of the figure."[32]

. . . . .

The flattened-breast silhouette did not entirely escape criticism. Objections were made on aesthetic grounds and assertions were put forth that flat-chested women were "unnatural." Enid Bisset and Ida and William Rosenthal were three such dissenters. Together they devised and marketed a bandeau with a center-front elastic inset to sell with the dresses they manufactured in their small New York shop in the early 1920s. When they realized in 1922 that customers were more interested in their brassieres than their dresses, they began to manufacture the brassieres exclusively under the Maiden Form label. Within fashion generally, designers also moved toward a subtle cupping of the breasts because the flattening brassieres pushed the breasts back under the arms, causing a bulge of flesh to appear there. This bulge worked against the desired straight effect, and perpendicular darts were inserted in brassieres to keep the breasts flattened in front of the body.[33]

As the vogue for flattened breasts faded in the late 1920s, bandeaux brassieres that supported the so-called natural shape of the breasts gained favor. Like the Maiden Form design, such bandeaux included a center-front inset or seam that created some breast separation. By the end of the decade, many of these brassieres also uplifted the breasts to some extent. Uplifting bandeaux brassieres usually had no boning and were made of all sorts of colored fabrics, including silk, cotton, and the newly developed "artificial silk," or rayon. The Sunnysilk fabric of one uplift model featured in the 1931 Sears, Roebuck and Co. catalog is described as "all silk material that re-sembles radium and wears so well." However, the "uplift" of this period must be seen in relation to turn-of-the century nonstructured brassieres worn with early topless corsets and to the flattened effect of the preceding era. Although the uplift trend began in this era, over the next two decades, it reached a popularity and dimension unimaginable in the 1920s.[34]

Manufacturers sold the uplift concept to women as a means of correct-ing the damage caused by breast binding, though without accepting any cul-pability. As a trade journal explained, "It has been admitted by most brassiere manufacturers that the incorrect *wearing* of the too straight-lined brassieres caused quite a bit of damage as far as sagging muscles and dropped busts, and . . . efforts are being made to counteract this by uplift models" [emphasis added]. A 1927 Model Brassiere Company advertisement informed readers that "Medical Science in a late treatise on bust ailments, states—'Much of the serious bust troubles of to-day have been caused by flattening the busts and so breaking the tissues. The scientific purpose of a brassiere is to support the bust and to correct drooping.' " The following year, an advertisement for the A.P.-Uplift brassiere designed by "Mme. Poix" noted that this model "gives *upward, converging* support and produces the youthful contour that Style demands. Eminent physicians endorse its hygienic, healthful, pain-relieving qualities." Thus, drooping breasts, which two decades earlier conformed to the fashionable low bosom, became a fashion and health problem that women could resolve in the post-flattened-breast period by buying and wearing brassieres. As a result of brassieres' new healthful function, *Corsets & Brassieres* could report in 1930 that the brassiere had come "into its own."[35]

Uplift became associated paradoxically both with the continuing 1920s preoccupation with the look of youth and the emerging 1930s trend toward restoring the "womanly figure."

> Now that the stylists or whoever is responsible for the new fashions have "sold" women everywhere on the idea of the molded silhouette and especially the exposition of the well rounded, uplifted, youthful bust line, that which a while ago seemed very daring, seems quite natural and women who could never make themselves flat-chested enough are flaunting whatever curves they may possess and rushing to foundation garment departments for brassieres that will give them above the waistline the contours of a "Winged Victory."[36]

Warner's vice president Lucien T. Warner concurred: "The masculine era in woman's dress has passed and feminine curves are in."[37]

At the time of its introduction, uplift was asserted to be a " 'Flapper' model" by the *Corset and Underwear Review* "because the younger generation of today are not particularly keen for the heavy, conforming type of corseting . . . there is a desire to have . . . freedom and style, and the 'uplift' vogue gives them all of this and more." Trade journalist Gertrude L. Nickerson thought the uplift trend beneficial because she blamed "the boyish form craze . . . for the ugly slouch of some of our youth. For when they couldn't flatten the bust completely they found by bringing the shoulders slightly forward it helped to efface it all together." Nickerson refers here to the infamous "debutante slouch," a rebellious youthful female posture of the early twentieth century that defied expectations that fashionable upper-class women would impart an "imposing . . . authority of appearance." Yet Nickerson advises that "male youth serve as the standard for the men, and . . . women take their standard from our girls," forgetting that older women also took up the debutante slouch. And, though women of all ages should maintain what Maiden Form described as "the natural, young, un-spoiled bosom," doing so might include "an uplift operation" ("if Madame is of the privileged class and of sufficient courage"), about which Nickerson had recently learned in Paris.[38]

Young women possibly ceased to find the slouch a satisfactory rebellious posture when their mothers affected it, so they turned to uplift as a more difficult feat for older women to imitate. Focusing on the breasts to assert youthful independence was also encouraged by fashions that abandoned the cinched waist as well as the curved hipline of the early twentieth century while continuing to display the "upper part of the figure, whether thru the transparent material . . . or the more close fit." Flattening drew notice to the bust by the simulation of absence; this further attention meant that a dec-orative brassiere was "generally [a flapper's] first real piece of 'grown-up' lingerie." However, while flattened breasts might also safely desexualize, uplift provided a potentially more dangerous alternative.[39]

As brassiere designers became more expert in providing uplift for women of all sizes and ages, the young and slender found new ways to dis-tinguish themselves. Observations that the appeal of uplift brassieres lay in their "purpose of daintiness" changed quickly into warnings about the "bizarre" designs of "extreme" uplift, which proved "that the psychology of woman is beyond human comprehension." In addition, extreme uplift posed a threat to conventions of modesty and propriety. "The younger girl is just as determined to outline her bust as she was to flatten it some months ago. . . . Consequently one finds the pointed cup effect . . . [which] is neither a lovely fashion, nor a decent one." Evaluating the two styles, commenta-tors characterized the "well-rounded, standing bust line" as "more conser-vative" and the "pointed French effect" as "ostentatiously calling attention to the bust. Such a show is vulgar and should be avoided if one would be classed among the refined women of the world." The Model Brassiere Com-pany advised that "the stylish brassiere must accentuate but not exagger-ate." Slim young women were also characterized as "the most particular and hardest to please" in brassiere sales, because they preferred both delicate bandeaux and uplift structure.[40]

Uplift appealed to manufacturers because the new style prompted pur-chases and because uplift brassiere design relied less on the ever-shifting placement of the waistline than earlier designs had. Freedom from style trends in corsets, girdles, and outerwear fashions worn below the bust increased retail stability and confidence in wholesale purchasing of product lines.[41] In the early 1930s, brassiere companies produced an increasing number of brassiere styles that provided uplifted breasts for all sorts and sizes of women's bodies. As one trade journalist remarked, "The modern brassiere comes in an infinite variety of shapes and contours so that women may disguise nature's deficiencies in absolute comfort." Uplift brassieres produced a slimmer appearance because they reduced the appearance of thickness around the middle torso and removed bulk from the waistline area. Thus, although the "womanly figure" might have been fashionable, the "matronly" look was highly undesirable. This redefinition of "woman-liness" reconstructed female bodies to fit a new complex standard of attrac-tiveness and erotic appeal that incorporated elements of youth and mature development.[42]

· · · · ·

Uplifted breasts became a distinctive feature of women's fashionable sil-houette in the 1930s. To shape women's breasts to this new standard, "more care than ever before [was] exerted on the designing of brassieres." "Cut with meticulous care," brassiere design now utilized "a host of ingenious and patented devices" to resolve the "great problem" of keeping brassieres in place. Shoulder straps received particular attention because of the prob-lems and discomfort resulting from the extra strain that uplift imparted. Two solutions were elastic straps and straps of adjustable length. In addition, the diaphragm, recently freed from restraint by lower-topped corsets, re-gained importance. Diaphragm bands on brassieres both secured brassiere placement and enhanced the definition of the bustline by restraining the flesh below the breasts.[43]

By 1933, *Corsets & Brassieres* no longer described extreme uplift in dis-paraging terms, reluctantly deferring to the greater expertise of other "fashion authorities": "The silhouette which accentuates width across the shoulders, partly by the prominent, lifted bust line; narrowness at the waist; and flatness over the diaphragm, is the one accepted by fashion authorities as the exponent of the 1933 mode. This means that the extreme uplift type of brassiere will be more in favor than ever and . . . there will be many new and unusual designs from which to choose. Brassieres moulding the bust to extremely pointed lines are numerous."[44]

Like perceptions of uplift, notions of "extreme" variations of "pointed lines" were relative. What seemed extremely pointed in 1933 did not ap-proach the peak of pointed brassiere cups that emerged in later decades.

Figure 17. As the number of styles proliferated, fashion industrialists promoted the concept of "brassiere wardrobes" and relied upon an increasing number of fashion authorities to control fashion changes. Experts, like those portrayed here, asserted the importance of up-lift for "good figure grooming," "perfection in figure molding," and "wonderful support, smart lines." *Ebony,* December 1950. Courtesy, Exquisite Form/VF Corporation.

However, pointed cups in the mid-1930s remained secondary in popularity to those that produced breasts "rounded, moulded, lifted to high, youthful contours." This occurred in part because rounded breasts and modified uplift seemed "more becoming" to the "full-busted figure." In addition, about 10 percent of women customers simply refused to wear the new style, and retailers were advised to keep suitable stock on hand for them.[45]

The desire to create the smoothly rounded lines of an idealized breast shape prompted further innovations in cup shaping and fabric selection. Maiden Form introduced brassieres with seamless cups in 1933, which the company called the Full Fashion. The name was an intentional reference to full-fashioned stockings, which tightly hugged the legs to produce a smooth and firm appearance. However, Maiden Form claimed the analogy carried only so far because "whereas stockings take the shape of the limbs, Maiden Form's 'Full Fashion' brassieres *control the bust*, mould it to conform accurately with the up-to-date woman's 1933 ideals of style and feminine beauty." According to the company, this brassiere's design fulfilled Maiden Form's "*single dominating ideal*, the glorification of the *natural* feminine figure." Within its first month on the market, the Full Fashion became Maiden Form's biggest seller to date.[46]

The use of two-way stretch Lastex fabric for brassiere cups, also inaugurated in the early 1930s, sought to ease conflicts between restraint and comfort, molding and movement, and uplift and "riding up." Lastex had been used in corsetry since 1931, and Warner Brothers Corset Company president John Field called its adoption "the greatest change in the corset field any of us have ever witnessed." Lastex brassieres were lauded for keeping their shape, even with multiple launderings, and for their ability to fit women who are "in-between sizes." Lastex brassieres thus had "a size range not obtainable with any other type of garment." Warner's described its first Lastex A'lure line of brassieres as a "second skin," which "softly mold[s] and gently uplift[s] the bust to Fashion's Silhouette."[47]

The trend toward separation of uplifted breasts spawned further innovations and fostered continual redefinition of the "natural" bustline. Patented devices and new designs improved artificial means to achieve a shape deemed "natural." Maiden Form introduced the Dec-La-Tay brassiere in 1933 "in answer to the new silhouette demand for *wide* as well as *high* lines." However, this demand was apparently so new that the company advised retailers "to show *first* any regulation Maiden Form brassiere . . . one that is not cut in a deep V-front. Point out that this brassiere holds the breast more or less *together*. Then put a Dec-La-Tay on the figure and demonstrate how it *parts* the breasts, without any hint of the crease that many women dislike." Within one year, Maiden Form offered five styles that created this "pulled-apart effect," defined as a "marked definition of the space between the breasts." The *Maiden Form Mirror*, a company publication for retailers, described these brassieres' purpose to bring the figure " 'back to nature' . . . because in the natural, young, unspoiled bosom, there *is* a distinct separation between the breasts, and it is this line which Maiden Form now glorifies."[48]

Uplift and separation ushered in greater use of wired sections for support and shaping. *Corsets & Brassieres* explained in 1930 that "tiny wired sections in . . . between the busts" were needed because "this section . . . must lie flat and stay in place, so that the contours of the bust may be more pronounced and outstanding." Thus, this important section between the breasts, a critical location in creating uplift and separation, received a great deal of design attention. Beautee-Fit Brassiere Company of Los Angeles patented a U-shaped wire insert in 1938 to "afford greater separation of the breasts and so achieve a more natural contour." However, use of wired brassieres declined during World War II, presumably because of wartime restrictions on the use of metals for consumer goods. In 1946, the production of wired brassieres resumed in increased numbers and styles, and sales were strong.[49]

Innovations in cup construction helped achieve the desired pointed effect. In 1935, Hollywood Maxwell debuted the important V-Ette Whirlpool brassiere, with "spiral-stitched uplift." *Corsets & Brassieres* claimed that the brassiere's "circular flange . . . uplifts in a superb fashion and results in a healthful circulation." Maiden Form's 1938 Chansonette, which became the best-selling brassiere in America in a 1955 prepackaged form, worked on a similar principle but created a circle out of spokelike sections to form what the company called "pointed roundness." Also in 1938, Beautee-Fit introduced its "loop-over" stitching, which circled the breast cups, in the Intrigue brassiere. Circle-stitched cups ultimately became so popular that special sewing machines with multiple needles were constructed to mass-produce them.[50]

The fashion for uplifted breasts increased sales of brassieres, as they became a requisite foundation—or even a "stern necessity"—for achieving the breast shape demanded by outerwear designs. Rising brassiere sales in the early 1930s enabled many companies to prosper during the Depression. Maiden Form, for example, reported "record breaking sales" in 1931. "The sale of foundation garments has not been materially affected by general business conditions," because, according to Maiden Form, "Looking beautiful is life itself to a woman, and she will hesitate long before economizing on comparatively inexpensively priced foundations which maintain her figure charm." Joseph Bissett, the company's general sales manager, found "corset departments to be the most cheerful" during a 1932 sales trip, where some departments were "not only maintaining last year's figures, but were frequently far ahead." That year, Maiden Form expanded operations in its large Bayonne, New Jersey, plant, which the company had built in 1929. Not all brassiere companies performed this well during this period. The long-established De Bevoise concern folded into the Royal Worcester Corset Company, and Gossard took over "the United States and Canada agency" of the English Kestos Brassiere Company in the mid-1930s.[51]

. . . . .

The proliferation of brassiere designs and styles in the early 1930s led to one of the most significant developments in twentieth-century brassieres: breast cups in graduated sizes. Warner's produced the first brassieres with Type A, Type B, Type C, and Type D cups in 1935, which the company later referred to as alphabet brassieres. These standardized cup sizes replaced brassiere lines individually named and styled to designate size and shape. Maiden Form, for example, had marketed the Etude for "the junior figure," the long-line Overture for "the mature figure," the Variation for "small and average figures," the Intimo for "the medium to full figure," and the Re-mold for "the pendulous bust." The Bali Brassiere Company quickly imitated Warner's patented cup sizing, and within the next few years, many other manufacturers followed suit.[52]

Graduated cup sizing drew upon the figure-classification schemes that corset companies used to promote their brands. Saleswomen were familiar with the concepts and practices of figure typing through corset training schools, promotional print materials, and actual corset fittings. Figure typing re-envisioned the female body and altered the experience of this body as both subject and object. Women's familiarity with figure-classification schemes in corsetry facilitated acceptance of the simplified brassiere-cup typing on sales floors, in fitting rooms, and, after purchase, in their bedrooms at home.[53]

Figure-type standardization worked in tandem with typologies fostered by advertising that targeted women. In the 1920s, for example, the cosmetics industry promoted types of facial features and personality. One company named its products Cleopatra, Mona Lisa, Godiva, and Colleen and included illustrations of each type in its magazine advertisements. The seductive headline "Which of These Alluring Types Are You?" encouraged readers to identify with one of these types and then to select the corresponding product. Such typologies aimed to give the shopper the feeling of an individualized experience, though she was actually purchasing standardized products. The advertisements complemented the personality and attitude tests in women's magazines that offered further inducements to self-typing. These tests asked the reader a series of questions, which she then scored to discover her fashion identity or a problematic feature of her personality.[54]

The relentless promotion of actors by Hollywood studios' public rela-

Figure 18. Figure types led to standardized cup sizes in brassieres, first introduced by Warner's in 1935. Standardized sizes supposedly eliminated the need for trained saleswomen. *Corsets & Brassieres*, February 1946. Courtesy of Special Collections, Gladys Marcus Library, Fashion Institute of Technology. Courtesy, Warnaco Inc.

tions departments, a means of increasing movie theater attendance, generated additional female typologies. A succession of female stars, from Theda Bara ("vamp") and Clara Bow ("It" girl) to Carole Lombard ("screwball") and Olivia de Havilland ("all-American girl"), were seen as innovators sparking a host of imitators or as the consummate expression of an existing category. The increasing circulation of the notion of "types," and of stories about stars' personalities and performances both on- and offscreen, increased audience members' identification with their preferred type. A 1939 *Movie Mirror* article discussing *The Women*, for example, focused entirely on the five female types the magazine identified in the film and asked the reader, "Which of these five types is yours?" The film itself encouraged this line of thinking by introducing each actress's character along with an image of an animal, such as a black cat, fox, lamb, and owl, in a reverse anthropo-morphic personality typology.[55]

The connection between figure types and screen types was not only ide-ological and discursive but also materially grounded in contractual rela-tionships between brassiere manufacturers and Hollywood studios. Since the early twentieth century, the garment industry had been well aware of the important style-setting power of the stage and screen. Brassiere manu-facturers that sought to benefit from association with the stage and screen included the Los Angeles–based Hollywood Maxwell company, which con-solidated its relationship with Paramount Pictures in 1935. The companies' agreement provided for the exclusive use of Hollywood Maxwell brassieres in Paramount movies and for mutually beneficial retail promotion on that basis.[56]

The need of Hollywood studios for foundation designs that met the unique demands of film costumes and camera angles strengthened the brassiere industry, particularly those firms based in Los Angeles. In addition to Hollywood Maxwell, companies like Renée of Hollywood advertised their brassieres in 1937 with the slogan "Worn by the Stars." As one trade journal explained, "In many instances a garment is designed for a special motion picture star in a new picture, and when it has proved successful under the discerning eyes of camera men, directors, and other minions of the cinema . . . that bandeaux is ready to be launched as consumer mer-chandise." The Sho-Form Brassiere Company of Los Angeles claimed that its head designer kept "in constant touch with the Hollywood film studios, developing for every woman brassieres which assist them in emulating the figures of picture stars." Actress endorsements further encouraged this de-sire, as did brassiere style names like Actress, Glamour, and Starlight, as well as brassiere advertisements in movie fan magazines.[57]

Women's identification with the typologies generated by standardized cup sizes, advertising, and film promotion engaged them in what critical theorist Theodor Adorno called pseudo-individualization: "Concentration and control in our culture hide themselves in their very manifestation. Un-hidden they would provoke resistance. Therefore, the illusion and, to a cer-tain extent, even the reality of individual achievement must be main-tained. . . . pseudo-individualization . . . [endows] cultural mass production with the halo of free choice or open market on the basis of standardization itself." Thus, cup sizes not only standardized and rationalized breasts but also implicated women in a process of pseudo-individualization. Corset and brassiere fittings were a primary way to educate female customers about figure typologies. A woman's identification as a 36B or 40D, whether by herself or by others, became a component in the construction of her individual, embodied subjectivity. However, such identification actually incorporated women's bodies and psyches in structures of standardization, literally inscribing them upon their flesh.[58]

As companies replaced their complex line of style and size names with numbered chest measurements and lettered cup sizes, they de-skilled the work of brassiere saleswoman. Foundation departments between the 1920s and 1950s were usually the most profitable in the store, and that fact, along with knowledge of merchandise and fitting procedures, elevated these saleswomen's wages and status. After cup sizing took hold, saleswomen no longer needed a wealth of information about each company's lines to assist and fit customers. As *Corsets & Brassieres* explained, "The theory is that the customer can pick the style of brassiere she likes and then find a garment in the set that fits her figure exactly."[59] Retailers benefited because it weakened saleswomen's power to demand high wages. Standardized sizing also permitted retailers to merchandise prepackaged brassieres in department store "bra bars," which enabled customers to select bras without any sales assistance. Playtex was one of the first companies to launch fully into a line of prepackaged brassieres; Maiden Form was one of the last.

Maiden Form also resisted cup sizes until 1949, when the company could no longer afford to stand alone. Six years earlier, the popularity of cup sizes had prompted Maiden Form to defend its sizing policy. In switching, the company asserted that "we would be betraying our customers, because we would be abandoning the principle which has *made* Maiden Form what it is today—the principle of *individual* designing." In 1948, the company tried to head off the inevitable by sending charts to retail stores, hailing them as "the greatest invention since the tape measure!" The charts explained in detail Maiden Form's style and size configurations and argued for the typology's superiority to "A-B-C" classifications. However, the next year Maiden Form produced Maidenette, a style aimed at younger women unfamiliar with past sizing strategies, in graduated alphabet cup sizes. By 1955, Maidenform, which had adopted the one-word spelling a few years earlier, had four cup-sized styles to stock its self-service bra bar, which the company called a "silent . . . salesperson" and placed in over 4,000 retail locations. Sears, Roebuck and Co., whose longstanding mail-order catalog was also a sort of "silent salesperson," also resisted across-the-board standardized cup sizing until the 1950s. Its 1948 catalog edition featured Maiden Form bras, as well as its own Charmode line, in figure-type styles. The catalog's inclusion of parenthetical notes like "(often called 'B' cup)" in style descriptions indicated the imminence of Sears's conversion to graduated cup sizing.[60]

The proliferation of standardized cup sizing suffused the corset and brassiere industry, as well as commercial mass culture, with the ideology of figure types and a rationalized female body. This permeation had several important consequences. First, the body divisions that had begun with the vogue for uplift and separation escalated. Measurement of both the width and the depth of breasts intensified the separation of fleshy breasts from the solid chest and the division of the breasts into two malleable parts. Initiated by the turn-of-the-century development of a specialized garment for the breasts, these processes of separation fragmented the formerly singular bosom of the female torso. The sheer fabrics and tight fit of 1910s fashions displayed and highlighted this area of the body, recently freed from the corset, and focused attention on its new undergarment, the brassiere. This attention furthered the segmented vision of the torso and the detachment of breasts from chest. After the 1920s' intensifying focus on repressing the breasts within binding garments, the incorporation of a center-front brassiere seam by the end of the decade initiated a type of breast shaping that emphasized separation. Uplifted breasts in pointed cups further dismembered the female body. As a 1941 advertisement for Beautee-Fit Company's new Swirl brassiere explained, "each breast is separate in its own swirl; at last attaining not only complete separation of breast from breast, but also freedom of breast from *body*."[61]

Freedom of breast from body was also achieved by "gay deceivers," pads or objects that women could place in their brassieres to augment their bustlines. In the mid-1930s, an increasing number of these products became available to women who wanted to appear larger breasted. Warner's Gay Deceivers, for example, were round bust pads made of layers of net fabric that drew on G. M. Poix, Inc.'s 1932 patented Cuties. According to the manufacturers, women could wear these pads "without anyone, even the wearer, being conscious of them." The growing popularity of such products prompted Los Angeles designer Madelon Louden to expand distribution of her Nue-Dé "bust forms" to East Coast stores in 1935. Described by the slogan "Perfect as Nature Itself," Nue-Dé forms "originated in a motion-picture studio in Hollywood" and were made of "flesh-colored chiffon that is shaded slightly darker over the natural looking tip," and came in five sizes, from "rosebuds" to "surgicals." Hollywood Maxwell produced its 1935 Hucatel Forms of "crocheted angora . . . in larger sizes than last season's bust tips," an indication of the decade's amplified standards for desirable breast

PERFECT AS NATURE ITSELF
Nue-Dé
(new-day)
BUST FORMS
created by
MADELON LOUDEN
6636 HOLLYWOOD BOULEVARD   HOLLYWOOD, CAL.

Figure 19. Nue-Dé Bust Forms were "perfect as nature itself." *Corsets & Brassieres,* May 1935. Courtesy of Special Collections, Gladys Marcus Library, Fashion Institute of Technology. Courtesy, National Corset Supply House.

size. By 1940, the Sears catalog offered two styles of Flatterettes, pocket bras that held bust pads made of "whipped Latex" or "shirred net." Instructive "before" and "after" illustrations demonstrated how these products augmented the breast silhouette to create a fashionable look.[62]

.   .   .   .   .

The emergence of uplifted breasts in the 1930s as a critical factor in fashionability, and breasts' increasing elevation, projection, and importance in the 1940s silhouette, occurred within a multifaceted social and cultural context. Fashion imperatives included slimness and youthfulness; pulling the breasts up created a slimmer appearance at the midsection and waist, whereas uplift and separation became essential components of the youthful look. Yet fashion also made a contradictory return to the "womanly figure" at the end of the 1920s, partly in reaction to the "boyshform" that emphasized the curves afforded by breasts and hips. This complex reconstruction of fashionable femininity based on idealized elements of both youth and maturity made the brassiere a necessary, and thus ubiquitous, undergarment for twentieth-century American women. By the late 1930s, the ritual of obtaining one's first brassiere was well inscribed into American culture as a memorable rite of passage that every woman would experience. In addition, the virtually inaccessible combination of youthful and mature body features increased the incidence of breast-enlargement surgery in succeeding decades, because this procedure provided a sure means of achieving both a slim figure and large firm breasts.

Analysis of the social and economic circumstances of the 1930s, in which the slim figure with large breasts first emerged, and of the 1940s, when it became dominant, is crucial to understanding why uplift became popular when it did. During the Depression of the 1930s, massive unemployment among men caused high levels of anxiety. In addition, because some sectors of the economy that employed women suffered fewer job losses than those that employed men, in many households women retained the ability to provide income when men didn't. The predominantly female workforce at Maiden Form's expanding company during this period is one case in point. The return to a "womanly" silhouette, which came into fashion alongside the slow acceptance of trousers for women, suggests that uplifted breasts played a part in assuaging gender concerns. A 1933 *Corsets & Brassieres* column noted, for example, that "as the figure remains feminine above the waist, in the current silhouette, so the demand for brassieres and bandeaux becomes more insistent." This statement clearly associates femininity with the molding of breasts into a distinctive shape that draws the gaze. This phenomenon became increasingly important during the 1940s, when, with men at war, women assumed roles and duties formerly performed by men. This reversal in what was considered acceptable work for women, which took place on a home front marked by the absence of large numbers of men, helped blur gender distinctions, despite the efforts of manufacturers and the state to convince women that their newfound capabilities should exist only temporarily during the war. Women's greater use of trousers for work and leisure activities at this time also meant that attention continued to be directed to the part of the anatomy "above the waist" for the purpose of maintaining female difference. Large, uplifted breasts constructed female difference not only in the silhouette they created but also in the gendered cultural practices that women's use of specialized garments like pointy uplift brassieres entailed.[63]

Brassiere trends in the 1940s and early 1950s intensified developments that had occurred during the 1930s. Uplift and separation in "bras," as they became known in the late 1930s, became more extreme, and devices to achieve these effects proliferated. Maiden Form described this intensification as "outlift," explaining that "outlift as well as uplift . . . means a bosom well accented through the middle and with a breadth of separation which extends to the very tip of each breast." The slim hipline and elongated torso of the early 1940s further accentuated the projection of the breast silhouette.[64]

During World War II, brassiere designers coped with the loss of rubber for elasticized fabrics and metal for wires by introducing design innovations and using stiffer cotton. Manufacturers promoted sturdy brassieres for war workers as practical garments that were necessary for support and health. *Corsets & Brassieres* recommended specialized local advertising in areas with defense plants to inform workers of the availability of brassieres that suited their needs. The trade journal also suggested planning a "fashion show for defense workers," which would not only show what the "well dressed defense worker wears in the factory but what she wears when going out at night." This "brassiere wardrobe idea" relied upon the expectation that "since defense workers have more money to spend they will be more receptive" to the idea of owning several types of brassieres. The industry also worked to intensify demand among women in the military by asserting the need for "impeccable foundations under uniforms," because "trimness and training go hand in hand."[65]

Representations of "practical" brassieres for defense workers and women in uniform coexisted with wartime pinup photographs that emphasized their subjects' breasts. Legitimized as troop morale boosters, and seen as a distraction from the hard, deadly, and chaotic circumstances of war, pinups represented the soft, the pleasurable, the domestic, and the controllable. The iconography of wartime pinups—long torso, long legs, and firm, uplifted breasts—drew on the association of breasts and legs as central features in erotic presentations of women's bodies that had prevailed since the nineteenth century. In the 1940s, pinups reflected the fashionable body shape of this period, especially as depicted by the Petty and Varga "girls" who became standard features in calendars and in *Esquire* magazine in the mid-1930s. A recurrent pinup pose depicted a woman with arms behind her head and elbows extended outward. This pose raises the breasts upward, and, by removing the arms from the torso, emphasizes the silhouette of breast projection.[66]

In 1945, Maiden Form held a pinup contest at its Bayonne factory in response to a request by Johnny Powasnik, a Maiden Form worker then serving in Germany in the 978th Engineer Maintenance Company. Each self-selected contestant submitted a photograph to the six-month-old company publication for employees, *The Maiden Forum*, in hopes of winning the soldiers' favor, $5 from management, and either free lunch for a week in the plant cafeteria or a carton of cigarettes.[67] *The Maiden Forum* published forty-seven snapshots in May, and the June issue contained a front-page letter from Johnny describing his comrades' reaction: "Never was the morale so high like it was the day I put the paper on the bulletin board! They just went nuts! . . . All day and all evening the boys talked of how all the girls are getting all set to either have their pictures taken or can't wait to read the results of our sweetheart! . . . We are on pins and needles to see the next issue."[68]

The soldiers in the 978th had to wait just one month to find out that #20, Shirley Levine, was the overwhelming selection not only of their company but also of several other Maiden Form employees' military units. Additional photographs of the "pin-up queen" and "G.I. sweetheart" graced the July issue, along with declarations from "G.I.'s all over the globe." Comments came from Johnnie Kowalski's outfit at the Naval Training School in Indianapolis, Leo Rosenthal's Company H 505th Parachute Infantry, Hilly Rosenthal's 562nd Squadron 388th Bomber Group in Europe, and John Campion aboard the USS *Charger*, Division A. In addition, Johnny Powasnik described the 978th's decision-making process: "After many heated arguments, several black eyes, two men in the hospital, long hours of debating, much drooling of the mouth, the wolves of the 978th howled number *twenty* as our Sweetheart."[69]

Shirley Levine's selection was probably due in part to the better quality of her photograph, a clear medium close-up showing an attractive and smiling young woman sitting on the ground in a park. She is wearing a relatively tight-fitting light-colored short-sleeved shirt and dark shorts. Tucking her legs to one side, Levine leans slightly on one hip, propping her body up with her right arm. With her chest projected outward by this pose, her prominent breasts are center frame. Yet despite entering this contest, Levine protested her selection in a *Maiden Forum* article that described her body, interests, and personality. She claimed, "Jeepers, I'm not the Pin-Up type!" The article responded to Levine's protest by characterizing her as "typically the American Girl," a type that includes "a figure that could aptly be described as 'well-stacked.'" The discussion and images generated by this contest demonstrate the centrality of large breasts to pinup iconography and to the American ideal figure of the 1940s. They also testify to how deeply this iconography permeated even noncommercial representations and the preferences of ordinary people, who in this instance, ironically worked at a brassiere factory. In listing Levine's prizes for winning the contest, the *Maiden Forum* first noted "the power and glory attached to being the Sweetheart of the 978th Engineers." Levine's selection reveals how power and glory were also attached to possessing large breasts.[70]

When Johnny Powasnik returned to Bayonne in November, 1945, he gave further details about the 978th Engineers' response to the pinup contest. His comments disclose that a woman's achievement of power and glory through provocatively positioned large breasts could not only be tenuous but even dangerous. Powasnik "received the issue with the winning pictures of *Shirley* [when] en route from Marseilles to the Philippine Islands." Having only one copy, he "posted it up on the ship's bulletin board, where 15,000 G.I.'s viewed it." The reaction was so strong that Powasnik said, "I hate to think what would have happened to *Shirley* if she were there." Yet he also notes that "the boys told me to be sure I passed on their very best regards to *Shirley*, and also a kiss."[71]

A few months after Johnny's Bayonne visit, the *Maiden Forum* began running a monthly pinup photograph of a female factory worker. Although the accompanying information on the pinups did not differ substantially from previous "Staff Profiles" of the largely female workforce, which the "Our Pin-Up for [month]" feature replaced, the photographs did change. The photo booth–style head shots of earlier columns gave way to full-body shots, which often focused on legs or chest. At one point, a professional photographer began taking the pictures of the women profiled in the magazine. The female worker selected each month tended to conform more to dominant notions of youthful beauty, enhanced by lighting, poses, and angles typical of fashion and pinup photography. As the pinup feature came to the end of its run, the photographs returned to images of women of ordinary appearance and were shot once again by nonprofessional photographers. At its height, however, the transformation of the "Staff Profile" into the "Pin-Up," undoubtedly a result of the pinup contest held at the factory, changed the way Maiden Form workers viewed themselves and each other.[72]

· · · · ·

Visual, discursive, and material partitioning and detachment of the female body encouraged cultural fetishism of breasts, which had been a prominent component of American gendered culture since the late 1930s. Although the division of the body works against women's stated yearnings for oneness, this contradiction finds resolution when the part becomes the whole through fetishization. Fetishization diffuses the sense of detachment by highlighting disparate elements—such as the breasts and legs of pinup iconography—to produce a caricature of wholeness. This process was at work in 1937, when Lana Turner's breasts first electrified male movie patrons.

The body of Lana Turner further elucidates the history of the brassiere because of Turner's oft-noted personification of Hollywood glamour, as well as her articulated desire to construct such an image. Costar Mickey Rooney called her "Baby Glamour" in 1938, and the Academy of Contemporary Arts voted her "the most glamorous woman in the history of international art" in 1951. In 1966, a film review described her as "the glitter and glamour of Hollywood; a symbol of the American Dream fulfilled. Because of her, being discovered at a soda fountain has become almost as cherished an ideal as being born in a log cabin. . . . To reject her is to reject the Dream itself." Turner later remarked, "Forsaking glamour is like forsaking my identity. It's an image I've worked too hard to attain and preserve."[73]

Lana Turner's embodiment of glamour originated in her celebrated breasts. The career of Jane Russell, another film actress whose celebrity was galvanized by attention to her breasts, further illustrates the connection between glamour and women's breasts. Russell's first screen role was in the ill-fated Howard Hughes film *The Outlaw*. The movie began shooting in 1941, but director Hughes's continual tinkering with the film, along with industry and state censorship of its sexual scenes, delayed release for five years. In the interim, however, Russell became famous not by appearing in any other movies but by a continual stream of publicity stills orchestrated and distributed by Hughes's publicist, Russell Birdwell.[74]

In these stills, Russell usually posed in the low-cut blouse she wore in *The Outlaw*. In the best known of them, she reclines on a haystack. This scene, along with other shots of her walking or bending over, emphasized and revealed her breasts in a way not previously seen in mainstream publications. In 1942, the film-industry magazine *Boxoffice* commented with surprise that Birdwell had released the statement "Jane Russell possesses the most beautiful bust in Hollywood." It pointed to "all the censure of photographs published in national magazines some months ago and widely indicted as being too revealing of Miss Russell's voluptuousness." Such censure notwithstanding, in 1945, *Collier's* magazine called Russell the "Queen of the motionless pictures" because of the enormous amount of attention she had received after widespread circulation of her photographs. This attention included Russell's selection as "official hostess" by soldiers at Camp Roberts, a two-day visit to a United States Naval Training Station (documented by a spread in *Look* magazine), and selection as the "favorite movie star" of the Army and Navy in 1941. Her popularity as a pinup during World War II rivaled that of Betty Grable and Rita Hayworth. In 1945, the *Los Angeles Times* characterized Russell as "the girl who made pin-ups pin-ups."[75]

One of the photographs in *Look* testifies to Russell's pinup appeal. A smiling soldier sits on his bunk in front of Russell's photograph while knitting a sweater for her. The caption includes the odd comment, "His progress is slow as his tent mates have been jealously hiding his needles." The comment undoubtedly makes an association between the attention garnered by Turner's sweatered breasts in 1937 and Russell's recent and similarly won notoriety. However, the tent mates' jealousy indicates a sort of displacement had also occurred: to hold Russell's sweater was to hold her breasts. That the sweater became a stand-in for breasts in the 1940s is clear in a 1949 *Los Angeles Times* report of a Paris hotel incident involving Russell that described her as "of Hollywood sweater fame." This description indicates the displacement from breast to sweater via the conflation of Russell with Turner.[76]

Published commentary about Russell from the early 1950s reveals that the process of erotic diffusion via displacement from body part to clothing did not end with this movement but rather continued to subtly shift. A *Quick* magazine photo caption reads, "Jane Russell is caught by a candid camera in a rare photograph that shows her without the usual careful pose and low-cut gown but not without glamour." And Hedda Hopper wrote in a 1953 column, "Since Jane had more than an average girl's glamour her publicity was slated toward sex. As a result she was built into one of the greatest illusions Hollywood has ever created." Both comments suggest that large breasts are a site for the production of glamour and a place from which this magical power transforms the woman, in this case Jane Russell, as a whole.[77]

The displacement and erotic diffusion seen in the movement from breasts to sweater to glamour is not only a movement away from the body, from flesh to object to intangible aura, but also a movement toward the body. Glamour returns to the body, infusing it with eroticism. Glamour is thus a mechanism that eroticizes objectification and reconstructs the female body as an object of desire. The desired object is the "Thing" that Lana Turner recognized at her first viewing of her cinematic body. The erotic object/thing attracts the desiring gaze and inspires fantasies of possession. Attaining this power that glamour confers, however tenuously, also explains Turner's change of heart and ultimate enthusiasm for her own objectification. Turner's ambitions, which included a successful film career as well as

Figure 20. The slogan "Building You Up" plays on the power accorded large, uplifted breasts in the postwar era. *Corsets & Brassieres,* January 1946. Courtesy of Special Collections, Gladys Marcus Library, Fashion Institute of Technology. Courtesy, Felina.

numerous love affairs, took place within prohibitive social and cultural structures. She mediated the contradictions she encountered by embracing the formation of her body as glamorous.[78]

The mingling of glamour with large breasts, an identification that began in this period, perhaps explains the perpetuation of large breasts' appeal to American women. Large breasts enhance a woman's ability to attract male desire because they symbolize a haven of maternal nurturing and are appealing fetish objects in themselves. But the erotic diffusion offered by glamorizing large breasts moves beyond the assumption that women desire large breasts simply because of their attraction to men. Large breasts' appeal for women may lie instead with the power conferred by the glamour that attaches to them. This power includes the illusionist's power to captivate even though she, as well as her audience, knows it's all a trick. Women's desire to infuse their bodies with the power created by glamour is not merely a means to strengthen their attractive force for men but also a method to enhance their power as a force to be reckoned with in themselves.

4 The Meaning of Black Lingerie

The sexual life of adult women is a "dark continent."

Sigmund Freud, *The Question of Lay Analysis,* 1926

Look! . . . She has black bras on the line and black underwear. . . . She didn't buy them for my son—she's fooling around with somebody. . . . that's how you . . . always tell.

Brooklyn housewife in *Clotheslines* (Roberta Cantwell, 1981)

After the stabbings, [she] allegedly fled . . . in a black negligee, authorities said.

City News Service, 2003

Early twentieth-century mass-produced undergarments were predominantly white. This was reflected in the name "White Goods Workers" given to New York City's Local 62, which formed during the mass strikes of 1909 known as the "Uprising of the 20,000." Within the clothing industry, white goods manufacture was also known as the "women's trade" because 95 percent of its workers were female. The use of both terms—*white goods* and *women's trade*—to refer to the production of apparel clearly linked with female bodily difference parallels the close association of American femininity with whiteness.[1]

White goods included petticoats, drawers, slips, corset covers, and combination garments made of cotton, linen, or silk. More expensive undergarments worn at the turn of the century, an era dubbed "the cult of chiffon," were also predominantly white or made of unbleached linen or muslin.[2] Silk ribbons in pastel shades of pink and blue often provided colored accents as ties and bows. These adornments, and the effusive flounces of lacy trim on elegant white undergarments, gave the term *lingerie* a further specialized meaning. Previously a designation for a range of garments made of linen, *lingerie* began to denote exclusively women's undergarments, and only those finely made.

Prosaic white goods and elite chiffon lingerie can be and were erotic garments despite prevailing views, which persist today, notably in bridal gowns, casting white apparel and the white women who wear it as respectable, if not virginal. Nonetheless, the development of oppositional cultural meanings for white goods and black lingerie intriguingly corresponds to the history of meanings attributed to white women's and black women's bodies. The view commonly held today that black lingerie confers on its wearer a particular charged eroticism thus raises questions regarding dynamics of race and sexuality, as blackness and black bodies have for several centuries in Western culture been linked to deviant and particularly lascivious sexuality, while whiteness and white bodies—and white lingerie—have been associated with sexual purity. Investigating the meaning of black lingerie in light of this history generally, and, more specifically, considering the purported heightened and transgressive sexual nature of black women within the larger context of changing attitudes about female sexuality during the cult of chiffon era when Victorian moral structures dissolved, suggests that in the twentieth century wearing black lingerie became a form of racial masquerade.

Racial masquerade has been central to the development of American culture, from the immensely popular theatrical blackface performances of the nineteenth century to more recent fashions, music, and visual arts that imitate or take inspiration from African and African American culture. Scholars have correctly characterized blackface performance as racist misrepresentation and exploitation that broadly disseminated harmful, distorted perceptions of African Americans to white audiences and prohibited African American performers from representing their own experiences. However, Eric Lott, in *Love and Theft*, points out the dual nature of racial masquerade as both homage and co-optation. Drawing upon such scholarship, this chapter explores whether, and if so, how, wearing black lingerie worked as a racial masquerade akin to blackface. Evidence from a range of sources suggests that black lingerie allowed women, especially white women, to express, and their bodies to convey, the eroticism attributed to black women via a safely contained and removable black skin.[3]

Yet investigating the history of black lingerie raises other questions as well. The historic relationships between sex, death, black fashion, and the female body also help explain the turn-of-the-century emergence of black lingerie's erotic signification. By the nineteenth century, black was well established in Western culture as a color of mourning and of Christian renunciation of the body. Nevertheless, over the course of that century and into the twentieth, black became a color of female fashion. The "little black frock" that Henry James noted in 1902, a phenomenon especially associated with Coco Chanel after her 1926 black day dress appeared in *Vogue*, became an essential component of urbane women's wardrobes. By 1944, *Collier's* magazine declared "black underwear, a hussy fashion in the last war," a "sellout" for "Navy officer's wives" and every man's "wife or sweetheart." The "boys who buy it . . . like black lingerie because it's feminine, alluring, and more than a little bit wicked." Sandra Cisneros's late-twentieth-century poem "Black Lace Bra Kind of Woman," which celebrates a woman so dressed "who serves up suicide in every kamikaze she pours. . . . A tease and a twirl," affirms the persistence of powerful connections in American culture between black lingerie, sex, and death. Furthermore, the varying and at times conflicting connotations of black clothing in the United States include two centuries of signaling bourgeois male sobriety, servant status, and bohemian opposition. Exploring the history of black lingerie thus requires untangling multiple agents and locations of cultural change and meanings and analyzing their widely scattered documentation. These include striking differences of signification in the spheres of production and consumption, a topic I address at the chapter's conclusion.[4]

· · · · ·

Black lingerie's appeal for white women may appear obvious, as an attractive contrast of light and dark. Yet we cannot assume that any culture would view such a contrast favorably. Even in Victorian America, whatever the actual effect, black mourning dress aimed to represent and support women's turning away from earthly pleasures to engage in respectable grieving. As for twentieth-century aesthetic concerns, English dress-advice author Mrs. Eric Pritchard counseled in 1902, "It is nothing unusual for this strong contrast to swallow [fair women] up altogether." In the 1920s, women were warned, "Black is unbecoming at any age if worn with a muddy complexion." Thirty years later, *Women's Wear Daily* recommended navy blue for "any customer who objects to black next to her skin." This advice indicates black was not always seen as a becoming contrast to light-colored skin. Moreover, women with darker skin, including African American and Mexican American women, shared European American women's interest in wearing black lingerie.

Black undergarments may seem desirable to all women for another reason—because they show dirt less readily and do not need to be laundered as frequently. Yet Pritchard warned regarding black outerwear, "Unless you are in mourning I advise you to avoid wearing black for it is apt to get a brownish hue towards the end of a journey." Her concern might reflect the continuing unreliability of dyed fabrics in her time. Black mourning dress, for example, was easily stained and notoriously often ruined by rain and moisture. Further, corsets made of dyed fabrics became more widely available only in later nineteenth-century decades. Thus, women did not wear black corsets until the beginning of the turn-of-the-century period in which black lingerie acquired its modern, erotic meaning.[5]

In those transitional years, when white women claimed new forms of sexual expressiveness, they drew upon the style and practices, both real and imagined, of African American women. Dominant stereotypes that linked blackness with lascivious sexuality, along with the sexually affirming expressions and conduct found within African American culture, were important resources for white women's new behaviors, manners, and moral codes. During that period, African American women worked to improve and enjoy their lives while continuing to suffer from characterizations of their behavior as pathological. With this context in mind, it is also possible to further consider whether wearing black lingerie became a form of racial masquerade.[6]

From the beginnings of the slave trade and during the time that slavery developed into an institution within the United States, racialized understandings of blackness and whiteness evolved to suit the need to maintain mastery and servitude. Winthrop Jordan points out the ideological implications and gendered associations of these colored meanings in his now-classic study *White Over Black: American Attitudes towards the Negro, 1550–1812*. Key to English definitions and connotations of white and black were understandings of female beauty. Even before the Elizabethan era of European initial engagement with Africans, lily white and red rose together marked the English ideal of feminine attractiveness. Ideas equating whiteness, particularly white femininity, with beauty, purity, and virtue, and long-held Western views linking blackness with disfigurement, depravity, disease, and dirt, were used to justify African enslavement and subjugation of peoples of color.[7]

As slavery in the United States became a principal component of the nation's economic structures of labor both bound and free, racialized understandings of blackness and whiteness persisted. These ever-developing meanings of whiteness and blackness had particular consequences for American women of all races. English, and later white American, constructions of African and African American sexuality as debased and unrestrained, ascribed to blackness and black women an excessive sensuality that transgressed white middle-class norms. Views that positioned Africans next to animals on a "chain of being" and placed Europeans at the top also linked black people with less-than-human sexual behavior. These concepts worked in complex ways to shore up white and male structures of domination—for example, by allowing male slave masters to sexually assault enslaved women with impunity. Maintaining control over sexual and other meanings of whiteness and blackness was critical to slave owners' ability to engage in sexual violence while retaining their status as Southern gentlemen. By ascribing lasciviousness to black women, white men could blame the irresistible lure of their color and bodies rather than admit to conscious exploitation of the women's vulnerable state. Moreover, as a mirror image of the Victorian ideal of white female passionlessness, assumptions about black women's sexual nature, by constructing an opposite category, helped define the contours of white female purity. Put to great use in subjecting white women to the "double standard" that accorded privilege to white men, this ideology created a powerful pretext of defenseless white females to justify lynching black men after slavery ended.[8]

Throughout the nineteenth century, medical texts, scientific discourses on anatomy and race, and visual and literary cultural representations presented black women's sexuality as animalistic, lustful, and deviant. Descriptions of black women's sexual difference that focused on their supposedly more primitive breasts, genitals, and buttocks sought to prove that Africans were a distinct, and distinctly lower, race than Europeans. Such depictions denigrated and dehumanized African women by linking them to animals and "freaks" of nature.[9]

The most striking example of the focus on black women's sexual body parts is the discourse generated by the 1810 exhibition in London, and later dissection in Paris, of a South African woman named Saartjie Baartman (1789–1815), widely known in Europe and the United States as the Hottentot Venus.[10] Until this time, display of black female bodies for commercial purposes had primarily taken place at slave auctions. Auctions had sexual overtones, as naked or nearly naked black women, already subject to widely held beliefs about Africans' lascivious sexuality, were shown and prodded to demonstrate their labor value and reproductive capacities. Given that such displays of the female body clearly violated standards of white female modesty, black women's exhibition at slave auctions reinforced white supremacists' beliefs about the women's debased sexual natures.[11]

The exhibition of Baartman, who was brought to England by enterprising businessmen, added a new dimension to the commercial display of black women; its purpose was to entertain a paying white audience, and Baartman earned wages for her performances. For an extra fee, viewers could poke at her main attraction, her large buttocks. "The Hottentot was produced like a wild beast," reported a sympathetic spectator, "and ordered to move backwards and forwards and come out and go into her cage, more like a bear on a chain than a human being." The *London Times* commented on her costume, "She is dressed in a colour as nearly resembling her skin as possible. The dress is contrived to exhibit the entire frame of her body, and spectators are even invited to examine the peculiarities of her form."[12]

Baartman's appearances were a great sensation and inspired newspaper accounts, bawdy songs, and lewd caricatures.[13] A similar response occurred in Paris, where, after three years of performances in London and the English provinces, Baartman's employer left her with an entertainment entrepreneur who exhibited wild animals. The show included claims about Baartman's lascivious and aggressive sexual desires. Prints of her image were for sale, and a one-act vaudeville musical comedy about the effect of her presence ran for thirteen months.[14]

Yet Baartman's most intensely scrutinized "performance" was before three prominent scientists who summoned her to their Paris research facility in March 1815. After a three-day examination, the men concluded that Hottentots, being more similar to orangutans than to "Negroes," were barely human. However, the investigators were unable to obtain "the most complete account possible of the anomaly of her reproductive organs."[15] While interested in her buttocks, known by the scientific term *steatopygia,* the scientists were far more intrigued by her genitalia, which had not been on public display. Hottentot women reportedly had a greatly elongated genital skin flap, or labia. Known in Latin as *sinus pudoris,* which translated as "veil of shame" or "drape of decency," the skin flap was known popularly as the "Hottentot apron." Since the seventeenth century, Western observers, including Voltaire, had speculated about the apron, debating its placement and function and wondering whether it was present at birth or resulted from manipulation of the tissue for cultural reasons. But Baartman refused to allow close scrutiny of her genitals. Only after her death in December 1815, most likely of smallpox after a misdiagnosis of pleurisy, did her genitals become available for close study.[16]

The police permitted Baartman's body to be delivered into the hands of Georges Cuvier, chair of anatomy of animals at the Museum of Natural History and secretary of the Académie des Sciences.[17] Cuvier had a plaster cast made of the body and dissected Baartman's corpse. Present at the March examination, Cuvier now eagerly assessed her genitalia. Having preserved Baartman's genitals in a manner that "left no doubt about the nature of the apron," his 1817 report began, "There is nothing more celebrated in natural history than the Hottentot apron, and at the same time there is nothing which has been the object of such great argumentation."[18] He described Baartman's labia minora as looking like "two fleshy, rippled petals" that "to-

Figure 21. An 1814 French caricature depicts "La Belle Hottentote" amid leering French spectators. Courtesy of the Bibliothèque nationale de France.

gether . . . form a heart-shaped figure. . . ." Also finding her hand "charming" and foot "alluring," Cuvier put forth a view of Baartman's body that was infused with eroticism. Yet Cuvier overall found Baartman to be "monstrous" and "the most primitive of all humans . . . the missing link between humans and apes."[19]

Baartman's plaster cast, skeleton, and genitals were put on display in the Musée de l'Homme for over a century after her death. In 1926, museum director Professor Verneau claimed, "[her] enormous steatopygia . . . excites many of the visitors to our collection." Photographs of her body cast were still on sale in 1949. Eventually, Baartman's remains were placed in storage. However, not until January 2002 did an act of the French legislature permit the return of Baartman's remains to South Africa, in response to requests first made by the postapartheid government in 1994. Her remains were finally buried there in August 2002.[20]

Like the long afterlife of Baartman's commercial exhibition in the Musée, Cuvier's report on Baartman provided a blueprint for Western anatomy texts, which reproduced images of Baartman's genitalia and buttocks for decades. Josiah Clark wrote in his 1855 *Types of Mankind*, for example, that Hottentot "females often present two very remarkable peculiarities or deformities, viz., humps behind their buttocks, like those on the backs of dromedaries, and a disgusting development of the *labia pudendi.*" As Sander Gilman has pointed out, for Western readers, Baartman "existed only as a collection of sexual parts" that would "summarize her essence" and, most importantly, "serve as the central image for the black female throughout the nineteenth century." Moreover, in that century's debates about the nature of beauty, American writers referred repeatedly to the Hottentot Venus in iconic terms to explain female attractiveness. One writer worried about the demise of absolute beauty standards and argued "there will be nothing either beautiful or ugly and the Hottentot Venus will equal the Venus de Medici." In this sense, Baartman, in her persona as the Hottentot Venus, also served as a central nineteenth-century image that explained white women's beauty by embodying its opposite.[21]

Such views, which mirrored scientific thought and were used to legitimize colonizer nations' subjugation of indigenous peoples, perpetuated damaging ideas about both white femininity and black sexuality. Nineteenth-century medical studies describe prostitutes in terms similar to those used to describe women of African descent, thereby encouraging readers to assess both groups as sexually deviant. Medical examinations of white prostitutes' bodies noted their large buttocks as indicators of pathological sexuality, thus linking them to black women. As a result, black women's characterization as deviant and diseased was further consolidated. Moreover, the growing social legitimacy and power of physicians and scientific experts often gave them influence over public policies, influence that could adversely affect their objects of study.[22]

The realm of culture also bolstered racialized ideas about female sexuality. Nineteenth-century paintings relied upon and perpetuated Western associations of black women with eroticism. Artists commonly signaled the sexual availability of white women by including a black woman, usually a servant, in the frame. The best-known example of this practice is Manet's *Olympia* (1863), in which a black female servant attends to a nude woman—wearing only a slim black ribbon tied in a bow around her throat—who reclines provocatively upon an unmade bed. Paintings of the orientalist genre, in which Western artists depicted women in imagined Arabic scenes of harems and slave markets, also incorporated black female figures to signify lighter-skinned women's sexual availability. Similarly, black female servants appeared in Western operas and novels to mark sexually illicit encounters between white characters. In addition, associations

Figure 22. Marlene Dietrich strikes a provocative pose in *Blonde Venus* (1932). Courtesy of the Academy of Motion Picture Arts and Sciences.

between white prostitutes and black females found frequent cultural representation. Well into the twentieth century, the film *Blonde Venus* (1932) demonstrated this phenomenon, not only in the notorious "Hot Voodoo" song and dance performed by its star, Marlene Dietrich, first in an ape costume and then in a huge blonde Afro wig, but also later in the film when her character becomes an increasingly destitute prostitute aided always by a black female servant.[23]

The association of black female bodies with eroticism in scientific, medical, and cultural discourse and in practices of enslavement and exploitation is indisputable. But connecting that association with the meaning of black lingerie and asserting that wearing black lingerie in the twentieth century became a form of racial masquerade involves several further considerations. One is to investigate how meanings might "leap" from bodies to clothing and from clothing to bodies. Another is to find out more about the redirection of eroticism from black women to white women. A closer look at visual, literary, and performance works by African, African American, mixed-race, and white working-class women, from the time of the initial performance of the Hottentot Venus to a century after her death provides evidence of both these processes.[24]

A one-act play staged at Paris's Théâtre de Vaudeville in 1814, *La Vénus hottentote, ou haine aux Françaises (The Hottentot Venus, or Hatred of French Women)*, reveals anxieties about how the lascivious reputation and eager spectatorship of the Hottentot Venus in Paris might affect white women's attractiveness to white men. The play debuted just two months after Baartman's arrival and ran for thirteen months. In the play, the beautiful and spirited widow Amelia disguises herself as a Hottentot to win the affections of her cousin Adolph, who has resolved to wed a "savage" after his first two French wives betrayed him. He visits relatives in their countryside château to avoid contact with charming yet cruel Frenchwomen, whose beauty is rivaled only by "Native American women and Hottentots."[25]

The play describes the Hottentot as the "Venus" who is an "amazing" spectacle but also "a frightening beauty," "barbarous" and "grotesque." Yet though the Venus "will never inspire love," she has stimulated new fashions, for "all our ladies have already ordered for this winter dresses and overcoats in Hottentot styles." When Amelia assumes the "brilliant costume of the Hottentots," she explains in song that "For a young innocent woman, still well naive, It will be embarrassing, To undertake such a task; but once one is a widow, One knows how to go about it." The ruse begins when Amelia meets Adoph disguised as Liliska, a Hottentot.[26]

Adolph falls immediately for her masquerade—and for her. T. Denean Sharpley-Whiting, in *Black Venus: Sexualized Savages, Primal Fears, and Primitive Narratives in French*, notes the "ease with which Amelia is able to perform as Baartman," a facility that evokes "another artistic, literary motif and preoccupation popularized in the nineteenth century: white women as 'closeted' sexual savages." This motif appears elsewhere in the play. A guest teases a servant as a "little savage" when she pinches him after he tries to kiss her. Initially insulted, the servant later concludes about Liliska, "You are a savage, I see, All in fact like me. They say. . . . That in your country they eat men; But in your eyes, miss, I read not a trace of cruelty. And you will eat them I can see that, Just like me." Aligned with scientific thought that found all women inferior to men and closer to animals, this exchange affirms the savage nature of all women.[27]

As the play concludes, a portrait of the real Hottentot Venus exposes Amelia's true identity. But happily, though her uncle finds it "a shame she is not a savage," Adolph is still smitten and wishes to marry her. In the last song, verses sung by each character address lovers, art dealers, and jealous husbands and all end with the plea "Do not abandon France"—that is, by choosing savages over Frenchwomen.[28] Yet as Sharpley-Whiting points out, "Difference and sameness are thoroughly confounded in the vaude-ville." The play uses the Hottentot Venus to reassert Frenchwomen's beauty, charm, and status as the proper mates for Frenchmen, but it is Amelia's ability to masquerade as the Venus that proves this. The savage lying within all women is the secret of their erotic appeal, and being a Hot-tentot, or simply dressing like one, makes this evident. Yet in this guise, Amelia outsmarts Adolph to provide him with what he really needs and wants.[29]

In this 1814 play, black women's dress signifies their essential eroticism and is a vehicle for transferring that quality to white women. When Amelia puts on the Hottentot costume, she accesses the Venus's erotic and exotic appeal to white men. In Saartjie Baartman's performances as the Hottentot Venus, she wore a costume that resembled her skin as nearly as possible. De-signed to produce the effect of nudity and highlight her ascribed erotic per-sona as "a lusty negro wench," the stage costume created a second, remov-able skin for Baartman. This alluring association of clothing and skin made a deep impression upon spectators, lingering long after her performances ended. In 1873, the U.S. consul to Mauritius, an island off the coast of south-ern Africa, related his fascination in "a Hottentot woman washing clothes. . . . I found all the descriptions I had ever heard of the Hottentot Venus beaten to fits by reality. . . . She was dressed in a skin, of some ani mal made very soft, and tightly drawn around her person from the waist to the knee, so that of course a perfect outline of her form was very visible." With his perceptions shaped by previous accounts, the consul eagerly an-ticipated and triumphantly achieved a clear view of a Hottentot woman's body, whether clothed or not. In his mind, too, all Hottentot women were Hottentot Venuses—that is, sexualized female bodies on display for the pleasure of male spectators.[30]

Western female desire for the Hottentot costume referenced in the play gives voice to white women's fantasy of wearing the skin of black women, at least temporarily. The Hottentot costume inspired Amelia's successful plan to win the affections of Adolph and energized fashion trends with its novelty and erotic associations. The play was prophetic in regard to the lat-ter. English foreign correspondent George Sala, whose books were pub-lished in the United States, commented in 1858 that it was "only twenty years since [ladies] borrowed a fashion from the Hottentot Venus." He was referring to the inflated skirts worn by "fashionable ladies." Fourteen years later, the *Ladies Repository*, a periodical published by the Methodist Episcopal Church of Cincinnati, warned readers, "Whether a gown swells out into the hoops of the great tun of Heidelberg, or projects backward like the reverse side of the Hottentot Venus, it is alike hideous." In addition to seeing her body parts used to explain the primitive, bestial, and hideously deformed nature of African women, the Hottentot Venus as Western icon was also a provocative amalgamation, both repugnant and attractive, of dark skin, difference and sameness, sexual availability, and extravagant fashions.[31]

The core of Hottentot eroticism was the much-discussed apron, the extended labia minora. An apron is also an article of clothing, and Saartjie Baartman was famously caricatured wearing a small apron that shielded her genitals from spectators who were fascinated by the mystery of their shape and size. It is well worth considering the apron's erotic meaning in association with a related figure of male desire and fantasy, the domestic servant. Baartman herself worked as a domestic servant in South Africa, and, during the nineteenth century, an increasing number of domestic servants worked in middle-class households. By 1880, 54 percent of American women who earned wages in cities worked as domestic servants. Similar trends were evident in Europe.[32]

The widespread entrance of female domestic servants into Victorian households generated novels and memoirs that expressed erotic fantasies and experiences with maids and governesses. In the summer of 1837, Nathaniel Hawthorne recorded his pleasure in watching and fantasizing about a female servant working in the house he visited for a month in Augusta, Maine. "She . . . may be seen standing over her tub, with her handkerchief somewhat displaced from her white bosom, because it is hot. Often, she stands with her bare arms in the water. . . . In the afternoon, very probably, she dresses herself in silks, looking not only pretty but ladylike, and strolls around the house, not unconscious that some gentleman may be staring at her from behind our green blinds."

Hawthorne imagines the servant deliberately displaying herself, while working, for middle-class men's viewing pleasure. Other writers expressed the common fantasy and actual experience of young boys' sexual initiation by female servants. Servants in charge of children often slept in their rooms, washed and dressed them, nursed them when sick, expressed affection, and doled out punishment. As Freud wrote, "It seems to have been my fate to discover only the obvious: that children have sexual feelings, which every nursemaid knows." Anne McClintock suggests that female domestic servants may have used sexual relationships with their charges to exercise power, secure children's dependence or compliance, or find sexual pleasure in a world that denied them acceptable opportunities to do so elsewhere.[33]

Most importantly, female domestic servants were subject to sexual harassment and seduction by the adult man of the house. Whether or not male heads of households had grown up themselves with nursemaids and harbored erotic fantasies about female servants, as employers, they wielded a great deal of power over servants' lives. Moreover, class status also bore sexual meanings, much as racial categorization ascribed erotic qualities to women of African descent. A woman who worked for wages violated middle-class norms of respectable femininity. She was not a "lady." As a result, the dominant culture seldom made a distinction between women who worked for wages as domestic servants and those who worked as factory workers, shop girls, or prostitutes. Stories of domestic servants of easy virtue and narratives of servants seduced and abandoned by male employers found wide currency. According to Timothy Gilfoyle, mid-nineteenth-century New York newspapers, such as *The Weekly Rake* and *Whip*, published "salacious stories of milliners and servants picking up men and bringing them to nearby brothels" and offered images of servants "in vulnerable or revealing poses." An 1842 *Whip* illustration, "The Chambermaid," depicts a lecherous employer holding a candle in one hand and grabbing his female servant around the neck with the other while she is sweeping. Positioning the broom handle held by the maid between the master's legs implies her familiarity with sexually pleasing conduct. Enslaved African American domestic servants remained the most vulnerable of all household workers. "The Victorian splitting of women into whores and Madonnas, nuns and prostitutes has its origins," McClintock concludes, "in the class structure of the household." And, as has already been well established, this splitting had racial dimensions. As W. E. B. Dubois astutely observed in 1899, the degraded status of domestic service in the United States was rooted in its association with the involuntary servitude of African Americans.[34]

The servant's dress and apron clearly signified her status within the household. Sexologist Krafft-Ebing commented on the erotic qualities of this quintessential servant's garment. "At a time when dress was establishing a veritable barrier between the sexes, the apron evoked a feminine undergarment and suggested easy intimacy." Krafft-Ebing does not mention here the importance of class status in conveying the sexual meanings of aprons. Yet according to Alain Corbin, in France, "the fetishism of the apron compelled certain prostitutes to appropriate the attitude of young domestic

servants when they worked in the streets." Sharpley-Whiting also suggests
the possibility that when a working-class woman in the late nineteenth century "fastened the apron around her waist, she was affixing a highly
charged sexual article from another era about her person; her subsequent
sexualization, whether or not she was actively involved in the sex trade,
constituted a residue of the urges and repressions associated with Baartman-
mania." A 1923 French advertisement that plays upon the iconic sexual
meanings of aprons and black female bodies supports this line of thought.
The advertisement depicts a highly eroticized female figure of African descent emerging from the wooden box in which she has been mailed from
Martinique to France. She is wearing only a maid's cap, large jewelry, and a
white apron that does not fully contain her large, full, and round breasts.
The caption reads, "Are you looking for a maid? Bamboulinette comes to the
rescue." The illustration more than implies the multiple duties expected of
the domestic servant and her apron. The enduring American male sexual
fantasy of the "French maid," seen in images promoting the 2006 film
Friends with Money, attests to the persistence of erotic associations with
domestic service and aprons.[35] Echoing the 1842 *Whip* illustration, star Jennifer Aniston—costumed in a short black dress and white apron—holds a
vacuum cleaner hose between her legs.

· · · · ·

In the decades after Saartjie Baartman's death, a new form of popular entertainment in the United States, minstrel shows, became the most common
commercial entertainment venues to portray African American women.
However, actors portraying African American women typically were cross-
dressed white men in blackface. These racial and gender masquerades were
part and parcel of minstrelsy from its earliest days in the 1830s. Female impersonators became, according to Eric Lott, "enormously popular in the
1840s" and contributed to minstrelsy's growing audience, which reached its
height between 1846 and 1854. Performed in Northern cities, the shows had
an audience that was primarily white, male, and working-class, although in
the 1840s, an increasing number of white women also attended. The mi-
sogyny expressed in songs and sketches cast with female impersonators is
not quite as well known as is the racism endemic to minstrel shows. But
here, too, Lott's "love and theft" thesis applies. Minstrel portrayals ridiculed
and denigrated African American women but also acknowledged their sexual attractiveness, creating both fascination and repulsion much as the performances of the Hottentot Venus had. The black female body might be
imagined as grotesque, but even so represented, it could still portray sexual

desire, romantic longings, and the difficulties of sustaining loving and erotic relationships. In minstrel shows, Lott points out, "White men were routinely encouraged to indulge in [sexual] fantasies about black women." And surely the white male newspaper reviewer who in 1842 found the impersonators so convincing he believed he was being entertained by "a strapping pair of colored ladies" from whom "fine fun may be expected" was not the only audience member to "see" an attractive black woman onstage rather than a cross-dressing white male actor in blackface. Clearly, African American women were widely represented in this popular form of nineteenth-century theater, however distorted their portrayal was.[36]

Minstrel shows directed attention to the skin color of black women in songs and skits that presented the darker "buffalo gals" and lighter mixed-race "yellow" or "yaller" gals. The latter were usually the female characters who provoked the most sexual desire. Intriguingly, the Hottentot Venus was also described in the mid-nineteenth century as a "mulatto woman," complected like "a person 'affected with jaundice'—'a yellowish-brown, or the hue of a faded leaf'—'a tawny buff, or fawn-color.' " Views of her sexualized, albeit diseased, body perhaps changed as the culture increased its focus on the erotic qualities of lighter-skinned African American women. The mixed-race gal of minstrelsy echoed the figure of the beautiful, light-skinned mulatta often written about in fiction in the nineteenth and twentieth centuries by both white and black Americans. In these novels and stories, known as racial melodramas, the mulatta's mixed-race blood inevitably leads to her death. An unhappy narrative closure was so common that this character, who embodied the violence or "sin" of miscegenation, is known as the "tragic mulatta." She appeared in many well- and lesser-known texts, including Harriet Beecher Stowe's *Uncle Tom's Cabin* (1852), Kate Chopin's "Desiree's Baby" (1893), and Pauline Hopkins's *Contending Forces: A Romance Illustrative of Negro Life North and South* (1900). Minstrel shows also featured black female characters who suffered tragic and untimely deaths.[37]

Though beautiful light-skinned African American women's fate in fiction remained tragic, an alternative iconic presentation of mixed-race women emerged in the new commercial entertainment forums of vaudeville, nightclubs, and cabarets in the late nineteenth and early twentieth centuries. These venues highlighted the mulatta's sexual attractiveness and energetic spirit rather than her tragic origins or demise, by casting her in the new role of chorus girl. The "café au lait" chorus-line dancers drew upon white standards of beauty in presenting lighter-skinned black women with straight hair. However, they also played on the sexually transgressive nature of miscegenation, an act both illegal and morally suspect, and in the South, deadly dangerous for black men, who were lynched with alarming frequency. Yet in the urban North during this turn-of-the-century period of changing sexual attitudes and practices, viewing the bodies of café au lait chorus girls was a new form of exciting entertainment. Especially for white audience members, the danger and transgression associated with mixed-race female bodies—and mixing with them—became a new source of pleasure rather than cause for fear or shame.[38]

According to Donald Bogle, all-black revues in the 1890s, such as *The Creole Show* (1890) and *Octoroon* (1895), featured "the light-bright-damn-near-white kind of black beauty." Typically, tragic mulattas in literature were Creole women, but now they were also onstage displaying their "exotic" beauty to great effect. Staged on or near Broadway, these shows were the first such revues to appeal successfully to white audiences. In 1903, *In Dahomey* became the first all-black show to open in a premier theater on Broadway. The novelty and appeal of café au lait chorus girls and "dusky belles" did not go unnoticed. But rather than casting actual light-skinned black women for the very first Ziegfeld Follies in 1907, Follies Girl Grace LaRue sang "Miss Ginger of Jamaica" in café au lait blackface. The lyric "I'm full of spice, sporty but nice" refers to the singer as "an elegant importation" recognized for "doing things up brown." The risqué sexuality conjured by terms like *sporty* and by dusky skin color made the song distinctive, and it was a hit with white audiences. As Linda Mizejewski has noted, "Café au lait makeup became a standard sexual mask for the more daring Ziegfeld Girls' performances."[39]

Black revues' rising popularity among white audiences in 1910s New York City influenced their white counterparts. As the Follies became virtually an annual event, Ziegfeld constantly looked for new ways to attract audiences. Like other producers, he hired black songwriters and choreographers to infuse shows with uptown entertainment sensibilities. In 1914, Ziegfeld bought some of the acts featured in the *Darktown Follies* produced by J. Leubrie Hill from 1913 to 1916, but he hired African American performers to teach dance moves to his white Follies cast. Yet influence went both ways. In 1922, when Ziegfeld first promoted the Follies with the Glorified American Girl, this icon was immediately countered in an all-black revue, *Strut Miss Lizzie*, which claimed to be "Glorifying the Creole Beauty."[40]

In 1921, the hit *Shuffle Along*, later famous for introducing Josephine Baker, brought black revues back to Broadway, and other shows, such as *Runnin' Wild*, *Blackbirds*, and *Hot Chocolates*, followed. A 1922 Follies song referenced the growing presence of "pretty choc'late babies" on the Great White Way. In "It's Getting Dark on Old Broadway," according to Mizejewski, a "lighting effect caused the chorus girls and their white costumes to take on a brown tint as they danced, so they were instantly transformed into dusky belles. . . . At the conclusion of the number, the voice of singer Gilda Gray rose 'in a deep and shuddering ecstasy' to the cry that ended the song: 'Getting darker!' " Although some 1920s white critics complained that blacks' performing in what they considered white shows undermined blackface traditions, an increasing number of whites enjoyed themselves at "black and tan" clubs in Harlem and attended Broadway shows in which African Americans were both onstage and in the audience. The popularity of racially diverse clubs continued to rise despite the possibility that police, who utilized every available excuse, might stage a raid.[41]

During the same period that café au lait chorus girls appeared in black revues and café au lait blackface chorus girls appeared in white revues, another form of racial hybrid, the "coon singer," emerged. Popularized between 1890 and 1910 and performed both in blackface and without it, female coon singers, or "shouters," were white or ethnic entertainers who sang songs typically sung by African American women performers, imitating these singers' style. Anna Held, an early Ziegfeld star who performed in the producer's shows even before the first Follies in 1907, sang coon songs and performed the cakewalk dance in the 1890s. Yet she did so in front of a backdrop with cut-out holes that, according to Held's memoir, each revealed "the woolly head of a Negro." As she sang, "thirty-three black noggins swayed . . . to the rhythm of the song." The cakewalk itself was reported to have emerged from African American slave culture as a mocking imitation of white cotillions. By 1903, African American singer and dancer Aida Overton Walker was a featured performer in a black vaudeville show, where her modern version of the cakewalk, danced to ragtime music, sparked a cakewalk craze among white society women in New York City. As with café au lait blackface acts, the spreading popularity of the cakewalk reveals how white women emulated black women's style in reformulating norms of sexual attractiveness, feminine bodily display, and energetic fun.[42]

Coon singers drew on comedy and conventions of minstrelsy to perform songs that expressed overt female sexual desire. Jewish immigrant Sophie Tucker, who became known as the "World-Renowned Coon Shouter" and initially performed in blackface, incorporated black performance styles with Yiddish inflections in her popular persona as the "red hot momma." As with minstrelsy generally, blackface makeup, or just its performative style, allowed whites to express emotions and perspectives in song and movement they were unable to otherwise. Coon singing particularly licensed the representation of female sexuality because of the long characterization of black women's heightened, licentious sexual natures. Black female vaudevillians and twentieth-century African American blues women popularized female assertions of sexual desire and romantic disappointments with authenticity. More complex amalgamations of African American women's out-front style by European American female entertainers followed coon singing, such as the performances of theater and film actress and writer Mae West, well known for her challenging sexual persona, risqué quips, and narrative racial themes. Literal racial masquerade also remained important in Hollywood cinema, in such performances as Judy Garland's café au lait blackface song-and-dance numbers in the 1941 musicals *Ziegfeld Girl* and *Babes on Broadway*.[43]

Further opportunities for racially hybrid spectatorship and identification for American women emerged in the late nineteenth century and persisted for decades. In scientific and cultural realms, the growing importance of the (non-white) "primitive" and of "primitivism" defined both the advances and missteps of industrial civilization. Looming large in the developing arenas of anthropology, avant-garde art, and popular literature, as well as in scientific discourses on hierarchies of race, the primitive provided Western thinkers and artists points of departure for self-satisfaction and self-criticism. White women's distinctive relationship to the primitive helps explain black lingerie's growing erotic signification in this period. Both avant-garde art and pulp fiction celebrated and promoted the association of Western female bodies with primitive peoples, especially Africans. U.S.-born artist Man Ray's striking 1926 photograph "Noire et Blanche," for example, depicts Kiki, a light-skinned European woman, holding a black African mask beside her own pale face, resting one cheek on a table. Despite the play of light and dark, the photograph emphasizes similarities between her face and the mask, such as the pencil-thin eyebrows and smooth surface, and is one of many examples of avant-garde art that evoked the sexual allure of white women by association with Africa.[44]

In popular culture, the character Jane in the original *Tarzan* novels by Edgar Rice Burroughs, written in the 1910s, and in the films that followed, especially the well-known 1930s versions starring Johnny Weissmuller and Maureen O'Sullivan, conveyed the special excitement of a beautiful white woman's sensuality unleashed in the jungle. This perspective is stated blatantly in their second film, *Tarzan and His Mate* (1932), when Martin (Paul Cavanagh), an unscrupulous Englishman, shows up in their African idyll with his ivory-hunting business partner, Jane's nice ex-boyfriend Harry

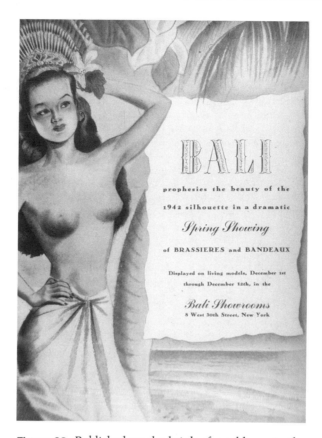

BALI

prophesies the beauty of the
1942 silhouette in a dramatic
Spring Showing
of BRASSIERES and BANDEAUX

Displayed on living models, December 1st
through December 12th, in the

Bali Showrooms
8 West 30th Street, New York

Figure 23. Published on the brink of world war in the Pacific, this advertisement drew on the American cultural fascination with lighter-hued women of color and the heightened eroticism attributed to "primitives." *Corsets & Brassieres,* November 1941. Courtesy of Special Collections, Gladys Marcus Library, Fashion Institute of Technology. Courtesy, Sara Lee Corp.

(Neil Hamilton). Harry brings Jane some slinky dresses and a phonograph, hoping they'll lure her back to "civilization." As she changes from her leather bra and loincloth in a tent that illuminates her silhouette to the peeping Martin, he tells Harry, "She's priceless! A woman who's learned the abandonment of the jungle and yet she's at home in Mayfair. . . . You lucky pup." With Harry temporarily away, Martin exclaims to Jane, "You know. You're a fascinating little savage," before suddenly grabbing and kissing her. Clearly, the danger, heat, and exposure of the jungle have infused the "civilized" white woman's body with extraordinary and overwhelming erotic appeal. The scene ends when Tarzan returns, and, also stimulated by her dress, stockings, and perfume, sweeps the happily willing Jane off into the trees.[45]

Tarzan is among many texts documenting that associations of blackness, sexuality, and transgression continued long past emancipation. Walter Benn Michaels argues that once slave status no longer formed a legal basis for upholding black inferiority, biological and cultural explanations of racial difference took on greater importance. The separate but equal doctrine upheld in the 1896 Supreme Court decision *Plessy v. Ferguson* codified that difference as irreducible. Antilynching activist Ida B. Wells, as well as more recent feminist critics Jacquelyn Dowd Hall and Valerie Smith, point out how the pretext for lynching—the protection of white women's virtue—also perpetuated conceptions of black women's lascivious sexuality. As Smith argues, the invisibility of black women in discussions of interracial rape not only normalizes the sexual abuse that African American women suffered under slavery but also "constructed black women as sexually voracious. If black women were understood as always to be available and willing, then the rape of black women becomes a contradiction in terms."[46]

Well into the twentieth century, the linking of blackness with unbridled passions that endangered black men and women persisted. Simultaneously, American women were able to engage in multiple forms of racial hybridity and racial masquerade during the turn-of-the-century period in which modern sensibilities edged out Victorian standards of morality. Light-skinned European American women represented and enacted the break with the Victorian past by being entertained by, if not taking on the performance style of, mixed-race actresses and fictional characters, female coon singers, café au lait performers, and blues women, whether they were actually African American or wearers of racial disguise. Some women also identified with fiction and nonfiction texts about light-skinned women engaging with Africa. In the United States, African American women and their culture, in addition to working-class women and their culture generally, were at the leading edge of social change, helping to reconstruct middle-class sexual morality and standards of respectable conduct. During this period, black clothing became increasing fashionable, black undergarments became more available, and black lingerie began to convey a higher erotic charge.

The influence of the Hottentot Venus in the early nineteenth century and the popularity of the hybrid visual, literary, and performance cultures as the century ended and a new one began suggest that racial masquerade, a central feature of American culture to this day, provides a significant means of understanding the larger context in which the new meaning of black lingerie in the twentieth century emerged. A further question arises. How is it that meanings may "leap" from bodies to objects and from objects to bodies? Studies of costume and fashion provide myriad examples and diverse evidence from around the globe of how apparel transmits to its wearer gender identity, sexual availability, class position, group membership, occupational status, and cultural affiliation, among other significations. The various, and at times contradictory, cultural interpretations lent to bodies from their clothing reveal the arbitrary, unfixed nature of such significations. More specifically, undergarments—which are worn closest to the naked body, are often made of sensuous, skinlike fabrics like silk, and are designed to cover, if not accent, the female body parts most closely associated with sexuality and gender difference—have long been known and utilized as objects of sexual fetishism. Sexual fetishism, along with the commodity fetishism of objects of capitalist mass production, imbues intimate apparel with a life of its own, detached from the agents and conditions of its manufacture and ostensible purpose. Sexual fetishism and commodity fetishism of undergarments thus are mechanisms that allow meanings to leap from bodies to objects. And, when those garments are repositioned on bodies, their reconfigured meanings may leap back from the objects to those bodies as well. Though forged in the exploitation of enslaved women and their continuing construction as pathological after the Civil War, the cultural practices of racial hybridity that emerged in the world of commercial entertainment, from the performances and theatrical representation of the Hottentot Venus to the café au lait dancers and coon singers, provided mechanisms for transferring meanings from objects to bodies and from bodies to objects. The fetishized meanings and particular historic, cultural constructions of blackness, black female sexuality, and black clothing form an important context for understanding the changing meaning of black lingerie.[47]

· · · · ·

One functional explanation for wearing black lingerie is simply that black undergarments were necessary under black dresses to conform to dominant fashion sensibilities. Indeed, black undergarments grew in importance as black became a highly significant and prevalent color of dress for women in the nineteenth century, primarily due to extensive mourning rituals that bore most heavily upon widows. These rituals included strict regulations regarding behavior and dress. Yet just what constituted proper Christian observance of a loved one's passing, which Karen Halttunen has shown was a central component of asserting middle-class status, was not without controversy.[48] Nineteenth-century minister Henry Ward Beecher admonished, "Christians are wont to walk in black, and sprinkle the ground with tears, at the very time they should walk in white, and illumine the way by smiles and radiant hope."[49] An 1886 *Harper's Bazar* columnist remarked, "Nothing in our country is more undecided in the public mind than the etiquette of mourning. It has not yet received that hereditary and positive character which makes the slightest departure from received custom so reprehensible in England." Though requirements for women to wear black for long periods persisted, some critics faulted women who too closely adhered to extensive mourning-dress rituals, charging them with displaying conformity to fashion and social custom rather than expressing sincere bereavement and sorrow.[50]

Nineteenth-century middle-class men already dressed primarily in black business suits, and Victorian mourning rituals did not alter their attire substantially. According to Pat Jalland, until 1850, men added only a black mourning cloak, "while black gloves, hatbands, and cravats were sufficient thereafter." Costume historian Lou Taylor states that by 1900, men wore only a crape armband for as little as three months, or up to one year. (Crape was an expensive silk fabric that emitted an unpleasant and reputedly malevolent odor.) In keeping with this briefer mourning period, widowers were able to respectably reenter society and remarry much more quickly than widows were.[51]

In contrast, the standard mourning period for widows was two and a half years. Deep mourning lasted one year and one day, followed by twelve months of second mourning. The last six months were known as half-mourning. Each mourning phase had different rules of dress. Widows in deep mourning wore dresses made of dull, unreflecting fabrics such as bombazine, a silk-wool blend, which were covered in black crape. Widows also wore black bonnets, accented by black crape streamers in back, and black crape veils over the face. All other outerwear, such as gloves, were made of dull black materials, and only black jet jewelry could be worn. During second mourning, dresses could be made of black silk and other fabrics, with less black crape required for the first nine months and no crape for the last three months—also known as ordinary mourning—and widows' caps were no longer necessary. In the final six months of half-mourning, mourning costumes used lighter yet still somber colors, such as mauve and gray. Mortality rates and mourning rituals, even with shorter requirements for deaths other than one's husband, could mean a woman dressed in black dress for lengthy periods.[52]

WINTER CLOAK.   WIDOW'S COSTUME.

Figure 24. *Peterson's Magazine* (February 1883) depicted the stylish mourning dress for a Victorian widow. Courtesy of Jennifer Thompson, http://homepage.mac.com/festive_attyre.

Beginning in the 1840s, the bereaved could shop at stores that sold only mourning clothes, such as Besson and Son of Philadelphia, rather than dye their clothes or turn to a seamstress. In addition to sales staff, mourning manuals, fashion magazines, and advice books provided guidance in mourning etiquette, deportment, and dress. In *Manners and Social Usages* (1884), Mrs. John Sherwood explained that mourning dress was a traditional sign of respect for the dead and a means of signaling one's bereaved state. Sherwood avowed, "A mourning dress does protect a woman while in deepest grief against the untimely gayety of a passing stranger. It is a wall, a cell of refuge." Black clothing was not the only means of providing, or enforcing, such refuge. Widows and the bereaved, especially female mourners, were expected to remain at home and decline invitations to socialize, especially at weddings, festive parties, and the theater. Mourning etiquette forbade widows from fully reentering society, let alone remarrying, for up to two years. Clothing was one barrier to attending parties and festivities, because the black-clad female mourner's appearance in itself was thought to diminish the enjoyment of others. Consequently, conforming to mourning-dress requirements was also a means of enforcing female seclusion.[53]

Taylor finds the "origins of widows weeds" in the "shapeless drapery" and color of early Christian nuns' costumes and sees further material links between nuns and widows in wealthy widows who "founded and maintained" early convents in Europe. In subsequent centuries, widows often ended up in convents for the remainder of their lives. The association between nuns and widows persisted over time. An 1886 American magazine article advised women mourners to replace the black crape veil with "thin nun's veiling" for health reasons. Sherwood's 1884 conception of a widow's wish to enter a "cell of refuge," and the real withdrawal of widows from society, also evoked the seclusion of convent life.[54]

Nuns' habits and seclusion in convents were fundamental to the doctrine and enforcement of sexual abstinence for nuns and also symbolically represented withdrawal from earthly marriage. Similarly, black mourning dress marked the end of a woman's marriage and enforced her social seclusion. The union that began in bridal white ended in widow's black. Moreover, loss of one's husband resubjected widows to prohibitions against sexual activity, because prevailing moral codes proscribed sex for unmarried women. Furthermore, widows in Victorian America were much less likely than widowers to enter second marriages, thus ensuring for most, as with nuns, sexual abstinence or risky illicit relationships for the remainder of their lives.[55]

Given the cult of true womanhood, which made sexual purity central to

respectable womanhood, and the cult of mourning, which identified grieving as the most sacred, pure, and genteel of all sentiments, that relatively
few widows remarried reinforced chastity as a respectable norm. After all,
a second marriage not only required a woman to depart from the virtuous
respectability of mourning but also marked her as a woman who had possessed more than one sexual partner during her life. Second marriages thus
potentially carried a suggestion of impropriety that widowhood, which
Philippe Aries described as the "symbol of inconsolable sorrow," did not.
Queen Victoria was the best-known advocate, by example, of chaste widowhood. Her husband, Prince Albert, died in 1861, when Victoria was
forty-two. She remained a widow in mourning until her death forty years
later. Some American women, such as the young widow Josephine Shaw
Lowell, who married in 1864 and lost her husband in the Civil War less than
one year later, did the same.[56]

Despite the reverence, respect, and compassion that widows received because of their grief and their loss of a loved one and household provider,
Western culture has a long history of anxiety about and ridicule, and sus-
picion of widows. Christiane Klapische Zuber, Allison Levy, and Nicole Pellegrin find these contradictory cultural meanings grew out of widows' am-
biguous social status and signification. The widow was a marker of male
absence and the bearer of her husband's memory; thus, she both reminded
men of their mortality and embodied their wished-for remembrance. Yet
upon her husband's death, a widow also emerged from his direct control and
authority to assume a more independent, and thus anomalous, position
within the gendered social hierarchy. Multiple views of widows as "decrepit,
dependent and dangerous," including the iconic foolish widow who easily
succumbs to and then marries a fortune hunter and the scandalous "merry
widow" who happily flaunts sexual mores, abound in several centuries of
Western culture, including poetry, fiction, advice books, sermons, operas,
songs, and films. Widows' sexual conduct, appearance, and demeanor were
central to respectable bereavement, and surely ridiculous and demeaning
characterizations provided enforcement mechanisms as well as sources of
entertainment.[57]

Because asexuality was a central feature of the respectable widow, not
surprisingly, assuming the mourning costume also required women to alter
the style of their undergarments, the apparel most closely associated with
sexuality. According to Taylor, mourning dress required the bereaved to
wear "additional top petticoats of black" over "the usual layers of white petticoats." Yet, although petticoats, especially top layers, might be visible when
a woman walked or sat, "the usual plain white chemises, drawers and un-

derpetticoats were sometimes slotted with black ribbon." In other words, even undergarments that ordinarily remained hidden from public view were ornamented in black to observe mourning. These undergarments slotted with black ribbon, the first items of clothing put on while dressing and the last removed while undressing, may have reminded widows most of all that their sexual life was suspended, perhaps forever. Furthermore, the Victorian emphasis on sexual purity for women, and the moral uncertainties and real difficulties for widows in securing subsequent marriage partners, surely lent a transgressive aura to romantic involvements by and with widows, heightened by their status as "sexually experienced, yet unavailable." Prohibitions against widows' active sexuality, along with wider cultural associations of sex and death, discussed below, suggest that black petticoats, chemises, and drawers and underpetticoats trimmed with black ribbon were the first garments to link black intimate apparel with forbidden, transgressive—and therefore heightened—sexuality.[58]

.   .   .   .   .

Examining explicit commentary and cultural representations concerning the relationship between sex and death in Western culture allows fuller exploration of how widows' black dress, petticoats, and ribbon trim on undergarments may have contributed to black lingerie's emerging erotic signification. Three major psychoanalytic theorists—Sigmund Freud, Jacques Lacan, and Georges Bataille—maintained that links between sex and death are central to the human psyche. Although Freud's analysis of the erotic aspects of what he termed the "death instinct" does not tell us what Victorians thought about widows, mourning dress, and sexuality, it does reveal the links between sex and death that he observed in turn-of-the-century Western culture, when black lingerie began to take on its erotic signification. Lacan and Bataille's ideas built upon Freudian insights. The interest and findings of these influential thinkers document the importance assigned to erotic aspects of death within Western culture that is well worth considering.

Freud concluded that in addition to the basic instincts of hunger and love, there was also a death instinct. The former, which he incorporated with sexual instincts as Eros, preserved both individuals and species. However, the death instinct, Thanatos, led "organic life back into the inanimate state." Considering that without "exception . . . everything living dies for *internal* reasons—becomes inorganic once again—then we shall be compelled to say that *'the aim of all life is death.'* "[59]

Freud found that the two instincts especially worked together in the "ejection of sexual substances in the sex act. . . . This accounts for the likeness of the condition that follows complete sexual satisfaction to dying, and for the fact that death coincides with the act of copulation in some of the lower animals. These creatures die in the act of reproduction . . . after Eros has been eliminated through the process of satisfaction."[60] Furthermore, the death instinct "escapes detection unless its presence is betrayed by its being alloyed with Eros." This alliance occurs most recognizably in sadism and masochism, which are "manifestations of the destructive instinct (directed outwards and inwards), strongly alloyed with eroticism." For Freud, the destructive erotics of sadism and masochism provide the "noise" that makes the death instinct most observable and thus available for analysis. The indisputable phenomena of sadistic and masochistic behaviors clearly establish a link between eroticism and death.[61]

In the mid-twentieth century, Lacan's reconsideration of Freudian thought makes central the concepts of lack and loss. Lacan found identity constructed around these concepts, shaped by repeated attempts to fill the void and heal the scar left by separation from the maternal body and the experience of existence as separate beings. As Ellie Ragland writes in *Essays on the Pleasures of Death: From Freud to Lacan*, Lacan theorized that a "*palpable* void lies at the heart of language, being, and body. Thus, it is loss that drives life." She suggests that Lacan also "distinguishes between a 'first' death of the biological body and a 'second' death, marked by rituals of mourning."[62]

Lacan's insights regarding the structural similarities between the unconscious and language afforded new ways to analyze psychoanalytic evidence. His key premise that "the unconscious is structured like a language" opened up possibilities for linguistic and semiotic study of the psyche. Literary critic Elizabeth Bronfen explains that for Lacan, language "allows for a differentiation between self and Other . . . and points to the truth of human existence as that of lacking, of being split. . . ." In other words, becoming a "speaking subject" is essential to individuation but also references the loss of primordial unity with the mother. Language is further suffused with loss because it is the absence of a thing, or the desire for something not present, that motivates speaking. Moreover, words can never fully bring something into being, and yet, significantly, words replace the things they represent. This unavoidable inadequacy and replacement are further forms and experiences of loss.[63]

To Lacan, the construction of a wholly differentiated and unified self is an illusion. Upholding illusory wholeness and masking loss through the search for stable meanings and repetition of pleasurable moments based on fixed fantasy "attaches us to stasis." As Ragland interprets Lacan, these efforts ultimately only "offer the fixity of 'death' . . . turning Eros into Thanatos." Moreover, as Lacan crucially points out, satisfaction is the enemy of desire; in other words, satisfaction puts an end to desire. Thus, for Lacan, ultimately "all drives are death drives."[64]

Georges Bataille, Lacan's contemporary, wrote widely on eroticism and death. *Death and Sensuality: A Study of Eroticism and the Taboo* (1962) opens by explaining the fundamental coupling of reproduction and death using the example of a single cell. In dividing into two new cells, a cell destroys itself. Overall, reproduction creates separate, discontinuous beings, whereas death returns bodies to continuity. Yet between birth and death, humans experience disruptions to discontinuity, and these moments are allied with death. Sexual experiences especially generate such disruptions because erotic desires and sexual fusion dissolve "individual isolated discontinuity" and substitute "a feeling of profound continuity." Thus, "reproduction leads to the discontinuity of beings, but brings into play their continuity; that is to say, it is intimately linked with death."[65]

Bataille suggests that people seek erotic moments to overcome isolation. But ending isolation and wrenching us out of discontinuity is an act of violence "that leaves us gasping." Hence, "there are widespread and staggering possibilities of harmony between erotic urges and violence." Bataille argues, in "essence, the domain of eroticism is the domain of violence, of violation. . . . The whole business of eroticism is to strike to the inmost core of the living being, so that the heart stands still." And, although sexual activity rarely results in death, "the exhaustion following the final paroxysm is thought of as a 'little death.'" The act of satisfying sexual urges violently demolishes barriers of self, with sexual climax experienced as "a minor rupture suggestive of death."[66]

Bataille further links death and sex as two "sanctified domains" subject to fundamental taboos and rituals. Transgression "suspends a taboo without suppressing it," and while dangerous to stability, is necessary to achieve "the feeling of freedom that the full accomplishment of the sexual act demands." Finding the "essence of eroticism . . . in the inextricable confusion of sexual pleasure and taboo," Bataille asserts that taboo always evokes sexual pleasure, and sexual pleasure always evokes taboo.[67] Bataille also links sex with decay because decay results from death and yet has "procreative power." The growth of plants and plant eaters, for example, depends on and benefits from the process of decay. Decay's duality inspires both repulsion and attraction, as Bataille finds embedded within the repulsion of death a "consciousness of life . . . of self." Eroticism—"assenting to life"—brings "us back from repulsion to desire." However, the anguish of eroticism is the awareness that "death, and death alone, constantly ensures the renewal of life."[68]

Despite different emphases and conclusions, Freud's, Lacan's, and Bataille's work on sex and death, summarized briefly here, assigns deep significance to this relationship in their core analytic frameworks. Freud's thought built a foundation for others seeking to understand the profound meanings, causes, uses, and consequences of death and destruction within a psychic economy that he understood to be organized primarily to enhance pleasure and sustain life. For subsequent theorists Lacan and Bataille, the fractured ego was not an aberration but a norm. More importantly, the conclusions of all three underscore the critical position of eroticism and destruction in Western culture in the nineteenth and twentieth centuries and thus prove helpful in considering historic cultural representations of death and sex from that period. A sense of this larger context is critical to considering whether black mourning dress contributed to black lingerie's emerging erotic meanings.

Freud, Lacan, and Bataille put forth their ideas in a historical context suffused by associations between sex and death. One of Freud's students, Otto Weininger, wrote an influential book in 1903 linking sex and violence well before Freud published his views on Thanatos. In *Sex and Character*, Weininger argued, "All that is born of woman must die. Reproduction, birth, and death are indissolubly associated; the thought of untimely death awakens sexual desire in its fiercest form, as the determination to reproduce oneself. And so sexual union, considered ethically, psychologically, and biologically, is allied to murder." Similarly, G. J. Barker-Benfield notes that numerous U.S. and European medical authorities envisioned the body as a finite container of vital fluids or essences and equated semen with blood. In tracts about the need to conserve semen to maintain male health, they recommended male sexual continence. Associating ejaculation with death, it was likened to a potentially dangerous form of bloodletting.[69]

As men lost sperm to female sexual partners, an increasing perception of women as deadly vampires sucking the life out of unsuspecting male victims appeared in a wide range of medical, literary, visual, and popular-culture texts—analyzed closely by Bram Dijkstra—that addressed issues of health, sexuality, evolution, eugenics, women's rights, and imperialism. Even biological studies of insects like the praying mantis, which kills her mate after copulation, drew upon the broadly held association of sex and death embodied by the newly sexualized woman. Similarly, the language of fantasy literature, which depicted wild jungle queens whom the hero must

Figure 25. This iconic figure embodies the Western cultural association of female sexuality and death: *Salome*, by Pierre Bonnaud (1865–1930).

domesticate or be destroyed by; mass circulation of eroticized images of well-known treacherous women like Medusa, Delilah, Judith, and Salome; and countless reproductions of anonymous female figures depicted as deadly snakes, sphinxes, and spiders spread ideas about deadly women. By the late Victorian period, the vampiric female had become an integral feature of American culture.[70]

The nineteenth-century aesthetic that related femininity and death is epitomized famously by Edgar Allan Poe, who wrote in 1846, "The death of a beautiful woman is, unquestionably, the most poetical topic in the world." Many agreed: representations of beautiful dead women permeated Victorian British and American literary and visual culture. Bronfen explains the unremitting appearance of the fetishized figure of the female corpse in psychoanalytic terms, considering together understandings about death and gender difference. Points of correspondence powerfully link the female body with death and loss, such as the early childhood experience of the absent or withdrawn maternal body. Yet although the female body signifies lack, it is also a locus for the "fantasy of a fusion or intact union" resulting from the desire to heal or mask the traumatic scar of separation. This ambivalent status underscores the feminine position—like the subjective experience of death—as indeterminable and unknowable through language.[71]

The cultural associations of beauty and love with femininity also link women and death. As Bronfen explains, women are objects of male desire, according to Freud, in three forms: "the mother, the beloved chosen on the pattern of the mother, and mother earth, who will receive him again." Meanings overlap because beauty evokes death both as its opposite and in its perfection, which masks the "inevitability of human decomposition." This illusion explains beauty's ability to deliver pleasure. In addition, the viewing position of the corpse is significant territory for feminization of death. The corpse is an object that lies passively to be looked at; it is unable to see, whereas the mourner can gaze actively at the corpse. These relationships also describe the iconic passive female and active male spectatorship positions within male-dominated culture. Bronfen convincingly finds in this correspondence an "implication [that] the corpse is feminine, the survivor masculine."[72]

The power of spectatorship also explains the dubious position and transgressive nature of widows. Yet a thick nineteenth-century culture of female sacrifice and self-negation—from the deathbed scene in *Uncle Tom's Cabin* to Snow White's body on display; literary and visual portraits of sick, dying, and dead women by Hawthorne and Wharton, among others; and images of sleeping women, collapsing women, consumptive women, fatally ill women, and drowning women—perpetuated links between femininity, death, and eroticized female passivity, invalidism, and annihilation. Cultural ties that joined beautiful, white female bodies with immobility, illness, and death functioned much like the ideologies that cast African and African American women as sexually deviant through association with disease and disfigurement. Though carrying significantly different social effects, the blackness of death and decay surrounded them all.[73]

· · · · ·

The transition from Victorian "household nun" to twentieth-century "vamp" took place as the New Woman publicly asserted her talents in politics, athletics, education, and the workplace, and ideas changed about female sexuality, particularly its role in forging lasting, happy marriages. Whereas Dijkstra forcefully argues that female vampire figures emerged from a masculinist backlash that demonized women's growing power, many young women, especially after the immensely popular 1915 Theda Bara film *A Fool There Was*, embraced the fashionably dark vamp style—dark dress, dark hair, and darkly made-up eyes—as a way of asserting their sexuality and expressing a desire to resist, or even vanquish, male domination in their personal lives.[74]

The move to vamp black became possible because the growing presence of black outerwear for women in the nineteenth century due to extensive mourning rituals merged with the growing sensibility that dressing in black was fashionable. Multiple factors expanded fashion-conscious women's black wardrobes. First, by the 1820s, interest in the white high-waisted neo-classical fashions had dissipated, refocusing attention on color in women's clothing. With the midcentury development of new technologies for dying fabrics, these colors, black among them, became ever more vivid and available. In addition, increasing mechanization of dress production extended possibilities for creating fashionable dresses in black. After the Civil War, *Godey's Lady's Book, Harper's Bazar,* and Sears' mail-order catalog all featured fashionable dresses and corsets in black for mourning and general wear.[75]

By the 1860s, and increasingly thereafter, the design of mourning dresses more closely followed fashion trends, thereby boosting mourning dress sales. Mourning etiquette was also in flux by the late nineteenth century. Though Taylor finds a "vast increase . . . in mourning dress" wear and an expansion of mourning etiquette to include rituals for more distant relatives' death, other sources point to shorter mourning periods and relaxation of some regulations. *Collier's Cyclopedia* in 1882 still advocated the two-and-a-half-year Victorian standard, while *Harper's Bazar* in 1886 advised a reduced widow's mourning period of eighteen months and reported "in England it is somewhat lightened in twelve." Sales of crape were in decline by the 1880s, indicating changes in mourning requirements.[76]

Most women still accepted wearing black for long periods but chose to remain fashionable during bereavement. An 1898 *Woman's Home Companion* article, "Latest Styles in Mourning Attire," noted, "Today frills abound quite as much on the dressy mourning-gown as on any other style of dress," and advised, "Black organdy dresses . . . are pretty summer mourning." Advice in the 1890s that "if you attend the theater or any place of public amusement while you are in mourning—and that is your prerogative—never wear a mourning veil" shows how adjustments in costume requirements accommodated breaks with past practices regarding seclusion. These new attitudes certainly blurred boundaries between women's mourning costumes and fashionable dress, undermining the idea that a female mourner's wearing of black signaled her removal from worldly pleasures. Though particular fabrics and veiling still symbolized mourning, the growing wear of black evening dresses with low décolleté necklines that were unacceptable for daytime particularly confounded the notion that women in black were secluded in chaste sorrow.[77]

Theatrical costumes also fostered black fashion. In the late nineteenth century, theatrical entertainment gained importance and respectability. The notoriety that plays and actors garnered via printed reviews and society journalism amplified their influence on fashion. Journalists also reported that female audience members were more interested in actresses' costumes than in the artistic merits of plays. Rich women even reputedly sent their maids to plays on fact-finding missions before attending themselves to avoid being outdone by actresses. In addition to journalistic accounts, paintings by Mary Cassatt and novels by Edith Wharton portray the theater as a site of costume display for female audience members as well as actors. And actresses, such as the famous Sarah Bernhardt, often wore gowns of black velvet in their heroic and dramatic roles. Evidence that such costumes moved offstage appears in an 1890 issue of *Harper's Bazar*, which presents "a black velvet evening gown" as one of a dozen "Evening Toiletries."[78]

Paintings of wealthy women dressed in fashionable black attire also appeared in the late nineteenth century, modifying the long tradition in Western art of widows' portraits. Artists' heightened interest in the dark aesthetic and interiors of seventeenth-century Spanish painter Velázquez, and a vogue for Spanish culture, inspired portraitists and subjects to represent the sheen of black silk, glisten of black satin, and furlike texture of black velvet, because in Velázquez's Spain, fashionable women wore black. Depending on the dress design and subject, nineteenth-century paintings of women in black show that the color can be a severe choice, an ordinary fashion option, or a risqué sensual statement.[79]

The most controversial painting in its time of a fashionable woman in black is John Singer Sargent's portrait of Madame Gautreau, who, though American-born, was a well-known Parisian woman of fashion.[80] In the painting, known as *Madame X* after a furor erupted during the painting's exhibition at the 1884 Paris Salon, the famously alluring Gautreau wears an extremely low-cut black dress constructed of a velvet bustier and satin skirt held up only by two slim, jeweled shoulder straps. Parisians found the full-length portrait shocking, and even repulsive, for a number of reasons. Standing in a twisted posture in a dark room, Gautreau leans back on one arm perched upon an ornate table. Turning away from the spectator to reveal her renowned profile, a diamond tiara in her hennaed hair, she unabashedly displays her body, adorned in a provocative, form-fitting dress. Though her fashionable appearances had been reported in society columns for some time, especially since her 1878 marriage to a wealthy French businessman at the age of nineteen, some saw in her image a defiant, arrogant, and vulgar embrace of the role of *"idole"* or "professional beauty." Others were offended by the rendering of her famously complected—and generously displayed—skin in lavender, purplish-blue, and ghostly white alabaster hues. After the uproar, Sargent stated that he merely painted what he observed, as Gautreau always wore skin powder of rice or noxious chemicals and was noted for rouging the tips of her ears as well as her lips.[81]

Critics of the painting found Madame Gautreau looked more like a corpse than a living beauty. Art historian Susan Sidlauskas explains, "Gautreau . . . flaunted a sensuality that was undermined by death and decay." Cosmetics at the time were associated with morbidity, not only because of the bloodless white complexion that powdering produced but also because of their dangerous chemical ingredients, such as arsenic and lead. Common side effects of their use included "facial trembling, even paralysis"; thus, "with her lavender pallor, Gautreau did not simply allude to death and decay: she embodied them." Contemporary assessments support this analysis. One reviewer said that Gautreau's skin "more resembles the flesh of a dead than a living body." Even Sargent's friend Ralph Curtis penned in a letter, "I was disappointed in the color. She looks decomposed." Repulsed, French commentator Henri Houssaye sharply criticized the painting: "The color pallid, the neck sinewy . . . the hand is deboned. The décolletage of the bodice doesn't make contact with the bust, it seems to flee any contact with the flesh."[82]

Male spectators conventionally expected in the act of looking to possess the displayed female body. Actively revealing herself as a self-made object "to-be-looked-at" disrupted Gautreau's objectification. Instead of being passive like a corpse to the spectator's gaze, the beautiful object draped in sensuous black was infused with haughty subjectivity. Though outraged reactions to *Madame X* did not focus upon the blackness of Gautreau's gown, Anne Hollander observes, "As a female affection for elegant dress, besides its self-conscious theatricalism, [nineteenth-century] black clothing had (and still retains) its connotations of fatal sexuality. A lady in black is not only dramatic and dignified but also dangerous."[83] Together, the multifaceted objections to *Madame X* associated fashionable blackness with beauty, morbidity, sexuality, and death.[84]

Figure 26. John Singer Sargent's *Madame X* (1884) portrays a scandalous woman in black. Courtesy, The Metropolitan Museum of Art, Arthur H. Hearn Fund, 1916 (16.53).

The public's reception of other paintings of women in black exposed confusion about whether women so dressed were in mourning or merely in fashion. Sargent's 1882 painting *Lady with the Rose* depicts the tightly corseted Charlotte Louise Burckhardt wearing a black satin dress. Below the form-fitting bodice, the skirt puffs out over crinoline bustles. Black satin bows tied together at the skirt's front reveal a black velvet petticoat. Black net covers skin bared by a low, squared neckline and satin elbow-length sleeves, and black-net ruffles further embellish collar and "cuffs." Burckhardt stands in front of a light-colored curtain, facing the spectator with a bemused expression on her face while her extended left hand "offers to view," in Henry James's words, a single white rose. Her other arm bends at her waist, her hand folded back. One critic who praised the well-received portrait described it as a "young girl . . . dressed in mourning in the very latest mode." Though aware of trends in fashion and art, he remained confused about the meaning of Burckhardt's black dress. Another critic's comment resonates with the connective leaps between black dress, black skin, death, and white women's sexuality explored in this chapter. He found the painting's essence in the "rose of yellow white, greenish at the core . . . washed of all fresh and pure origins . . . which exhales poisoned perfumes. This rose is a feast for the eyes. Why aren't the hands of the woman black?"[85]

An 1881 portrait by James McNeill Whistler, *Lady Meux*, provoked similar confusion. Whistler painted about twenty portraits of women in black between 1870 and the early 1890s. Lady Meux was a controversial woman in English high society, having had a career as an actress and a known affair before marrying into one of England's wealthiest families. Elite women declined to include her in their rounds of "visiting," an important social ritual among ladies. In her portrait, Lady Meux wears a black velvet, close-fitting, and simply designed sleeveless evening gown with a long white fur cloak draped over one shoulder. The dress hem seems to merge with the dark space she stands in. On her right hand, she wears a black glove, trimmed with black net or lace, that extends just below her elbow. The same trim edges the dress's neckline and shoulders. She also wears an extravagant matching set of diamond tiara, necklace, and bracelets. Yet despite Lady Meux's notoriety and the current fashion for black evening gowns, one reviewer described Meux as "dressed in deep mourning" and her attire as a "young widow's costume." This painting, like Burckhardt's portrait, also evoked confusion about skin color. In a letter, Whistler referred to Meux's portrait as a "beautiful Black Lady," blurring the distinction between clothing and flesh. Together these comments show how particular representations of white women in black elicited both the morbidity and sensuality associated with blackness in Western culture, and the ease with which differentiation between black dress and black skin can vanish.[86]

By 1905, when *Madame X* was publicly exhibited for only the second time, in London, and certainly by 1915, when it was displayed at the Pan Pacific Exhibition in San Francisco, the furor and scandal associated with the painting had dissipated. Gautreau died that year, and in 1916, Sargent finally sold the painting to the Metropolitan Museum of New York, declaring it "his best work." The public life and history of *Madame X*, from its shocking debut in 1884 to its entrance into the canon of great American art in 1916, coincide with a great transition in attitudes toward women's sexuality and female bodily display. The meanings and uses of women's black dress also changed during this time frame. The fashionable "little black dress" emerged as a distinct departure from black mourning dress, and the sexual sophistication that such dresses openly signaled endowed the black lingerie that women increasingly wore under them with a highly charged erotic significance.

Lingering confusion about whether black dress represented sophisticated fashion or fashionable mourning illustrates the uneven development and potential fusion of cultural connotations. In the 1936 film *My Man Godfrey*, Carole Lombard's attractive, black-clad, high-society character is greeted at a party with the question "Why the shroud?" Similarly, *Madame X* remained a potent icon of sexual transgression well into the twentieth century. Jean Louis, the costume designer for the 1946 film noir *Gilda*, starring Rita Hayworth in the title role, drew upon *Madame X* as the inspiration for the black dress that Hayworth wears in the most notorious scene in the film, in which she sings "Put the Blame on Mame" in a nightclub. Notably, each verse in the song explains how a particular woman's extreme sexuality—either too hot or too cold—caused catastrophe. Most disasters described in the song, such as the Chicago fire of 1871 and the Manhattan blizzard of 1888, took place during the era of Sargent, Gautreau, Whistler, and Meux. Gilda's dress retains the shape of Gautreau's in *Madame X*, though Jean Louis made it strapless in the contemporary 1940s mode, enhancing the sense, especially while Gilda dances, that, as in the painting, the "dress flees from the body." This impression becomes almost literally the case when Gilda begins a striptease to goad her abusive second husband, Johnny (Glenn Ford). Images of Hayworth in that strapless black dress dominated publicity for the movie, with many ads featuring the moment when Johnny slaps her following her removal from the stage. The film further connects transgressive female sexuality, black dress, violence, and death in another scene. When

Gilda and Johnny marry, she is still wearing black dress in mourning for her first husband, who apparently committed suicide after murdering a business rival.[87]

In the 1940s, costuming femme fatales such as Rita Hayworth in fashionable black was a well-established practice. Black had been solidly in vogue since the mourning periods following Queen Victoria's death in 1901 and the death of her son King Edward nine years later. Related to the larger turn-of-the-century confusion about whether women in black were mourners à la mode or merely fashionably attired, early twentieth-century representations of widows conflicted with and played on the idea of widows as icons of chaste, dignified sorrow. In 1901, American magazine illustrator Charles Dana Gibson published *The Widow and Her Friends*, a humorous series of illustrations with captions that tell the story of an attractive young widow's tough adjustment made more difficult by the unwanted attention she receives from male admirers. When the widow, wearing a black dress with deep décolletage, finally goes to a dinner party, "Some Think That She Has Remained in Retirement Too Long. Others Are Surprised That She Is About So Soon." Though she remains impassive, two men seated on either side of her are entranced; the women sitting next to them are irked and suspicious. After "She Is the Subject of More Hostile Criticism," and the object of unfortunate notoriety, "Miss Babbles Brings a Copy of a Morning Paper and Expresses Her Indignation and Sympathy over a Scurrilous Article." After the scandal, the widow enters a convent, but even there, she is subject to the desiring gazes of male clerics. Gibson's young widow is indisputably a sexually attractive and dangerously disruptive social force.[88]

Franz Lehar's commercially successful operetta *The Merry Widow* also centers on the power and sexual magnetism of widows. As in Gibson's illustrated tale, in *The Merry Widow*, the sexual knowledge and availability of widows are important components of their allure, as well as of the narrative itself. Opening in Vienna in 1905, London in 1906, and New York in 1907, *The Merry Widow* played at the New Amsterdam Theater for more than a year and has not disappeared from popular consciousness since. Made into a Hollywood movie three times—1925, 1934, and 1952—and staged at New York's Metropolitan Opera House in 2004, the operetta taps into a persistent cultural interest in attractive widows and the sexual tensions they inspire. Lehar's merry widow is a wealthy woman from a tiny European country whose royalty and subjects fear will marry a foreigner, thus bankrupting the country's state treasury when her fortune enters her second husband's hands. A native count is prevailed upon to woo her, but he prefers the nightclub dancers at Maxim's. Naturally, after several misun-

Figure 27. The disruptive widow in black "is the subject of more hostile criticism." Charles Dana Gibson, *The Widow & Her Friends* (1901). Courtesy of University of Southern California, on behalf of the USC Library Department of Special Collections.

derstandings a happy ending ensues, as the count and the merry widow are actually attracted to each other. The narrative speaks to the power that women commanded as widows rather than wives and also shows the challenge that risqué entertainment poses to traditional authority. In the 1905 operetta, a problematic baroness takes on the disguise of a Maxim girl, but in the 1952 film, Lana Turner as the widow enchants the count with her dancing and chorus-girl costume at Maxim's. This alteration is in keeping with the twentieth-century construction of American femininity as "naughty but nice," the advertising slogan of the Warner's Merry Widow corset, which the company introduced in conjunction with the film's release.[89]

In the early twentieth century, the long-standing Western tradition of ridiculing and conveying ambivalence toward widows also remained in force. In a 1904 illustration, Gibson depicted a stout older woman looking coquettishly across the room during a formal party toward a man speaking in confidence to someone, who asks, "Are Your Intentions Toward the Widow Serious?" "Oh, Very," he replies, "I Am Going, If Possible to Get Out of Marrying Her." In 1910, *Cupid's Cyclopedia* humorously defined widows as "the most dangerous variety of unmarried female." The caption

Figure 28. *The Evening American* spoofs early twentieth-century Merry Widow mania (1908). Courtesy of the Academy of Motion Picture Arts and Sciences.

Figure 29.
Glamorous Lana
Turner poses in
her black corset
during the film-
ing of *The Merry
Widow* (1952).
Courtesy of the
Academy of
Motion Picture
Arts and Sciences.

for an illustration of a demure Gibson-like young woman reads, "Type (A
Widow) Found the World Over / Very Dangerous to Man."

Long perceived in Western culture as a disruptive force, widows clearly
remained a concern for some American men in the early twentieth century,
with their fearsome sexuality and power. Though different in tone, a similar view expressed centuries before in an early modern text still advised
widows not to remarry, though " 'It is bet[ter] to marry than burn.' . . . And
let them get such husbands as be according for widows to be married unto,
nor young men, wanton, hot, and fully of play, ignorant and riotous, that
can neither rule their house nor their wife." Amorous and potentially powerful, widows needed the discipline of husbands who could assert proper
male control.[90]

. . . . . .

Widowed or not, women found that black frocks became "an absolute necessity for afternoon and evening" in the early twentieth century. So de-

clared fashion adviser Mrs. Pritchard, who identified two types of black dresses—neither related to mourning—in her 1902 book *The Cult of Chiffon:* those of "beauty" and those of "utility." For women on limited budgets, she recommended, "If you cannot afford many [dresses], have one really good black frock, and combine beauty with utility." Though she advised a small purchase of "jet or lace" to enhance the dress's attractiveness, she cautioned, "The black dress must be very beautiful to be a study in harmony, and, above all, it must never jingle." As "for the important question of evening dress," Pritchard insisted, "You must have a really good black one."[91]

Pritchard stated that white was the preferred choice for undergarments, finding the "predilection for everything white . . . a pretty cult." However, she encouraged "women [who] look their worst in white" to consider colors such as "blue, pink [and] yellow." Pritchard then added,

> Dare I whisper also of a strong fancy amongst many immaculate people for black undergarments? This affectation is chiefly noticeable amongst Americans. . . . I fancy I hear exclamations of "What a horrid idea," but I assure you that the people who adopt a peculiarity of this description are seldom deterred from wearing what they wish by such a domestic detail as the washing bill. There is something curiously effective about black silk, silk gauze, or finest cambric, trimmed with beautiful white lace. This is an extravagant notion, and would be in most instances generally unbecoming, so it need not be taken seriously into consideration.[92]

Concern about the meaning or perils of black undergarments is evident in undergarment trade journals. At times, trade reporting referred to black without comment. In January 1910, for example, the *Women's & Infants' Furnisher* included "popular brassieres in black and in white" among items carried in the "well-equipped" store department, and some styles of petticoats advertised by Gimbels in 1915 were available in black only. In the mid-1910s and into the 1920s, when sheer black dresses became fashionable, black undergarments were increasingly seen as necessary components of proper and stylish dress.[93] A black brassiere and slip underneath such a dress provided appropriate modesty by conforming to fashionable construction of the ensemble. Yet, more often, the fashion press suggested that black was a bold alternative. *Women's Wear Daily* continued to identify black undergarments as "daring," "different," and a "novelty," whereas *Corsets & Lingerie* characterized demand for black as "small," "spasmodic," and "striking."[94]

Although women favored white undergarments at the turn of the cen-

Figure 30. This black bandeau was made in 1915. With permission of the Royal Ontario Museum © ROM.

tury and for many decades thereafter, a shade introduced in the 1910s became the leading alternative the following decade. Known as "flesh," this color was a pink or peach tone, obviously limiting the range of skin colors it referenced. Brassieres in this color were worn underneath transparent blouses for an elegant, though risqué, "nude" effect. According to London *Vogue*, women in 1916 greeted "brave soldier-boys" in sheer and lacy "glad mad undies of tooth-paste pink" with "black chiffon as a dashing alternative." After the war, pink was the "prevailing color," and together with white, still considered "daintier" than black. *Corsets & Lingerie* thus characterized the "vogue for black lingerie . . . as entirely a French innovation and one which the American would be most unlikely to adopt because of her innate daintiness." This association of Frenchness with high-fashion styles and overt sexuality likely stemmed from multiple sources, such as the courtesan tradition, the leadership of Parisian couturiers, and the racy reputation of French literature and popular culture. Cancan dancers in 1880s Paris linked Frenchness, style, and risqué sexuality with black lingerie because they were required to wear black silk stockings, and more importantly, black silk drawers. Identifying black lingerie as French positions pink and white daintiness as safely modest, in both the appearance and implied sexual behavior of its wearer.[95]

The various ways in which undergarment trade journals treated the color black belies uncertainty about the meaning of black undergarments. For trade journalists advising manufacturers and retailers about production and purchases, this meant demand might not be reliable as well. They need not have worried, because the popularity of black frocks continued to soar in the 1920s. The *New York Times* reported in June 1921 that "chic women adopting all-black costumes with lilac chapeaux" were everywhere in Paris.

> At the Chantilly racetrack, the Claridge and the Ritz tea rooms and on the Rue de la Paix there is an overwhelming percentage of smart Frenchwomen, as well as wealthy American and English visitors, wearing black silk gowns. . . . Every gown is cut alike, sleveless [sic], V-necked and with only a big-linked gold chain, set with large opals or other stones, marking the waist line. . . . Elbow black gloves are worn, revealing bare upper arms, and black satin sandal slippers, cut away to almost nothing, with the sheerest of stockings to complete the costumes.

Famed designer Paul Poiret, who was "seeking to reintroduce corsets and colorful costumes," disparaged the trend by evoking older associations of black with servants' dress and with death. "Women are wearing uniforms now. . . . They all look like mourning, wearing ropes of pearls and solid black."[96]

Three months later, while *Corsets & Lingerie* downplayed the demand for black, *Women's Wear Daily* reported on the "decided increase in the use of black for undergarments" with an article and a half-page illustration captioned "The Vogue for Black in Silk Lingerie." The paper disclosed that orders by "representative large stores throughout the country . . . appear to indicate that they are being purchased for stock as well as for display purposes," and that "black is also selling well for fall underslips." The seven models and sets in the illustrations range from an exotic "black satin brocaded crepe petticoat fringed with monkey fur" to "vest and bloomer set of black georgette and lace." A "slip for wear with tunic blouse of black canton crape or crape black satin" further indicates declining distinctions between fashionable black and mourning dress, because black crape earlier had been the fabric most identified with mourning.[97]

Figure 31. Reflecting her husband's and child's approval of her corseted figure and sophisticated, fashionable black dress, the mirror reinforces the woman's status as "to-be-looked-at." *Corsets & Lingerie*, October 1921. Courtesy of Special Collections, Gladys Marcus Library, Fashion Institute of Technology.

Returning from Paris in October 1921, New York fashion entrepreneur Herbert Deutz's claim that Paris was "making strong efforts to break away from black and is . . . tired of the simple dresses" would prove to be off the mark. Editors at *Vogue* were equally confused, declaring in November 1921 that "Black Is Still the Favourite . . ." and in December "The Reign of Black Is at an End." However, a 1922 Macy's department store ad resolved the dilemma by incorporating the questionable desire for black underwear in its "January Sale of Black and White," explaining, "We welcome *black* to this traditional event, for word from Paris is that black has found a permanent position in the intimate wardrobe." Four years later, in July 1926, *Vogue* still reported that "Black Grows Steadily in the Favour of Paris." And in October of that year, *Vogue* published the famous illustration of Coco Chanel's long-sleeved, just-below-the-knee black dress, declaring, "Here is a Ford signed Chanel—the frock that all the world will wear." Though the trend had been building for years, this press attention enshrined Chanel as the creator of the "little black dress." Certainly, Chanel's designs, stature, and penchant for black further popularized the black dress and, as *Vogue* predicted and promoted, helped make it a cornerstone of American women's wardrobes. Moreover, the high-fashion cachet of Chanel and *Vogue* furthered the aura of feminine sophistication in this look. A key component of the urbane femininity embodied in the "little black dress" is sexual knowledge. The increasing presence of fashionable black outerwear meant that stylishly dressed women were both reclaiming this knowledge as respectable and enjoying the vestiges of transgressive pleasure that wearing black in this manner could bring. Furthermore, Chanel's new use of fabrics like jersey for women's dresses and suits and her championing of costume jewelry meant that the tools for dressing in this chic, sexually aware, sophisticated, and stylish manner were widely available.[98]

Representations of women in a range of cultural forms serve as indexes for modes of fashion, along with changes in public concerns, taste, moral sensibilities, and the meanings ascribed to clothing. Women in states of undress are stock images in a wide range of elite and popular visual media. Undergarments worn by women in Victorian erotic images are predominantly ordinary white goods made of the muslin fabric that most women wore. Apparently, pornographers preferred white bloomers because the garments afforded a view of women's pubic hair, which black undergarments did not. In E. J. Belloq's circa 1912 photographs of New Orleans prostitutes, some wear black stockings, but black was also the color most commonly worn. It is possible, however, that black stockings may have conveyed sensuality. In the early 1920s, when women wore flesh-colored stockings with the new shorter skirts, couturier Lady Duff Gordon advised women to "stick to black stockings and long slinky dresses if they wanted to get—and hold—their men." Yet Duff Gordon's comment may not so much express appreciation for past modes of feminine sensual attraction as reflect changes in the signification of black lingerie that emerged during and especially after the turn of the century.[99]

Evidence for this shift appears in the 1943 best seller *A Tree Grows in Brooklyn*, a semiautobiographical novel noted for its detailed re-creation of life between 1901 and 1919. Francie, the teenage working-class female protagonist, asks her brother to buy her a "black lace dance set" for Christmas in 1916. Her brother disapproves of the purchase and, rather than have to ask for it himself, gives Francie the two dollars she needs to buy "the coveted dance set—panties and brassiere made of scraps of black lace held together by narrow black satin ribbon." Black lingerie from this period in costume archives substantiates author Betty Smith's (1896–1972) date and description. When the siblings return home, "Mama let loose her 'Oh my!' of astonishment," but isn't perturbed when Francie hopefully asks, " 'Do you think that's what fast women wear?' " Instead, she responds,

> "If they do, I'm sure they all come down with pneumonia. Now let's see: What'll we have for supper?"
> "Aren't you going to *object?*" Francie was disappointed because mama wasn't making a fuss.
> "No. All women go through a black-lace-drawers time. You came to it earlier than most and you'll get over it sooner."

In a new female rite of passage, "black-lace-drawers time," wearing black lingerie for the first time, signaled a change in sexual status and the first experience of eroticism. Young women actively embraced, and even flaunted, their sexuality by imitating, they hoped, the dressing practices of "fast women" such as Charmion, an innovator in the modern art of striptease who wore "black net underthings" in her famous turn-of-the century act. Mama's measured response downplayed her daughter's new urge for sexual rebellion. The purchase of such black undergarments by working-class youths with their own wages, and discourse about them, belonged to a post-Victorian world.[100]

Almost sixty years later, a similar exchange between feminist theorist bell hooks (b. 1952) and her mother shows the persistence and pervasiveness that donning black lingerie holds as a pivotal ritual in a young woman's coming of age in America. In *Memories of Girlhood* (1996), hooks remembers her Southern upbringing in both first and third person. She writes that her grandfather is "a man whose skin is the color of soot and other wonderful black things, things they love—shoe polish, coal, women in black slips. She cannot wait to grow up and be a woman who can wear black slips, black dresses. Black is a woman's color—that's what her mama tells her. You have to earn the right to wear the color black."[101]

Hooks begins to earn that right in the anecdote that follows, in which she is offered popcorn in exchange for a kiss while wandering with her brother through an impoverished "cracker" neighborhood. Though warned by her parents to stay away from the dangerous racists who live there, she accepts the offer on a dare by her brother.

> She gives the kiss, gives him the popcorn for already she is ashamed. She knows better, knows that kisses are for friends and other loved ones. She fears the history in this exchange. White men taking black girls, black women, the word they do not understand but hear the grown-ups use: white men raping black women. After eating the popcorn he assures her that he will tell as soon as they are home, that she will be punished. Rushing home, running through the dark, she hopes the punishment will wipe away the feeling of shame.[102]

Mixing the "natural" black color of skin and coal with the manufactured black of shoes and slips leads hooks to the naturalized, cultural meaning of women's black dress as a sign of sexual maturation. The anecdote of the kiss brings history to bear in showing that for African American women, earning that maturity holds the potential for violence, suffering, and shame. Here too, then, the sexual knowledge epitomized by women's black slips and dresses is associated with destructive power and ideologies of race.

In *An Offbeat Social History of Women's Clothing, 1950 to 1980*, Ellen Melinkoff further confirms the significance of wearing black for young women in the 1950s. In this collective memoir, she describes the impact of seeing Audrey Hepburn in movies and magazines wearing beatnik black turtlenecks and stretch pants as well as perfect sleeveless black dresses at cocktail and evening lengths. Melinkoff writes that she could not "live without a black dress in the closet for any and all emergencies. . . . It symbolized sexiness and adulthood. Black on young girls was frowned upon. Our mothers told us we would look like old crones in it and forced us into namby-pamby pastels. *They* (and we also) knew black had power behind it. A first black dress was a significant event, a coming out, and no mere girl could pull off such a severe color." In the book, Carolyn Zucker also recalls, "My mother would tell me that a sixteen-year-old shouldn't wear black, but I did. And I'd put my hair in a French twist so I'd really look sophisticated."[103]

The twentieth-century association of black lingerie with "fast women" described by Betty Smith, and young women's tendency from the 1910s to the 1950s to link it with the power of sex and transgression, is significant. As new meanings of black lingerie emerged, an increasing number of erotic and pornographic images of women appeared that differed from those of the Victorian era. Black lingerie began to be featured in such images, which were widely available for purchase and especially proliferated after 1920. Black lingerie's identification with disreputable sexuality and commercially available female bodies surely heightened the eroticism attached to it. One erotic photograph taken circa 1928–29 depicts a woman in short black underpants, black garter belt, and stockings. She stands with legs somewhat astride, one in front of the other, each of her hands holding the opposite, bent upper arm behind her head. This posture curves her back, raising and projecting her breasts forward. The only thing covering her upper body is a black strap that goes around her neck, extends down between her breasts, and attaches to her underpants. The woman's stylized face, with thin, drawn eyebrows and darkened lips, looks away from the spectator, gazing over her right arm. Her arch look underscores the commercialized association between black lingerie and illicit sexual availability.[104]

Images of sexual women in black lingerie also began to appear in more mainstream fare. Jean Harlow's earliest notable film appearance was a "featured bit" in the 1929 Laurel and Hardy silent short *Double Whoopee*. In the film, Laurel and Hardy play inept doormen on their first day working at a ritzy hotel. When the elegant and beautiful platinum-blonde hotel guest arrives in a taxicab, she takes Hardy's arm; she is wearing a slinky black ensemble composed of a spaghetti-strap camisole top with lace trim at the neckline and a long, silky skirt. A sheer black scarf is draped around her neck. As Harlow and Hardy walk into the hotel lobby, the distracted Laurel shuts the taxicab door on Harlow's dress. No one initially notices that when the cab pulls away from the curb, it also pulls away her skirt. In a scene shot from behind as Harlow sashays confidently forward into the hotel, the camera reveals Harlow clad only in her low-back camisole top, black lace step-in drawers, black garter belt, black stockings, and black shoes. While waiting at the reception desk, Harlow turns toward the camera, her scarf strategically placed across her body, and finally realizes her dress is half gone. Horrified, Harlow grabs Laurel's doorman's coat and rushes off, comically revealing that Laurel wears only a union suit beneath his coat.[105]

Although scenes of young women in lingerie were common in mainstream 1920s films, *Double Whoopee* is an early example—and perhaps the first—in which the actress wears black rather than light-colored lingerie. Harlow would appear again in black lingerie in her first real screen role, in *Hell's Angels* (1930), a World War I drama that cost director and producer Howard Hughes millions to complete. Harlow plays devious girlfriend Helen who comes between two pilot brothers, one in search of a nice girl to marry and one a playboy. In a scene revealing what the *Los Angeles Evening Herald* described as Helen's "amorous, predatory" character and Harlow's "sultry temperament," Helen invites the playboy brother up to her apartment. After asking him whether he "would be shocked if [she] changed into something more comfortable," Harlow returns to the living room wearing only a clingy black negligee with white trim at the collar and cuffs. The fact that Harlow changes into black lingerie after uttering a line that became a potent cinematic cliché of female seduction is significant.[106]

Despite Harlow's small amount of screen time, advertisements for *Hell's Angels* prominently featured her. One ad reproduced a photograph of Harlow "half-reclining on a divan, her alabaster arms outstretched to a man in uniform" underneath the word " 'SEX.' " A poster advertising the film's screening in downtown Los Angeles sometime after the movie's extravagant Hollywood premiere positions a larger, full-body photograph of Harlow in black lingerie between head shots of the film's two male stars. In the image, Harlow doesn't wear the black negligee she wore in the film but a much more revealing black lace combination garment, composed of a camisole and thigh-high step-ins, that hugs her torso and reveals her bare shoulders, arms, and legs. Underscoring her act of self-display, Harlow extends her arms away from her body, holding out a black lace wrap that forms an alluring backdrop for her seductive posture. With hips tilted slightly to her left side and her left foot raised at the heel, she bends her left knee provocatively forward, leaning in toward her right leg. Harlow's posing in scanty black lace conveys the obvious sensual appeal of her role in the film that launched her screen career.[107]

In 1932, Harlow appeared again in a black negligee, in *Red-Headed Woman*, in which she plays one of her most brazenly sexually assertive roles. The actress who personified and popularized the sexual allure of platinum blonde hair, and who favored white dress and home furnishings, appears also to be the earliest well-known figure in popular culture to embody and act out the erotic and transgressive meanings of black lingerie. Harlow's notorious screen persona, dubbed the original "bombshell," evoked the destructive power of female sexuality, and of the dangerous blonde dressed in black. In doing so, she popularized the coupling of black lingerie with openly erotic expression.[108]

Lingerie scenes in movies continued unabated in the 1930s and 1940s, featuring female stars with more ordinary levels of sex appeal than Jean Harlow. In 1933, *Motion Picture* reported that actress Jeanette MacDonald was "tired of being the screen's leading lingerie model" due to work in films such as the 1932 *One Hour with You*, in which she was "comparatively clothed in a series of transparent negligees," and the 1931 *Don't Bet on Women*, in which "Jeanette maintained the step-in touch by pursuing Edmund Lowe in a very wispy bit of black lace." The fan magazine noted that although "certain elements have always regarded the undraped figure of the

Figure 32. Jean Harlow wears black lingerie in *Double Whoopee* (1929) in an early—and perhaps the first—appearance of black undergarments in a Hollywood movie. Courtesy, Photofest.

Misses Jean Harlow, Clara Bow, Alice White, et al., as sheer sex displays, Jeanette's brand of décolleté has always passed in the category of the piquant. It's daring, and a little bit naughty, of course, but it's sex with a chuckle. Jeanette's innately 'nice' personality has always removed any vestige of the objectionably risqué from even bathtub scenes."[109]

A similar sensibility that nice girls wear "transparent" and "wispy" black lingerie is central to the 1930 film *Our Blushing Brides*, Joan Crawford and Anita Page's follow-up to *Our Dancing Daughters* (1928). Two of the six images from the "movie 'undie' parade" (a fashion show in the film) that appeared in fan magazine *Photoplay* featured black lingerie. One caption reads, "Blonde Gwen Lee, in black chiffon and lace nightie and robe that make her look like a fairy tale princess." Within the context of wider display of women dressed in white or pastel-colored "exquisite" and figure-revealing undergarments, black lingerie could be an "elegant" alternative.[110]

Yet costuming "nice" girls like MacDonald and the always good "fairy tale" princesses in black lingerie indicates a new type of feminine construction, which fully flowered in the 1950s. Twentieth-century women were to be both "a wee bit naughty but so nice," as a midcentury corset advertisement succinctly put it. Black lingerie enabled respectable American women to display bits of naughtiness, perhaps for their own pleasure as well as their husbands'. Mary McCarthy (1912–89) describes that possibility in her best-selling novel *The Group* (1963), for which she drew upon her life and those of her female classmates after their graduation from Vassar in 1933. In one passage, Norine tells Helena about her visit to a physician to resolve sexual problems with her impotent husband, Put, who is unable to make love to a "good woman."

> "He was pretty much of a Behaviorist. When I explained Put's sexual history, he advised me to buy some black chiffon underwear and long black silk stockings and some cheap perfume. So that Put would associate me with a whore. And to try to get him to take me that way, with all my clothes on in the afternoon, when he got home from work. . . . It was almost a success. I went to Bloomingdale's and got the underwear and stockings." She pulled up her sweat shirt, and Helena had a glimpse of a black chiffon "shimmy" with lace inserts.

Though black lingerie failed to save this marriage, the prescription indicates a belief that, due to black lingerie's association with illicit and therefore exciting sex, a healthy dose might keep husbands and wives happy.[111]

Two other midcentury cinematic representations provide a measure of black lingerie's transgressive character. In the early 1930s, Fleischer Studios'

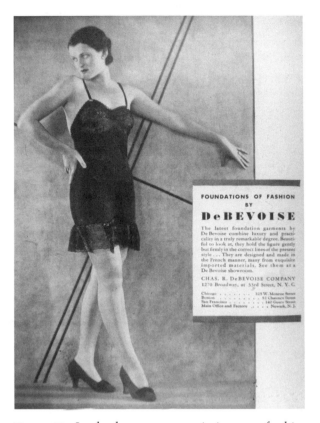

Figure 33. In the late 1920s, erotic images of white women in black undergarments began to appear in mainstream print culture, such as this provocative pose in black lingerie "made in the French manner." *Corsets & Brassieres,* November 1930. Courtesy of Special Collections, Gladys Marcus Library, Fashion Institute of Technology.

Betty Boop cartoons presented the sexually expressive animated star in a short black strapless dress that revealed a black garter on her left leg. In addition, a number of cartoons put Boop in situations that exposed her shapely body in her underwear. Her sexuality, reputation for naughtiness, and erotic appeal were such that Boop was the subject of unauthorized eight-page "dirty" comic books in the 1930s that depicted her sexual experiences more broadly. After the film industry instituted self-censorship in 1934 via the Hays Code, Boop's animated skirts lengthened and her garter disap-

peared. In addition, the outrageous sexual displays and racy narratives in
the fifty or so Boop shorts between 1930 and 1934 shifted to stories that
placed Boop in more domestic situations, until her cartoon career ended in
1939.[112]

Race also was a factor in Boop's identity. Boop cartoons made inspired use
of jazz music and jazz musicians, such as Cab Calloway. Though Boop's Jewish creators laced the cartoons with jokes and references that established her
as a Jewish immigrant daughter, her skin darkens in some cartoons, such as
"(I'll Be Glad When You're Dead) You Rascal, You," a jungle tale that includes the music and voice of Louis Armstrong. Moreover, in a 1934 lawsuit by once-popular singer Helen Kane, who was the obvious inspiration
for Betty Boop's distinctive voice and look, Fleischer Studios successfully
defended itself by screening a film of African American entertainer Baby
Esther singing a song with the lyric "Boop Oop a Doop," which had become
a signature Betty Boop phrase. Baby Esther's manager also testified that
Helen Kane and her manager saw Baby Esther's cabaret act in 1929. As
scholar Robert G. O'Meally has said, "Boop herself had, as it were, a black
grandmother in her background." Betty Boop thus provides another midcentury cultural marker of the admixture of race, African American culture,
sexuality, and black dress. Moreover, as a judge in another mid-1930s Boop
copyright lawsuit described her, "There is the broad baby face, the large
round flirting eyes, the low placed pouting mouth, the small nose, the im-
perceptible chin, and the mature bosom. It was a unique combination of in-
fancy and maturity, innocence and sophistication." In other words, Betty
Boop, while dressed in short, garter-revealing black, clearly embodied the
"naughty but nice" ideal of twentieth-century American femininity.[113]

Black lingerie made news—and almost inspired litigation—again in
1941, when established character actress Binnie Barnes played a typical supporting role in *This Thing Called Love,* which starred Rosalind Russell. The
New York Times review noted the "frequent appearances of Miss Russell in
delectable negligees," but Barnes received unwelcome headlines after she alleged that director Alexander Hall had duped her into appearing in the film
in a "black lace bra and panties" and threatened a lawsuit against Columbia
Pictures. Hall, Barnes claimed, promised that she would be seen only in silhouette while wearing black undergarments onscreen. Barnes and her new
husband objected to that scene but did not pursue their case after published
reports about her complaint included the shot from the movie of Barnes in
black lingerie. A few years later, though still risqué, Paulette Goddard's black
nightgown would "double for an evening gown" in the 1943 wartime
drama *So Proudly We Hail.*[114]

Women were not only wearing black lingerie in novels and movies. From the 1930s on, manufacturers produced, and retailers offered, more black undergarments to meet rising demand. Maiden Form reported a "big boom in black foundations" in 1937.

> For years, most women have had at least one black slip in their wardrobe and have found it to be practically indispensable. Apparently, many women are now having the same idea about a black foundation garment and about black brassieres: at least one of each makes an excellent "standby" to fall back on for those costumes for which anything except a black brassiere or a black foundation is not exactly right. In increasing numbers, fastidiously dressed women are demanding black in their foundation departments. Fashion emphasis on black outer apparel also tends to increase the popularity of black foundations. Consequently, there are more black numbers in the Maiden Form line than there have been in some time.[115]

During World War II, as with many consumer goods, demand for black lingerie exceeded supply. Maiden Form warned retailers in 1942, "Black is scarce these days," and two years later, *Women's Wear Daily* reported "Heavy demand for black lingerie continues unabated. Most buyers are still having trouble keeping enough black in stock." Though female shoppers also found black "practical . . . for traveling," the evocative qualities of black lingerie predominated. In the late 1930s and 1940s, both *Vogue* and the Sears mail-order catalog promoted black lingerie and foundations with the themes of "black magic" and "enchantment," a stratagem that would find intensified commercial attention in the 1950s when an "increased selection of black styles" in foundations was available. In 1952, *Women's Wear Daily* reported that white constituted 90 percent of undergarment sales and black, 10 percent.[116]

From the mid-twentieth century, black undergarments became both normalized within the American woman's wardrobe and further fetishized as naughty objects representative of illicit sex, as such fetishism itself became more mainstream. By the 1980s, black punk-rock fashion sensibilities became widely popular, including the use of underwear as outerwear, torn and pinned-together apparel that revealed undergarments and skin, overt bodily restriction through black leather dog collars and corsetry, and neo-retro body shaping such as extremely pointy bras. Steve Miller's 1982 hit song "Abracadabra" included the lyrics

> I feel the magic in your caress
> I feel magic when I touch your dress,
> Silk and satin, leather and lace
> Black panties with an angel's face.

The song reaffirms the close association between garment and body, especially for constructing sexual allure, and it also speaks to black lingerie's assumed erotic quality. Together, these meanings enable "black panties" to transform the angelic woman into an alluring temptress.[117]

. . . . .

The 1999 comedy *Ten Things I Hate about You*, which set *The Taming of the Shrew* in a contemporary high school, reaffirmed the sexual meaning of black underwear for another generation. While foraging through the bedroom of Kat, the teenage shrew, her sister and her sister's boyfriend respond to finding "black panties":

—What does that tell us?
—She wants to have sex someday, that's what.
—She could just like the color.
—You don't buy black lingerie unless you want someone to see it.[118]

And plenty of young women wearing low-cut trousers and thongs in the early twenty-first century certainly do want someone—if not everyone—to see their underwear. Giving voice to the connection between open expression of sexual desire and the display of black underwear, Shadee Malaklou proclaimed herself to be a "black lace bra kind of woman" in her January 2004 column in Duke University's student newspaper. She urged Duke's "Southern belles" to wear black lace bras and have "little black books" as a means to end the double standard of sexual conduct. Her proposal prompted heartfelt exchanges about female sexual expression in American youth culture.[119]

Throughout the twentieth century and into the twenty-first, women engaged in many sorts of struggles over the meanings of white and black. In the early 1920s, African American women like Mabel Durham looked for employment in New York City as sewing-machine operators, seeking to join the largely Jewish and Italian immigrant women who made white goods. On several occasions, Durham found an employer willing to hire her, only to have other workers refuse to let her stay, one likely reason being their fear that her hiring would drive down wages. Finally, in 1922, she found employment sewing slips at a place where her coworkers tried to ensure that she would receive pay equal to theirs. Not wishing to risk losing her hard-won job by confronting the boss when told by her primarily Italian and Jewish immigrant coworkers that she earned $2 less a week than they, Durham decided that displaying her skills would eventually earn her equal wages. Her strategy succeeded within two weeks, and soon thereafter she became lead operator in the shop.[120]

Eleven years later, Durham's boss was stunned when she and most of the other workers joined an ILGWU-organized general strike. Durham was also surprised when her coworkers elected her shop chairlady. These garment workers trusted Durham because she had often used her favored status, as well as her ability to express herself, to successfully articulate their needs to the boss. Durham had also questioned the Local 62 representative about the allocation of dues at the first organizing meeting. When the union representative responded that dues would go to office expenses, charitable contributions, and education programs, she was satisfied with the answer and joined. Durham later noted that although she was never treated badly by her boss, she believed that all workers deserved better.[121]

Mabel Durham and many other African American women remained a sizable minority among undergarment workers throughout the 1930s and 1940s. The union leadership at this time was committed to including African American workers on union staff and representative committees. Durham's life profoundly changed as a result. After marriage and a stint in the Women's Army Corps, Mabel Durham Fuller returned to work producing undergarments in 1945. Local 62 manager Samuel Shore then asked Durham Fuller, a long-standing member of the local's council, to attend a special year-long course at Harvard University for selected members from a variety of unions. This course, like other "workers colleges" held at universities across the United States, prepared members for union staff positions. Shore recruited Durham Fuller not only for her proven organizing skills and dedication to the union but also because he felt it important to integrate the union's staff. The racial and sexual politics of the ILGWU throughout this period were complex, with Jewish and Italian immigrant men largely controlling the union nationally as well as holding major staff positions locally. Yet these men held progressive notions about a wide range of social issues, including a belief in challenging racism. Shore's desire for an African American presence on the Local 62 staff was in line with national ILGWU political tendencies.[122]

Durham Fuller's successful tenure as assistant education director and then education director of Local 62 lasted until her retirement in the 1970s. She organized classes for union members and planned cultural events, which later included tours of the United States, Europe, and Israel. Nonetheless, the respect and recognition that Durham Fuller received in Local 62 did not protect African American undergarment workers from discrimination

Figure 34. Mabel Durham Fuller, the education director of the International Ladies Garment Workers Union Local 62, speaks at a union meeting in the late 1950s. Courtesy, UNITE HERE Archives, Kheel Center, Cornell University.

in other situations. African American women found work at the many northern undergarment firms that either moved entirely to the southeastern region of the United States or opened additional factories there in search of nonunion workers who would accept lower wages and no benefits. Records of organizing drives at these shops tell heart-wrenching tales of the racism of white employers and white coworkers. However, union organizers also reported instances of cooperation and solidarity between black and white women workers.[123]

Subtle forms of racism also persisted in the supposedly more tolerant racial climes of New York and New Jersey. African American undergarment workers often found a pile of black undergarments stacked next to their machines when they returned from vacation or sick leave. Sewing black thread on black fabric is obviously more difficult and tiring than doing the same work on a

Figure 35. The ILGWU's antiracist politics included this 1960 protest against segregation by Local 62 members outside a Woolworth's in New York City. Photograph by Mabel Durham Fuller. Author's collection.

lighter fabric. Thus, working with piece rates or quotas made work on black undergarments less than desirable. Some shops paid a differential for working with black undergarments to compensate for the extra time and effort they required. Yet even when this was the case, as at Maiden Form's Bayonne, New Jersey, plant, African American women often came back to work after an absence to find a bundle of black brassieres by their machines.[124]

This form of discrimination brings the connections between blackness, sexuality, and transgression full circle. The view that African American women's sexuality transgressed notions of white femininity and propriety linked black lingerie with eroticism. Yet ironically, producing these transgressive commodities was undesirable and tedious. Furthermore, when African American women sewed more than their fair share of black undergarments, the meaning of black lingerie shifted from eroticism to exploitation, though both meanings centered on racial difference. This largely hidden meaning of black lingerie, known only to workers at the site of production, is emblematic of how the meanings of intimate apparel diverge in the separated realms of production and consumption.

. . . . . .

The meaning of black lingerie changed over time and location. Changes in fashion and style, new trends in mourning etiquette, shifts in gendered and racialized understandings of female sexuality, and the full development of mass production and consumption of women's clothing all helped identify black lingerie as overtly sensual and worn as a sexual invitation. Black clothing's primary nineteenth-century function in women's outerwear of signaling mourning deeply imbued the color with a distinctive meaning that underscored cultural associations between and anxieties about sex and death. In the early twentieth century, the link between black apparel and grief and solemnity dissipated when women wore the color publicly in fashionable styles, as well as in matching lingerie underneath their clothing and next to their skin. At the same time, cultural associations of blackness and black people with sexuality and unbridled passions, such as those found by Walter Benn Michaels and Toni Morrison in the fiction of F. Scott Fitzgerald, Ernest Hemingway, and Willa Cather, shaped views and maltreatment of African Americans, marking them as people who lacked self-restraint. Still, when white women challenged Victorian codes of female sexual conduct, they drew upon the style and practices of black women—and the blackface tradition—in constructing modern alternatives that allowed for both "naughty and nice" behavior, or at least their appearance.

Correlations between blackness and death were not entirely antithetical to erotic meanings. Not only have sex and death been complexly linked in multiple arenas from popular culture to medical texts and psychoanalytic theory, but black women's sexualized bodies were seen as both highly charged and dangerously diseased. In addition, turn-of-the-century perceptions of Africa cast it as a primitive place that was both wildly fecund and suffused with decay and death. During that era, when mourning practices and fashions in dress were in transition, confusion about whether women in black were sexually experienced widows or attractive women of fashion also linked blackness, death, and sexuality, as did the long-standing fetishizing tendency for women's clothing to signify and stand for, if not replace, the female body.

The early nineteenth-century French play in which the widow Amelia becomes a seductive primitive by assuming the Hottentot's clothing provides striking evidence of how phenomena largely considered separately—such as fashion trends, racial masquerade, and the association of widowhood with heightened eroticism—overlapped. More than a century later, as black clothing became fashionably sophisticated in its own right, Josephine Baker was one of a number of performers who confused critics about their racial identities. Drawing upon Baker's sexy performance style and the fascination such confusion evoked, Marlene Dietrich's role in *Blonde Venus*, suggests Mary Ann Doane, presented blackness as a removable "erotic accessory" in the "commodification . . . of white female sexuality." Such cultural fusions, racial hybridity, and objectifying mechanisms undoubtedly suffused black apparel, particularly the intimate garments that clothed women's breasts and genitals, with greater power to convey meanings. Culled from a range of overlapping significations, those texts and practices that melded the sexually practiced and yet forbidden widow dressed in black with the alluring eroticism associated with dark skin established the power of black lingerie to signify illicit sexuality. They also propelled the potent sensibility that black lingerie possessed a heightened erotic charge imbued with the potential to leap to the body it adorned. A description of Fifi, a stripper at the notorious Minsksy's burlesque house, illustrates this notion: "The black net that clung to her skin from toe to breast covered her but it could not conceal her. The figure that swayed upon the runway, . . . turning upon itself and thrusting out of itself, was all Fifi, pure Fifi, the black of her and the white of her."[125]

5 The Invisible Woman

Intimate Apparel Advertising

Brevity is the Soul of Lingerie.

Dorothy Parker, 1934

In August 1936, S. H. Camp, president of Camp Corsets of Jackson, Michigan, a leading manufacturer of "scientific corsets," purchased a model of a female body manufactured in Europe. Camp correctly assessed the promotional potential of this nude transparent model that revealed the "complete structure of the female human body and its organs." He brought it to the United States, arranged for its exhibition at the New York Museum of Science and Industry, and hired a manager for a Camp Transparent Woman national tour. By September 1937, Camp advertisements in magazines such as *Vogue, Parents, Good Housekeeping, Hygeia,* and *Woman's Home Companion* boasted that over two million people had seen the "most publicized woman in the world," news of which had also been "broadcast over national radio chains." After the tour concluded, the Camp Transparent Woman went on permanent exhibition at the Chicago Museum of Science and Industry. By 1941, Camp claimed, more than eighty million people had seen this marvel, including sixty-five thousand members of the medical profession, who "studied it in detail."[1]

The Camp Transparent Woman's promise of resolving mysteries of the female body long viewed in Western culture as deeply enigmatic may explain her popularity. Yet the Transparent Woman's association with corsets is further suggestive. With a name derived from the French *corps,* or body, and insertion of pliable "bones" into sturdy fabric, corsets alter the size and curve of the torso by enveloping and displacing flesh. The imperfect body disappears as corset laces tighten, and with fitted placement of the outer dress, the female body further dissolves literally into a mere "figure."[2] Corsets thus ostensibly make female flesh vanish.

Though remarkable, Camp's Transparent Woman was not the first nor the last such figure seen by Americans. Transparent and invisible women regularly appeared in twentieth-century images in which undergarments seem to be worn, though by a female body that is not visible. The thrust of absent hips, the curve of hollow backsides, and the fullness of missing breasts infuse the empty garments with an erotic corporeality. Other illustrations and photographs created a similar effect by placing the body in shadow and the undergarment in light or by portraying incomplete bodies or cut-off body parts. These images make female bodies and women's subjective experiences harder to see. Such disappearing acts and their larger cultural meanings are central to the operation of gender, sexuality, and power in the United States.

The long use of invisible women in intimate apparel advertisements demonstrates how effective this graphic figure was both as a sales tool and as a cultural metaphor. Certainly, as the body disappears in such images, the object/commodity appears in greater relief. On a pragmatic level, drawing attention to the garment for sale was undoubtedly the intent of the fashion-industrial complex of manufacturers, retailers, fashion publications, and advertising agencies. However, the practice had other consequences as well. Intimate apparel representations construct female bodies as sexual objects of a male gaze and elevate these commodities' role as signifiers of feminine eroticism.[3] Together, these interrelated processes of objectification and fetishization diminish the significance of three-dimensional female flesh, limit the range of significations possible for the female body, and attenuate the female subject's ability to assign meanings herself. Importantly, such constraints undermine possibilities for collective critiques and for challenges to social structures that restrict women's opportunities.

The invisible woman was not the only visual convention and theme of intimate apparel advertising that appeared consistently from the 1910s to the early 1950s. Throughout this period, undergarment promotions frequently depicted erotically charged scenes of narcissism, voyeurism, exhibitionism, and fetishism by incorporating images of windows, mirrors, and pinup poses. In addition, ad copy linked undergarments with health, beauty, youthfulness, and fashion and used key twentieth-century advertising concepts of modernity and commodified self-transformation. One ad in the 1910s, for example, promoted the "transforming power of Model Brassieres" to fulfill women's desires for "a charming figure," and another by the Futurist Company announced the arrival of "woman's modern undergarments." Yet although such themes were constant during these five decades, others came and went. A preoccupation with "daintiness" permeated ads in the 1910s and 1920s, anxieties about maintaining femininity while taking on potentially masculinizing responsibilities and work arose during World War II, and increasing references to magic, witchery, and dreams were common in the postwar period.[4]

Figure 36. Crossed out, the female body disappears in this 1940s foundation ad. *Corsets & Brassieres,* February 1946. Courtesy of Special Collections, Gladys Marcus Library, Fashion Institute of Technology.

Though the goal of advertising is to increase product sales, it is not essential to evaluate sales results nor to determine advertisers' and ad agencies' intent to analyze the methods of intimate apparel advertisers and the consequences of those methods. Certainly, intimate apparel advertisers want female consumers to believe that purchasing and displaying their products will endow them with attractive qualities like beauty and glamour. Yet although advertisers may not always consciously produce images of fetishized and objectified female bodies, they ultimately benefit from these effects, both directly, in increasing sales, and indirectly, in maintaining the desirability of particular commodities and of gendered consumption. Success encourages repeated use of these selling methods and their further inscription into American culture. Powerfully embedded in the culture of daily life, such signs circulate meanings about gender and sexuality that go far beyond their commercial context.[5]

Often assailed as a major instigator of the objectification of women's

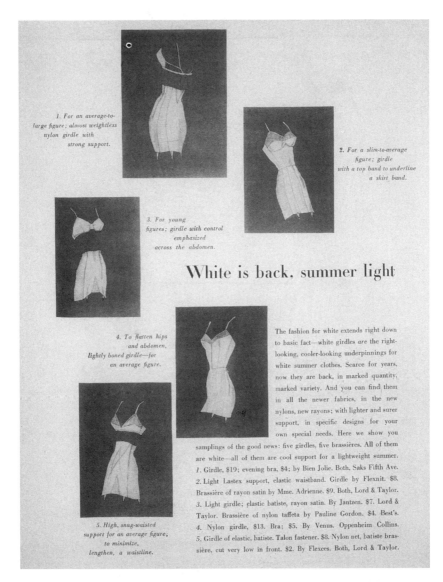

1. For an average-to-large figure; almost weightless nylon girdle with strong support.

2. For a slim-to-average figure; girdle with a top band to underline a skirt band.

3. For young figures; girdle with control emphasized across the abdomen.

White is back, summer light

4. To flatten hips and abdomen, lightly boned girdle—for an average figure.

The fashion for white extends right down to basic fact—white girdles are the right-looking, cooler-looking underpinnings for white summer clothes. Scarce for years, now they are back, in marked quantity, marked variety. And you can find them in all the newer fabrics, in the new nylons, new rayons; with lighter and surer support, in specific designs for your own special needs. Here we show you samplings of the good news: five girdles, five brassières. All of them are white—all of them are cool support for a lightweight summer.

1. Girdle, $19; evening bra, $4; by Bien Jolie. Both, Saks Fifth Ave.
2. Light Lastex support, elastic waistband. Girdle by Flexnit. $8. Brassière of rayon satin by Mme. Adrienne. $9. Both, Lord & Taylor.
3. Light girdle; elastic batiste, rayon satin. By Jantzen. $7. Lord & Taylor. Brassière of nylon taffeta by Pauline Gordon. $4. Best's.
4. Nylon girdle, $13. Bra; $5. By Venus. Oppenheim Collins.
5. Girdle of elastic, batiste. Talon fastener. $8. Nylon net, batiste brassière, cut very low in front. $2. By Flexees. Both, Lord & Taylor.

5. High, snug-waisted support for an average figure; to minimize, lengthen, a waistline.

Figure 37. A May 1947 *Vogue* article illustrates the use of invisible women. Copyright © 1947 Condé Nast Publications.

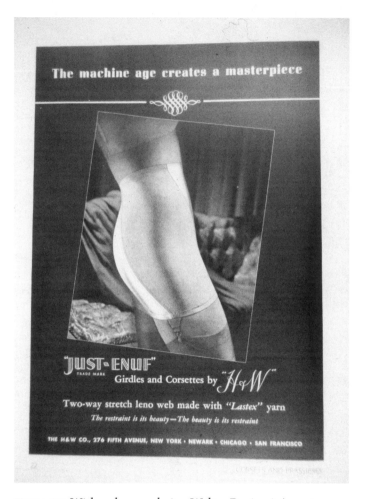

Figure 38. With a slogan echoing Walter Benjamin's contemporaneous essay on art in the "age of mechanical reproduction," this ad presents a truncated, girdled female torso set within an intimate boudoir scene as a modern masterpiece. *Corsets & Brassieres*, April 1938. Courtesy of Special Collections, Gladys Marcus Library, Fashion Institute of Technology.

bodies, advertisements notoriously sell idealized femininity as well as the products necessary to construct it, and they use women's sexuality to heighten the allure of commodities for male consumers, such as cars and liquor.[6] For feminist critics, such advertising images are proof of women's sexual subordination and degraded status as decorative appendages to men. Yet embedded within the concept of objectification lies the notion that a nonauthentic body as object replaces an autonomous body as subject. In this sense, an alternative female body exists but remains invisible, especially to mass culture's male gaze. Objectification thus requires both the disappearance and reconstruction of women's bodies. From the early twentieth century, the business of selling intimate apparel expanded the context for fetishizing female bodies and feminine undergarments. However, as an analysis of ad images and text shows, it also offered possibilities for female readers to subvert their status as object and fetish.

Building upon feminist critiques of visual culture, including the iconography of Western painting, photography, pornography, dance, and Hollywood films, in addition to advertising, and upon historical accounts of the advertising industry, this chapter examines how intimate apparel advertising became a potent vehicle for objectifying women's bodies.[7] Scenes of women dressing, bathing, and lounging together from both elite art and pornography commonly offered a view of women in undergarments and provided an established repertoire of postures for commercial emulation. In addition, as Steven Marcus suggests, pornography and advertising share a similar purpose, to stimulate the body to act.

> Literature possesses . . . a multitude of intentions, but pornography possesses only one. . . . [Pornography's] success is physical, measurable, quantifiable; in it the common pursuit of true judgement comes to a dead halt. . . . [It] falls into the same category as such simpler forms of literary utterance as propaganda and advertising. Its aim is to move us in the direction of action . . . [and] although pornography is obsessed with the idea of pleasure, of infinite pleasure, the idea of gratification, of an end to pleasure . . . cannot develop.

The history of advertising also tells us about the early influence of movies on advertising texts and images, such as use of cinematic "close-ups" and movie-star endorsements. Utilizing methodologies of film analysis that consider framing, cutting, and lighting techniques in addition to narrative and plot clarifies how processes of objectification work both within images and in the act of spectatorship.[8]

Viewing intimate apparel advertising within the longer history of female objectification in Western culture is particularly useful because the highly

educated white, Protestant, professional men who worked in the burgeoning advertising industry in the early twentieth century clearly drew upon
well-established images in creating ads. However, admen expressed ambivalence about using images because they evoked the hucksterism and
charlatan quality of patent-medicine ads and bottle labels from which these
elite professionals sought to distance themselves. The continuing use, long
after her death, of Lydia Pinckham's image and endorsement on the tonic
that bore her name was one of many such scandals that haunted advertising in this period. Yet the lure of images remained compelling, even as the
proliferation of advertising in daily life made it harder for a single ad to attract and hold consumers' attention. This was true even for proponents of
"reason-why" advertising, who favored advertising based on facts and
logic. However, reason-why ads often included illustrations of products and
representations of intended users and authoritative figures to produce an
aura of common sense that enabled readers to justify purchasing one brand
over another. Reason-why advertising thus cannot be entirely separated
from its presumed opposite, the image-centered "atmosphere" ad.[9]

Although some historians see the two approaches as alternate and cycli-
cal, the methods coexisted. Agencies used reason-why or atmosphere ads to
sell different sorts of products and to define themselves. Becoming well-
known for using one strategy or the other was a way for an agency to advertise its services to potential clients. Moreover, some intimate apparel advertising used both strategies, because, even early in the century, the visual
appeal of these garments was a central selling point. Although some ads depicted garments on their own, most portrayed them on female figures that
inevitably represented particular constructions of femininity. These ads
therefore invoked "atmosphere" rather than "fact." Perhaps, then, the tactic of the invisible woman suited admen's need to maneuver among the demands and standards of their industry. By withholding parts of the female
body, they could represent a greater "truth."[10]

· · · · ·

Intimate apparel advertisements first appeared in women's magazines in the
1870s. The explosion of this medium after 1893, when magazines became
dependent primarily on advertising rather than subscriptions and sales for
income, increased the presence of undergarment ads in print circulation.
The 1895 founding of the trade journal *Women's & Infants' Furnisher* also
stimulated the reproduction of intimate apparel advertisements in women's
magazines, because the coordination of wholesale and retail promotion became an important tool for merchandising brand-name goods nationally.[11]

The invisible woman of intimate apparel advertising first surfaced in 1914, but not without controversy. According to Warner Brothers lore, some publications refused to print the company's first drawing of the Redfern Corset Lady, a female figure wearing Warner's Redfern corset over a chemise, presumably because editors considered it too erotic. Viewed from the side, this bare-shouldered figure's fallen chemise straps rest upon her rounded upper arms, while she crouches on shod feet and addresses a small dog standing on its hind legs. The woman's parted knees and legs establish not only her three-dimensionality and ability to balance while corseted but also her erotic positioning. In the revised drawing ultimately accepted for publication, "Warner's removed everything possible except the corset." However, as the company notes in its 1964 ninetieth-anniversary publication, the amended version was both "modest and sensational" because the disappearance of shoulders, arms, upper torso, thighs, and calves did not prohibit erotic speculations; indeed, the lack of these body features encouraged them. Though much of the figure had disappeared from the ad, a *New York Tribune* columnist paid poetic tribute to the beauty of the Redfern Corset Lady, concluding, "Far away discretion's chain I throw, Lady, for I feel I know you better than most any other girl I know."[12] Paradoxically, this columnist's lack of information about a woman's body becomes a source of knowledge about her. His comment implies that bodily erasure enables objectification and allows the male onlooker to impose a simulation of female subjectivity.

Three years later, *Harper's Weekly* contributor Oliver Herford used the Redfern Corset Lady to ridicule elite women's activities. He humorously suggested that society columns use this type of graphic to illustrate the life and deeds of "the Society Lady." Herford draws a connection between "The New Advertising," which displays women's bodies and their intimate apparel, and women's greater public presence.

> The Corset Lady . . . specializes on the corset she is created to display, leaving other excellent points which might distract the attention to the imagination. The Society Lady, on the other hand, does not desire to advertise her corset, her only object is to advertise herself. . . . In the accompanying pictures of Mrs. Seymour Fentolin—at the Ball, the Opera, Palm Beach, and the Flatiron Building—we have tried to show how by eliminating all superfluous sartorial distractions the conscientious observer may arrive at some pleasing mental conceptions of the real Mrs. Seymour Fentolin.[13]

Herford's illustrations of a partially invisible yet obviously nude Society Lady provided a means for containing women's greater public visibility in

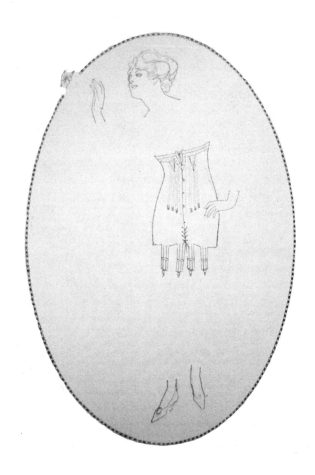

Figure 39. This ad features the invisible Redfern Corset
Lady. *Vogue,* April 1915.

the 1910s as pleasure seekers, workers, progressive reformers, consumers, and suffragists. Constructing women as sexualized objects that are subject to the probing male gaze muted modern women's threat to masculine privilege.[14]

The invisible woman of intimate apparel advertising inspired Herford's erotic vision of nude women in public. His fantasy also unintentionally comments on the blurring of distinctions between explicitly erotic images and advertising images of women in this period. Ironically, men's exclusive access to erotic images of female bodies declined as such images proliferated. In addition, women's greater appearance in and claims to public space in the 1910s lessened male control over the circumstances of viewing women's bodies. As Herford notes, by placing the invisible woman in the service of advertising, companies put more emphasis on the object for sale than they would if the advertising figure were fully represented. However, because women purchase most commodities, a different meaning exists for male spectators, for whom the displayed female body also becomes an object for visual consumption.

Many corset ads in the 1910s eschewed the sensational visual appeal of figures like the Redfern Corset Lady and used reason-why techniques to extol the benefits of this controversial garment. However, some ads relied on both reason and atmospheric imagery. A 1915 ad explained why "the women of the world choose Gossard corsets": "The only reason that there are a few countries still without Gossard Corsets is because demand has always exceeded the supply. And why? Many reasons come to our mind, but there is one which covers them all: 'Figure improvement usually means health, and health always means beauty. The Gossard Corset, which laces in front, assures an immediate figure improvement with its attendant joys—health, beauty and comfort.' There you have the reason."[15]

An illustration of a fashion parade of beautiful women, identified by country of origin and dressed in impressionistically drawn chemises, detailed line-drawn corsets, and high-heeled shoes, surround this appeal to reason. Floating in heavenly space, the figures provide a different type of entreaty. Their coy facial expressions of self-fulfillment, emphasized by graceful gestures that end in self-referential touching of the body, form an appeal based on sensuality, physical attraction, and erotic satisfaction. The visual dissimilarity between these figures and their realistic corsets invokes the corsets' disciplinary function of imposing restraint upon such feelings, whereas the made-up faces and curved figures eroticize such discipline.

This ad also bases its appeals on the unique qualities of the Gossard brand, including a claim to fashion authoritativeness and an invitation to join the "vast army of women" who belong to the "Gossard family" world-wide. We might more accurately, therefore, classify this ad as "reason-why not" advertising, because the numerous reasons it suggests seek to overwhelm any opposition. The ad reveals the difficulties of using reason-why techniques to sell underwear and foundation garments, as defending their use required constant reformulations to justify continued purchase.

Assuming the necessity of undergarments is one method of constructing reason in ads. Yet ads also contain implicit or explicit critiques of undergarments that undermine such logic. If "there is no dread or discomfort to a Mysteria" reducing corset, buying this brand rather than others that cause such problems is quite sensible. Yet common claims such as "no 'hiking up'; no strain thru the crotch," "no ugly crease marks," and "won't ride up . . . the magic inset . . . entirely eliminates the annoying discomfort of bones" indicate that these garments were generally very troubling. By mentioning dread, discomfort, and strain, such ads suggest that wearing this apparel may not be reasonable at all.[16]

Amid the widespread public debate in the 1910s about the benefits or harmful effects of corsets, some advertisements spelled out the ills corsets could inflict: "Dame Fashion has a new world to cater to. It must heed the call of those who say 'Leave us our health. Do nothing to tamper with our natural shapes and proper functions. Leave our livers free to act, our blood free to circulate, our limbs free to move. We wish to be active and vigorous and above all we desire to remain young and healthy as long as we can.' To you we say, 'Wear the Frolaset.'"

Other ads, which linked modernity to women's vocal demands for change, strove to persuade readers that purchasing the featured undergarments enabled them to share in a critique of previous cultural and physical repression: "Think of the 'Girl of To-day.' No longer a cramped, unnatural figure with hampered limbs and mincing tread. . . . The athletic girl chooses a Bon Ton Model because the lines of her corset must follow in perfect accord the contour of active body and rippling muscles. . . . Modern ideals of natural grace and beauty of form find their fullest expression in the wearing of Bon Ton Corsets."[17]

Advertisements for other undergarments also broached such appeals. On the eve of the achievement of women's suffrage, an ad connected the wearing of Futurist combinations to emerging political and sexual liberties: "Emancipation from undergarments that irk and bind, that is the promise Futurist keeps. So softly fitting, it gives lithe freedom to one's every movement. Daintily feminine, it is a delight to dress over. Futurist has entered the discriminating boudoir, a welcome guest." Redefining women's propriety within consumption equated freedom of movement with ease of dressing, while sexual behavior remained circumscribed by gearing newly legitimated sensual feelings toward purchasable objects rather than persons.[18]

Advertisements often couched appeals in terms that spoke to the contradictions of contemporary social relations. One such category of advertising played with the dichotomies of "freedom and support" and "restraint and control." In the immediate postsuffrage period, a College Girl corset ad explained that control is organic to the female body, posing a counterargument to demands for freedom. The "natural 'lines of control' which give shape to the human form . . . are the spine, the lines of the supporting pelvic basin, and the thigh. . . . College Girl corset construction parallels those lines exactly." Similarly, ads highlighting fashion concerns imbued corsetry with desired freedoms and needed control: "Let's determine to be beautiful, but let's not sacrifice one iota of our freedom. . . . That means a Modart Corset, of course." By incorporating women's desires for freedom, such ads sought to maintain acceptance of restraint in achieving a stylish silhouette.[19]

Yet intimate apparel advertisers of the 1920s struggled to restore the dominance of beauty and style as dressing concerns. Critiques of dress that elevated the importance of freedom and comfort undermined the coupling of beauty and pain, and propriety and restraint, that had supported foundation sales. The Kenlastic fabric company suggested that "the freedom of the modern woman is fully expressed in the . . . Brassiere Cor-Set . . . a model that gives you the right body support without restriction." "This new freedom in corsets," the company also assured, means women are "in no way . . . conscious of any slightest restraint."[20] Manufacturers, by denying that their products physically restricted wearers or by disavowing conscious awareness of such restriction, enabled emancipation and fashionable restraint to coexist.

The shorter ad copy of the 1930s and 1940s succinctly expressed these now-familiar claims in slogans like "Controlled Uplift . . . the New Freedom Bra" or simply "Control and Freedom." Further explanation was unnecessary: freedom could be "youthful," "sleek," "unhampered," or even "forever." However, even with "Freedom under Control," the Lite manufacturing company exclaimed, "Lady alive! This is blessed freedom at last," indicating that, indeed, freedom promised is freedom denied. Advertisers thus modified guarantees. When you "scarcely know you're wearing a girdle" or "hardly know you're wearing" a Delineator bra, freedom results from a denial of knowledge. A further retreat was evident in Carter's Foundations offer of only "a new sense of freedom." And, whether Silf-Skin's [sic] conclusion that "the birds in the air are no freer than you" is a sad com-

Figure 40. This ad combines commonly seen themes of fantasy, freedom, and high art suggested by ballet poses. *Vogue*, May 1947.

mentary or a utopian vision, Blue Swan Lingerie's "Fantasy in Freedom" slogan navigated such difficulties by distinguishing happy illusions from more binding reality. Ad placement could enhance similar conceptual appeals. A 1952 "equalizer bra" ad resonated with the themes in *Ebony* articles: an African American woman wearing the bra stands below the slogan "Now . . . all women are created equal," with "created" slashed out and replaced with "made."[21]

Intimate apparel ads emphasized beauty for many decades.[22] Some 1920s ads bypassed issues of freedom and comfort by referring only to products' pleasing visual effects. De Bevoise described its products as "brassieres that beautify," and Model Brassiere touted its bra as "everywhere noted for its beauty—worn by noted beauties everywhere." Lily of France went one step further in the mantralike "The Lily of France is the beautiful corset worn

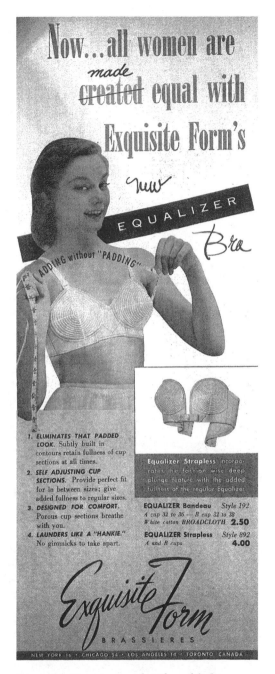

Figure 41. Drawing on the idea of fashion as a democratizing force, this ad appeared during the nascent era of civil rights activism, six months before *Brown v. Board of Education* was first argued before the Supreme Court. *Ebony*, May 1952. Courtesy, Exquisite Form/ VF Corporation.

by beautiful women to make them more beautiful." However, as one 1931 ad explained, "Life is still a beauty contest . . . but the rules are new." Beauty might not have to mean discomfort, but it did mean work on "a symphony of self-improvement . . . that can only be accomplished with . . . professional assistance." Whereas control had earlier been naturalized as organic to the body, beauty was now externalized as a constellation of commodity effects performed on the body. "Feminine beauty as an individual creation" meant "that the enjoyment of beauty is a matter of choice—not of chance." By fostering a sense of expanding opportunities for women, copywriters framed intimate apparel advertisements within a language of options and freedoms that encouraged women to achieve "a figure from which all natural imperfections have been removed." Technological assistance for this aim became especially crucial in the postwar era when heightened concerns about the potential loss of femininity helped remove women from higher-paying jobs. As one 1944 ad explained, "Beauty alone is not sufficient. . . . Laboratory research . . . prolongs . . . beauty . . . beyond present expectations." This point was also clear in advertising images that showed female figures emerging from test tubes in intimate apparel laboratories.[23]

. . . . .

A 1950 Bali Brassiere Company ad stressing beauty asserted, "Beauty is no accident! It's carefully made up . . . of the shape of your hair, the color of your lipstick, the flair of your clothes." Selling the Bali brassiere as integral to this orchestration of appearance required the active participation of the female consumer, because "like every beauty secret . . . you must discover it yourself . . . in the fitting room." The world of "beauty secrets" thus relies upon the complicity of the customer in constructing a specialized beauty epistemology that defines knowledge as mystery, and upon her absorption into a practice in which shared information is privileged and confidential. Such information must remain so because "the world's best kept secret" is not only the "Très Secrète Inflatable Bra" but also the notion that exhibiting femininity, analyzed since the mid-twentieth century as a masquerade, requires work.[24]

A photograph of a brassiere-clad woman removing a carnival mask in the Très Secrète ad underscores the edgy, persistent concern of intimate apparel advertisements with feminine masquerade.[25] Because of intimate apparel's central role in constructing this masquerade, secrecy, hidden knowledge, and magical practices form important advertising themes, surfacing regularly in ads promoting appearances that, they insist, must convey both knowing and not knowing. Intimate apparel is especially emblematic of this contradictory foundation of beauty knowledge because although undergarments are usually hidden by outerwear, the silhouette they create depends upon the type of undergarments worn. Intimate apparel is thus both seen and not seen, in the sense that, for example, it is usually clear whether or not a woman is wearing a brassiere. "The secret behind the new silhouette," which a 1947 Francette Foundations advertisement addressed by touting a "private wire" sewn into its combination garment, may not really be a secret after all. Being at once revealing and concealing may indeed be the "definite need" that the Gossard "Secret Panel satisfies . . . as no other girdle ever could."[26]

Mystery and secrecy are often invoked and then resolved within ads. This process reproduces the state of both knowing and not knowing by retaining information within a covert realm known only to adepts. Copy from the 1920s through the 1950s, such as "But what is the secret of keeping a youthful figure as you go on in life? The answer is—the right kind of corset" and "Double diagonal pull. The real secret of the French look," suggests categories of secret knowledge about the alchemies of preserving youth and becoming "French." The merging of technological and occult knowledge, an important part of twentieth-century beauty epistemology, is clear in "Suspants . . . mysteriously hugs your waist whether you bend, twist or stand on your head. The secret is the new 'pivot-point' bias pattern" and in "Here's A'Lure! It's a love of a bra! The secret . . . Warner's exclusive all-elastic bands." Other information remains a confidence only shared between advertiser and purchaser: "Shhh! they're padded . . . but no one will ever know."[27]

The evocation of magic dispensed with the need for facts. Slogans such as "Weight simply disappears in a Mysteria reducing corset," "This new magical brassiere makes women young in bust beauty!" and "Complete figure magic is yours with Toni Lee—the honest to goodness Built-In Brassiere-Top Slip" assume no need to spell out actual methods. Furthermore, blending secrecy with magic can stem lingering questions: "Its secret magic laces give you a fresh custom-made fitting every day." "Our secret! Double diagonal power-pull. . . . Works wonders. Inches vanish like magic." One ad that combines secrecy, magic, and confidentiality appears to provide all the answers: "Magically, beautifully, naturally—your bust appears fuller, lovelier under all your fashions in Peter Pan's exciting new Hidden Treasure. No gadgets, no devices—never a fear of detection. The secret's in the patented 'Magicup.' Keeps its shape—and yours."[28]

After World War II, related concepts such as miracles, dreams, fantasies,

witchery, and spells became even more common in ads. Paranormal explanations of the effects of wearing intimate apparel were no doubt related to
the reimposition of a constricted waistline in fashionable dress. This style,
named the New Look in 1947, brought back boned foundation garments,
even for young women, to create a feminized silhouette that reenvisioned
gender divisions that had been muted by the mobilization of women's labor
during World War II. The greater importance placed on marriage and maternity in this period reformulated gender distinctions, leading to concep-
tualizations of men as unwilling partners and women as tricksters ever
ready to "trap" them. Intimate apparel ads supported this idea in their construction of the female body as lure and of women as adepts who use undergarments as tools of sorcery to gain power over men. A mid-1950s ad exemplifies this trend: "Do you know this woman? She's the femme fatale
who invoked the cosmetic arts, but whose figure evoked no admiration.
Then she was transformed by Peter Pan black Magic which raised her spirits, and enchanted her friends!" Similarly, although "Warner's Merry
Widow makes you the most bewitching charmer of any evening," sorcery
could benefit the wearer more directly: "See how Warner's witchery weaves
a spell of breathe-easy comfort, keeps you breathlessly beautiful."[29]

Glamour is an overarching category in which ads incorporate "time-
less" skills such as charm, magic, and occult practices as well as allusions
to style, grace, and sexual attractiveness. References to glamour appeared
as early as the 1910s in *Vogue*, though glamour did not become a staple of
intimate apparel descriptions until the 1930s. In that decade, ads ascribed
glamour to commodities ranging from "Every-Day Foods in a Glamorous
Guise" to "Marly [perfume] . . . men are in your debt for the glamor you
lend to women." A 1933 shoe advertisement conveys the novelty of using
this approach by asking, "What is this thing called Glamour?" and offering an intriguing answer: "A magic quality—an aura of grace and beauty
that bewitches—charms—enchants. Glamour! You see it in a beautiful
woman—in a precious gem—in all things that have beauty and perfection. . . . I. Miller shoes, too, possess glamour." This definition objectifies
and commodifies the "beautiful woman" by equating her with "a precious
gem" and by constructing the magic aura of glamour in both as "natural."
Yet significantly, made as well as found objects like precious stones may
"possess glamour." By ascribing the capacity of ownership to objects like
shoes, ads implied that whether or not the reader has innate beauty and
perfection, she might possess glamour by purchasing and displaying
glamorous commodities. The "Secret Charm," as Celebrity Bra Inc. explained, is "the bra that makes glamour fully yours." The magic of glam-

Figure 42. This visually compelling image effectively combines motifs of female masquerade, secrecy, magic, and the transformative power of intimate apparel. *Harper's Bazaar* (November 1956).

our makes the rare common, while maintaining an aura of wondrous exceptionality for all who possess it.[30]

Advertisements that asserted the glamour of intimate apparel focused on beauty, perfection in fit and silhouette, allure, and elite status to give their claims credence. New York fashion models used "Fortuna Flatums for Figure Glamour . . . 'neath glamorous clothes." The models' credo, "My figure is my fortune," explained the meaning of the Fortuna style name, and the stakes involved, and implied the slippage from body to figure to commodity that the process of objectification entails. Mass production allowed democratic participation in this process: the "Equalizer Bra in 'adding without padding' . . . adds glamour" to all women. The many appeals to glamour in postwar intimate apparel advertising also suggest a growing desire for and the availability of glamour for purchase, as a means of enhancing attractiveness.[31]

As the Manhattan Undergarment Company pointed out in its assertion

Figure 43. This intimate scene evokes the erotic glamour of women in high-fashion, tightly fitted girdles. *Ebony,* May 1953. Courtesy, Exquisite Form/VF Corporation.

that "a slip can be glamorous if it fits properly," precision is essential to achieve glamour. The Newform slips promised to do so and thus "glorify your figure." According to such ads, a woman can achieve glamour by literally conforming her body to commercial standards not unlike those that define the output of mass production itself. In these ads, women become glorified and glamorous by submitting to the status of commodity, because these transcendent qualities facilitate the transition from subject to object.[32]

Intimate apparel "miracles" offered powerful possibilities for self-transformations. A young woman and her mother found the life-changing miracle of Gossard corsets in a 1919 full-page ad that used the style of magazine fiction.[33] In 1933, when suggestions of miracles might be especially appealing because of the severe depression, Vassarette foundation garments had "miraculous powers of restraint" though they were "feather-light little things." Rubber Products, Inc., promoted Lastex fabric as "The Miracle Yarn That Makes Things Fit" in the 1930s and 1940s, while other 1950s garments provided "heavenly comfort."[34] Miracles thus came unexpectedly, from a higher authority that dispensed pleasure to women. In these formulations, women accept technological knowledge on a faith that links spiritual joy with binding garments.

· · · · ·

Intimate apparel ads that incorporated the notion of dreams invited more active participation by female readers. These ads drew upon an important cultural convention; defining human dreams in terms of commodity purchase and ownership had played a powerful part in shaping mass consumption since the mid-nineteenth century. According to Rosalind Williams, entrepreneurs constructed new commercial spaces like department stores and trade expositions as materialized "dream worlds," thus merchandising consumer goods as realized fantasies. Moreover, Williams asserts, the act of marketing fantasy caused dreams to lose their "liberating possibilities as alternatives to daylight reality." The pervasive presence of commercialized dreams in daily life overwhelmed their radical potential by uniformly presenting consumption as the fulfillment of fantasies.[35]

During this postwar period, for example, one ad claimed that a Perma-Lift girdle "curves you and molds you, and holds you like a dream"; others suggested that "Barbizon's Nylon Satin [is] Dream come-true fabric" and that a "Warner-Wonderful girdle or corselette" can "accent your charms, give you the most intriguing silhouette you've ever dreamed of." Such copy assumed that women dreamed of enhancing their physical attraction by wearing figure-shaping garments and promoted the view that women could easily fulfill their imaginative desires through commodity purchase. However, this motif also resonates in the anxious dreams of advertisers. For example, a 1952 *Vogue* advertisement for the Brand Names Foundation, which called itself a "Non-Profit Education Foundation," asked, "Who is the Girl in the dreams of ten thousand men?" The foundation conceded that "unlike most dream girls she is very real! She lives and breathes—and buys! For she is you—the American consumer." Furthermore, she is "the one in the dreams . . . of America's brand manufacturers . . . the one for whom they are constantly dreaming up new products . . . to make . . . the consumer happy with the things they make." Concluding with a paean to the buyer's "freedom of choice," a result of "free competition," this ad revealed the concerns underlying industry efforts to align American women's dreams with their own.[36]

In August 1949, Maidenform launched perhaps the best-known "dream campaign" to advertise its brassieres. The first ad featured the almost predictable slogan "I dreamed I went shopping in my Maidenform bra." It was illustrated by a photograph of a woman shopping, who is fully dressed with the exception of her blouse. All of the company's dream ads portrayed women in a similar manner, exposing each woman's Maidenform bra to magazine readers as well as to spectators within the ad scenes. The campaign was so successful that Maidenform used the dream idea until 1967. In one two-month period in 1950 alone, dream-theme ads appeared in dozens of magazines, including *Harper's Bazaar, Seventeen, Glamour, Ladies' Home Journal, Cosmopolitan, True Confessions, Modern Screen, Woman's Home Companion, Good Housekeeping, True Romance,* and even *Parents.* The ads' popularity inspired traveling fashion shows at department stores nationwide. Numerous store-window displays used mannequins with blowups of dream ads as backdrops. Within a year of launching the ads, Maidenform could claim that the "dream fantasy" had become a "national catchword." Satirized by comedians and used as a basis for daring outfits at costume parties, the ads had indeed entered American popular culture.[37]

Dream themes in early 1950s Maidenform ads included the ordinary and the fantastic, the trivial and the ambitious. "I dreamed I went to the flower show" and "I dreamed I went sightseeing" lay within the purview of acceptable feminine behavior, as did "I dreamed I danced the Charleston" and "I dreamed I went to the theater." The spectacles evoked in these themes double the voyeuristic impact of the ads' visuals. The Maidenform woman is a spectator at the events depicted in the ads, but, due to her state of undress, is also a spectacle herself. Other dream themes pushed the bounds of permissible feminine behavior. "I dreamed I was a toreador," "I dreamed I was a lady ambassador," and "I dreamed I was a lady editor" invite fantasies about, and perhaps criticism of, the types of job opportunities available to most women readers at the time. Though the images of half-dressed women fulfilling these career desires undercuts readers' ability to take these dreams seriously (as does the modifying "lady"), these Maidenform ads gave expression to women's employment fantasies at a time when many white middle-class suburban housewives—some of whom had worked during the war—were feeling unhappily confined at home. Though a growing number of working-class and professional women worked for wages in the 1950s, the Maidenform dream images marked women's frustrated ambitions since they largely validated readers' beliefs that a person who wears a brassiere may never do more than dream about such adventures and challenges, and that even if she succeeds, her male coworkers will always be aware of her bodily difference—and limit her opportunities—whether she wears a blouse or not.[38]

In the 1950s, sexual fantasy provided another outlet for women who felt constrained by domesticity and saw limited openings for well-paid and challenging employment. The Maidenform ads certainly drew upon the quite common fantasy—or nightmare—of appearing undressed in public. However, as one critic points out, women in these Maidenform ads are "surprisingly uninhibited," exhibiting no embarrassment, shame, or fear about their incompletely dressed state. The ads are not unlike the 1910s ads featuring the Redfern Corset Lady, which, by stimulating spectators to imagine what women look like underneath their clothes, encouraged a view of women in public as sexualized objects. Thus, the ads worked to contain women's public presence in the 1950s through objectification and through fantasies that eroticized female desires for better opportunities.[39]

· · · · ·

An emphasis on the difference between female and male bodies is central to Maidenform fantasies of public undress, in which breasts are the primary objects on display. In contrast, the restraint of female flesh and suppression of intractable difference, emphasized in ads that promoted reduction, pointed to the disappearance of women's bodies. Reduction of flesh was an explicit concern of many foundation-garment ads in the 1910s and 1920s. Rubber garments were particularly marketed for their minimizing ability. "Girdle pants," for example, "reduce the limbs, hips, abdomen, and as far above the waist-line as desired." La Resista promised readers, "You can be slender as you wish" wearing a "Perspiro-Massage Band for dissolving abdominal fat." Many such ads used reason-why approaches, as in "The idea

I dreamed I was
a lady editor in my

maidenform bra

Nice work if you can get it... making headlines in a *Maidenform*® bra! What a glamorous means of support... I'm so well-rounded, such a fabulous figure in fashionable circles. No wonder I get such a lift from this dreamy bra!

Shown: Maidenform's *Allo-ette*® 2-inch band in white satin; also available in nylon taffeta or marquisette, and broadcloth ... from 2.00. Send for free style booklet, Maidenform, N. Y. 16.

There is a *maidenform* for every type of figure.

®Reg. U. S. Pat. Off. ©1951, Maiden Form Brassiere Company, Inc.
Costume: Mr. John, Shoes, Julianelli

Figure 44. This ad from Maidenform's signature campaign describes both the elusive "dream" job and the accessible mass-produced brassiere as a "glamorous means of support." *Harper's Bazaar*, March 1951. Courtesy, Maidenform.

of reducing by a rubber garment is unquestionably correct. Doctors endorse it on hygienic grounds; women find it restores youthful slenderness." Bon Ton went further, asserting that "dead tissue and waste matter are eliminated" by its reducing corset. The importance of this disappearance should not be underestimated. As Bon Ton also noted, "What a world of difference in the loss of just a Few Small Pounds."[40]

The decline of the 1920s flapper silhouette meant a return to waist definition in the 1930s. Perfolastic proposed in 1933 that "now is the ideal time to reduce," backing its claim with testimonials from satisfied users of the Perfolastic reducing girdle. " 'I reduced from 43 inches to 34½ inches' writes Miss Brian. . . . 'The fat seems to have melted away' . . . writes Mrs. McSorley." By the late 1930s, inducements for reduction were not always so direct, and advertisements often used puns. The wholesome underwear firm Carter's challenged readers to "Waist away in good form." Its "teens group" of foundation garments had "a pet hate on waistlines. Stubborn thighs, rebel torsos and obvious rears, too. . . . What's more, you can depend on them to do something about it. In a velvet-glove manner, tho." Though perhaps less overtly painful than an iron-fisted method, Carter's description of the resistance of young female flesh to its own evisceration is nonetheless disturbing.[41]

After World War II, Warner's pledged "to give you the new small waist with utmost comfort." In this period of increased waist constriction, companies promised to "whittle" and "make little of your waist" and extolled the virtues of "belittlin' you [to make] the most of your charms." The importance of such "waist-cinching" in maintaining a youthful appearance is captured in Jantzen's 1952 ad slogan "Take two inches off your age!" These jaunty suggestions conceptualize the body as an object subject to partition. Certain bodily areas are defined as excessive and dispensable; others are to be controlled and disciplined. In this case, the redefinition of beauty standards in terms of a small waist and youthful appearance distracts readers from the sinister implications of repeated calls to women readers to "waist away."[42]

. . . . .

The use of "invisible women" in advertising also encouraged the diminution of female bodies, beginning with the Redfern Lady created in 1914 because of censorship concerns. The hidden nature of undergarments, and their dual status as seen and unseen, explains one aspect of invisible women's popularity and longevity. When undergarments reshape the body, the silhouette they form masquerades as the "natural" body. Ads using this device comment on the concern that underwear, and the duties it performs, be revealed and thus expose the wearer's beauty as fraudulent. The Redfern Wrap-Around, for example, "eliminates the difference between the real and the ideal, between your own figure and the silhouette of fashion. But its presence is unsuspected." "Beauty . . . seen and unseen" might also be best achieved without the sense of touch, as in the "Kickernick Idea in Underwear . . . Clothing is comfortable only when you can not feel it." This ambivalence about the sight and touch of underwear in marketing was evident in many advertisements with invisible women. Renditions of bodily transparency, disappearance, dismemberment, and mutilation; graphic placements of the body in shadow and in "negative" outline; and the portrayal of undergarments on a body that is not visible all document ongoing preoccupations with the status of the female body, the meaning of representations of undressed women in nonpornographic mass media, and the construction of female spectatorship.[43]

Foundation manufacturers used transparency to promote underwear sales both before and after the Camp Transparent Woman appeared in the 1930s. Modart's 1915 series of ads afforded views of its front-laced designs by showing them on fully dressed women whose clothing was transparent in critical areas. These illustrations of stylish women in darkly colored dress give the spectator "X-ray vision" in that the white outlines of the corsets appear like the bones in radiological photographs. Again, here is the equation of corset/*corps* (body) and stays/bones so as to objectify the body by confusing it with a commodified garment.[44]

A 1921 P. N. Practical Front Corset ad depicts a different sort of transparency. The ad lauds the corset's fit, declaring that "it is as though there were an invisible fitter of rare cleverness constantly at hand in Madame's own boudoir." The transparent "phantom fitter" attends to Madame's laces while standing within a dressing table and bending forward from a mirror. Other ads use two or more figures to convey transparency. Warner's series of Le Gant girdle ads from the mid-1930s show two female figures wearing foundation garments, stockings, and high heels. The women appear in various situations, such as dressing for skiing or bowling. To convey the movement possible in the Le Gant girdle, the ad shows one figure crouching while the other, a transparent figure, stands. In one 1935 ad, the crouching figure retrieves a ball of yarn that the standing figure has dropped while knitting. A Gossard series of ads in the late 1940s shows a woman enveloped by her own large and overpowering shadow, and a 1947 Alene Bra ad depicts a transparent woman through whom the spectator can see two partially drawn companions.[45]

In addition to transparency, shadows and darkness abound in intimate apparel ads. A 1923 Model Brassiere ad depicts "the concealed cause of the attractive Silhouette" in a drawing of a woman's silhouette illuminated behind a curtain. In addition, numerous photographic images place bodies dressed in undergarments in deep shadow. Such images most often obscure heads and faces, though limbs regularly receive the same treatment. These body parts are also apt to be missing from the multiplicity of photographic and line-drawn ads that depict incomplete female bodies and torsos. From a marketing standpoint, these tactics keep the spectator's focus on the area of the body most relevant to the garment of interest. Yet such representations also underscore the additionally self-serving division of the body into parts that the viewer can scrutinize individually for flaws. Parts that do not measure up, as most never do, can be rectified through the purchase of the proper corrective garments. The mutilation implied in the commercial portrayal of partial, half-dressed female bodies, the analytic dismemberment that women must perform, and the reshaping that garments achieve all come to the fore in a 1924 Snuggleband ad. The soft, almost impressionistic, focus of the photograph reveals a woman's body from her mouth to her upper thigh. She wears a shiny white Snuggleband girdle and drapes a scarf around her shoulders. Her bare chest reveals no hint of breasts or nipples; this advertiser dealt with "extraneous" body parts by dispensing with them altogether.[46]

That shadows and silhouettes imply disappearance is clear in a 1929 Model Brassiere Company advertisement for its combination foundation garment Scanties. The drawing of a woman in a Scanty and high heels fronts a series of ever-lighter shadows that gradually disappear behind her. However, this image, and ads with images of a woman both dressed and undressed, illustrates that wearing such garments is the only way for the female body to be seen. In many of these latter ads, the dressed figure is in shadow, whereas the underwear-clad figure is in light.[47]

Disappearance of flesh also finds expression in ads that depict the body "in negative," in both drawn and photographic representations. In drawn versions, the body is a dark silhouette with white outlines and wears white garments. Often faces are complete blanks, with no features whatsoever. A variant portrayal shows the drawn negative woman with a hand in front of her face, a common gesture in ads.[48] Negative reversal of the body, images that obscure the face with hands or shadows, and regular exclusion of faces and limbs undermine these depictions as portrayals of fully realized female subjects. Instead, these images represent female bodies as commodified fantasy objects upon which readers can project their own facial image.[49]

· · · · ·

Figure 45. The corselette name, Shadow Garment, underscores the placement of this woman in shadows, a common practice in intimate apparel ads. *Corsets & Brassieres*, April 1928. Courtesy of Special Collections, Gladys Marcus Library, Fashion Institute of Technology. Courtesy, Warnaco Inc.

Invisible women like the Redfern Lady appeared in intimate apparel depictions through the early 1950s. They were particularly common in fashion magazine articles on the latest trends in undergarments, rather than in advertisements themselves, though ads and articles often featured the same merchandise.[50] Companies advertised in fashion magazines to get mentioned in fashion articles, and often the articles and ad copy were indistinguishable from one another. Articles and ads thus reinforced each other in fashion magazines' overall aim of influencing fashion trends. Research on the way that women read magazines supports the idea that ads and articles

Figure 46. Depicting women as "negatives" undermines their status as fully realized subjects. *Corsets & Brassieres,* December 1933. Courtesy of Special Collections, Gladys Marcus Library, Fashion Institute of Technology.

were equally important sources of information for readers. Particularly since the 1920s, when ads were more fully interspersed among articles, ads and articles were equally effective in catching the attention of readers looking through magazines. This pattern was especially evident in fashion magazines, given that the central purpose of these publications is display and description of garments currently available for sale.[51]

Invisible women in advertisements and fashion layouts also facilitated the graphic presentation of narcissism, voyeurism, exhibitionism, and fetishism. These sexualized categories of looking and possessing describe erotic relationships between subject and object, viewer and viewed, and owner and possession. Though ads for all sorts of products drew upon these

Figure 47. The body appears in parts: in this ad, flowerpots take the place of women's heads, and female torsos appear without arms. *Harper's Bazaar*, October 1956.

relationships to induce sales, the sexual associations of intimate apparel meant that ads for these products were more likely to incorporate eroticism. Understanding how intimate apparel advertisements positioned the underwear-clad female body in erotic relationships is important to understanding how these ads provided pleasure for female viewers.

Mirrors, which are overt signals of narcissism, appeared frequently in undergarment advertising. In *Captains of Consciousness*, Stuart Ewen notes the widespread use of mirrors in advertisements of many products for women in the 1920s. He suggests that women viewed themselves critically in these mirrors, ever reminded that their survival depended on maintaining an appearance attractive to men. However, although mirrors certainly serve this self-negating function, they also facilitate women's narcissistic pleasure. And though portrayals of women gazing at their reflections provide a stunted view of spectatorship, they create spectatorship nonetheless. Thus, the pleasure women take in narcissistic self-gazing grows out of the more general pleasure of active looking. The numerous images of women viewing their reflections in handheld mirrors suggest that the women depicted have made an active decision to engage in this activity. Moreover, by representing women's pleasure in viewing female images, these ads double

Formfit Girdleieres

Figure 48. This 1920s mirror scene illustrates the pleasure of viewing oneself. *Corsets & Lingerie*, May 1925. Courtesy of Special Collections, Gladys Marcus Library, Fashion Institute of Technology. Courtesy, Jockey International, Inc.

the activity of the female magazine reader, and thus validate her pleasure in selecting images of women for her own viewing enjoyment.[52]

Mirror images of female figures also appear in ads that have no visible mirror to explain the duplication. These renditions supported female readers' view of the magazine as a mirror for their own reflection. They also suggested that readers did not always see idealized magazine images of fashionable women in self-critical terms or as anxiety-producing triggers for unfavorable self-comparisons. Instead, female readers might derive pleasure from seeing these images as reflections of themselves. A deceptively complex 1929 Poirette ad illustrates this possibility. The purported reflection of a stylishly drawn figure in corset, stockings, and heels extends over the "edge" of a surface that at first appears to be two-dimensional. The figure's surprising three-dimensional folding over evokes the magazine page itself, which readers are invited to enter through pleasurable fantasy.[53]

Few intimate apparel ads openly represent the self-critical aspect of mirror gazing. One 1921 ad that does, portrays a woman before a mirror that contains her husband and child's reflection instead of her own. The woman in this ad knows that her position within her marriage and household depends upon maintaining conventions of dress and body shape. Numerous other ads include a freestanding or wall-hung mirror that the woman in the ad ignores or views nonchalantly. Such images reinforce the idea that mirrors are ever-present sources for self-criticism. Yet these mirrors also invite female readers to see the magazine page as mirror. In some 1910s and 1920s ads in which women seem unconcerned about their appearance, mirrors show no reflection whatsoever. The resulting empty spaces allow readers to place their own images within the page, and may signify the narcissistic pleasure that mirrors offer. One 1915 ad depicts a woman with her back to a darkened mirror that is hung behind a drawn curtain. She engages the reader in a languorous look, perhaps presenting a self-satisfied postmirror moment, as she holds a long-stemmed rose across her lips.[54]

Women in intimate apparel ads are generally enthralled with their reflections and appear to enjoy mirror gazing thoroughly. Their autoerotic pleasure is emphasized in many ads that show women touching themselves while viewing their reflections. Some women caress their large freestanding or hanging mirrors or lovingly lean against their own images. Advertisements thus widely present narcissistic behavior as a gratifying, absorbing, and valid activity for women. And although ads certainly seek to tie narcissism to commodity consumption, these images of self-directed pleasure sometimes overwhelm the ads' directives to buy things. As in the ancient myth from which the term *narcissism* derives, one can at times simply enjoy oneself and one's reflection.[55]

Advertisements that construct the female reader as voyeur are less clear-cut in their assignment of pleasure. The call to voyeurism is evident in numerous intimate apparel ads that place underwear-clad female bodies in front of open windows and doorways. Some ads present these portals abstractly, as a series of well-spaced cross-hatched lines or empty window-frame-like apertures behind the female figure. Other, more detailed ad images, such as explicit windows with drawn or sheer curtains, emphasize that the woman is vulnerable to exposure. This vulnerability makes the invitation to look an uneasy one. As readers, women may enjoy the privileged position that voyeurism allows, in which the viewed object unknowingly reveals intimacies. However, identification with the depicted woman may provoke anxiety regarding the unwanted presence of a hidden observer. This hint of danger might be pleasurable for some women readers, especially as fantasy, but nevertheless it links pleasure to potential harm. A 1941 Formfit Foundations ad betrays this fear in the startled and anxious expression of a young woman caught in brassiere, girdle, stockings, and heels as she is about to step into her slip. A bowed female head with closed eyes strangely set in the upper corner of the ad seems to acknowledge female readers' inability to look without identifying with the viewed object. The voyeurism that intimate apparel ads offer female readers is thus not reliably pleasurable, because they may be able to participate only as viewed objects in possible peril.[56]

The construction of women "to-be-looked-at" may enhance a female reader's voyeuristic pleasure by allowing her to usurp the powerful position of viewing subject and temporarily abandon her usual position as viewed object. The female reader's familiarity with being an object on display might also render the danger in these images less threatening. In other words, she is all too accustomed to intrusive perusals. However, the partially dressed state of the female figures in intimate apparel ads would likely be unsettling not only because they suggest obvious vulnerability but also because the garments they promote are designed to correct bodily defects and hide them from public view. Such images thus reinforce the idea that women must choose their undergarments carefully, a concept that is compatible with advertising's goal of stimulating sales.[57]

Advertisements that place women in picture frames also incite voyeurism. Some of these frames clearly are to be read as apertures—or even keyholes—to intimate scenes. Explicit keyholes appeared in intimate apparel advertising as early as 1882 in an oft-reproduced trade-card image that shows a woman peering through a keyhole to discover "why Mrs. Brown has such a perfect figure." Seventy years later, a woman peers through a keyhole to find out "What goes on in her dressing room?" She sees a woman in brassiere and slip holding a telephone in one hand and a hand mirror in the other while standing in front of a louvered window with drawn curtains.[58]

Ads without keyhole voyeurs could still convey a peeping sensibility. A 1923 ad gives the impression of such secretive viewing: an octagonal frame contains a woman clad in chemise and bloomer while she sits in an easy chair and examines another undergarment. Similar intimate scenes appeared in rectangular, oval, and other geometrically shaped frames. Frames underscored the intentional exhibition of such female figures by equating them with framed paintings or photographs. However, because of the nature of intimate apparel, these ads afford views of private moments. Moreover, the framing of a figure within the magazine page doubles the spectacular nature of the female body as an object to be viewed.[59]

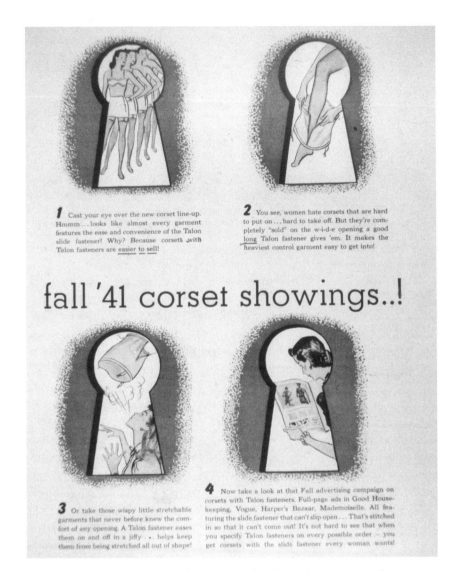

1 Cast your eye over the new corset line-up. Hmmm...looks like almost every garment features the ease and convenience of the Talon slide fastener! Why? Because corsets with Talon fasteners are easier to sell!

2 You see, women hate corsets that are hard to put on...hard to take off. But they're completely "sold" on the w-i-d-e opening a good long Talon fastener gives 'em. It makes the heaviest control garment easy to get into!

fall '41 corset showings..!

3 Or take those wispy little stretchable garments that never before knew the comfort of any opening. A Talon fastener eases them on and off in a jiffy . . helps keep them from being stretched all out of shape!

4 Now take a look at that Fall advertising campaign on corsets with Talon fasteners. Full-page ads in Good Housekeeping, Vogue, Harper's Bazaar, Mademoiselle. All featuring the slide fastener that *can't* slip open . . . That's stitched in so that it can't come out! It's not hard to see that when you specify Talon fasteners on every possible order — you get corsets with the slide fastener every woman wants!

Figure 49. Keyholes and window frames heighten the position of magazine readers as voyeurs enjoying the culturally reinforced pleasure of secretly looking at undressed women. *Corsets & Brassieres,* July 1941. Courtesy of Special Collections, Gladys Marcus Library, Fashion Institute of Technology. Courtesy, Tag-It Pacific.

Intimate apparel advertisements also displayed female bodies in implicit or explicit performance. As one comely corset model said in a 1915 ad, "Here I am. . . . I knew you would be interested to see how I look. That's why I posed for this picture."[60] This figure and numerous others like her demonstrate cognizance of being on display and appear to take pleasure in their nearly naked state of exposure. In some senses, exhibitionism provides a preferable location for the viewed object, especially when it allows expressions of defiance or erotic power along with apparent acquiescence to dominant conventions of physical beauty and dress. When these options are not available, the female body more completely takes the form of a commodity, including that of labor power.

Exhibitionist rather than voyeuristic ad images include stage curtains instead of window curtains, spotlights, performance accessories such as fans or drapery, and theatrical postures and settings. These exhibitionist images draw on a range of visual and performance-art conventions. The model's eyes may also directly engage those of the reader, conveying awareness of the onlooker's presence. This address is distinct from voyeuristic portrayals in which models are shown to be self-involved and oblivious to potential peepers. The self-conscious posing of the exhibitionist model clearly contrasts with the postures of privacy assumed by a spied-upon woman. However, a 1949 *Ebony* ad conveys both pleasure and concern about expected scrutiny: "Hits of the Season starring YOU . . . in captivating bras, designed for admiration" that give "you the glamorous lines of your favorite star . . . to win the most critical audiences!"[61]

Frames in intimate apparel ads facilitate exhibitionism as well as voyeurism. Explicitly drawn picture frames around women construct them as objects of art meant for viewing. "Painterly" renderings of female figures, connoted by simulations of brush strokes or Western high-art schools, mark these bodies as self-consciously exposed. Alternatively, posing a woman dressed in underwear next to a framed portrait of another woman suggests that the model also is an exhibited *objet d'art*. In one 1947 ad of this type, a woman whose hair and accessories evoke the manner of Degas stands before an imitation of one of this well-known artist's famous ballet scenes. Other ads place women alongside female statues or in an artist's studio. Feminist art critic Marcia Pointon notes the prevalence of such scenes in the Western high-art tradition, analyzing the way in which they express the artist's creative mastering of the female form, an achievement that conferred both masculinity and proficiency upon the male artist. The predominantly male commercial artists who drew such images were borrowing from this tradition, but they were perhaps also participating in it to confer similar status on their own artistic efforts.[62]

Advertisers'—and advertising agents'—desire to associate their products with the elegance and cachet of high art is also evident in ads that draw upon the performance arts. For example, intimate apparel ads throughout the period often presented women in corsets and slips assuming balletic poses.[63] Yet the display of female bodies in intimate apparel ads can blur distinctions between high and low performance arts. Thus, elite magazines like *Vogue* might run both "high-art" ads and ads featuring popular performance arts. Some photographic portrayals of underclad women exhibiting themselves evoke the "naughty" postcards in mass circulation since the nineteenth century. One such 1921 photographic image, of a woman in knickers and camisole glancing over her shoulder toward the spectator while pressing her body against a wall, very nearly duplicates a postcard image from the same period. Women also appear in photographic layouts reminiscent of "girlie" calendars. The "Allure in Action" of a 1947 girdle in one ad is certainly not only the "miraculous Kuron" but also the woman in brassiere, girdle, and stockings who strikes a pose similar to those in the now-famous early work of Marilyn Monroe.[64]

Multiple female figures in ads conjured the musical and chorus lines of Broadway. A 1923 photograph shot from above prefigures the cinematic work of Busby Berkeley, showing women and girls lying in a huge semicircular series of partitioned cloth compartments. A more common use of multiple bodies depicts identical female figures lined up to display variations of a particular undergarment style. These lines of bodies, like chorus lines or the replaceable bodies in Busby Berkeley's stagings, downplay distinctions among the women in the ads. Repetition of models seems to signify not only the mass duplication of commodity objects but also the degraded status of labor power as commodity central to their mass production. The duplication of idealized images within the ads thus conveys the figures' dual status as commodity objects and industrial workers, equated here with replaceable machine parts. Thus, the figures retain little sense of the personal or erotic power that exhibitionism offers.[65]

The conventions of the pinup appeared repeatedly over the years in intimate apparel advertisements. The pinup, signified by specific postures such as raised elbows with hands held behind the head and jutting of breasts or hips, often engages the spectator's gaze with a seductive come-on. Such gestures of sexual invitation and readiness let us know that the pinup intends to exhibit her body. Yet raised elbows held behind the head also widely signify surrender. Combined with the pinup's usually standardized look and body type, this

Figure 50. This ad appropriates the erotic style of illustrated pinups in midcentury calendars and men's magazines like *Esquire*. *Corsets & Brassieres*, June 1941. Courtesy of Special Collections, Gladys Marcus Library, Fashion Institute of Technology. Courtesy, Jockey International, Inc.

emblem of capitulation conveys submission to the spectator's desires. Thus, the pinup's exhibitionism is not often an autonomous pleasure.[66]

•   •   •   •   •

Images of pinups, as well as those of undressed female exhibitionists generally, typically assume that the spectator is male. However, male voyeurs rarely appear in intimate apparel advertisements. In a 1911 ad, a man in a union suit peers from behind a curtain to watch his underwear-clad wife buttoning up their daughter's Munsingwear. Though the man is barred from fully entering the scene, his identification in the ad text as a family member condones his presence. The ongoing difficulty of fully presenting male onlookers is evident in two 1952 ads. In one illustration, male heads appear in a cloud above a female figure dressed in a padded bra and half-slip. The lines drawn around the cloud, which give it the appearance of a cartoon bubble, suggest that these male onlookers exist only in the woman's imagination. Another ad shows only half of a man's head as he views the demurely curvaceous "fit to be eyed" woman in a swimsuit with a built-in Hidden Treasure bra. Wholly representing male voyeurs is clearly problematic for women's fashion magazines, despite the publications' critical interest in maintaining female readers' construction as "to-be-looked-at."[67]

Several theorists have commented on the ways in which women's magazines imply the presence of male viewers without visibly representing them. Their analysis reveals how female objectification occurs within the homosocial world of women's magazines despite the absence of depictions of male voyeurs. Erving Goffman notes that women in advertising generally seem to be "playing at" what they are doing rather than seriously engaging in tasks like men do. The frivolous nature of female activity is conveyed in their off-center stances, relative stature and frame placement next to men, and gestures of submission and protection, which connote dependence and possession. Pervasive images include women who are smaller than men, who lean upon men for support, and who do not occupy a central place in the image. Roland Barthes describes women's magazines as defined by male absence, representing a world entirely formed by the male gaze. In other words, though men do not appear in these magazines, the editorial and ad content primarily address female concerns about attracting male attention, love, and visual approval.[68] These two critiques are mutually supportive because, even within the homosocial magazines, women's stances often depict their subordination to men. Thus, women readers are meant to see the models, and themselves in reflection, through the lens of the male spectator.

Avoidance of full representation of male spectators carries important implications for female spectatorship as well. Most importantly, it implies that women may direct sexual attention toward each other. This implication applies to the depicted women as well as to the woman spectator, who must not only consider herself in terms of male pleasure but must also identify with erotic feelings the display of women's bodies may arouse. Laura Mulvey's well-known analysis of visual pleasure in cinema suggests the possibility of this dual position for women. Subsequent essays by Mary Ann Doane, Tania Modleski, and Linda Williams draw out additional disturbing, subversive, and conflicting meanings of female spectatorship. Diana Fuss uses Lacanian psychoanalytic theory to articulate the female spectator's duality, distinguishing between the desire to *be* the woman or to *have* the woman. She points out that though fashion magazines attempt to produce "a female subject who desires to be desired by men," the magazines also constitute a "socially sanctioned structure" that encourages women's voyeuristic pleasure in looking at female bodies that are often displayed in "sexually provocative poses."[69]

The potential for eroticism, and thus homoeroticism, in intimate apparel ads is obviously quite high given undergarments' close association with sexuality and the naked body. However, since the 1910s, advertisers have used many tactics to dispel the homoerotic impulse among the female readers viewing images of women grouped together in their underwear. Typical features of these ads include averted eyes between the models, postures and graphic design that suggest distance, and the cutting off or incomplete portrayal of body parts. Ads also depict women alone, turned away from the viewer. The common practice in outerwear ads of showing women touching each other is never reproduced in intimate apparel ads. These methods of constructing invisible women in ads undermine the female spectator's desire to *have*, while encouraging her desire to *be*. The invisible woman, then, is also the female spectator, whose own body disappears to fill the empty spaces on the page.[70]

. . . . .

Mail-order catalogs as well as magazines brought intimate apparel images into homes across the United States. The Sears, Roebuck catalog included undergarments among its many products, thus affording views of partially dressed female figures to readers in search of many types of goods. However, the class of intended catalog readers altered the representation of female bodies and of intimate apparel. Unlike upscale magazines like *Vogue* and *Harper's Bazaar*, Sears, Roebuck emphasized durability and price value in the undergarments displayed in its catalogs. Because these catalogs cater to a less wealthy clientele, visual and written presentation is more clinical than that of women's magazines and conveys realistic detail. Some cutaway views of foundations are like medical drawings of the human anatomy that show the layers of muscle, tissue, and bone. Standardized faces and bodies keep the focus on the garments for sale. The desire for luxury, which along with sexuality is a key association with lingerie, is not ignored but adapted—for example, in slogans such as "Low Priced Luxury." Beauty is defined in concrete terms rather than as an artistic ideal, in phrases like "beautifully shaped," and "dainty, yet serviceable fabrics." The problematic

Figure 51. The models' averted eyes dispel the homoeroticism of imagining two women together wearing sexy lingerie. The ad copy also addresses the perennial "pretty-or-practical" fashion dilemma. *Vogue*, July 1944.

realities of the "stout figure" and "maternity supports," never mentioned in *Vogue*, are confronted and resolved.[71]

The concepts of fantasy, such as dreams, magic, miracles, and witchery, do not appear in the Sears catalogs. Such notions perhaps conflicted too directly with the catalog's construction of working-class concerns as primarily practical. However, concepts of fantasy are central to the catalogs of Frederick's of Hollywood, a mail-order firm established in 1946. Frederick's catalogs are similar to the Sears catalogs in the class of readership they address and in their use of detailed drawings and explanations of brassiere engineering, emphasis on value, and standardization of facial and body features. However, they differ in substance. Rather than evoking grace and

Figure 52. Sears catalogs stressed value and provided clinical detail of garments for mail-order clientele. *Sears, Roebuck and Co. Catalogue,* 1931. Courtesy, Sears Brands, LLC.®

Figure 53. The early catalogs of Frederick's of Hollywood emphasized erotic excitement and fantasy. *Frederick's of Hollywood Catalog*, 1957. Courtesy, Frederick's of Hollywood.

propriety, Frederick's displays women in sexually inviting pinup poses that feature impossibly narrow waists and large, uplifted, and pointed breasts. The overall sense is one of continual excitement, enhanced by the chorus-line poses, which impart unceasing movement. These women embrace the molding of their bodies, unlike the Sears women, who don brassieres out of propriety, modesty, or the need to be "modern"; and unlike the *Vogue* women, who seek to embody cultural ideals of beauty, control, and freedom. The embrace of bondage appears to release the Frederick's women into a frenzy of pleasure. This satisfaction is short-lived, though, because fashion itself allows, encourages, and depends on women to continually try on, purchase, and discard identities. However, this restless search for pleasure contains the subversive thread of revealing women's continual dissatisfaction with the choices proffered.[72]

Interestingly, intimate apparel ads in postwar *Ebony* mixed upscale, practical, and erotic modes, offering some of each type as well as hybrids. Containing a range of articles on serious political and social topics, the arts, individual achievements, entertainment news, and sensational stories akin

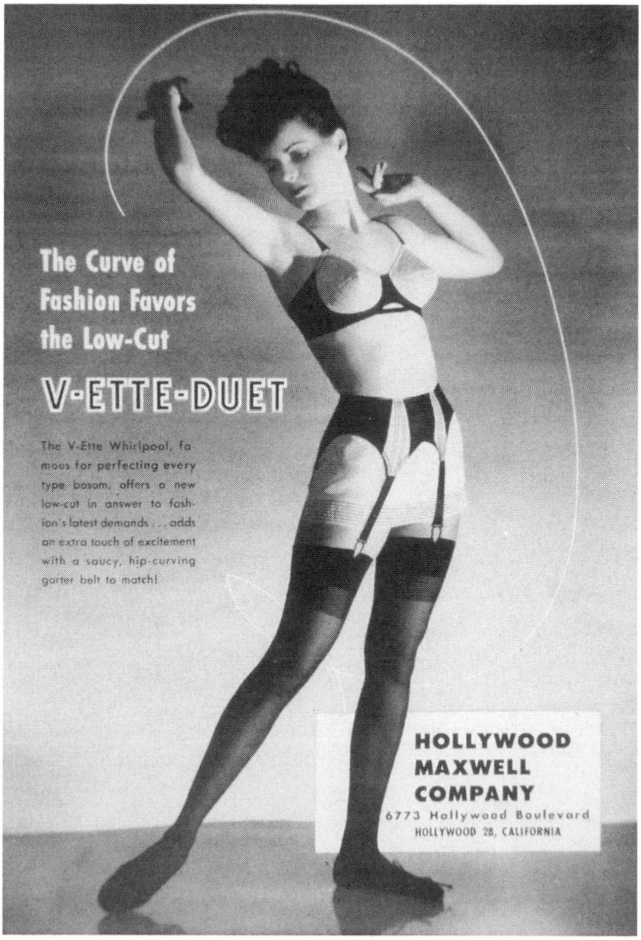

The Curve of
Fashion Favors
the Low-Cut
V-ETTE-DUET
The V-Ette Whirlpool, famous for perfecting every type bosom, offers a new low-cut in answer to fashion's latest demands . . . adds an extra touch of excitement with a saucy, hip-curving garter belt to match!
HOLLYWOOD
MAXWELL
COMPANY
6773 Hollywood Boulevard
HOLLYWOOD 28, CALIFORNIA

Figure 54. Adding "an extra touch of excitement with a saucy garter belt," this image, with a whiplike line encircling the model in her fashionable two-toned "whirlpool" circular-stitched bra, indicates the growing acceptance of fetishistic representations of intimate apparel within mainstream postwar culture. *Corsets & Brassieres,* February 1946. Courtesy of Special Collections, Gladys Marcus Library, Fashion Institute of Technology.

to those in its sister publication, *Tan Confessions,* this magazine for African American men and women included many advertisements for goods available via mail order from small companies, especially for brassieres and sexy lingerie. Mail-order brassiere and girdle ads often explained and visualized in clinical detail the benefits of wearing these garments, as did Sears catalog pages, but the magazine also ran ads for extreme pointed brassieres and "transparent" lingerie that were similar to the Frederick's ads in their emphasis on sexual excitement. These goods—unlike lightening creams and hair products—were not uniquely marketed to African Americans, and seeing them modeled on African American women, both drawn and photographed, suggests the models' incorporation within mainstream consumerism. Yet the distinct experience and appearance of African Americans remained important in this magazine, even in intimate apparel ads, indicated perhaps in the many references to the goods' "French" quality. The construction of Frenchness as a desirable attribute possibly acknowledged and also mitigated real barriers to full participation in the American marketplace. It posited a transnational consumer identity associated with a country well known to *Ebony* readers as more tolerant, if not enthusiastically appreciative of, African Americans and their culture.[73]

Changes in the mode of female undergarments marketed to diverse American women in the twentieth century created garments of a specialized nature that measured and covered parts of the female body in new ways. This process, and the graphic use of invisible women and cut-off bodies, worked to encourage the fetishization of lingerie. Once the woman is cut into parts and can be represented by exaggerated breasts or a focus on the crotch, the representation of a body part by the brassiere or G-string is only a step away. This movement of the sign away from the body makes the part ever more the apparition of the whole. Lingerie then becomes anthropomorphized—*it* is sexy or excites—and animates the qualities in the living body whose arousal depends upon lingerie's awakening caress. The metaphors of magic in lingerie advertisements encourage but also recognize the transformative erotic power these garments confer.[74]

The invisible woman appears in many guises: as graphic device, as the passive body that disappears underneath the fetishized garment, and as the female spectator whose identity is subsumed by the magazine image and whose lesbian desire is defused. She is also the garment worker whose conditions of employment remain outside the frame of the advertisements that tout the product of her labor. She is all around us, for, as designer Christian Dior explained in his definition of lingerie, "real elegance is everywhere, especially in things that don't show."[75]

6 The Production of Glamour

Intimate Apparel Workers and Union Culture

Having staged "Pins and Needles," one of the most successful musical comedies ever to hit Broadway, and having inaugurated a workers educational program that reads like a college curriculum, and having indulged in such didos as dressing its pulchritudinous pickets in expensive evening gowns, the Los Angeles branch of the International Ladies Garment Workers Union has firmly established itself in the public mind as the "glamour girl" of Labor Unions.

Los Angeles Citizen, February 21, 1941

In 1909, the first undergarment local formed in New York City under the auspices of the International Ladies Garment Workers Union (ILGWU). The working lives of these union members spanned key social and conceptual divisions that developed along with the ready-to-wear industry at the turn of the century. For the mass production of clothing both stands at and crosses over the boundary between the culture of consumption and the business of production. Its dual names—the "garment industry" and the "fashion industry"—suggest a place of importance in both spheres but also raise questions about the implications and effects of this distinction. The term *garment industry* evokes the unglamorous world of exploitation, tiresome repetitive work, anonymity, machinery, dirt, and dingy workplaces, whereas *fashion industry* evokes the glamorous world of beauty; artistic self-expression; fame; highly paid designers, models, and photographers; glossy magazines; and the excitement of shopping. Constructing these worlds as distinct highlights the seductive aspects of apparel manufacture for the consumer, thereby increasing the pleasure that female shoppers can take in purchasing and wearing new clothing. Consumption practices are in this way distanced, if not divorced, from their unsavory and negatively judged origins. Ironically, this may also endow workers in the fashion industry such as poorly paid sales clerks with the sheen of cultural capital while undergarment workers in a unionized shop who receive higher wages remain dully tainted.[1]

Female undergarment workers' lives as sewers and shoppers and makers and wearers of mass-produced intimate apparel bridge the economic and cultural divide between the fashion and garment industries and between the production and consumption of intimate apparel. Commodification of labor and objects makes it literally easier to equate apples and oranges, and even blurs the distinctions between these commodities and the workers who pick, process, or sell them. Nonetheless, in some moments, what workers produce and where they work matter very much. Garment workers in New York City and Los Angeles, for example, displayed fashion sensibilities directly linked to their position within the urban apparel industry. These workers' claims to fashionable dressing affected their understandings of the meaning of their work and of the culture of glamour. Workers also explored what glamour and fashion could be and could mean in their daily lives.

How female undergarment workers and their union responded to, invested in, and redefined glamour for themselves opens a window on the relationship between production of goods and production of culture. As Nan Enstad also has shown for the early twentieth century, working-class women's interest in fashion and popular culture could fuel, rather than distract from—as male labor leaders typically believed—their aims as union members. In that era, groups like the Women's Trade Union League (WTUL) and Consumer's League resisted the harmful effects of distancing production from consumption by organizing boycotts of unsafe products made under abusive conditions and by distributing lists of decent companies. At the same time, suffragists self-consciously exploited the new world of consumer culture for political purposes. Similarly, in the 1930s and 1940s, workers affiliated with the ILGWU staged a musical revue in New York, fashion shows in Los Angeles, and innovative picket lines nationwide. In the 1950s, a national ILGWU advertising campaign to promote the union label asserted working-class notions of fashion and taste. These events took place amid larger struggles to define the meaning of democratic citizenship and the meaning of consumption during the tumultuous midcentury experience of economic depression, war against fascism, and subsequent peacetime affluence—a trajectory that Lizabeth Cohen identified as leading to a "consumer's republic." These ILGWU activities and the published commentary about them countered the understandings of fashion and female bodily display that appeared in conventional media. Union members drew upon established ideas of glamour and the female body in public to further their aims as workers and to legitimize their claims as fashionable citizens.[2]

·   ·   ·   ·   ·

Nine years after the 1900 formation of the ILGWU by Jewish male cloak makers in New York City, thousands of female garment workers took to the streets in pursuit of improved working conditions and wages. The 1909 Uprising of the 20,000 included approximately two hundred intimate apparel workers who, with the help of WTUL activist Rose Schneiderman, formed White Goods Workers Local 62. White goods included lingerie such as petticoats, drawers, slips, corset covers, and combination garments made of cotton, linen, or silk. One WTUL organizer described the largely Jewish workers who made these garments as "the youngest, the most ignorant, the poorest and most unskilled group of women workers who ever went on strike in this country."[3]

Commercial manufacture of women's lingerie began in the 1880s but did not fully constitute an industry until the first decade of the twentieth century.[4] It rapidly grew. By 1909, Bloomingdale's was manufacturing underwear for sale in its department stores, and between 1913 and 1919, the number of white goods shops almost doubled. The expansion of undergarment production and sales occurred for the same reasons that ready-to-wear outer garments became increasingly available: a growing number of women wage earners bought rather than made clothing, new styles and new technologies further enabled mass production of garments, and a huge influx of immigrant women provided a ready source of cheap labor.[5] In addition, setting up a garment shop required little investment but could prove quite lucrative. The garment trades therefore provided an attractive entry point for those who aspired to business ownership.[6] According to a 1913 National Cotton Garment Manufacturers Association (NCGMA) report, the white goods business was one of the easiest garment fields to enter: "It does not take any capital worth considering for anyone to set himself up in business as a manufacturer of this kind of underwear. He need have but a few sewing machines, some muslin, and some embroidery. With the help of a few seamstresses, he can at once set to work and enter the competitive field. As a matter of fact, the competition in our trade is intensely keen . . . primarily [because] such a large percentage of the cost of production consists purely of labor."[7]

Access to materials, markets, and labor made New York City the chief producer of lingerie in the United States in this period. In 1913, 246 of 389 such shops nationwide were located there. Philadelphia, Boston, and St. Louis were distant runners-up, with 17, 13, and 12 firms, respectively. By 1919, 637 shops were in operation nationwide, with a total workforce of 19,225.[8]

New York City Local 62 was largely inactive until January 1913, when white goods workers took part in a general trade strike organized by the ILGWU. Schneiderman was instrumental in securing the funding necessary for Local 62 to participate in the strike, persuading union officials and the Strike Committee of the WTUL to support the local's efforts. Her belief in the possible success of this endeavor was not based purely on faith; as a paid WTUL staff member, Schneiderman had been organizing white goods workers for the past two years, along with United Hebrew Trades organizer Samuel Shore. Schneiderman, Shore, and Local 62's financial secretary, Mollie Lifschitz, believed that the potential for unionization of these workers was high, and their view proved to be accurate. About half of the fourteen thousand white goods workers in New York City left their machines and walked to strike meeting halls across the city.[9]

Workers on the picket line, many of whom were teenagers, suffered indiscriminate arrests by police and assaults by female thugs hired by employers, who hurled obscenities, swung their stone-laden purses at strikers' heads, and carried scissors to chop off workers' long braids. Strikers kept their spirits up by singing the "Song of the White Goods Workers":

> At last all New York's White Good toilers,
> Just dropped the life of Slavery,
> And went to join the "Golden Soil"
> Of the Union's Bravery. . . .
>
> We're getting beaten by policemen,
> With their heavy clubs of hickory,
> But we'll fight as hard as we can
> To win "Strong Union Victory."[10]

Besides their singing, the strikers were buoyed by the support of society women, who held benefits, posted bond for those arrested, and joined picket lines in what was popularly known as the "Mink Coat Brigade," and by the attentions of prominent physicians, who administered medical aid to the injured. Progressives like Wisconsin Senator La Follette's daughter Fola and students from Barnard and Wellesley also joined picket lines, and New York City Mayor William Gaynor warned employers against the use of violence. Even Theodore Roosevelt paid a short visit to the strike headquarters to announce his dismay about working conditions and workers' treatment on the picket line. In addition, New York police commissioner William Baker received so many complaints of false arrest that he pulled some officers from the area and reprimanded others for their rough treatment of strikers.[11]

Local 62's six-week strike resulted in a February 17 agreement with the newly formed Cotton Garment Manufacturers Association of New York (CGMA) that reduced the work week from sixty hours to fifty and established a minimum wage of five dollars per week, extra pay for overtime, and four paid holidays a year. Employers also assumed all expenses for materials and power and agreed to the "preferential" type of union shop common to garment-industry settlements in this era. Though less powerful than closed shops, preferential shops would give union members preference in hiring. Among the innovative aspects of the agreement were provisions for a "white sanitary label" identifying garments as union made, a ban on child labor, establishment of "wage-scale boards" to standardize wages and promote efficiency in production, and a fixed two-year term.[12]

In March 1917, the renewed agreement covered eighty-four employers and approximately sixty-five hundred workers, representing about half of the workers but only one-third of the employers in New York City.[13] Thus, as with the national CGMA, larger businesses were more likely to join the association. According to a 1915 Department of Commerce study, the NCGMA represented almost "80 per cent of the entire value of business done in this trade," which amounted to between $30 million and $40 million per year. Although CGMA employers initially resisted the union, the labor contract standardized wage scales and thus stabilized the trade by making competitive pricing more reliable. This provision primarily worked to the advantage of larger producers who could afford higher wages in exchange for the greater return they would enjoy with stable retail prices. Smaller producers could still undercut New York City association members by paying lower wages, but their goods had less effect on prices and profits because of their smaller market share.[14]

White goods workers also organized during this period in cities such as Chicago and Boston. However, victories like Local 62's proved difficult to duplicate outside of New York City. White goods workers and dressmakers in Chicago, for example, formed Waist, Dress and White Goods Local 59 in 1912. The WTUL sent Rose Schneiderman to Chicago in the spring of 1914 to help boost membership, but after a year, Local 59 membership had increased only from one hundred to one hundred fifty. The ILGWU then sent New York organizer and future head of the union education department Fannia Cohn to head up the local. Cohn was arrested soon after her arrival during a strike in August 1915 of glove workers because police arrested both strikers and white goods workers in the area on their way to their jobs. This indiscriminate police action garnered workers the favorable attention of the Chicago press and of high-profile visitors like longtime labor organizer Mother Jones. The strike ended with a union contract, hundreds of new union members, and the founding of the separate White Goods Local 60. Yet by November 1916, the local's declining membership forced it to merge once again with the dressmakers. A 1917 strike attempt to revive the organization of white goods workers ended in failure, as manufacturers obtained court injunctions that severely limited workers' rights to strike and to picket. These limitations, plus hundreds of arrests and contempt citations, forced the union to call off the strike.[15]

The organization of corset workers also had mixed success in the early twentieth century in Illinois, Massachusetts, Connecticut, and Michigan. The production of corsets was distinct from the production of white goods because of the different materials, skill, and techniques it required. White goods manufacturers knew that lingerie's sales appeal depended on style and trimming. In fact, these manufacturers were known for stealing design ideas so quickly that one shop's competitive style edge might last only a few days. An emphasis on style trends in white goods also lowered expectations of durability. These relatively inexpensive and lightweight garments only had to last through the current season.[16]

Corset manufacturers faced different expectations. Although style played a part in corset sales, the most important selling points of corsets were fit, wear, and effectiveness. The design and construction of these shaping garments were more complex than for lingerie, and entering the corset field required more capital investment and more technical expertise. Expenditures for corset makers, especially for "quality" lines, were also more likely to include advertising, because even in this early period, brand-name recognition was an important element in sales. Because of these distinctions from lingerie production, corset enterprises were on average larger than white goods shops. In 1919, a comparable number of employees in the United States—18,415 corset workers and 19,225 undergarment and petticoat workers toiled in 188 and 637 factories, respectively.[17]

Differences between the production of white goods and corsets did not translate into better working conditions or wages for unorganized corset workers. In 1905, workers at Kabo Corset Company in Aurora, Illinois, went on strike to increase their wages from a mere twenty-five cents a day. The recently formed Chicago WTUL supported their efforts by raising strike funds and encouraging clubwomen in the region to boycott Kabo corsets. Linking workers with consumers proved effective; the company responded to the strike and boycott threat by doubling wages. Satisfied with the results of this dual strategy, Kabo workers formalized their association with the WTUL by affiliating as a local with the Chicago League.[18]

Michigan corset workers formed an ILGWU-affiliated local after a spontaneous strike of eight hundred workers at the Kalamazoo Corset Company in 1911. Surprised company officials quickly signed a one-year agreement, but when the agreement expired, they decided to fight the union. Firing union officials and activists, the company provoked a strike that lasted from March to June of 1912.[19] The ILGWU first sent organizer Josephine Casey to lead the strike, in part because she was, like most of the Kalamazoo workers, an American-born white woman. Casey hoped to win the support of middle- and upper-class women by invoking moral concerns about workplace safety and maintaining a demure presence on picket lines. Unfortunately, Casey did not realize that the overlapping networks of business leaders and their wives in the relatively small community of Kalamazoo would make cross-class alliances unlikely. Though the strike had the support of organized labor, the rest of the community remained indifferent.[20]

To break the deadlock, Casey defied an injunction and landed in jail. The ILGWU then sent Pauline Newman, a Jewish immigrant and the first woman hired by the union as a full-time organizer, to lead the strike. Newman negotiated an agreement that workers narrowly approved, but at a cost. Key provisions guaranteeing the rehiring of strike leaders were rewritten in the company's favor. Even so, the company did not honor the agreement, and Local 82 protested by organizing a consumer boycott. In 1915, when new owners bought the company in receivership and reestablished the business, they did so without union contracts. Despite this setback, the Kalamazoo corset workers were successful in advancing the cause of women garment workers generally. Their struggle drew national attention, and at the following ILGWU national convention, male delegates passed resolutions supporting general strikes in the waist and dress industry and in the women's trades.[21]

In 1915 also, corset workers in Bridgeport, Connecticut, reduced working hours from fifty-five to forty-eight, increased wages, and abolished charges for needles after a spontaneous walkout that led to the formation of ILGWU Corset Workers Local 33. Bridgeport had developed into a center for quality corset production after Warner Brothers established its headquarters there in 1874. In July 1919, more than thirty-seven hundred workers at the Crown Corset, George C. Batchellor, La Resista, Birdsey-Somers, and Warner Brothers companies went on strike to win a forty-four-hour work week, a 25 percent wage increase, and a closed-shop agreement. Similar demands were also being made by other Bridgeport workers, including machinists, weavers, and employees at Bryant Electric, Columbia Graphophone, and Hawthorne Manufacturing. The corset workers did not seek cross-class support from clubwomen or the WTUL. Instead, relying on the strength of the citywide labor movement, they won a 20 percent raise in pay, a reduction in hours, and other concessions, though not a closed shop. When the strike ended, the *New York Times* reported, "DeVer C. Warner says his factory is not unionized and the labor leaders say they are satisfied."[22]

Though increased production of garments during World War I brought ILGWU membership to a new height in 1918 of 129,000 members, the next decade saw a steady decline. Membership dropped to 77,600 in 1922, and by 1927, the union numbered only 27,000 members nationwide. The postwar slump occurred because of the transition from a wartime economy and lowered peacetime demand for garments, and also because of intense struggles between communist members newly vitalized by the Soviet revolution and the established leadership, which was satisfied with its moderate vision of trade unionism and intimidated by the Red Scare that tore apart locals and decimated their ranks. In Los Angeles, for example, the largest local disbanded entirely to circumvent a communist takeover. The subsequent formation of a new local brought the total Los Angeles ILGWU membership to only 75.[23]

Changes within the industry also contributed to the ILGWU's decline in the 1920s. Rising union membership in the 1910s coincided with a growth spurt in the ready-to-wear industry. A postwar depression halted that growth, putting union members out of work, unable to afford dues. In addition, manufacturers responded to the greater regulation of factories—which had resulted from ILGWU efforts and urban reformers' campaigns against homework in tenements and unsafe working conditions in shops—by sending work out to contractors rather than producing garments themselves. The rising importance of style and merchandising of 1920s apparel also expanded contracting as manufacturers sought flexible production structures that could quickly shift from making limited numbers of one style to making another. The system that emerged increased the number of "jobbers," garment businesses that designed and sold garments but arranged for their production with "outside" contractors. Contractors' primary expense was labor costs, and cutting wages was the principal means of beating the competition and getting orders. Workers suffered because manufacturing firms with in-house production were easier for unions to organize and police than were smaller contracting firms.[24]

The increasing use of "section work" and the intensified subdivision of labor in the 1920s also undercut workers' ability to organize. Especially suited to producing standardized garments, section work began in the mid-nineteenth century with the manufacture of men's work clothes and uniforms. Section work created "the constituent crafts of cutting, machine sewing, hand sewing, pressing and examining" and then divided the sewing process further, with each machine operator completing a different task instead of sewing one garment in its entirety.[25]

The greater complexity of fitting women's clothing delayed mass production of women's wear until later in the nineteenth century. Section work did not enter the commercial manufacture of women's clothing until the early twentieth century, and then it did so initially in branches less influenced by style changes. Undergarments were among the first types of women's clothing to be produced in this manner. As the lines of both outer and undergarments simplified in the 1920s, possibilities for section work increased. Manufacturers divided sewing operations further within the growing jobber/contractor system to accommodate expanding attention to fashion changes in clothing detail. In addition, section work benefited employers because operators required lesser skills to perform limited tasks, which meant lower wages.[26]

The jobber/contractor system created greater specialization within the industry as a whole because it separated production from the design, marketing, and sale of garments. This separation manifested geographically, as companies maintained elegant showrooms in Manhattan's garment district while locating production wherever it was cheapest to do so. Thus, New York City continued to be a leading fashion center where buyers could come from stores across the country to view and purchase the latest vogues. However, the growing practice of locating production elsewhere ultimately undermined New York's status as a center of apparel manufacturing. Moreover, this detachment of the material construction of garments from their aesthetic design and retail promotion severed cultural aspects of clothing manufacture from those of physical production.[27]

The terms *garment industry* and *fashion industry* mark distinctions between the separated spheres of material and cultural production of clothing and its meanings. Costume historian Claudia Brush Kidwell dates the origins of a differentiated fashion industry to the 1920s. In this decade, a key component of the industry, the fashion press, assumed a greater presence in the daily lives of most Americans. The *New York Times,* for example, hired fashion reporter Virginia Pope to cover the city's garment district for fashion news, and then, with Pope as fashion editor, became the first newspaper to include photography and sketches in its fashion coverage. Interest in fashion reportage spread nationwide. In 1926, over a hundred American reporters covered couture showings in Paris. Fashion's upgraded status as newsworthy heightened popular awareness of style changes. No longer would readers of fashion magazines be the only consumers exposed to the latest designs in wearing apparel. Newspaper coverage thus enhanced the power of fashion itself, making fashion awareness an important component of modern cultural knowledge.[28]

The interaction between the garment industry's flexible network of large firms and small shops able to quickly produce a wide array of styles, and the fashion industry's extensive media promotion and expanding national distribution system of mail-order catalogs, department stores, and specialty shops, quickened the tempo of fashion changes. Both industries required a "speed up" in apparel consumption to profitably make goods, make news, and make sales. However, the material distinction between the fashion industry and the garment industry that emerged from the jobber/contractor system served an ideological function as well. Detaching the design, promotion, and display of clothing from its drab production concerns heightened the pleasure of apparel consumption by enhancing fashionable attire's associations with purely aesthetic and sensual considerations. The separation of workers and consumers further obscured the factory conditions that had recently come into public view in the general strikes of the 1910s, and it advanced the interests of business owners by making cross-class alliances and their dual strategy of strikes and boycotts more difficult and thus less likely. In the 1920s, even the WTUL dispensed with such direct action strategies, opting to focus instead on legislative lobbying to improve conditions for female workers.[29]

· · · · ·

In 1929, 15.5 million dozen pieces of underwear made from purchased fabrics were produced in the United States, with a value of over $146 million. The "corsets and allied garment trade" produced almost 25 million brassieres valued at $18.5 million, just over 18 million corsets valued at $32.8 million, and 10.5 million combination garments valued at $21.6 million. Although most of these garments were still produced in the New York City metropolitan region, the membership of White Goods Workers Local 62 had dwindled to only a few hundred women by the end of the 1920s. Wracked by internal struggles, the local had also lost ground in the transition from underwear made of white goods to lingerie made of silk and rayon.[30]

Well aware that the undergarment trade was the third-largest branch of the garment industry, the ILGWU leadership realized the importance of revitalizing Local 62. In 1931, at the suggestion of President Benjamin Schlesinger and General Secretary David Dubinsky, the union appointed Samuel Shore, who had left the labor movement in the early 1920s, executive supervisor of the white goods local. Shore instigated an organizing drive, which, despite the adverse economic situation, netted the union twelve hundred new members by September 1931. Shop owners formed a new organization the following month, the Lingerie Manufacturers Association (LMA), to negotiate an industrywide settlement with Local 62 and therefore head off a general strike. Signed in November, the new agreement, and the renewed union strength it represented, put New York City undergarment workers in a good position to take advantage of the federal support of unionization and collective bargaining ushered in by Franklin Roosevelt's election to the presidency the following year, despite attempts by the LMA to deflect the impact of both.[31]

In 1933, the passage of the National Industrial Recovery Act empowered the National Recovery Administration (NRA) to establish codes standardizing wages and working conditions in various industries. The LMA successfully petitioned the NRA for a separate code for the undergarment trade, after assuring the union that its cooperation would result in higher standards for workers. Yet once the separate code was achieved, manufacturers proposed much lower standards than those promised. Local 62 responded by "writ[ing] its own code" and calling a general strike in September 1933. The twelve thousand workers who walked out shut down production in both high- and low-end shops throughout New York City. After three weeks, the local signed agreements with the LMA and also with the newly formed Allied Underwear Manufacturers Association, producers of rayon and lower-priced silk garments; the United Underwear Contractors Association; and the Corset and Brassiere Manufacturers Association.[32]

The strike brought significant wage increases and reduced hours to undergarment workers, but many of the provisions of the Undergarment Code remained unresolved. Most important to Local 62 was the right to have representatives on the Undergarment Code Authority, the board that would oversee and adjudicate code enforcement, and to have wage classifications included in code provisions. The union won these concessions after seven months of negotiations, and the Undergarment Code finally went into effect in May 1934. However, despite outnumbering labor six to one on the Code Authority, the manufacturers sought to deprive Local 62's representative of the right to vote on matters before the board. Though the manufacturers initially were successful, the union's vigorous protest ultimately won the local two voting positions.[33]

Depression economics, federal labor legislation, and fashion trends brought substantial changes to the undergarment and corset trades in the early 1930s, restructuring the industry. A number of long-time firms did

Figure 55. A young woman is detained and led away from a strike scene, circa mid-1920s. Courtesy, UNITE HERE Archives, Kheel Center, Cornell University.

not survive. Yet though the increasing pace of style changes and use of flexible production methods heightened chaotic aspects of the industry, the Undergarment Code provided a measure of stability. Corset firms that successfully navigated the technological and stylistic changes of this period particularly benefited. After Local 62 updated its name to the Undergarment and Negligee Workers, the Corset and Brassiere Manufacturers Association convinced newly elected ILGWU president David Dubinsky to create a separate Local 32 for corset and brassiere workers in 1934. However, even with the loss of these members, Local 62 stood as the third-largest local in the ILGWU. By 1935, Local 62 had 10,330 members, 2,307 of whom belonged to Local 32. The diverse women who made up this membership now included immigrants from Italy and Syria, African Americans, native-born white women, and Christians, Muslims, and Jews.[34]

The growing strength of the ILGWU nationally, and in the undergarment and corset trades in New York City, allowed the union to advance the social, health, and cultural programs it had begun in the 1910s and esta-

Figure 56. Well dressed Local 62 members visit the Museum of Science and Industry, 1934. Courtesy, UNITE HERE Archives, Kheel Center, Cornell University.

blished at both national and local levels. In the 1930s, garment workers could go to a union health center, tuberculosis sanitarium, or vacation resort; join sports, drama, music, and literary clubs; and take classes in English and other subjects. Local 62 manager Samuel Shore, for example, hired an education director to coordinate after-work activities and instituted the local's journal, *Our Union*. The journal discussed strikes, explained settlements, and included a regular column of gossip from the shop floor about romances, weddings, births, illnesses, deaths, and other changes in undergarment workers' lives.[35]

New York City manufacturers responded to the union's robust presence by beginning their long exodus out of the city. Larger firms opened branches or moved operations entirely to nonunionized areas in the Southeast, West, and Puerto Rico. Small shop owners who were unable or unwilling to pay union wages also relocated to these areas. After the Supreme Court ruled the NRA and its codes unconstitutional in 1935, some undergarment firms simply moved to neighboring states like New Jersey, Pennsylvania, and

Massachusetts, where the union was not as strong and able to maintain code standards without federal mandate. By December 1935, *Women's Wear Daily* reported that New York manufacturers were feeling "the effect of the exodus" as they competed with the lower prices that out-of-town shops offered buyers.[36]

The union had some success in organizing these "runaway" workplaces. From the ILGWU southeast regional office in Atlanta, organizer John Martin reported to Samuel Shore in 1937 that "down in the deep south [there are] any number of underwear factories—at least a hundred of them. Some employing as many as 1800 people, others a little as 200." Martin, a long-time veteran of the labor movement who began his activism in the well-known conflicts of Ludlow, Colorado, described the arduous nature of union work in the region by telling Shore "if he thought Pa. was tough he just don't know 'Nuthin yet." However, Martin was able to assist undergarment workers in Virginia, Tennessee, and Georgia in securing improved wages and conditions with union contracts. He also found that "sometimes getting into a town even before a plant moves here will keep the plant from coming south." Martin may have preferred this strategy because, despite his past experience facing "the machine guns," he was stunned by the level of violence organizers faced in the South. In 1939, for example, an employer "brutally beat up" a white female union activist in Atlanta on the street in broad daylight. Another problem was the racial tension between white and black women workers. A local in Atlanta, for example, refused to let African American workers join. The dismayed Martin resolved the dilemma by creating a separate local for black workers. Though this solution violated the spirit of ILGWU opposition to racial discrimination, it drew upon the accepted tradition of separate locals for different ethnicities. Italian and Jewish cloak makers in New York City, for example, belonged to separate locals, as did "Spanish" dressmakers in Los Angeles.[37]

. . . . .

John Martin's reports painted a grim picture of garment manufacture and organizing in the South, far removed from the glamorous aspects of fashion production. However, despite the ideological, cultural, and economic separation between the fashion and garment industries, garment workers at times drew upon the power, allure, and growing glamour of fashion in this period to effect labor codes as well as dress codes. This approach was especially favored by ILGWU members in the late 1930s and 1940s who worked in the important fashion centers of New York City, the top-producing area nationally, and Los Angeles, its fast-growing West Coast rival. As big-city dwellers going to workplaces on 7th Avenue in New York and in the garment district in downtown Los Angeles, many female garment workers dressed in a fashionable urban style. Garment workers, however, had access to updated fashion information that other urban women did not. They could stay on top of trends not by reading fashion magazines like *Vogue* or *Harper's Bazaar,* but simply by going to work.[38]

At union shops in which piece rates determined wages, workers were especially attuned to the finer nuances of fashion changes. A new design of a collar or sleeve, for example, often brought immediate negotiations with the boss about the degree of difficulty that its construction entailed, and thus about the rate at which the work should be paid. If standing members of the piece-rate committee were not satisfied with the rates the boss offered, they called a union official down to the shop to continue negotiations. In addition, spontaneous group decisions to stop working until an acceptable settlement was reached were not uncommon. Clearly, ongoing attention to fashion changes by these workers was critical to their employment experience and earnings. And, given the seasonal nature of garment work, as well as the alternating periods of "rushes" and layoffs common to the industry, current fashion information helped workers plan schedules and expenditures around potential periods of unemployment or stretches of overtime shifts. For workers interested in stylish clothing, fashion knowledge at work was useful both for job considerations and personal dressing practices.[39]

Some garment workers copied patterns used in their shop, made alterations to suit their sense of style or body shape, and sewed garments for themselves, their family, and friends at home. These workers and their close associates could thus be wearing new styles, or innovative variations of them, before manufactured clothing reached retail stores. Members of New York City Dressmakers Local 22, known for its militancy and leftist politics under the longtime leadership of radical Charles Zimmerman, were particularly proud of their stylishly up-to-the-minute wardrobes. And, though undergarment workers might not have immediate access to outerwear patterns, the changes in underwear shapes they closely monitored did indicate changing directions in the fashionable silhouette. In addition, as with outerwear workers, undergarment shops' location in urban fashion and garment districts gave production workers ongoing exposure to emerging style trends.[40]

· · · · ·

Garment workers' sense of style came under wider public scrutiny when *Pins and Needles,* a musical revue sponsored by the ILGWU's Labor Stage as a cultural activity for union members, unexpectedly became a hit in New York. Workers such as Lydia Annucci of Undergarment and Negligee Workers Local 62 and Ruth Rubinstein of Corset and Brassiere Workers Local 32 who joined the cast of *Pins and Needles* rehearsed three nights a week after work for over a year before the show debuted in November 1937. After the revue garnered supportive notices in several New York daily newspapers, demand for tickets soared. To meet this demand, the ILGWU arranged for cast members to take leaves from their jobs so that they could perform on weeknights as well as weekends. In April 1938, the original company began a well-publicized national tour, while two additional casts were put together to continue performances in New York City. One of the New York companies performed for the general public in the evenings, and the other staged late-afternoon matinees for union members at reduced ticket prices. Ultimately, *Pins and Needles* became the longest-running Broadway musical of the 1930s.[41]

The novelty and appeal of *Pins and Needles* lay in its surprisingly adept amateur cast of garment workers and in musical numbers and skits that proved compelling to a wide audience. These songs and sketches provided a class analysis of American society and culture by exploring working-class life, problems, pleasures, and social interaction both on and off the job. As a whole, the revue upheld trade unions as vital and necessary institutions and championed the cooperative values, collective strategies, and class consciousness of the labor movement. It was also pointedly antifascist, condemning collaboration with fascists four years before the United States engaged in war with the Axis powers. In addition, *Pins and Needles* poignantly expressed workers' rights to happiness, love, sexual pleasure, and fulfilling recreation despite class inequities and exploitation. Moreover, the show critically surveyed a wide range of American culture by lampooning both consumerism and 1930s radical agitprop theater. And though the show unsurprisingly conveyed the ILGWU's acceptance of class divisions as inevitable and unalterable, it also hinted at a day of reckoning when workers would transcend inequities and overcome social divisions.[42]

Harold Rome's songs, and those by Marc Blitzstein, Arthur Arent, and Emanuel Eisenberg, evoked working-class concerns and perspectives with humorous, witty, and sensitive lyrics, which were set to the melodies and arrangements of the popular music of the time. In "Sing Me a Song with Social Significance," the second number of the show, female workers told male suitors that they weren't interested in "moonsongs of stars" or "ditties romantic." Instead, the men must sing about "wars . . . breadlines . . . front page news . . . strikes and last minute headlines" to gain the women's interest. The song connects political solidarity and sexual attraction, radically refiguring conventional understandings of why couples fall in love. This Harold Rome song became one of the most popular and well known of the show, not only because of its catchy melody but also because of its innovative lyrical take on romance. A reproduction of the sheet music even served as a backdrop for a fashion layout in *Vogue*.[43]

Several political sketches, as well as those about loving relationships, express sensitivity to gender issues, as do two Rome songs that link production and consumption. "Dear Beatrice Fairfax," sung by machine operator and radical activist Millie Weitz, alternates a litany of consumer goods and the eroticizing effect they promise with Millie's lament that, even though she uses the products, "nobody makes a pass at me." In "Chain Store Daisy," brassiere maker Ruth Rubinstein assumed the role of a brassiere salesgirl in a department store. The song describes the saga of a salesgirl who studied hard and made it to and through college only to find herself unemployed. Her only option, applying for work in a department store, requires her to submit to demeaning physical and psychological scrutiny by Macy's personnel staff. She gets the job and then has to contend with snooty customers and the ongoing work of making "the big things small and the small things bigger."[44]

"Dear Beatrice Fairfax" and "Chain Store Daisy" highlight working-class women's location at a juncture between production and consumption. In the first song, the narrator makes fun of women's attempts to produce themselves as marketable objects of desire through the use of consumer goods, but she also points out the absurdity of the transformations promised by products' advertisements. The latter song recognizes that the salesgirl's job facilitates and promotes consumption, though her status as an employee subject to the power of her bosses is clearly no different than that of the factory worker. The song also shows how women are objects of scrutiny both as workers and as consumers.

This mix of political commentary, romance, popular musical sounds, and comedy in *Pins and Needles* was extremely innovative and an important part of the revue's appeal. As one critic explained, "For the first time in the history of the labor theatre, entertainment, and not edification, has been made the watchword of a production. . . . The nature of 'Pins and Needles,' its special emphasis upon entertainment, can be seen from the fact that it boasts several boy-meets-girl numbers after the approved style of the musical revue." Another noted it as "so original, . . . so up-to-date that audi-

Figure 57. Brassiere factory worker and Local 32 member Ruth Rubenstein performs "Chain Store Daisy" in *Pins and Needles* (1937). Courtesy, UNITE HERE Archives, Kheel Center, Cornell University.

ences are sure to wonder why they never thought of placing lovers against a background of the CIO [Congress of Industrial Organizations] and the present industrial setup."[45] Critical praise also included the comment,

> Just because this is a labor production, don't think it is ponderously proletarian or solemnly left wing. It is delightfully original and clever, gay, spicy and as smart an intimate revue ever come. Of course, it is class conscious, but even a die-hard capitalist with a gout swollen foot on his workers' neck would be moved to mirth by the gleeful zest of this entertainment and be grateful for a refreshing theatrical experience that mingles gaiety with "social significance."[46]

Yet a large national audience responded not only to the show's entertainment value but also to the questions *Pins and Needles* raised about the effects of capitalist economic and cultural organization. That the cast members were factory workers brought the separation between production and consumption more sharply into view.

Dominant cultural forms maintain the division between production and consumption by obscuring, assuaging, or rationalizing the tensions, uncertainties, and alienation it provokes. Two cartoons published in 1938 articulated tensions on the fault line between production and consumption that *Pins and Needles* exposed. A *New York Times* cartoon depicted two male workers unloading dress forms from a truck parked across the street from a mobbed Labor Stage entrance. Large cars parked in front of the theater further distance the two workers from this site of cultural consumption, emphasizing the disjuncture between labor and leisure in class society. A *New Yorker* cartoon with the caption "The Theatre Guild counters the entrance of the International Ladies' [sic] Garment Workers' Union into theatrical production by introducing a ready-to-wear dress line" imagines the manufacture of dresses taking place inside a theater. On the stage, well-dressed young women labor at sewing-machine tables. Behind them, male designers confer with female drapers and sample makers preparing the next order, while a technician attends to stage lights. A line of women and one of men walk on separate narrow platforms off the stage into theater seats. The dark-suited men push carts hanging with finished dresses, while the women model a variety of dress designs for white-suited male buyers seated in the theater. The dress of both male and female actors reminds readers that though these people may be workers, they are not working class. In addition, even in this fantasy of reversal, only female actors perform as bodies on display.[47]

These images reveal how Americans experienced the estrangement between production and consumption not only in terms of business booms and busts but also on cultural and psychic levels. The separation between production and consumption articulated in the *New York Times* cartoon is familiar and real, though made more sorrowful by the workers' lack of pleasurable access to the theater their union membership created. The incomplete inversion expressed in the *New Yorker* cartoon, despite its conventional gender division of labor, provides a vision of self-directed manufacture in which dignified workers engage in all phases of production, enjoy using the products they make together, and command center stage.

The estrangement between production and consumption articulated by these cartoons formed distinctions between the garment industry and the fashion industry, in which conceptions of the glamorous and nonglamorous play key roles. Newspaper reviewers of *Pins and Needles* commented, though often in indirect ways, about the blurring of differences brought about by seeing honest-to-goodness factory workers acting on a theater stage in a broadly acclaimed musical revue. Critics continually felt com-

*The Theatre Guild Counters the Entrance of the International Ladies' Garment Workers'
Union into Theatrical Production by Introducing a Ready-to-Wear Dress Line.*

Figure 58. Responding to the success of the ILGWU musical *Pins and Needles,* this *New Yorker* cartoon jokes about the mixing of industrial and cultural spheres brought about by garment workers performing on Broadway (January 8, 1938). © The New Yorker Collection 1938 Carl Rose from cartoonbank.com. All Rights Reserved.

pelled to position the cast, particularly its female members, in one sphere or another, primarily by assessing cast members' beauty, glamour, and potential for professional employment as actors.

Reviewers of *Pins and Needles* often dismissed the ILGWU cast as "quite un-Broadwayish in appearance; no pretty boys and probably not a single Hollywood possibility among the gals. They look just like what they are—garment workers." This comment visualizes "garment workers" as an unattractive aesthetic category defined in opposition to those who typically appear on stage and screen. Other reviewers admired the talent and beauty of particular performers who seemed to transcend their proletarian status. For example, undergarment worker Ruth Rubinstein, called the "company glamour girl for looks and figure" and "star material," compared favorably to successful entertainer Fanny Brice.[48] By comparing Rubinstein to a well-known stage star, a reviewer not only could convey her performance style in familiar terms but also downplay her prosaic associations and reposition her in the sphere of culture and consumption.

Speculation about whether talented cast members would leave the garment industry for Broadway or Hollywood fomented discussion about distinctions between the glamorous and the nonglamorous. *Manchester Guardian* critic Marie Seton found *Pins and Needles* "the most outstanding example" of why "during 1938 the most successful plays on Broadway were almost entirely devoid of conventional glamour."[49] Yet personal accounts of how the show transformed cast members' lives emphasized the pleasure of leaving the factory shop for the stage. Twenty-one-year-old Lydia Annucci was one of several female players who agreed that being in *Pins and Needles* was "a beautiful interlude away from the undie machines." The caption of a newspaper photograph worthy of any Hollywood publicity department, showing Annucci and fellow cast members Rose Newmark and Rose Kaufman dressed in shorts and midriff tops and wrestling on a bed, read, "From garment workers to the drama, and they hope not back again." The accompanying article outlined the women's desire to continue on the stage. "Going back to dressing dummies would be a last resort," said twenty-five-year-old Newmark. She wanted to be "a truly great dramatic actress" but supposed her "chances aren't so hot." However, the article claimed, "she'd prefer her old job in the factory to either starving or having an office job." Newmark thus preferred acting when assessing a range of employment options available to her but did not place it in stark opposition to her former job, as this and other newspaper accounts suggested.[50]

Navigating the glamorous/unglamorous divide could mean embracing the democratic significations of the unglamorous. One critic found that "these folks are giving the stage a long needed stimulant. They are restoring the fun and the vital substance of the theater to the ordinary everyday American people."[51] A Hollywood-based reporter who saw the show in New York agreed, albeit by embracing a reversal of cultural norms: "The performers . . . were fresh and original. They didn't have the tricks of professionals. There wasn't one beautiful or pretty girl in the chorus. It was a great relief not to see everyone overstuffed with glamour."[52] Cleveland critic Winsor French expressed a similar sentiment, linking the show's aesthetics to performers' appearances. "The costumes are simplicity itself, the decor is almost non-existent and there are no glamour boys and girls with their names spelled out in lights, but the general absence of these ingredients, if anything, is an enormous relief."[53] And another critic confessed she'd "hate to see the *Pins and Needles* boys and girls become blasé stage folk, with a limited range of interests." Having brought a friend backstage with her who had "just returned from eight years in a border town in Austria . . . you should have heard the cast pepper her with questions about how things are over there. Later they turned the tables on your interviewer and asked pertinent questions about a columnist's freedom to print." This reporter disdained the glamorous realm as superficial and apathetic and was duly impressed by the intelligence and talent of well-informed, articulate cast members.[54]

Newspapers also reported more affirmatively on garment workers' glamorous transformations both onstage and off. Cast member Anne Brown, who appeared with Ruth Rubinstein in the "Chain Store Daisy" number, reported, "We never went to beauty shops when we worked in the factories. Now we go now and then. We want to look as good as we can for the sake of the show. For ourselves." Yet this article also reported that cast members "buy their clothing from factories—and are proud of it. . . . There wasn't a temperamental bone in the lot of them; no finery to be jealous of." This report thus presents an appropriation of glamour that is not in conflict with working-class solidarity and consciousness. Brown and other female cast members responded to the spotlight on their appearance as performers but determined the amount and type of attention they would devote to their public image.[55]

The success of *Pins and Needles* demonstrated to the nation that alternatives to dominant modes of production and consumption of culture and glamour could work. Despite the persistence of some commercializing aspects of the revue, including costuming female actors in undergarments, the show generated radical challenges to class-based limitations on individual life experiences and cultural access. It also provided a forum, both in the form of its presentation and the content of the show, for expressing working-class concerns, criticism, and pleasures. The inclusion of African American cast members in the national tour required theaters in cities like St. Louis to put aside segregationist seating policies because the troupe refused to perform unless such policies were revoked. The tour also challenged racial stereotyping in cities in which women of color had previously appeared onstage only as domestic servants.[56] Songs from *Pins and Needles* were also performed by workers outside the theater. For example, one group of strikers in San Francisco sang "Not Cricket to Picket," a satire of upper-class views of strikes, while on the picket line themselves.[57]

Putting garment workers onstage challenged the division between the glamorous culture industry and the unglamorous garment industry. Emerging from the collective strength and vision of unionized garment workers, *Pins and Needles* exposed, but also bridged, the production/consumption divide. The show enabled garment workers to produce alternative cultural meanings about the commodities they manufactured and about their status as industrial workers. As one cast member said to a Hollywood reporter when he told her he was returning home for a date with Marlene Dietrich, "*Nu*. What's Marlene Dietrich got that I haven't got?"[58] *Pins and Needles'* success provided garment workers and their working-class audiences with a powerful means to become producers of culture, by rewriting dress codes and labor codes from the factory floor, onstage, and in the public imagination.

. . . . .

One energetic and innovative union organizer who understood how rejoining the sundered connections between the fashion and garment industries could get workers what they hadn't got was Rose Pesotta. Sent to Los Angeles in 1940 by union president Dubinsky to fill in for hospitalized Pacific Coast director Louis Levy, Pesotta organized several highly publicized fashion events for the union during her two-year stay in Southern California.[59] Pesotta was known in labor circles and was familiar with the industry on the West Coast because seven years earlier, in her first assignment as a full-time paid organizer, the ILGWU had sent her to Los Angeles to organize dressmakers. The union was responding at that time not only to recent passage of New Deal labor legislation but also to the significant growth then taking place in Los Angeles's garment industry. As in New York City, the availability of a large population of immigrant women willing to work in garment shops for low wages was a critical factor in spurring the development of this industry. In Los Angeles, however, these women were predominantly Mexicans and Mexican Americans. Utilizing her perspective as an immigrant woman of Russian Jewish heritage in ways immigrant male organizers had resisted, Rose Pesotta successfully reached out to large numbers of Mexican immigrants working in nonunion shops, distributing leaflets in Spanish and broadcasting information over Spanish-language radio stations. Most of the two thousand workers who joined the union as a result of a tradewide strike in October 1933 were women who had never before been union members and who had been considered by male bosses and some male union officials to be passive and reluctant to challenge existing conditions and wages. Their activism, like that of Latina garment workers in Texas and elsewhere, defied these persistent, demeaning stereotypes. Pesotta's assessment that "Mexican girls and women" in the strike of 1933 "acted almost like seasoned unionists" acknowledged their readiness and abilities to join together as ILGWU members, an understanding that made her a more effective union leader.[60]

Pesotta's successful work with these women during the 1933 strike in Los Angeles was a major factor in her election the following year to the ILGWU's executive board. As with the tenures of Fannia Cohn, the first female vice president (1915–25) and Mollie Friedman, who was later elected to the position, the union's male leadership successfully enforced an unspoken rule that only one woman could serve on the board. Nonetheless, Pesotta, one among the group of dedicated, dynamic, and mutually supportive female union leaders, returned to Los Angeles in 1940 with greater clout and confidence, after spearheading many successful organizing drives in cities across the country and in Puerto Rico and Canada. Although Pesotta was reluctant to leave her assignment in Boston, the Los Angeles appointment was challenging and was worthy of her earned national stature as a union official and organizer. Not only was Los Angeles known generally as an antiunion town, but by the early 1940s, the rapid growth of the women's garment industry had far outpaced static union membership.[61]

American clothing manufacturers on both coasts benefited from the war in Europe, which shut down couturiers in Paris, undermining French fashion authority. For Los Angeles garment industrialists, this development offered an opportunity to challenge both Paris and New York as leading style centers. They culled the Hollywood film industry for cultural capital, direct sales to studio wardrobe departments, and opportunities for coordinated business ventures that could link the manufacture and promotion of clothing to a film's release and distribution. In addition, Los Angeles garment manufacturers seized upon American women's rising interest in "sportswear," clothing perceived as informal and comfortable, as well as upon the more formal glamorous outfits they saw regularly in movies. The local industry promoted both types of clothing as Hollywood-inspired style that women could best achieve by purchasing "authentic" garments made in California.[62]

Pesotta decided to organize the growing number of workers who were producing sportswear and undergarments in nonunion shops, thereby avoiding interference with Pacific Coast Director Levy's administration of male tailors or Los Angeles ILGWU official George Wishnak's leadership of the dressmakers. Yet Levy, a somewhat complacent union official who clearly did not possess anything close to the spirit, energy, and devotion Pesotta gave to the union movement, resented her independence. Levy had been in Los Angeles for about eighteen months and claimed credit for progress in straightening out union affairs. His relative indifference stemmed in part from a lack of confidence in the abilities of Mexican immigrant women and in the substantial contingent of white women from Oklahoma and other midwestern states who migrated to Los Angeles during the Depression to join and remain members of the union.[63]

Pesotta's energetic organizing talent, receptive membership, and her desire to overcome the union's less-than-favorable public image in Los Angeles led her to stage a picket line at the annual manufacturers' Market Week and Style Show during her first week in the city. Pesotta arranged for twelve female union members dressed in elegant evening clothes to carry picket signs protesting the substandard conditions in which the garments in the show were produced. As Pesotta later noted, the women were "all good looking, [and] they took on glamour with the change of attire." With their striking appearance, which Pesotta felt approximated the look of "Park Avenue debutantes," the protesters garnered supportive press coverage for the union, including photographs of the "picket line in evening garb alongside those of Hollywood models wearing gowns our members had made."[64]

Although this event was innovative, it drew on a long-standing tradition of women on picket lines dressing well to heighten the worthiness and appeal of their struggle for union recognition and working conditions. Archival photographs of ILGWU strikes nationwide in the early to mid-twentieth century reveal that many women dressed up for these public occasions. During the 1933 Los Angeles strike, for example, Pesotta had seen workers join the picket line "dressed in their best dresses, made by themselves, and reflecting the latest styles. Many of them were beauties, and marched on the sidewalks like models in a modiste's salon." The transformation of a picket line into a fashion parade also shows working-class women's awareness that their participation in a public demonstration put their bodies on display. Undergarment workers in particular evidenced a self-conscious theatrical flair, at times using the attention-getting tactic of wearing the type of intimate apparel they made in the factory over their street clothes. This political use of "underwear as outerwear" included one 1941 picket line of American Lady Corset workers on strike in Detroit who marched for their cause clad only in their combination corsets and stockings. Acting boldly on their understanding of the centrality of female bodily display to American culture, these women exploited this often-oppressive reality to advance their interests as workers.[65]

Figure 59. Striking American Lady Corset workers display underwear as outerwear on a picket line in Detroit, 1941. Courtesy, UNITE HERE Archives, Kheel Center, Cornell University.

Wearing underwear as outerwear on picket lines made visible intimate apparel's hidden figure-shaping and erotic qualities. The tactic also represented the usual obfuscation of production processes and working conditions from public consumption and the private nature of these goods. The picket line as fashion parade also disrupted the ideological separation of production and consumption by making evident working-class women's location at the critical juncture between these two spheres. Garment workers who did not "look like garment workers," to paraphrase one negative appraisal of *Pins and Needles* female cast members' pulchritude, blurred social and cultural boundaries. Embodying overlapping points of connection,

Figure 60. Fashionably attired Mexicana and Anglo brassiere workers walk the picket line in Los Angeles, 1941. Courtesy, UNITE HERE Archives, Kheel Center, Cornell University. Stan Boyd Press Photos, #37 AR 8 2293.

these working-class women's public presence undermined mechanisms that upheld hierarchical class relations by affixing dubious judgments upon garment workers' bodies and taste.

Dressing strategies on the picket lines emphasized workers' feminine qualities. Highlighting their attractiveness may have been a way not only to gain greater attention or encourage a more sympathetic view of their struggle but also to curtail potential violence. Lacking the measure of safety provided by the presence of middle- and upper-class women on picket lines in the 1910s, garment workers in the turbulent 1930s and 1940s who dressed up for picketing assumed a dual role. Appearing well-dressed and displaying the accepted feminine interest in following fashion muted the defiant nature of workers' refusal to accept employer-dictated working conditions and wages without diminishing their militancy in achieving improvements in the workplace.

. . . . .

A year after the Market Week picket, Rose Pesotta staged an even more elaborate event that merged fashion display with union goals. The Spring Fashion Show and Ball on March 1, 1941, at the upscale Biltmore Hotel in downtown Los Angeles responded to conventional Market Week fashion shows by featuring clothing lines produced in union shops. Manufacturers with union contracts donated the modeled outfits, happy to share in the publicity. In addition to the featured models—a mix of professionals and garment workers—Maurice's Rendezvous Orchestra provided music for dancing late into the night. Tickets for union members cost half the regular low $1.10 price, and so many members of ILGWU locals purchased them in advance that shortly after doors opened, the many people who came without tickets had to be turned away. Reporting on the unprecedented event by the local American Federation of Labor weekly, the *Los Angeles Citizen*, noted that it was also the first time members of so many locals and their relatives had come together. These garment workers made up most of the overflow crowd of more than two thousand, but elected officials like the district attorney and a representative of the mayor, prominent members of the labor community such as Central Labor Council officials, and well-known movie stars including Melvyn Douglas and Edward G. Robinson also attended. Screen actor Robert Montgomery, chair of the British War Relief Agency, showed up unannounced and spoke before the fashion show to thank the cloak makers for contributing their labor to make the several hundred coats that his war-relief organization had sent to Britain.[66]

The enthusiastic *Los Angeles Citizen* report on the evening described the fashion show as "a complete cross-section of fashions for the immediate future—from play-suits to super-formal wear." In conventional fashion-show style, the display ended with a bridal costume. The *Citizen* noted the favorable reviews by fashion editors of daily papers in Los Angeles, who seemed surprised "to learn that a Labor Union could stage such an elaborate and successful affair, and also that a Union would go out of its way to help the manufacturers in its industry." The male editor even found the fashion show—and the audience—exciting for men as well as for women. Reminding readers "that at least 90 per cent" of the audience were ILGWU members, he beamed, "And they were good to look at, take it from one who has had considerable experience along that line. While not a 'dress affair,' in the full sense of the word, the girls all outshine many of those who appear at 'real high society functions.'"

The editor took pride in union members' appearance as well as the fact that "costumes worn and shown were made by Unionists and bore the Label of the ILGWU." Bringing together the cultural practice of dressing with the production process, he understood the lasting meaning of the show as a call to "Lady Unionists and friends [who] will remember they can secure just as fine, if not better and up-to-date gowns, cloaks, etc., with the Label as without, and the workmanship is better." Similarly, dressmakers manager

George Wishnak did not distinguish between cultural and workplace activism within the union in his remarks to the gathering: "I know you are always ready to support the Union—always ready to fight for it—and always ready to show its strength, whether on the picket line or on the dance floor."[67]

Wishnak then expressed a deeply serious political message in the event's demonstration of workers' strength. "Through your efforts, industrial democracy has become realized in the garment industry, and I know that through your effort, democracy will never disappear from the face of the earth." Wishnak was, of course, alluding to the war in Europe and the destruction of democracy taking place there. The *Citizen* report also placed the fashion show in an antifascist context, comparing it to the Bal des Midinettes that Parisian garment workers held every spring before "the iron heel of Hitlerism crushed all the gaiety and beauty—as well as all the freedom—out of conquered France." Linking global politics, trade unionism, and fashion display, these labor spokesmen interpreted the show's significance in terms that transcended customarily gendered views of fashion as feminine, and thus trivial.[68]

Justice, the ILGWU's nationally distributed newspaper, provided a no less celebratory though perhaps less lofty appraisal under the heading "Glamour from Los Angeles": "As a piece of glamorous Union publicity, particularly in a partly hostile market like Los Angeles, it probably could not be excelled. . . . It has raised the Union's stature in the local industry, enhanced its stake in the market's destiny and has paved the way for wider Union appreciation and recognition in Los Angeles."[69] Glamour in this context provided an effective means of asserting union principles and validating union presence in the public sphere of a city in which achieving those goals had proved difficult. Yet questions remain about whether the centrality of female bodily display to the production of glamour ultimately undermined the ability of female workers to benefit from such glamorous union activities. Did such display irreparably objectify the very persons seeking to assert their rights as subjects? Were women union members unable to participate fully in trade unionism with such objectifying structures in place? These questions also make clear that the contradictions of glamorous union activism within the ILGWU stem not only from the larger context of the cultural institutions of female objectification but also from the contradictions inherent to the ILGWU's practice of trade unionism at midcentury.

The *Los Angeles Citizen* reported that the overwhelming success of the fashion show clearly would make it an annual event. Speculation about the next year's show focused on which larger hall the union would choose to accommodate all those who wished to come. Yet the show did not take place the following year, though several similarly elaborate dances and balls were held during the next few months to celebrate successful Pesotta-led organizing drives within the sportswear industry, including the important formation of a new local composed entirely of sportswear and lingerie workers at a large manufacturing plant, Mode O'Day. ILGWU president David Dubinsky attended, as did cast members of *The New Pins and Needles,* who happened to be in town for what became the final performances of the revue.[70]

In pursuing union recognition among the five hundred workers at Mode O'Day, Pesotta went against the advice and wishes of Levy. Her persistence, and tactics like the creation of a newsletter specifically for Mode O'Day workers, overcame the resistance of the owners and the fears of the largely white migrant workers, who ratified a union agreement by the end of March 1941. Shortly after the new local's formal installation in May, Pesotta heard that Dubinsky planned to send out a manager from New York to head the new sportswear locals in Los Angeles and Salt Lake City that she had worked so hard to organize. She protested to Levy and Dubinsky, "If I am qualified to organize these workers, negotiate for them, and sign a contract in their behalf with their employers, I hold that I am fully qualified to manage their locals." At the next General Executive Board meeting, held the following October, Pesotta learned that Dubinsky would not support her as manager and that she would be "eased out" of the Pacific region. One reason was that this region "was too small to have two vice-presidents." Knowing that several vice presidents worked together in New York City, Pesotta judged this an excuse for the union's male leadership to maintain unstated restrictions on appointing women as local managers. Levy's authoritarian streak might also have damaged any chance Pesotta might have had to win this unprecedented appointment. His subsequent conflicts with numerous union officials who were sent to work with him in Los Angeles indicate that he even had problems sharing power with men.[71]

Pesotta left Los Angeles in February 1942. Letters to Dubinsky from Mode O'Day workers who were devastated by Pesotta's departure did not alter the president's decision about their local's management. The following June, disgusted by the treatment of women within the ILGWU, Pesotta resigned from her position as a union organizer. She decided she would rather return to work in a garment shop than continue "doing the groundwork and pinch-hitting for others" without receiving the recognition and authority she felt she deserved. However, though none of the other General Executive Board members supported her views on the situation in Los Angeles nor shared her criticisms of the union's restrictions on female leadership, she maintained her position as vice president on the board until her term expired in 1944. To the dismay of the union's male leadership, Pesotta did not go quietly. At the ILGWU's 1944 national convention, Pesotta announced publicly that she would not seek reelection to the board because of its unstated policy of having only one female member.[72]

Louis Levy was more successful in his dealings with the board. His fellow board members not only supported his desire to remove Pesotta from Los Angeles but also his ambition to assume control of the new locals she organized. His tenure was lackluster. Not only were there no more glamorous fashion shows galvanizing the union movement in Los Angeles, but Mode O'Day Local 384 itself disbanded in less than six years. Contributing factors included Levy's problems with female staff members and his continuing difficulties relating to the female rank-and-file membership.[73]

The decline of the Mode O'Day local and the ongoing failure of the ILGWU's leadership to organize the increasing number of garment workers in Southern California makes clear that Pesotta's organizing strategies had made an enormous difference to the lives of women garment workers in Los Angeles. Yet the staging of the fashion show as a unique event also raises questions about the ongoing effectiveness or possibility of glamour as an organizing tool. After all, the impact of the fashion show and other ILGWU fashion events stemmed in part from their startling combination of glamour and pleasure with serious trade-union politics. Thus, perhaps the very nature of the fashion show meant it could not be sustained as an annual event to galvanize the labor movement. Pesotta noted her awareness of this probability in her memoirs. Commenting on the intervention of a policeman acting on behalf of the Biltmore Hotel to halt the glamorous Market Week picket line in 1940, she wrote, "If ever I wanted to embrace a cop who stopped a picket-line, it was then. I had been searching in my mind for some excuse to end the march before it became mere routine."[74]

Assessing Pesotta's sojourn in Los Angeles, however, suggests links between the union's persistent sexism that denied her a permanent appointment there and the retreat to less public, less energetic, and ultimately less effective organizing tactics. Therefore, the display of female bodies central to the union fashion show's production of glamour was a momentary assertion of female power within the union. Like the picket lines that enacted both protest and fashion parade, the fashion show drew upon dominant visual conventions that position the female body as "to-be-looked-at." Drawing attention to the bodies of female garment workers was an effective tactic for bringing a wider social gaze upon the circumstances of women's-clothing manufacture. Dressed provocatively in fashionable attire, workers proposed to both heighten and disrupt the pleasure shoppers and spectators took in the consumption and visual display of women's clothing by making the conditions of apparel production integral to the production of that pleasure.[75]

. . . . .

Almost twenty years after Pesotta organized the Spring Fashion Show and Ball in Los Angeles, the ILGWU embraced fashion and glamour as an organizing strategy on a national level. This tactical decision occurred after the union finally achieved a broad agreement with manufacturers to place union labels in garments made in union shops. Labels appeared in some garments early in the twentieth century, and the Blue Eagle symbol appeared briefly in many garments to certify compliance with National Recovery Act labor codes. Yet mandating labels in union-made apparel proved to be an elusive goal for the ILGWU for many decades. The late-1950s push for the label occurred in the wake of the federal government's efforts to place postwar limitations on union-organizing tactics; the 1947 Taft-Hartley Act was one such measure. The label thus provided a legal means of promoting the concept of trade unionism in the public sphere, as well as a way to pressure manufacturers to maintain union standards in the workplace. A 1958 agreement signed by the union and manufacturers nationwide resolved the central point of contention—the labels' cost—by requiring manufacturers to fund the purchase and stitching of labels within garments and requiring the ILGWU to fund a $2 million, two-year advertising campaign promoting labeled apparel. This agreement covered 105,000 ILGWU members in nine states.[76]

Longtime union vice president Julius Hochman headed the Union Label Department created in 1958 to coordinate the advertising campaign. Hochman, who believed strongly in broadly publicizing union principles and in "selling" the concept of organized labor, outlined two approaches for convincing consumers of the advantages of purchasing labeled goods. One focused on the union as a social institution and highlighted the ways the ILGWU benefited society as a whole; the second featured ILGWU-manufactured products and linked the production process to fashionable consumption. Though the union pursued both types of promotion, Hochman preferred the latter strategy and authorized its implementation via advertisements, free distribution of brochures, and films.[77]

Examining the logic behind, and the documents created by, this fashion strategy reveals fault lines in the production/consumption divide and con-

Figure 61. "Be right in style with the ILGWU label" is the theme for this 1962 parade float. Courtesy, UNITE HERE Archives, Kheel Center, Cornell University.

traditions in the ILGWU's position in the garment and fashion industries. The union's fashion strategy expanded the ILGWU's claim as a working-class institution with the power to influence taste as well as factory conditions. Yet the union's claims in both spheres were also limited. Although the trade union's social-democratic vision clearly improved working conditions and enhanced members' lives, it also ultimately supported a system of clothing manufacture that perpetuated the inequitable and uncertain employment status of its rank-and-file members, as well as their denigrated status in the dominant American culture. Moreover, the union's male-dominated leadership continued in this period to frustrate the ambitions of its largely female membership, such as the Mexican American, Anglo, and immigrant women garment workers who went on strike in Texas in 1959.[78]

By that time in the late 1950s, the ILGWU was a strong organization, representing approximately 77 percent of apparel workers nationwide.[79] Emerging from this shop floor foundation, the union-label advertising campaign helped assert an ILGWU presence within the social relations of consumption. The campaign's promise of advancing union goals thus further implicated the ILGWU within dominant ideologies and practices of consumerism. Yet just as the union's position as a bargaining partner with manufacturers both enhanced and limited possibilities for profound changes in workers' lives, the union-sponsored fashion texts both promoted and offered an alternative to conventional notions of fashion and female bodily display in the United States.

Julius Hochman understood that jobs, and thus union membership, depended on women consumers' fascination with changing styles. In his view, anything the union could do to stimulate this interest, and thus stimulate the industry, was good for the union. Furthermore, Hochman saw fashion as the central propelling element of the apparel industry, and as a central facet of women's lives: "It is to the woman not just a product, but a part of the excitement of her life, a part which she likes to follow. Therefore, the union should make fashions the vehicle of which it shall sell its social cause."[80] Hochman's appraisal of women's relationship to fashion was certainly one that manufacturers, retailers, and fashion magazines relied on and promulgated. Yet linking fashion to labor's "social cause" did add a degree of difference from the ideologies of dominant fashion institutions; this difference was especially evident in the ILGWU's understanding of fashion in its pamphlets and films promoting the union label.

Hochman hired fashion consultant Eleanor Lambert to write and produce the union's fashion-label–promotion materials. Lambert was a major and highly respected figure in New York fashion; she worked as a publicist for designers, and, among other accomplishments, had "commandeered" from the silenced French in 1940 an international "best-dressed list" of elite, wealthy women, a tradition she continued until a year before her death at one hundred in 2003 and for which she became most famous. In 1959, she and an assistant began writing a series of illustrated booklets for the union. *How to Be Well-Dressed* was followed the next year by *Your Trousseau and How to Plan It, How to Dress Your Little Girl, College Wardrobe: A Guide to the Right Clothes for Women's Colleges, Coed Schools, Big Universities, Your Dream Wardrobe and How to Make It Come True: A Fashion Guide to Young America,* and *Glamour Guide (The Wonderful New World of Lingerie and Loungewear).* Advertisements and promotional write-ups in newspapers and fashion magazines apprised readers of the booklets' availability and told them how to receive the publications by mail. Individuals, retailers, women's clubs, and community groups all requested booklets, and the union sent out 338,000 copies of the initial seven booklets within the first year of distribution.[81]

Much of the text in these booklets reproduced the type of fashion advice common in women's magazines of the period, advising readers on the styles and colors that could make them appear longer, shorter, or thinner, for example, and offering suggestions for special events like dates, weddings, and formal occasions and for everyday wear at school, home, or work. Booklets also offered practical information about dress sizing and care of clothing, as well as tips on "smart" shopping. The fashion sensibility was decidedly middle-class, with warnings, for example, against wearing high heels with slacks or wearing a scarf in the city instead of a hat. The booklets also contained assumptions about wifely desires to share one's life "with a man you want to please in every way" and advised college girls not to "spend your campus life in pants [because] men are looking for *girls*, not other boys for dates." Yet fashion in women's lives did not revolve totally around male attention. The "career girl" received the highest praise, as "the girl with the chance to live up to the full potential of what American fashion provides in style and quality."[82]

Lambert included a reproduction of the union label in each booklet, along with an explanation of its significance as a "symbol of decency, fair labor standards and the American way of life." She also identified the series as part of the union-label campaign, and "in the ILGWU tradition of community service and active concern for the welfare of all Americans." Most of the initial booklets gave little additional information about the union. However, the introductory section of *Your Dream Wardrobe* explored the link between the ILGWU and fashion more fully. Drawing on the booklet's title theme and addressing young women, the introduction portrays the history of teenage sweatshop workers at the turn of the century, their struggles to improve harsh working conditions, and current benefits of union membership as examples of "how to make dreams come true." Linking the production and consumption of clothing in this manner altered the conventional advertising theme of fulfilling one's wishes through the purchase of consumer goods, instead giving the act of consumption a history and making its contemporary practice a self-conscious act within a context of known social relationships.[83]

Though the connection between production and consumption lay at the heart of the label campaign's meaning, Lambert and her cowriters did not develop this concept, perhaps because it resonated more with an earlier twentieth-century ideal—which Lizabeth Cohen calls the "citizen consumer"—that had become difficult to articulate and imagine within the postwar consumer world. The choice to emphasize consumption rather than its link with production may also indicate the lessening interest of comfortable and aging male union leaders in the hard work of organizing garment workers, who, once immigration restrictions were lifted in 1965, increasingly were immigrant women from Mexico, Central America, and

Asia, with whom the leadership was unfamiliar. Though Taft-Hartley limitations and greater movement of production offshore caused membership to decline and portended the return of sweatshops to America a few decades later, the ILGWU in the 1960s was still over four hundred thousand strong, was respected and politically influential, and provided a decent standard of living and significant benefits to its members.

Yet the ILGWU's label campaign still offered an alternative view of fashion consumption. Especially in the first booklet, *How to Be Well-Dressed*, and in *Your Dream Wardrobe*, Lambert's response to the question "What Is Fashion?" for example, describes fashion as a system in which all are implicated but in which all can take pleasure. Though presenting fashion as a source of female pleasure served the ongoing sales goals of magazines and manufacturers, this union publication legitimized body self-decoration and display as a source of female pleasure at work and in other spheres of life. The union's democratic view valorized fashion as a "modern art form" that "everyone can practice," a "big business," and "an important part of our national life and culture." These comments dignified and lent significance to women's garment work, as well as infusing such work with the cachet of aesthetic sensibilities. Moreover, they argued against trivializing women's interest in apparel consumption and display by reformulating what was often characterized as an individual weakness as a source of national strength and pride.[84]

The first fashion film that Lambert produced more richly explored the ideas mentioned briefly in the booklets. The opening sequence of *The Fashion Picture* depicts a series of three models, the second of whom is a stout older woman. The film's female narrator describes the older woman's suit in phrases similar to those she uses to characterize the outfits modeled by the two other slim, young blonde and brunette models, though with the additional comment that her look "is purely wonderful in all sizes and for all ages." This inclusive view of fashion and of the fashionable continues throughout the half-hour film. Though younger and slimmer models predominate, older and larger women also appear and receive attention in the narration. Their bodies are not problematized through an emphasis on figure faults that need particular clothing styles for correction but are depicted as fashionable and dignified. The narrator's tone expresses knowing delight in describing the stylish possibilities available in "size 18½." Her vocal inflection subtly indicates a shared awareness with the viewer that larger sizes are not usually presented in this manner. Moreover, including children, teenagers, younger and older women, and a range of "the well-to-do to those who have to watch the pennies" within the context of fashionability in itself defies the conventional segmentation used by the fashion press to make distinctions between the fashionable and the unfashionable. *The Fashion Picture* keeps a range of women in view while acknowledging a diversity of apparel needs and desires.[85]

Early in the film, narration and images describe the apparel production process, depicting participants ranging from designers and store buyers to cutters, operators, finishers, and pressers. This section lasts about five minutes, during which the narrator discusses the "modest little label that speaks volumes, that tells you these skilled garment workers work with pride and pleasure, that they were glad to make your dress," and describes the "International Ladies Garment Workers Union, one of the country's most respected organizations." The union is not only a "productive and stabilizing force in industry" but also a "pioneer in workers' education and health and welfare programs . . . a leader in community service and in aiding the cause of democracy throughout the world." Moreover, the "450,000 members . . . sign their work with the ILGWU label because they want you to know it was produced by men and women who, through their union, have won fair standards, the dignity of a voice in their own conditions of employment, a respected place in their communities." Images of male and female European Americans of diverse ethnicities and African American women intent on their work in garment shops accompany this narration, connecting bodies and faces to commodities that consumers usually viewed in stores, divorced from their productive origins. And, although the assertion of garment workers' "pride and pleasure" was more utopian proposition than reality, it did offer a critique of most people's working conditions by presenting an alternative view of what work could and should be. Situating a discussion of work within the film's primary context of fashion display evoked the pleasurable possibilities of reintegrating production and consumption.

A central feature of *The Fashion Picture* is its appropriation of high culture. The narration and visual presentation make explicit comparisons between the clothing modeled in the film and painters like Gauguin and Van Gogh, and it analyzes modern architecture's effect on contemporary fashion. In addition, models appear in museum-like settings with touches of faux pre-twentieth-century elegance or minimalist modern decor and geometric backdrops. Calderesque mobiles decorate one sparse staircase on which models materialize in sequential jump cuts. Op-art special effects, some showing rounded and conjoined union labels spinning like balls, fill the screen to mark transitions between film segments. With this appropriation of high art and architecture and use of innovative visual effects, the union lays even further claim to the sphere of culture and consumption. In line with the union's offerings of educational and cultural programs that defied conventional boundaries between working-class and elite culture, this aspect of *The Fashion Picture* asserts workers' rights to aesthetic knowledge, beauty, artistic experimentation, and adornment. Without the elitist edge of *Vogue*, which also often linked high art and fashion, the film confounded categories by embracing elegance, glamour, and avant-garde aesthetics as central to working-class life and pleasure. Moreover, the union's version of these qualities, which remained associated with elites to maintain class definitions, was not mere imitation. Their formulation and presentation by the union in this film and in its programs was an innovative and inclusive mix of elements.

The Fashion Picture and subsequent Lambert films were shown at movie theaters and stores, on television, and to women's groups and schools. Audiences for the first four films exceeded twenty-one million people within three years. However, the later films became more conventional in their narration and presentation of fashion, with less emphasis on diversity and on garment manufacture. The fashion strategy as a whole also came into question in a report by Louis Harris and Associates, whom Dubinsky hired in 1961 to investigate the campaign's effectiveness. Though the fashion presentations smoothed relations between the ILGWU and the manufacturers whose clothes appeared in the films, the report indicated that direct appeals to women's social conscience were more effective with the public. Despite this conclusion, the union persisted in its use of a fashion emphasis to publicize the label.[86]

The early booklets and films, which were read and seen by a mass audience, put forward alternative understandings of the relationship between fashion and factory work and between production and consumption. The difficulty of sustaining discussion of these relationships is evident in recent efforts by sweatshop workers in Los Angeles, Central America, and Asia and by their advocates to affect sales of products. Though a national survey suggests that American shoppers would rather buy clothing produced under decent conditions, informing the public about which garments come from sweatshops is difficult, and getting consumers to consistently act on this information at the point of purchase is more so. According to the *Los Angeles Times*, one antisweatshop activist thinks that "it'll be a decade, if ever, before changes in consumer purchasing show up." The separation of production from consumption, and of the garment industry from the fashion industry, is a strategic mechanism for maintaining manufacturers' and retailers' power and limiting workers' ability to effect changes in the production of glamour.[87]

. . . . .

The ILGWU's use of glamour and fashion as an organizing tactic—whether in spontaneous local efforts by rank-and-file members and inspired organizers like Rose Pesotta or in nationally orchestrated advertising campaigns—had mixed results. The strategy certainly brought publicity and positive public attention to the union and its goals. However, despite the cultural capital the union accrued through staging fashion shows, disseminating fashion booklets and films, and, especially, through the unexpected success of staging *Pins and Needles,* the use of glamour brought forward the contradictions wrought by the heightened separation of production from consumption in the twentieth century. Within dominant culture, glamour helps ease the tensions generated by this division, a key component in the construction of class-based hierarchies of work, leisure, and identity. The glamour of the fashion industry enhances clothing's associations with pleasurable use and display by veiling the prosaic and exploitative environment of the garment industry.

Culture is an important arena for maintaining class difference and preserving dominant relations of production and consumption. The publicity generated by *Pins and Needles* and other union-sponsored activities that transgressed boundaries between the fashion industry and the garment industry exposed the constructed nature of inequitable divisions of labor and the social hierarchies they uphold. Intimate apparel workers who made public claims to glamour and fashion blurred those distinctions and disrupted naturalizing ideologies that limited workers' ability to shape the cultural meaning of the garments they made.

7   Return of the Repressed (Waist), 1947–1952

To *make* oneself an object, to *make* oneself passive, is a very different thing from *being* a passive object.

Simone de Beauvoir, *The Second Sex,* 1953

In February 1947, French couturier Christian Dior presented spring and summer fashions at his new salon. Dubbed the "New Look" by *Harper's Bazaar* editor-in-chief Carmel Snow, the Dior style featured a long and full skirt, rounded shoulders, and a cinched waist. This silhouette was a dramatic departure from the shape of women's clothing in the United States and Great Britain during World War II. In both countries, wartime shortages had prompted government regulation of fabric and materials that kept skirts straight and hems knee length. The crisis was more severe in Britain, where the "Utility" dress became the state-sanctioned fashion trend in 1942. In the United States, though Women's Bureau director Mary Anderson declared corsets essential to women's war work in factories, the government banned elastic from foundation garments. The effectiveness of such regulations was clear in lingerie manufacturers' plea to define certain robes as necessities rather than luxuries. Women, they argued, would need the robes during late-night or early-morning air raids.[1]

Pent-up desire for fashion changes has served to explain women's acceptance of Dior's new silhouette. Yet distinctions between New Look and World War II–era styles also provoked arguments against its adoption, and a short but pointed debate ensued. For many, the New Look marked a welcome return of peacetime femininity for women, but some viewed it as a step backward in women's comfort, convenience, and beauty in dress. It certainly was a lucrative trend for corset and textile manufacturers. The strongest opposition centered on American women's relationship to the fashion-industrial complex, and to their bodies, to male onlookers, and to the gender division of labor. Analyzing the history and meaning of the New Look debates thus provides a multifaceted perspective on midcentury dynamics of gendered fashion, power, and sexuality, a central theme of this book.[2]

Figure 62. Christian Dior's 1947 New Look emphasized sloping shoulders, a cinched waist, and a long, full skirt. Courtesy, The Metropolitan Museum of Art, Mrs. John Chambers Hughes, 1958 (C.I.58.34.30), and Christian Dior, 1969 (C.I.69.40). All rights reserved, The Metropolitan Museum of Art.

The revival of fashionable corsetry generated by the New Look—and consolidated by the introduction of the Merry Widow corset in 1952—points to a number of important issues discussed separately in previous chapters. The initial formulation of the New Look in France and its ultimate acceptance by women in America raise questions about women's "spontaneous consent" to wearing more restrictive clothing in this period and also about the gendered meanings ascribed to female dressing practices during the postwar years. In addition, closer examination of how American women constructed their New Look directs us to consider the shaping of dominant cultural forms like popular fashions as a process of negotiation between resistant consumers and an industry engaged in both active persuasion and accommodation. In the manufacture and sale of clothing, the fashion and garment industries produced ideologies as well as the goods necessary to achieve the New Look. And within the garment industry itself, both factory owners and organized labor had a stake in backing the New Look because it promised to increase both apparel sales and jobs. Thus, the New Look succeeded because of a number of French and American postwar economic and labor concerns; reformulating gender distinctions and relying on conventions of female bodily display became a means of resolving the difficult transition to a peacetime economy and culture.

.   .   .   .   .

The New Look's design and distribution came about as the French government, the French textile industry, and the Chambre Syndicale de la Couture Parisienne, the trade association of Paris couturiers, worked together to restore the luster and respect of French fashion after the Allied Forces liberated Paris in August 1944. Until that time, no one outside of occupied France had known that as many as one hundred couture houses had continued making high-fashion clothing under the administration of the Nazis for some twenty thousand customers. Couturiers explained this collaboration as a means of preserving civilian jobs during the war for their twelve thousand workers and of preventing the Nazis from removing the couture industry to Vienna or Berlin, as they threatened to do several times. Though the Nazis also granted couturiers special access to fabrics otherwise in short supply, the cheerful and relatively extravagant fashions available to upper-class French women, black marketeers, and high-ranking Nazis stationed in France were similarly rationalized as a blow against the spiritual oppression of fascism. Yet as costume historian Lou Taylor notes, "By the very fact of remaining open the couture houses, like the theaters, contributed to Hitler's overall plan for Paris." That was certainly the perspective of fascism's active opponents who refused to aid the Nazis in creating the veneer of respectability they occasionally utilized to cloak their viciousness.[3]

The first Allied fashion reporters to enter Paris after the liberation were shocked to discover the ornamental attire worn by city residents. Despite attempts by American officials to censor news about high fashion's survival during the Nazi occupation, word spread, and anger and accusations followed. Couturier Lucien Lelong, the head of the Chambre Syndicale, who negotiated with the Nazis under the occupation, presented his organization's perspective to representatives of the United States, Britain, and the French Resistance investigating French collaboration with the Nazis. Nevertheless, much of New York's fashion press was eager to restore the good name of French fashion to once again enjoy its pleasures. Edna Woolman Chase of *Vogue* led this contingent, and in December 1944, Lelong published a statement in the magazine explaining the actions of couturiers during the war. In addition, the French government was anxious to restore this important export industry in which domestic sales accounted for only one-fifth of yearly production. Thus, although many observers remained unconvinced of the couturiers' innocence, no collaboration charges were filed against any couturiers. Coco Chanel, who closed her business after the German occupation but spent the war as the companion of a Nazi officer, quietly moved to Switzerland.[4]

The Chambre Syndicale's campaign to restore French fashion's reputation and influence began with the introduction of post-liberation collections that favored simplified styles in the mode of wartime fashions worn in the United States and Britain. Uncertainty among French designers about style trends and continued fabric shortages impeded full revival of haute couture until Dior's 1947 show. During the war, Dior had designed clothing for Lucien Lelong, whose house, according to *Current Biography 1948,* "was a favorite of the Germans during the Nazi occupation." With the backing of French textile magnate Marcel Boussac, who was reportedly looking for a designer who would restore Parisian fashion prominence and jump-start French textile sales, Dior opened his own salon in 1946. Dior's 1947 collection promptly accomplished both of Boussac's goals, though not without controversy. Although the international debate in the press and on the airwaves helped organize opponents of the New Look, it also garnered Dior's collection extensive publicity.[5]

Opposition to the New Look came from a range of sources. The British government and women's wear industry, still coping with the war's devastation, determined that the New Look's excessive fabric requirements posed a threat to peacetime reorganization. In fact, despite the ultimate popularity of the New Look, British regulation of clothing continued well into the 1950s because of the severe economic dislocations caused by the war. The Utility Scheme lasted until 1952, and other price and production controls continued until 1955. In a 1947 compromise proposal that sought to allow Britain to profit from the New Look without jeopardizing the home market and textile supply, Stafford Cripps, president of the British Board of Trade, suggested that British designers supply long skirts for export but keep skirts short for the domestic market. However, in 1948, representatives of three hundred dress manufacturers petitioned the Board of Trade for a ban on long hemlines.[6]

In the United States, well-known Hollywood designer Gilbert Adrian voiced high-profile objections to the New Look. Adrian was widely credited with creating the upscale version of the wartime silhouette, with its squared and padded shoulders, trim suits, and skirt hems set just at or below the knees. By 1947, Adrian had branched out from movie-costume design at MGM studios, where he had worked since 1925 and was especially noted for defining the look of actors such as Joan Crawford, Greta Garbo, and his wife, Janet Gaynor. He left MGM in 1942 to produce clothing designs for national retail sale in better department and specialty stores from his unionized shop in Los Angeles. Considered a pioneer of "California couture," Adrian, through his opposition to the New Look, evoked the ongoing rivalry between the United States and France for fashion preeminence. During the war, the stature of American designers in New York City and Los Angeles benefited from the silencing of France. Yet competition also existed between the East and West Coasts for style leadership, and the primary location of the national fashion press in New York City often meant that Los Angeles designers received short shrift. This situation surely weakened the possibility that Adrian's negative appraisal of the New Look would dispel any of the eagerness with which the New York City–based fashion press awaited the French revival.[7]

Adrian's rejection of the New Look was certainly based in his aesthetic and financial investment in a mode that had suddenly become passé. At the presentation of his August 1947 collection in Los Angeles, he advocated resistance to being "bullied." "As I prefer women to look slim and elegant rather than dowdy and dumpy, I cannot prescribe to the sloping shoulder or padded hip. Why any woman wants to return to ugliness for the sake of change is more than I can comprehend. To this nonsense I must give reassurance that no woman has to do anything today she doesn't want to . . . we fortunately are still living in a free country."[8] Many Americans agreed. A Gallup poll found the combined national membership of Little Below the Knee clubs to be three hundred thousand, and in September 1947, *Women's Wear Daily* reported male opposition to the disappearance of the leg in Baltimore, Maryland, and Lafayette, Indiana. That month, Dior faced protesters in Chicago, who picketed outside a hotel luncheon in his honor, and in Dallas, Texas, where he was accepting a design award from the Neiman-Marcus department store. He also received angry letters in Paris from American husbands dismayed at his success in "disfiguring" their wives.[9]

Dior remained unshaken by this opposition: "Once they have seen it they will be convinced. The short skirt was a fashion of the German occupation—a warlike interpretation of women's clothes. The new lengths represent a freedom from restriction—a natural result that cannot be

Figure 63. Gilbert Adrian is best known for his 1940s suits with square-shouldered jackets and straight skirts. Courtesy, Museum Associates/LACMA, Gift of Mrs. Houston Rehrig. 2005 © Museum Associates/LACMA.

stopped."[10] Yet Dior's version of freedom from wartime restriction dictated specialized corsetry that constricted the waist, abdomen, and hips. The designer's couture creations often included a layer of boned foundations within the structure of the garments themselves. American corset and foundation manufacturers knew that mass-market versions of the New Look, which began production within months of Dior's initial February show, would not include this feature. Women would need to purchase waist cinchers and other revived fashionable corsetry to create the New Look for themselves.

By November, American fashion economists predicted that 1948 corset sales would "certainly equal and probably surpass the all-time highs of 1947." Yet though they recognized the importance of the New Look to sales increases, they cautiously declined to peg this growth to unstable fashion trends. Instead, they considered the phenomenal growth in foundation sales since the late 1920s, during which time brassiere production quadrupled and that of corsets and garter belts more than doubled, to be evidence that women accepted foundations as "essential to proper comfort, posture and health," and "because they afford the illusion of slimness." Looking beyond the New Look, corset manufacturers intended the many marketing campaigns they had waged since the 1920s to keep women in some form of foundation indefinitely.[11]

Corset makers had good reason for confidence. Restriction of the female body provided continuity between wartime and postwar silhouettes. Even the apparently striking differences between Dior's and Adrian's collections did not make them opposites. Both designers, for example, used asymmetricality for effect and took inspiration from high-culture artists like Dali and Picasso, respectively. Most importantly, whereas the New Look resurrected the need for waist cinchers, looking smart in an Adrian suit had required tightly girdled hips to achieve a smooth, straight skirt line. Thus, Adrian's objections to the New Look, like those of most other critics, did not focus on body restraint but on the silhouette shape and the long, full skirt. Similarities between Dior and Adrian increased within a few years of the New Look's introduction, as both men modified their designs. Dior shortened hems somewhat and added a straight-skirt option, while Adrian produced dresses with fuller skirts that emphasized a narrower waistline.[12]

American designer Claire McCardell provided an alternative to both Dior and Adrian. In fact, Betty Friedan entitled her 1955 *Town Journal* magazine article on McCardell "The Gal Who Defied Dior." McCardell first worked in New York as a ready-to-wear designer in the 1930s. Though her job was to make mass-market versions of Paris styles, in 1937, McCardell wore one of her own designs to work. A buyer who happened to see her in the showroom ordered three dozen dresses in this design, which became known as the "Monastic" dress. The simply draped dress, which had no seamed waistline and was to be worn with a self-adjusting belt, became the first McCardell fashion hit.[13]

McCardell's success continued in the 1940s. Her locally inspired designs held her in good stead during the war, when Parisian style ideas were no longer available for New York firms to copy. After a stint working for Hattie Carnegie designing exclusive, custom-made clothing for the wealthy, McCardell returned to her preferred medium of creating affordable, attractive, long-lasting, and comfortable clothing for American women on a mass scale. As the chief designer and co-owner of Townley Frocks, McCardell pioneered the use of cotton and denim fabrics for dresses, simplified clothes fastenings for easier dressing, put pockets in skirts, and designed the popular "Popover" dress for women to wear while they did housework, tended their wartime victory gardens, and entertained at home. These accomplishments earned McCardell the Neiman-Marcus award the year after Dior received it.[14]

Many commentators claim that the New Look was wholly Dior's invention after the war. However, prewar fashions of 1938 and 1939 had begun to feature full skirts, and Dior himself had designed such shapes at that time and during the German occupation of Paris. In addition, McCardell and other designers presented longer and fuller skirts in the postwar period. Dior's extreme formulation of the style, impressive costume artistry, flair for presentation, and ability to manifest these qualities with Boussac's extensive financial backing brought him extensive acclaim as the New Look's originator. The hubbub after Dior's presentation of the style also created a favorable climate for the New Look's widespread adoption.[15]

Despite the fashion industry's—and often fashion history's—preoccupation with origins and originality, the critical question about the New Look is why American women quickly embraced the New Look silhouette, with its waist-cinching requirements and its acknowledged symbolic meaning as a "return to femininity." However, embracing Dior as a fashion dictator or genius obscures the broader context of international politics, economics, and fashion in which the New Look emerged and thrived. As with corset use generally in the twentieth century, women's "spontaneous consent" to wearing New Look foundations did not occur without prompting. The interests of corset and textile manufacturers, the fashion press, and dress manufacturers eager to make wartime wardrobes obsolete all contributed to the ultimately favorable reception for the New Look in the United States.

In accepting the overall New Look silhouette, women were certainly taking pleasure in turning away from fashions linked with the devastation and privation of war. Yet women's purported desires for renewed femininity in this period are crucial to explore. As this book has shown, wearing foundations and undergarments not only constructed gender differences but also displayed compliance to their conventions and boundaries. And although women may have donned these garments to heighten feelings of sexual pleasure and desire, the way in which undergarments expressed and satisfied such pleasures cannot be entirely divorced from larger ideological structures and institutions that fetishized and objectified women's clothing and bodies. Such structures at this historical moment, for example, naturalized the use of women's bodies as a symbol for the end of hostilities and connected particular configurations of femininity with "normalcy." In addition, very real needs certainly heightened women's concerns about attracting male attention in the postwar reorganization. Millions of return-ing servicemen needed jobs at the same time that government production orders were dwindling. Reestablishing gender divisions of labor that had blurred during the war eased the shift to a peacetime economy by dimin-ishing women's opportunities to secure higher-paying and more challeng-ing work. Complying with conventions of femininity in dress and manner was a long-standing means of attracting a husband and obtaining the eco-nomic benefits of marriage—challenges that were especially important for women living in an era in which they could not easily support themselves.

Another significant question is how American women put on their New Look. The view of Dior as a fashion genius or dictator not only denies the larger forces of cultural hegemony at work in the acceptance of the New Look—in terms of the location and force of top-down persuasion—but also overlooks female resistance and fashion-industry accommodation. Certainly, the increased emphasis on a small waist fueled sales of cinchers and other re-strictive foundation garments. However, many mass versions of the New Look were not as constricting or as cumbersome as Dior's original design. For example, a 1948 *Harper's Bazaar* fashion spread on clothes for college stu-dents entitled "The Now Look," characterized styles of the previous year as "extremes and excesses" that had "gladdened the funnymen of stage, screen and radio." The styles of 1948 would retain the small shoulder and waistline and the long skirt, but without "all extra bulk and billow and balloonery."[16]

By 1949, Dior was dismayed at the interpretation of his New Look seen on the streets of America. "American women have misunderstood. I de-signed a long skirt for cocktail wear. That does not mean it is for street, of-fice or sports wear. I designed one skirt; your American manufacturers made it the style for all women. . . . You can overdo a good thing."[17] What Dior missed, as have commentators on the New Look who analyze its acceptance as evidence of women's ridiculous devotion to fashion or to their oppressed state, is that long skirts and petticoats also free women from the tyranny of slim hips and close public scrutiny of their legs. Though female members of the "Below the Knee Club" may have enjoyed the freedom of shorter hems and perhaps male appreciation of their legs and hips, other women clearly welcomed additional cover.

Some women indeed appropriated the new length without taking on the more constricting features of the New Look. Angela Partington examined postwar family photographs and found that working-class women con-structed a more comfortable version of the New Look silhouette. In addi-tion, these women often mixed elements of pre- and postwar fashion in put-ting together their outfits. Though Dior or other fashion arbiters might

Figure 64. A Local 62 member (far right) wears her stylish take on the New Look for a union skit (1952). Courtesy, UNITE HERE Archives, Kheel Center, Cornell University.

have disagreed, these women identified their costumes as fashionably New Look. Moreover, Partington argues that rather than viewing such outfits as "watered down" versions of the New Look, we should see them as deliberate revisions in which working-class women "articulate[d] their own specific tastes and preferences . . . by using the cultural codes of the mass-market fashion system."[18]

· · · · ·

The reaction of the International Ladies Garment Workers Union to the New Look was similar to that of the manufacturers with whom it had labor contracts. ILGWU Undergarment and Negligee Workers Local 62 memos exude excitement at the increased production of petticoats and corsets that kept workers employed and preserved their status as dues-paying union members. However, the ILGWU may have been especially relieved to see the emergence of the New Look silhouette because of another trend that began in 1947, the Taft-Hartley Act, which brought a new look to postwar labor legislation and negotiations and was a blow to unions.[19]

When the Republican-controlled Congress that had been elected in 1946

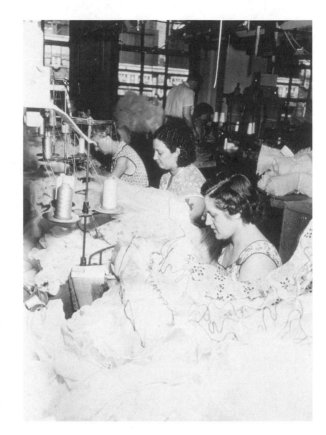

Figure 65. Undergarment workers sew the new postwar fashion of full, frilly petticoats. Courtesy, UNITE HERE Archives, Kheel Center, Cornell University.

overrode President Truman's veto of the Taft-Hartley Act in 1947, it marked the end of an era for organized labor. Limiting the rights the federal government had guaranteed to workers under the New Deal labor legislation of the 1930s, Taft-Hartley restricted the methods that labor unions could use in organizing workplaces and in maintaining their right to collective bargaining there. It allowed states to enjoin unions from requiring new workers to join their locals, effectively permitting states to outlaw the closed shop, and it authorized the president to declare a "cooling-off" period during contract negotiations, in effect prohibiting strikes for eighty days. In addition, the legislation held unions financially responsible for any court penalties imposed at the conclusion of strikes for violations of labor agreements, whether those strikes had been authorized by the union or not. Moreover, union officials were required by the act to sign loyalty oaths affirming they were not communists for their union to receive government enforcement, through regulatory bodies such as the National Labor Relations Board, of their right to organize. This latter provision created division throughout the labor movement, prompting union officials and members to weigh First Amendment considerations against the desire to protect hard-won gains—and future victories—in wages, working conditions, and benefits.[20]

Ultimately, the effects of the Taft-Hartley Act outlasted those of the New Look for members of Local 62 and other undergarment workers nationwide. Local 62's membership peaked in the late 1950s before beginning its slow decline through the next several decades. The increasing movement of production "offshore" to Puerto Rico, Mexico, Central America, and Asia also diminished the presence of the ILGWU in the American garment industry. Though the garment industry continued to flourish in cities like Los Angeles, many of the largely immigrant workers found themselves working in nonunion shops under conditions similar to those faced by other immigrant women at the turn of the century.

. . . . .

The New Look glamorized corsetry and the constricted waist through its association with haute couture and the Allied victory, yet paradoxically, its popularity also made corsets' status as fetish object more ordinary. Many American women particularly sought to reduce their waists for special-occasion dressing, and the common use of corsets to construct the unique pleasures of proms, weddings, and New Year's Eve parties brought these restrictive garments back into the mainstream of American public as well as private life. The success of the Merry Widow corset, a 1950s reimagining of Victorian corset design by Warner's, illustrates the widespread interest in corsets as sexual fetish objects after the war. It was both a nostalgic throwback and an up-to-date means of eroticizing the female body via restriction. Although the Merry Widow ultimately incorporated a range of styles, from short to long line, its early versions were boned, had attached garters, and extended from the top of the breasts to the top of the hips. In addition to its decorative functions, the Merry Widow constricted the waist and reshaped breasts and hips.[21]

In the well-established and profitable practice of linking fashion and film promotion, Warner's, as we have seen, introduced its new product with the release of the third high-profile Hollywood film version of Franz Lehar's operetta *The Merry Widow*. A silent version directed by Erich von Stroheim in 1925 starred Mae Murray and John Gilbert, and a black-and-white sound film directed by Ernst Lubitsch in 1934 cast Jeanette MacDonald and Mau-

Figure 66. Gina Lollobrigida gets laced into her fashionable 1950s corset for *Beat the Devil* (1953). Courtesy, Photofest.

rice Chevalier in the lead roles. Set in 1900, the lavish 1952 Technicolor version starred former "sweater girl" Lana Turner as Merry Widow Crystal Radek and Fernando Lamas as her suitor Prince Danilo.[22] In the movie, Turner makes several appearances wearing a corset shaped like Warner's Merry Widow rather than one that actually reflected the style worn at the turn of the century. As a grieving widow, Turner wears black, in one scene wearing only her black corset (see figure 29). This scene and one in which she wears a beautiful black nightgown with black lace trim highlight the seductive and erotic qualities of Turner's body. Though playing a widow who sincerely mourns her husband, Turner wears black costumes that enhance rather than mute her striking sexual attractiveness.[23]

Ironically, only when the widow assumes the character of Fifi, a prostitute who works at the Paris nightclub Maxim's, does Turner wear white. Danilo had been ordered by the king of his tiny, poor, but still elegant country to seduce and wed the wealthy widow, who has been invited to the castle ostensibly to honor her husband's memory. After discovering the plan to use her wealth to pay off the national debt, Crystal flees to Paris before she is to meet Danilo. Sick of fortune hunters and wanting to enjoy life again, the widow initially changes personas with her assistant. However, in seeking to discover the true character of Danilo, she follows him into Maxim's, which she can enter alone only as a working girl. After ripping some lace from the top of her white dress, the widow convinces both cohorts and customers, including Danilo, that she is Fifi.

Back at her Paris hotel, dressed only in her white corset, Crystal realizes that Danilo has followed her. Angry and yet attracted to the handsome and charming Danilo, Turner at one point leaves her room to give him a piece of her mind, only to return when she suddenly realizes she is not fully dressed. This incident evokes the familiar fantasy (or nightmare) of appearing in public undressed and heightens film viewers' attention to Turner's tightly corseted body. However, because Turner's body is clearly one of the central attractions of the film, the scene underscores the Merry Widow corset itself as erotic fetish. Similarly evocative is the 1947 Playtex Living Girdle, which, in its name, embodies the transformation of pliable flesh into appropriately feminized form, thereby bringing the objectified and therefore fetishized body to life. In the postwar, New Look era, restrictive clothing, particularly undergarments, still infused the female body with erotic meaning.[24]

Lana Turner's costumes in *The Merry Widow* also play upon conventional midcentury understandings of blackness and whiteness, giving them material shape in black and white lingerie. Turner wears seductive black when playing the morally upright and sincere widow, and she wears white when assuming the false persona of the licentious prostitute. But the central meaning of this reversal in typical understandings of white and black undergarments may be less concerned with changes in contemporary meanings of whiteness and blackness than with the sexual objectification of women's bodies generally. As I discuss in chapter 4, black undergarments not only conveyed the status of mourning but also reflected the sexual knowledge and experience of a married, though now widowed, woman. The eroticization of white undergarments that takes place in *The Merry Widow* transforms the purity and modesty associated with white undergarments into another potential source of fetishized pleasure.

The film's corset scenes resonated with 1950s notions of femininity and sexual attractiveness, in which women needed to be both naughty and nice whether dressed in black or white. The notorious extreme-uplift bras with pointy, circle-stitched cups; girdles made from unyielding synthetic fabrics that tightly pressed the legs together; and heightened attention to "magic" and "witchery" in undergarment advertising of this era also helped mainstream intimate apparel's status as sexual fetish in American culture. Moreover,

Figure 67. This Merry Widow corset ad foregrounds feminine masquerade and the centrality of tight foundation garments as means of constructing the twentieth-century "naughty but nice" feminine ideal. *Life,* December 13, 1954. Courtesy, Warnaco Inc.

these trends furthered the expectation that American women would consider and construct themselves as "to-be-looked-at," whether they were fully dressed or clad only in their lingerie and shaping garments.

From the 1909 founding of Local 62 to the 1952 introduction of the Merry Widow corset, mass-produced, commercially advertised, nationally distributed, and widely available undergarments and foundations were worn by almost every woman in the United States. Their large-scale production, purchase, and display brought women garment workers and consumers into a transnational network of political, economic, and cultural interests. Fashion changes in this period resulted from negotiations between female consumers and primarily male manufacturers, advertisers, and retailers. Female garment workers and saleswomen also played an important part in determining the shape and meaning of fashion in daily life. All these historical actors drew upon, promoted, resisted, and transformed significant ideological constructs in asserting their fashion statements.

The evolving fabric, ornamentation, and design of undergarments—and their meanings—reveal how changing notions of femininity have found expression in the shaping of the female body, which is shaped as well by wider industrial factors and ideological concerns. Women submitted to the ever-changing array of constricting garments that remolded their flesh so as to construct themselves as silhouettes of fashionable feminine attractiveness. However, throughout the twentieth century, body constriction coexisted with evolving desires for comfort and freedom in dress. Female consumers' search for these qualities in their wardrobes drove manufacturers into a "corsetless panic" and powered the rise of sportswear. Yet by adapting their marketing strategies to promote new designs made from higher-tech materials, those who made their living from the satellite of undergarment and foundation industries were able to continue doing so. Thus, in 1947, *Women's Wear Daily* also described "the New Look in sportswear," and in response to women's increasing ability to wear trousers in the 1950s, manufacturers produced "Slackees," a long-line girdle with separate leg sections, to wear under trousers.

As long as body restriction and slimness remain central features of fashion, femininity, and female sexuality, American women will use some form of body-shaping garments. The fashion-industrial complex, deploying multiple means to uphold, foster, and cherish the objectification and fetishization of the female body, works to make sure that they do.[25]

Epilogue **Bra vs. Bra**

Feminist Intimate Apparel Art

> Who can doubt that the modern feminist is the direct outcome
> of the vanishing undie?
>
> **Alma Whitaker,** *Trousers and Skirts,* 1923

After the New Look became old hat, fashionable underwear again began to shrink in size and scope, but not in importance. Though undergarments were smaller, the rise of the feminist movement prompted closer scrutiny of the garments as profitable commodities and restrictive gender markers, and many women made their criticisms widely apparent. Countercultural and expressly women's liberationist dressing practices melded within these critics' rejection of confining foundation garments, objections similar to those made by turn-of-the-century corset opponents in the aesthetic and health and hygiene movements, and challenges mounted by high-fashion designers and tango-crazed youth in the 1910s. In the 1960s and 1970s, concerns about providing "natural" beauty, comfort, and health; unleashing the pleasures—and strengths—of the female body; enjoying popular music and fashion; and challenging traditional wisdom about respectable femininity all informed the shape and perceptions of women's underwear.

Although—contrary to urban legend—no bras were burned on the Atlantic City Boardwalk at the 1968 Miss America Pageant protest, participants unfurled the new critical perspective they called "women's liberation," and feminism has been closely associated with undergarments in the popular imagination ever since. The protesters threw bras, girdles, and other objects they found offensive into a "freedom trash can" but scrapped an earlier plan to burn the can's contents due to fire regulations. Yet mass-media reports often labeled feminists as "bra burners," a derisive moniker perpetuated by their opponents. Undergarments were a powerful symbol for both feminists and antifeminists for good reason. As this book has shown, intimate apparel shapes and sexualizes female bodies and figures centrally in women's conformity to particular, historic notions of embodied femininity. The "bra-burner" characterization fostered fear of and sought to dismiss feminist critiques by associating them with protests by Vietnam war resisters who burned draft cards, demonstrations of discontent by inner-city residents, and the trivialized feminine preoccupation with fashion. A century earlier, antifeminists had used a similar strategy in ridiculing the Bloomer Costume and the pro-suffrage women who wore it. With the vote won, and in the context of civil rights, antiwar, and countercultural movements, late twentieth-century feminists were better able to remain focused on transforming fashions they identified as oppressive and achieving political and economic gender-equity goals.

Since the 1960s, works by feminist artists that depict undergarments have pointed to a wider cultural concern as well as specifically feminist interest in undergarments and the striking symbolic power they wield. Paintings have long provided historians with detailed information about clothing worn during certain eras, as well as about their cultural meanings. This book thus ends with a brief look at the more recent past of intimate apparel by analyzing feminist art that documents the undergarments women wore and the importance of intimate apparel to the feminist imagination. Feminist intimate apparel art incorporates a range of approaches, from the anger, rejection of convention, and fiery performance style of 1960s protestors to works that evoke and critique the sensual promise, unintentionally hilarious images, commercially constructed romanticism, and sweatshop labor that Victoria's Secret has capitalized on since its successful launch in the late 1970s. This body of art also addresses the 1980s have-it-all Superwoman, who wore erotic lingerie underneath her business suit to demonstrate that career achievements and ascent to the glass ceiling do not undermine gender difference. This image was certainly a factor in the "underwear as outerwear" trend of that decade that is most closely associated with popular music icon Madonna. Further, intimate apparel art visualizes postmodern feminism's gender playfulness, attention to contradictions in theory and practice, and concerns about women's success qua success—particularly concerns about the divide between women who benefit from class, race, and heterosexual privilege and those who do not.[1]

. . . . .

The female body is, unsurprisingly, a major focus of feminist art. By representing the subjective experiences of female bodies, from the pleasurable to the painful, feminist artists reclaim the female body from its many centuries of objectification by male artists and its subjection to the male gaze in Western art.[2] In addition, their work recognizes that the female body, as artist Barbara Kruger points out, "is a battleground," a critical site of feminist struggle. Some of this struggle is to define the terms—and for artists, the visual terms—in which and through which we understand the experiences, sensations, agencies, and objectification of female bodies. Feminist artists represent menstruation, childbirth, illness, surgical procedures, sexual pleasure, sexual assault, aging and other corporeal topics, and in so doing, invent and make space for new subjects of legitimate aesthetic consideration and new images of female embodiment. Through such work, artists devise creative means of critiquing conventional and dominant views of female bodies, both in high art and in popular culture.[3]

The material culture of gender construction located at and situated by the female body is also important terrain for feminist artists. Clothing, jewelry, cosmetics, artifacts of women's reproductive capacities, and female rituals of daily life provide subjects and materials for representation.[4] Although many contemporary artists use clothing to represent the absent human body of abstract art, feminist artists have moved beyond this generic use because of the close association of female bodies with fashion, textiles, apparel, and the work of producing, purchasing, and maintaining wardrobes. That feminist artists of the early 1970s, as art historians Broude and Garrard point out, "prefigured the proliferation of clothing imagery in the 80s and 90s" demonstrates both the innovation of feminist art and its influence on the contemporary aesthetic generally; it also shows the striking importance of gender diversity in ensuring the creative vitality and proliferation of new tropes of visual representation.[5] In a further innovation, many feminist artists embraced the materials and methods of needle crafts traditionally associated with women's work. In doing so, they sought to critique Western culture's long denigration of these crafts as less valuable than the skills of high art and to validate a tradition of women's artistry not recognized in the dominant telling of Western art history. Judy Chicago's large-scale collaborative work *The Dinner Party* (1979) was certainly germinal, if not iconic, in this regard but did not stand alone. In addition, working with textiles and needle crafts became a means of portraying—via form as well as content—the "fabric" of women's lives. For some female artists, these skills are the most familiar grounds for self-expression and thus offer an important path to making art and becoming artists.[6]

Feminist artists express multiple themes in their representations of underwear: femininity, restraint, sexuality, fetishism, ambiguity, and the female body as object. Feminist intimate apparel artwork can be categorized as celebrations of the sensuous fabrics and erotic feel of lingerie, critiques and lampoons of dominant images of women's undergarments and their effects, and expressions of ambiguity about these essential components of daily dressing practices. In addition, some works foreground clothing and the body as text to be read, resisted, and rewritten. Artists use a variety of visual strategies: their work may be figurative or abstract, or it may use lingerie artifacts—or their simulation—as reworked material or as canvas, page, or framework.

Considering the bra-burning stereotype of early 1970s feminists, it is ironic that two works that focus on the beauty and sensual appeal of lingerie date from that period. However, Sherry Brody's *Lingerie Pillows* (1972) and Linda Burnham's *Satin Pockets* (1974), both created while the artists were students in the then-new Feminist Art Program at the California Institute for the Arts, highlight distinctly different aspects of this appeal. Brody's pillows are fresh, gleaming, and plump, whereas the elegance and allure of Burnham's pockets seem worn and fading; *Pillows* evokes lingerie's pleasurable promise and promise of pleasure; *Pockets*, the experience and memory of pleasure, or perhaps, disappointment. Yet both pieces speak to the erotic fascination of the fabric and ornamentation of silk, satin, and lacy lingerie, and both also rely on the well-established status of undergarments as fetish objects that stand in for the female body as a whole or in parts: *Pockets* fairly directly names the vaginal opening, whereas *Pillows* imagines the female body, particularly the breasts and pelvic region, as a soft resting place. Confounding the boundaries between mass-produced objects and singular works of art, an established practice of modern art by the 1970s, these early works of the feminist art movement use the material culture and needlework of the feminine sphere to assert their aesthetic value in the face of dominant views that trivialize these objects and skills, and thus the women who wear and sew them. The artists reference women's subordination and status as sexualized objects to claim their own status as subjects with the power to choose and use these objects for their own purposes of representation.[7]

The fetish quality of undergarments can also provide a basis for comedy. A long-standing method of dismissing feminist criticism and activism has been to assert that feminists lack a sense of humor. Feminist intimate apparel works that belie this stereotype include Margaret Harrison's *He's Only a Bunny Boy but He's Quite Nice Really* (1971), a pencil drawing that places Hugh Hefner, pipe and all, in a black front-lacing fetish corset. Kneeling on one leg with the other leg bent forward en pointe in sexy sandals, Hefner is depicted in a provocative position that reveals large nipples on his ample breasts and also exposes his bunny-head-shaped genitals. This drawing appeared in Harrison's 1971 one-woman exhibition in London that depicted role reversals of men and women in advertising and pornography.

The exhibit, one of the first feminist gallery shows in England, was deemed offensive and forced to close within a day of its opening.[8] This event shows that determinations of who has a sense of humor and who does not depend on who holds the power to define and police the line between humor and offensiveness.

Agitprop-style satire informs the takeoff on Maidenform ads by artist, activist, and former Madison Avenue advertising director Erika Rothenberg. A banner headline in the drawing, which appeared in the feminist art journal *Heresies* in 1983, proclaims that "men used to masturbate to our ads," and sits above a slightly ajar bathroom door. Commentary in smaller letters beneath the image reads, "We apologize for using sex to sell our products, and we solemnly promise: No more sexy photos! No more photos at all! Just good, clean underwear ads—the kind that no one will get excited over. Now you can say 'I fought pornography in my Maidenform bra.' " The final dig at Maidenform's signature advertising campaign is an absurd company slogan: "The lingerie against pornography."[9]

Rothenberg composed this satire in the midst of the feminist "sex wars" of the 1980s, during which an intensified critique of the effects of pornography on women's status and safety led to differences among feminists about the strategies necessary to protect women from sexual violence. She melds that concern with the feminist critique of women's sexual objectification in advertising. In the 1980s, Maidenform "updated" the Dream Campaign with photographs of half-dressed women surrounded by men at the sites of their newly won professional jobs. These images replaced the fantasy scenarios of the earlier ad campaign in which few male spectators appeared and the female figure stood alone in her "dream." The 1980s ads were widely criticized for trivializing women's success in breaking down gendered job barriers in this period and for encouraging a view of female employees as sexual objects rather than as competent colleagues. Rothenberg points out the pornographic fantasy embedded in the publicly acceptable, ubiquitous Maidenform ads by graphically describing men's sexual behavior in response to them, and she ridicules the backpedaling corporate response that fooled no one.[10]

A more recent work that literally expands upon but conceptually deflates the absurdity of culturally gendered overlays on human biology is Nancy Davidson's *Overly Natural* (1993). Two large weather balloons suspended from a ceiling are each "dressed" in a flouncy black net petticoat, one with a white underskirt and the other with a dark red underskirt. The tie securing each petticoat produces an indent that induces the viewer to see the balloons as exposed buttocks as well as the ovaries indicated in the piece's title.

The work is funny and gets the artist's point across effectively. Davidson uses excess in other works for its humorous effect. Enormous corseted and vividly colored weather balloons distill particular features of the known erotic content of these garments. The corsets transform the balloons into voluptuous hourglass shapes that viewers are bound to identify as female forms, thus revealing the process of female masquerade in dressing practices. In her art, Davidson embraces the archetypal fool or clown, finding in that role a powerful means of entrancing audiences and thus inducing them to consider the meaning of her work. In addition to making a corset measuring 204 inches to exploit the visual fascination with large scale, Davidson constructed *Maebe*, a white balloon inside a shiny blue corset with narrow black stripes, trim, and laces that suggests the cinematic presence of Mae West as saloon-hall prostitute. In *Elvissa*, she dressed a blue balloon in a white corset trimmed with white fringe. These works represent the corseting practices of Mae West and Elvis Presley, whom she sees as comparable masters of sexual masquerade. The pieces' titles and subjects point to the instability of gender identity: *Maebe* could easily become "maybe not" if differently shaped. Moreover, the two icons' embrace of fashionable display, assertive sexual expression, and loving that is both tender and tough challenges conventional gender dualities.

A number of feminist intimate apparel artworks use undergarments to depict the pain and trauma of the restrictive and narrow beauty standards that uphold male privilege and the profit motives of the fashion-industrial complex. Laura S. London's 1983 *Cosmetic Ritual Series* includes an untitled photograph of a woman in an ordinary white bra and bikini underpants. The image cuts off the body, beginning at the chin and ending midknee. Dead center, her hands pull a measuring tape tightly around her waist. The image is a painful reminder of the torturous practices women undergo to conform to beauty standards. Her hands are not relaxed, but neither do they convey extreme exertion. The action is thus familiar and well practiced. The undergarments are critical to the image, because they bring the body into culture in a manner that an unclothed body would not. In this image, the bra and underpants contain and desexualize the breasts and genital area, directing our gaze to the fettering process of measurement and restriction.

Shattered #12 (1980) and *Shattered Slip* (1985), mixed-media pieces by Nancy Youdelman, convey the fragility of the female body as it is subjected to these pressures over time. In *Shattered #12*, Youdelman de- and reconstructed a turn-of-the-century sheer corset cover, once off-white but now darkened from age, using glass, pins, a photograph, and glue. *Shattered Slip* evokes a similar effect with a pale green slip that still holds together, but just

Figure 68. In this untitled piece from her *Cosmetic Ritual Series* (1983), Laura S. London depicts the pain of restrictive beauty standards. Courtesy, Lucy Lippard Women Artists Registry Collection, Special Collections and University Archives, Rutgers University Libraries.

barely. The beauty of the pieces stems from their aching delicacy; somehow, despite all their cracks, they remain intact as identifiable items of feminine clothing and thus as signs of female bodies and women's lives. But their shattered state suggests that further movement or infliction of damage would result in utter disintegration.

The tension of vulnerability evoked by undergarments is also present in *My Mother Is Ill Again/Objectification*, Jenny Watson's 1991 oil painting on red velvet into which the depicted young woman's figure would just about disappear if not for the fact that her black bra and bikini underpants, black high heels, and puffy black hair keep her tied to the visible. Her torso, arms, and legs barely outlined in yellow, her hands behind her back, and her feet turned to her left at an almost impossible angle, the figure stands be-

Figure 69. Nancy Youdelman's *Shattered #12* (1980) expresses the fragility of the female body. Courtesy, Nancy Youdelman.

neath the yellow word *Objectification*. The velvet is laid upon a lavender canvas, though positioned off center to leave room on the left side for a handwritten note that reads, "My mother is ill again." The awkward position of surrender and instability, the dissonance of the texts, and the generic nature of the young woman's black lingerie of seduction and her bland doll-pretty face together construct an unsettling image of exposure: of her body, family secrets, social danger, unease, submission, dissonance, fragmented identity.

Dangerous sexuality permeates Nicola Russell's 1993 oil painting *Measuring Sensuality*. The fleshy, voluptuous, and wildly grinning figures of a dark-haired woman and a light-haired woman stand seductively on either side of the canvas, each dressed in variant ensembles of undergarments. The vivid red background incorporates black shaded areas that contribute to the chaotic sense of movement and frenetic energy of this image. Suspended in the air between the two figures is a speculum, positioned on its side to look like a quacking duck's head and floating above a microscope. Can sensuality be measured and quantified? These female caricatures suggest so, as they convey the generic quality of the components necessary to produce a sensual effect. The intrusive presence of quantifying devices also insinuates that the process of dissecting and measuring sensuality—which is gendered female—prescribes violence and violation of women's bodies.

Energy and tension emanate from the large, central female figures in two 1985 Ida Applebroog paintings; each woman is both assertive and restrained. Small multiple images on one edge of the work amplify these contradictions, competing for the viewer's attention and complicating efforts to understand the meaning of the singular figures. In *Two Women III (after de Kooning)*, Applebroog uses broad strokes to paint a large woman clothed in a brassiere and a long-line girdle, her arms outstretched, her eyes gazing upward, and her mouth wide open, perhaps in energetic song or in a shout of joy. Her arms are not fully drawn, and the left is overlaid with a border of four identical cartoonlike images of three men in swimming trunks lined up with beauty-pageant sashes. A phantom third nude female figure overlays the central figure's right arm, in a rough approximation of de Kooning, while an even sketchier fourth female figure, also nude, floats below the third. The large woman's teeth are sharp, and bits of red swirl around her chin, implying that the girdled woman's appetites are not so contained after all.

The second Applebroog painting, *Peel Me Like a Grape*, is a view from behind of a woman bending over, her grinning face peering back between her long legs, which are set widely astride and show that she is wearing high heels. She stands on a shiny surface that reflects her shoes and calves and also reflects the body of a birdlike figure with a long, pointed beak and a rooster's comb. Set above the central figure are four small drawings laid out horizontally across the top of the painting. Each is the simply drawn figure of a woman in brassiere, girdle, and gartered stockings, cut off midface and midthigh. The title of the painting is a lighthearted reference to seductive stripping, but the repeated figures at the top are mute and, with their hands behind their backs, assume a position of surrender. The painting does not reveal whether the central figure wears a confining garment, and if so, whether she wants it peeled off, nor does it make clear whether her grin is meant to please the spectator or to express her own pleasure; the submissive figures hovering above her detract from the possibility that she is fully in control.

Artists who use unexpected materials to construct simulations of intimate apparel can convey these garments' contradictory status as sources of pleasure and as vehicles of conformity and restriction. Mimi Smith has created a number of such lifesize works, including *Steel Wool Peignoir* (1966), *Girdle* (1966), and *Candy Bra* (1972). Feminist art critic Lucy Lippard credits Smith for anticipating the "feminist artist's fascination with clothing as an extension of the body and the life—a device that flourished throughout the seventies, was revived in the eighties, and is still going strong." She describes *Peignoir* as a "proto-feminist sculpture [that] is a witty commentary on women's work on a double level—sexual and domestic."[11]

In 1978, *Heresies* reproduced images of the two 1966 pieces alongside commentary by the artist. Smith explained her fascination with girdles:

> One of the most frightening articles of clothing that I can imagine is the girdle. . . . Its function is to mold one into society's ideal. It is completely dishonest. . . . It is an uncomfortable torture. It doesn't let a woman breathe. It sticks to her like an octopus. . . . This is why I used rubber bath mats with suction cups all over them to make my girdle. . . . As a punishment for getting old, [a girl] will have to wear a girdle. She will end her life being surrounded on all sides by rubber and elastic.

About *Peignoir*, Smith writes:

> The peignoir is made of lace, steel wool, and pink nylon. The choice of materials illustrates a cruel-gentle ambiguity. Pink nylon is a very soft, pretty material. Steel wool is not. It scratches you. It can cut you. There is cruelty in the peignoir in the fact that the steel wool is very deceptive. It was sewed to look like fur. One doesn't notice the danger until one gets close. . . . There is a whole mystique . . . built up around peignoirs. . . . They are the "something more comfortable" used for seduction. . . . I felt that a steel wool and nylon peignoir combines the reality of marriage with the romance of marriage.[12]

Willy Scholten's mid-1990s crocheted wire-filament brassieres also speak to contradictions and ambiguities in the pleasures and dangers of intimate apparel. The brassieres appear delicate but would not feel so if worn pressed against one's breasts. Scholten's work questions why women submit to painful practices, from breast-implant surgery to the wearing of uncomfortable brassieres. And many bras do, of course, contain underwires that poke and restrain. Scholten uses friends' worn bras as the models for her pieces and attaches a tag to each finished piece that contains a picture of its original owner. This tactic ties Scholten's critique to individual experience and because the bras' owners come in all shapes and sizes, contests prevailing narrow norms of beauty standards. Thus, Scholten refused an invitation to lend her sculptures for a fashion layout because she knew that such a context would be inimical to the intent of her work.[13]

Another category of intimate apparel art asks us to consider clothing and the body as texts to be read and pondered and as sources of visual pleasure. Works by Valie Export, Carol Hamoy, and Miriam Schaer also underscore a view of the female body and intimate apparel as canvas and artistic material for the reworking and rereading of gendered culture. Austrian performance artist Valie Export's *Body Sign Action* (1970) is a shockingly effective tattoo on her thigh of a garter pulling up the barest representation of a stocking—suggested by a brief angled line with a few dashes where it meets the garter to convey the tension of being pulled upward. The tattoo is a brilliant image of gender and sexuality as written on the female body and is a stunning depiction of how clothing inscribes femininity on women's flesh.[14] Carol Hamoy's 1998 *The Female Body* reproduces Margaret Atwood's short 1994 essay of that name on a range of "embellished" undergarments: brassieres, chemises, garter belts, and underpants. Atwood's essay is a wry commentary on experiencing her body as flesh and as a cultural construct. One part of the essay asserts that the "basic Female Body comes with the following accessories: garter belt, panty girdle, crinoline, camisole, bustle, brassiere, stomacher, chemise, virgin zone, spike heels, nose, ring, veil, kid gloves, fishnet stockings, fichu, bandeau, Merry Widow, weepers, chokers, barrettes, bangles, beads, lorgnette, feather boa, basic black, compact, Lycra stretch one-piece with modesty panel, designer peignoir, flannel nightie, lace-teddy, bed, head." Hamoy inscribed these words in black block letters on a 1920s-era pale peach combination garment with green trim, amplifying the meaning of the written text by merging it with the female body "accessory" it describes. Hamoy's *Underwhere* is a collection of turn-of-the-century camisoles upon which she has placed photographs of women artists. Working within the wider theme of women's clothing as a stand-in for the female body, these undergarments evoke intimate contact and thus provide a means for Hamoy to visually connect women's artistic expression with the physical sensation of embodiment mediated through gendered culture.[15]

Miriam Schaer's inventive and beautiful corset books most directly merge body, intimate apparel, and text. When Schaer first heard about "girdle books" in the mid-1980s, she immediately visualized books made from girdles and was disappointed she hadn't thought of this idea herself. When she discovered that the term referred to books with leather straps that medieval nuns tied to the cord—or girdle—they wore around the waist of their habits, she began work on her own concept. Through various means, Schaer

Figure 70. In *Underwhere* (1998), Carol Hamoy integrated photographs of women artists on a collection of turn-of-the-century camisoles. Courtesy, Carol Hamoy.

stiffens the fabric of bustiers, long-line brassieres, and corsets and transforms them into front and back covers inside of which she places small books and artifacts in spaces she carves out for them. When closed, each painted and molded garment takes on the form of the imagined woman who possessed it and, through daily wearing, impressed the shape of her torso upon it. Only when the girdle book is open are the interior objects and text visible.

Schaer uses her girdle books to comment on a number of themes, evident in each piece's title: *The Things We Do for Love* (1995), *Ancient Armor* (1996), *How Do You Compare?* (1996), *Mourning Prayer* (1998), *Love and Madness* (1998), *Housekeeping* (1998), and *Columbine* (1999–2000). The books are exquisite, providing luscious, poignant, and compelling structures in which to consider the subjects she addresses in them. The conventional distinction between decoration and substance in art vanishes in

Figure 71. Miriam Schaer transformed ordinary corsets into works of art in *Ancient Armor* (1996) and other girdle books. Courtesy, Miriam Schaer.

Schaer's books, because they are richly decorative and thoughtful, if at times also humorous, considerations of her selected topics. On the outer surface of *Housekeeping,* according to a *Fiberarts* discussion of her work, Schaer "painted and scribbled . . . line drawings of toilets, laundry, scrub brushes and brooms." The piece opens to reveal "an arch-shaped cartouche that frames a book made from the pages of the *Consumer Report Guide on How to Clean Anything*. . . . Small plastic toys spill from other circular recesses. . . . Open, the work resembles an altar piece or reliquary." Schaer creates a feeling of reverence with this collection of trivial and mundane objects through the rich colors and textures of their setting, but more importantly, through the act of opening the corset-book covers. This allows us to peer inside the woman whose life—and therefore whose body—is filled with the knowledge and experience of child care and cleaning. For the book pages in *How Do You Compare?* Schaer excerpted questions and multiple-choice answers from sex surveys. Removed from the context of the survey and placed in a structure that evokes the inner tenderness of sexual experience and vulnerability, these questions take on an ominous tone and echo Nicola Russell's concern about the potential violence of quantifying human sensations and intimate practices. Inside *The Things We Do for Love* (1995), Schaer compiled an extensive list of grouped verbs to evoke the complexities, dangers, and pleasures of relationships, such as "Allay Sate Strut Flourish . . . Annoy Incite Irritate Provoke . . . Tease Console Lash Inflame . . . Favor Spoil Cuddle Caress . . . Entice Tempt Invite Lure Bate . . . Deceive Bribe Defile Corrupt . . . Violate." Schaer's girdle books visualize the inscription of confining garments on women's outer flesh, as well as the effects of gendered culture on women's interior lives.[16]

Bra vs. Bra (1989) by Leslie Sharpe creatively tackles an important theme of this book, the joint consideration of production and consumption. Sharpe's exhibition book is humorous and critical in analyzing the meanings of brassiere advertising and use, as well as the exploitative conditions of brassiere manufacture. In *Bra vs. Bra*, Sharpe imagines alternative brassiere designs that exaggerate and transform the conventional brassiere functions of uplifting and molding breasts to highlight the artificiality of the breast shapes that brassieres construct. Why not have a "Pulley Bra" that allows women to point breasts in opposite directions or out to the sides? How about acknowledging the cultural conception of women's bodies and female sexuality as dangerous by wearing a "Spike Bra" that creates two large mounds on a woman's chest covered in pointy spikes? This bra can also serve as a weapon of self-defense, thereby providing a commentary on the precarious status of women in public. Moreover, it slyly mediates women's cultural obligation to construct themselves "to-be-looked-at" with the concomitant dangers of living amid the myriad representations of female bodies as objects of reified femininity. Yet Sharpe's work does not argue against artificiality nor advocate a mythic return to the natural; instead, it calls for brassieres "directed to women's pleasure and needs. Feathers . . . and satin could tickle our breasts. . . . Artifice should be made obvious and pushed to exaggeration; the insertable blow-up pad could be a 6 foot curly balloon or one twisted into the shape of a poodle. . . . Pointed bosoms should be frightening—they should really be weapons, either visually intimidating—or for women who need them, actual weapons."[17]

Sharpe addressed issues of brassiere production by including data about deplorable working conditions in the garment industry. She also wrote and sewed some of this information into brassieres to subvert the usual, expected detachment of commodities from their origins and conditions of production. In a brassiere made in the Caribbean by a U.S. manufacturer, for example, she inscribed facts about the Caribbean Basin Initiative, a Reagan-era measure that allowed U.S. companies duty-free entry for goods they manufactured there so that they could exploit the cheaper labor costs. In one bra, she simply sewed "I can't feed my family on $5.00 a day" to give voice, perspective, and embodiment to the otherwise anonymous, invisible worker who made the garment. Sharpe also conceptualized bras to assist worker resistance and organizing. Her "Mike Bra" has a pocket that contains a small tape recorder upon which to record "employers' promises/demands," and her "Speaker Bra" contains a sound system to "broadcast announcements & propaganda" on the job.

The title *Bra vs. Bra* underscores Sharpe's method of countering dominant intimate apparel constructions and representations with her own. The deceptive simplicity of her title reveals the powerful potential of feminist intimate apparel art and feminist criticism generally. Feminist humor, satire, ironic use of artistic materials, analysis of gender construction, critique of femininity, representation of personal experience, and visual strategies for mending the rent between production and consumption, which in turn sustains capitalist commodity manufacture, generates subversive intimate apparel knowledge and systems of meaning as well. Feminist intimate apparel art provides alternative and oppositional uses and significations for these garments, and thus new forms of knowledge about our bodies and about how we costume and live within them. Moreover, because intimate apparel functions as a fetish object or stand-in for the female body, these works portray the female body and its attendant material culture not only as a site of cultural contention but also as a site for feminist struggle. In this way, they suggest transcendent possibilities for imagining our bodies in new ways and modifying our cultural understandings of gender difference.

· · · · ·

A postscript: In April 2001, I received the following e-mail:

WOMAN ARTIST SEEKS BRAS ASAP

In late October 2000 I responded to a news item that a male artist was looking for a home for his large Bra collection. I have done artwork about female body image and gender issues for years and immediately jumped at the chance to have the collection. I called him and we spoke for about an hour. During our conversation I proposed my idea, a giant Bra Ball made of the thousands of bras wrapped up around each other; like a huge rubber band ball. I followed this conversation up with a formal letter. I discussed my idea with him at length. We met and discussed it further. He told me . . . he liked my idea best and was probably going to give them to me.

In December, I went up to his house to discuss logistics and see how many boxes of bras there were etc. After that meeting I wrote him a detailed plan of what how and when we could transfer the bras from him to me and other information about my plans for the BraBall, possible exhibition sites etc. He phoned me a week later to say that not only has he decided not to give me the bras but now he's going to make my Bra-Ball himself. He promised to give me "credit" for the idea but when pressed couldn't tell me exactly what that means. I sent copies of all my documentation to the reporter of that original news item and she ran a piece about our dispute in the [San Francisco] *Chronicle* (titled "Underwear Undercurrents"). . . .

The other artist has over 20,000 bras in his possession . . . and he claims to be . . . making "his" BraBall. I need bras ASAP. I'm asking everyone I know to please send as many bras (any size, color, condition) as you can. . . .

Thanks so much for your help with this unusual request. I can't tell you how violating it feels to have this man steal my idea for an art piece about female body image.

Sincerely,

Emily [Duffy]

I forwarded her request to my women friends, and sent her three similar bras of different colors of my own that I no longer wore because the elastic was stretched out, but I had saved because I loved the satiny, striped brocade fabric.[18] I was happy to contribute to a work of feminist intimate apparel art and to become further entangled in its analysis within my book on the history and meaning of intimate apparel in modern America. I find this story and this piece of feminist intimate apparel art an ironic and fitting conclusion to this epilogue, for the BraBall controversy is another manifestation of the competing uses, contested ownership, and conflicting sense of entitlement inspired by women's undergarments and their meanings, in this case crystallized in a dispute between a male artist and a female artist over material and intellectual property. Duffy's proposal for making art from twenty thousand bras is absurd, gives unified form to the detritus of worn-out clothing, and conjures the lives of the thousands of women whose brassieres construct the ball. The ubiquitous requirement that women wear brassieres opens up a range of interpretations for the BraBall. The ball can represent women's suffering in wearing uncomfortable brassieres but also evoke the neat piles of clothing left behind by Holocaust victims and the trauma of breast cancer (which many women shared with Duffy in the letters they sent with their bra donations). In turn, the stretched-out and stained maternity bras in the ball represent lives of nurturing and care. The BraBall communicates bodily experiences of constriction and gender conformity as well as lives of pleasure, play, defiance, and sensuality. The contradictions persist as feminists seek greater joys and pleasures by striving to understand, contest, and transcend the appeal of feminized material culture and its power to bind women in many ways.

Notes

These notes use the following abbreviations and shortened forms of collection locations: Fashion Institute of Technology (FIT); Kheel Center for Labor-Management Documentation & Archives, School of Industrial and Labor Relations, Cornell University (Kheel Center); Los Angeles County Museum of Art (LACMA); Margaret Herrick Library, Academy of Motion Picture Arts and Sciences, Center for Motion Picture Study, Beverly Hills, California (Herrick Library); Costume Institute, New York Metropolitan Museum of Art (Met); Costume and Textile Department, Royal Ontario Museum, Toronto, Canada (ROM); and Smithsonian Institution, Washington, DC (Smith).

INTRODUCTION

Epigraphs: Virginia Woolf, *Orlando* (Rahway, NJ: Quinn & Boden, 1928), p. 188. Lawrence Ferlinghetti, "Underwear," in *Starting from San Francisco* (Norfolk, CT: New Directions, 1961), pp. 33–35.

1. Tammie Smith, "Low-Ride Pants Bill Advances," *Richmond Times-Dispatch*, February 5, 2005; Tammie Smith, "House Passes Underwear Measure," *Richmond Times-Dispatch*, February 9, 2005; Alyssa Rashbaum, "Show Me Your Thong, Show Me the Money: Virginia Cracks Down on Pants," MTV News, www.vh1.com/news/articles/1496756/20050209/index.jhtml?headlines=true, February 9, 2005; Christina Bellantoni, " 'Droopy Drawers' Bill Seeks End to Overexposure of Underwear," *Washington Times*, February 9, 2005; "Low-Riding to Jail," *Times-Picayune*, April 24, 2004; Jan Moller, "How Low Can You Go? Panel Decides," *Times-Picayune*, May 7, 2004; Ed Anderson, "House Ditches Britches Bill," *Times-Picayune*, May 26, 2004; Bruce Ward, "Thong of the South," *Ottawa Citizen*, May 29, 2004; Bethany Thomas, "Memo to Britney: Lose the Low-Slungs," NBC News, http://msnbc.com/id/4963512/, May 13, 2004.

2. A striking twentieth-century example of dress codes as social control was laws prohibiting cross-dressing used to harass gay men and women. After the advent of the gay rights movement, these laws were largely eliminated. Jonathan Katz, *Gay American History: Lesbians and Gay Men in the U.S.A.* (New York: Meridian Books, 1992); Lillian Faderman, *Odd Girls and Twilight Lovers: A History of Lesbian Life in 20th Century America* (New York: Penguin, 1991). In addition to women generally, other groups with less structural power, such as youth and people of color, have been subject to anxiety about and efforts to control their dress. During the Zoot Suit Riots of 1943, for example, servicemen stationed in Los Angeles assaulted Mexican American youth who had developed a signature style of dress that differed from the norm. Edward J. Escobar, *Race, Police, and the Making of a Political Identity: Mexican Americans and the Los Angeles Police Department, 1900–1945* (Berkeley: University of California Press, 1999); Mauricio Mazon, *The Zoot-Suit Riots: The Psychology of Symbolic Annihilation* (Austin: University of Texas Press, 1984). Sharde Miller, "High Schools Wrestle with Clothes That Expose," *St. Louis Post-Dispatch*, August 12, 2004. The assistant principal also pulled on at least one girl's tube top to check for a brassiere and forced a boy wearing a toga to reveal his shorts. The vice principal disputes the number of girls' underpants she inspected, claiming she lifted three girls' skirts, not the "dozens" reported. "Parents Want School VP Out After 'Panty Check' at Dance," *Fresno Bee*, May 1, 2002; Eleanor Yang, "School Dance Incident Sparks Furor," *San Diego Union Tribune*, May 1, 2002; Eleanor Yang, "Demotion Possible for Assistant Principal," *San Diego Union Tribune*, June 16, 2002; "San Diego Principal Demoted for Thong Underwear Check," SFGate.com, June 18, 2002.

3. A 1921 trade-journal article that uses the terms *intimate apparel, intimate apparel departments,* and *intimate apparel group* (referring to a set of undergarments produced by a particular manufacturer) is the earliest reference to the term I have found. Their unbracketed use implies a previous assimilation into the language of dress. *Women's & Infants' Furnisher*, February 1921, p. 50. The United States Patent Office defines foundation garments as "devices which are specifically designed to fit the human body to protect, compress, support, restrain or alter the configuration of the body torso or a portion thereof, e.g., the female mammae, or those portions of the body lying below the mammae and extending along a line below the abdomen portion of the body to the region of the thighs." www.uspto.gov/go/classification/uspc450/defs450.htm.

4. Elizabeth Ewing, *Dress and Undress: A History of Women's Underwear* (New York: Drama Book Specialists, 1978), pp. 88–95, 113, 151, 158–59, 161; C. Willett and Phillis Cunnington, *The History of Underclothes* (London: Faber and Faber, 1981), pp. 87, 114, 125–26; Norah Waugh, *Corsets and Crinolines* (London: B. T. Batsford, Ltd., 1954), p. 87; Paul Poiret, *My First Fifty Years* (London: Victor Gollancz, Ltd., 1931), pp. 72–73. French designer Madeleine Vionnet also presented dresses worn without corsets at this time. François Boucher, *20,000 Years of Fashion: The History of Costume and Personal Adornment* (New York: Harry N. Abrams, 1987), p. 391. *The Future Out of the Past* (Con-

necticut: Warner Brothers Company, 1964), p. 47; *The Merry Widow,* directed by Curtis Bernhardt (MGM, 1952).

5. For more on the first undergarment local in the International Ladies Garment Workers Union (ILGWU), see Harry Lang, *"62": Biography of a Union* (New York: Astoria Press, 1940); Philip Foner, *Women and the American Labor Movement: From Colonial Times to the Eve of World War I* (New York: Free Press, 1979), pp. 368–72; Gertrude Barnum, "A Hungarian Girl's Impressions of America," *Outlook* 104 (May 7, 1913): 111–14; Rose Schneiderman, "The White Goods Workers of New York," *Life and Labor* 3 (May 1913): 132–36. The extensive records of Local 62 are in the ILGWU collection at the Kheel Center. See also chapter 6 for more on undergarment workers. Louis Levine, *The Women Garment Workers: A History of the International Ladies Garment Workers Union* (New York: B. W. Huebsch, Inc., 1924), pp. 219, 391; U.S. Department of Commerce, *The Women's Muslin-Underwear Industry* (Washington, DC: Government Printing Office, 1915), pp. 1–2; Roy B. Helfgott, "Women's and Children's Apparel," in *Made in New York: Case Studies in Metropolitan Manufacturing,* ed. Max Hall (Cambridge, MA: Harvard University Press, 1959), pp. 62, 69; Local 62 Collection, Box 12, File 1, and David Dubinsky Collection, Box 309, File 7B, ILGWU Archives, Kheel Center; United States *Census of Manufactures,* 1954 census. In addition to the undergarment employment statistics cited, 60 corset shops employed 2,879 workers in New York City in 1913. United States *Census of Manufactures,* 1920. The other 1913 and 1954 figures cited combine statistics for undergarments and corsets, which the census categorizes separately.

6. For works that articulate distinctions between culture, mass culture, and popular culture, see Walter Benjamin, "The Work of Art in the Age of Mechanical Reproduction," in *Illuminations* (New York: Schocken Books, 1969), pp. 217–52; Michael Denning, "The End of Mass Culture," *International Labor and Working-Class History* 37 (Spring 1990): 1–18; Antonio Gramsci, *Selections from the Prison Notebooks* (New York: International Publishers, 1971); Stuart Hall, "Notes on Deconstructing 'The Popular,' " in *People's History and Socialist Theory,* ed. Raphael Samuel (London: Routledge & Kegan Paul, 1981), pp. 227–40; Max Horkheimer and Theodor Adorno, "The Culture Industry: Enlightenment as Mass Deception," in *Dialectic of Enlightenment* (New York: Continuum Publishing Company, 1987), pp. 120–67. Andreas Huyssen, *After the Great Divide: Modernism, Mass Culture, Postmodernism* (Bloomington: University of Indiana Press, 1986); Fredric Jameson, "Reification and Utopia in Mass Culture," in *Signatures of the Visible* (New York: Routledge, 1990), pp. 9–34; Chandra Mukerji and Michael Schudson, eds., *Rethinking Popular Culture: Contemporary Perspectives in Cultural Studies* (Berkeley: University of California Press, 1991); Janice Radway, "Maps and the Construction of Boundaries," *International Labor and Working-Class History* 37 (Spring 1990): 19–40; Raymond Williams, *Marxism and Literature* (Oxford: Oxford University Press, 1977).

7. Elizabeth Ewing, *Dress and Undress;* Cunnington and Cunnington, *His-*

tory of Underclothes; Lois Banner, *American Beauty* (Chicago: University of Chicago Press, 1983); David Kunzle, "Dress Reform as Antifeminism: A Response to Helene E. Roberts's 'The Exquisite Slave: The Role of Clothes in the Making of the Victorian Woman,' " *Signs* 2 (Spring 1977): 570–79; David Kunzle, *Fashion and Fetishism: A Social History of the Corset, Tight-Lacing and Other Forms of Body-Sculpture in the West* (Totowa, NJ: Rowman and Littlefield, 1982); Helene E. Roberts, "The Exquisite Slave: The Role of Clothes in the Making of the Victorian Woman," *Signs* 2 (Spring 1977): 564–69; Helene E. Roberts, "Reply to David Kunzle's 'Dress Reform as Antifeminism: A Response to Helene E. Roberts's 'The Exquisite Slave,' " *Signs* 3 (Winter 1977): 518–19; Valerie Steele, *Fashion and Eroticism: Ideals of Feminine Beauty from the Victorian Era to the Jazz Age* (New York: Oxford University Press, 1985). Douglas Kellner, "Madonna, Fashion and Identity," in *On Fashion,* ed. Shari Benstock and Suzanne Ferriss (New Brunswick, NJ: Rutgers University Press, 1994), p. 179.

8. Christine Stansell, *City of Women: Sex and Class in New York 1789–1860* (Urbana: University of Illinois Press, 1982); Kathy Peiss, *Cheap Amusements, Working Women and Leisure in Turn-of-the-Century New York* (Philadelphia: Temple University Press, 1986); Susan Porter Benson, *Counter Cultures: Saleswomen, Managers, and Customers in American Department Stores 1890–1940* (Urbana: University of Illinois Press, 1986); David Kunzle, *Fashion and Fetishism;* Valerie Steele, *Fashion and Eroticism;* Maureen Turim, "Seduction and Elegance: The New Woman of Fashion in Silent Cinema," in *On Fashion,* ed. Shari Benstock and Suzanne Ferriss (New Brunswick, NJ: Rutgers University Press, 1994), pp. 140–58; Elizabeth Wilson, *Adorned in Dreams: Fashion and Modernity* (Berkeley: University of California Press, 1985); Kaja Silverman, "Fragments of a Fashionable Discourse," in *Studies in Entertainment: Critical Approaches to Mass Culture,* ed. Tania Modleski (Bloomington: Indiana University Press, 1986), pp. 139–52; Fred Davis, *Fashion, Culture and Identity* (Chicago: University of Chicago Press, 1992); Laura Mulvey, "Visual Pleasure and Narrative Cinema," in *Movies and Methods,* vol. 2, ed. Bill Nichols (Berkeley: University of California, 1985), pp. 304–15; Jane Gaines and Charlotte Herzog, eds., *Fabrications: Costume and the Female Body* (New York: Routledge, 1990). For an excellent discussion of major twentieth-century works of fashion history and theory, see Davis, *Fashion, Culture and Identity.*

9. Banner, *American Beauty;* Jackson Lears, *Fables of Abundance: A Cultural History of Advertising in America* (New York: Basic Books, 1994). Glamour is also analyzed by Theodor Adorno and George Simpson. Their view is that "he who is never permitted to conquer in life conquers in glamor." Theodor Adorno with the assistance of George Simpson, "On Popular Music," *Studies in Philosophy and Social Science* 9 (1941): 29.

10. Kathy Peiss, "Making Up, Making Over: Cosmetics, Consumer Culture, and Women's Identity," in *The Sex of Things: Gender and Consumption in Historical Perspective,* ed. Victoria de Grazia with Ellen Furlough (Berkeley: University of California Press, 1996), pp. 311–36; Tania Modleski, *Loving with a*

Vengeance: Mass-Produced Fantasies for Women (New York: Routledge, 1982); Susan Bordo, *Unbearable Weight: Feminism, Western Culture, and the Body* (Berkeley: University of California Press, 1993); Kathy Davis, *Dubious Equalities & Embodied Differences: Cultural Studies on Cosmetic Surgeries* (New York: Rowman & Littlefield, 2003). Antonio Gramsci, *Selections from the Prison Notebooks* (New York: International Publishers, 1971); Max Horkheimer and Theodor Adorno, "The Culture Industry: Enlightenment as Mass Deception," in *Dialectic of Enlightenment* (New York: Continuum, 1987), pp. 120–67; Andrew Arato and Eike Gebhardt, *The Essential Frankfurt School Reader* (New York: Continuum, 1982).

11. Gramsci, *Prison Notebooks*, p. 12; Raymond Williams, *Marxism and Literature* (Oxford: Oxford University Press, 1977), p. 110. See also T. Jackson Lears, "The Concept of Cultural Hegemony: Problems and Possibilities," *American Historical Review* 90 (June 1985): 567–93; and George Lipsitz, "The Struggle for Hegemony," *Journal of American History* 75 (June 1988): 146–50.

12. Sharde Miller, "High Schools Wrestle with Clothes That Expose," *St. Louis Post-Dispatch*, August 12, 2004.

13. Costume historians generally, and feminist critics particularly, have long understood the power of fashion to regulate and signify. My discussion here of fashion as a regulatory practice draws upon Michel Foucault, *The History of Sexuality*, vol. 1, *An Introduction* (New York: Vintage Books, 1978), and also upon Judith Butler's analysis of Foucault in *Gender Trouble: Feminism and the Subversion of Identity* (New York: Routledge, 1990). My analysis is in some sense a response to Butler's call for a "critical inquiry that traces the regulatory practices within which bodily contours are constructed [that] constitutes precisely the genealogy of 'the body' in its discreteness that might further radicalize Foucault's theory" (p. 133). Joan Scott, *Gender and the Politics of History* (New York: Columbia University Press, 1988); Roland Barthes, *The Fashion System* (New York: Hill and Wang, 1983); Roland Barthes, *Mythologies* (New York: Noonday Press, 1972), p. 9.

14. Steele, *Fashion and Eroticism*, pp. 6–8; Severa, *Dressing*, pp. 25, 185, 292, 300, and photographs on 243, 260, 263, 285, 325, 451, 478, 494, 497, 507. See also Erna Olafson Hellerstein, Leslie Parker Hume, and Karen M. Offen, eds., and Estelle B. Freedman, Barbara Charlesworth Gelpi, and Marilyn Yalom, associate eds., *Victorian Women: A Documentary Account of Women's Lives in Nineteenth-Century England, France, and the United States* (Stanford, CA: Stanford University Press, 1981); Bonnie G. Smith, *Ladies of the Leisure Class: The Bourgeoises of Northern France in the Nineteenth Century* (Princeton, NJ: Princeton University Press, 1981); and Nancy L. Green, *Ready-to-Wear and Ready-to-Work: A Century of Industry and Immigrants in Paris and New York* (Durham, NC: Duke University Press, 1997).

15. *Harper's Bazar* used the single *a* in *Bazar* until November 1929, when the magazine became *Harper's Bazaar*.

16. Severa, *Dressed*, pp. 3, 375; *Godey's Lady's Book*, January 1831, p. 1; January 1836, p. 1; "*Godey's* Paris Fashions Americanized," August 1849. Stella

Blum, ed., *Victorian Fashions & Costumes from Harper's Bazar: 1867–1898*
(New York: Dover Publications, 1974), p. v.

17. Alison Gernsheim, *Victorian and Edwardian Fashion: A Photographic
Survey* (New York: Dover Publications, 1981), p. 7. See also Herbert Norris and
Oswald Curtis, *Nineteenth-Century Costume and Fashion* (New York: Dover
Publications, 1998), pp. 147–48; James Laver, *Costume and Fashion*, 3rd ed.
(London: Thames and Hudson, 1995), pp. 186–88; Steele, *Fashion and Eroticism*,
p. 80; Boucher *20,000 Years*, p. 391; Blum, *Victorian Fashions*, introduction and
p. 227. On Wilde, see Lee Hall, *Common Threads: A Parade of American Clothing* (Boston: Little, Brown), p. 101; and Severa, *Dressed for the Photographer*, p.
380. The *Barnhart Dictionary of Etymology* dates the ascot at 1908, pp. 231,
698.

18. Farid Chenoune, *Beneath It All: A Century of French Lingerie* (New
York: Rizzoli, 1999), p. 18; Edward Warwick, Henry C. Pitz, and Alexander
Wyckoff, *Early American Dress: The Colonial and the Revolutionary Periods*
(New York: B. Blom, 1965), p. 13; Diana Crane, *Fashion and Its Social Agenda:
Class, Gender, and Identity in Clothing* (Chicago: University of Chicago Press,
2000).

19. Lorraine Gamman and Merja Makinen helpfully draw distinctions between anthropological, commodity, and sexual fetishisms in *Female Fetishism*
(New York: NYU Press, 1994) and further categorize sexual fetishisms as "or-
thodox" objects for bringing the fetishist to orgasm or "mild forms" for arous-
ing the fetishist and providing visual pleasure (59). Louis Rose, "Freudian
Fetishism: Previously Unpublished Minutes of the Vienna Psychoanalytic Society," *Psychoanalytic Quarterly* 57 (1988): 156. Laura Mulvey, in *Fetishism
and Curiosity* (Bloomington: Indiana University Press, 1996), explains the two
major foundational theorists of sexual and commodity fetishism: "The process
of disavowal (Freud) and estrangement (Marx) produces an over-valuation of
things." Therefore, "fetishisms . . . create social and sexual points . . . where relations between people are liable to become relations between things" (p. 3).
This fetishization occurs, according to Marx, because the exchanges central to a
capitalist economy depend upon assigning all goods a value that is easily trans-
latable into a money amount. Objects take on further social and cultural value
through their promotion and consumption. The labor power invested in making an object—the true source of its value—and the conditions of production are
estranged from and thus disappear under the weight of the monetary and cultural value assigned to it. Freud described sexual fetishism as the mechanism for
male disavowal of the lack of the mother's penis, the early awareness of which
stimulates the male's fear of his own pending castration. Fetish objects in this
sense substitute for or displace a female sexual partner, enabling the fetishist to
avoid the sight of female genitals that reactivates castration anxiety. See also
Michael T. Taussig, *The Devil and Commodity Fetishism in South America*
(Chapel Hill: University of North Carolina Press, 1980); and Emily Apter and
William Pietz, eds., *Fetishism as Cultural Discourse* (Ithaca, NY: Cornell University Press, 1993).

20. *US Economic Census,* Manufacturing Industry Series, "Women's and Girls' Cut and Sew Lingerie, Loungewear, and Nightwear Manufacturing: 2002," p. 3. William Leach's research indicates that the split between production and consumption was occurring by 1880. *Land of Desire: Merchants, Power and the Rise of a New American Culture* (New York: Vintage, 1993), p. 147.

CHAPTER 1. DRAWERS

This chapter appeared previously as "Erotic Modesty: [Ad]dressing Female Sexuality and Propriety in Open and Closed Drawers, 1800–1930," *Gender & History* 14, no. 3 (November 2002): 492–515; and also in Carole Turbin and Barbara Burman, eds., *Material Strategies: Dress & Gender in Historical Perspectives* (London: Blackwells, 2003).

Epigraph: Grace Margaret Gould, "What Is and Isn't Style," *Woman's Home Companion,* March 1914, p. 47.

1. *Our Dancing Daughters,* directed by Harry Beaumont (MGM, 1928).

2. See, for example, open-drawer artifacts 982.183.1 (ROM); 64.24C, 43.35B, 54.16 (Met); 81.121.7 (FIT); 58909, 243178.4 (Smith). Rosemary Hawthorne, *Oh . . . Knickers!: A Brief History of "Unmentionables"* (London: Bachman & Turner, 1985), p. 14. Men had worn some sort of drawers or breeches since the Middle Ages. Nineteenth-century drawers evolved from detachable breech linings. Some drawers had a slit in the back that often closed with ties or buttons to accommodate bodily functions. Flaps opening in the front continue to be a common feature of men's underpants. Edward Warwick, Henry C. Pitz, and Alexander Wyckoff, *Early American Dress: The Colonial and Revolutionary Periods* (New York: Benjamin Blom, 1965), pp. 246–47; C. Willett and Phillis Cunnington, *The History of Underclothes,* rev. ed. (1951; repr. London: Faber and Faber, 1981), pp. 31–32, 42, 53, 67, 80, 90, 109, 121; Philippe Perrot, *Fashioning the Bourgeoisie: A History of Clothing in the Nineteenth Century* (Princeton, NJ: Princeton University Press, 1994), p. 161; Gary Griffin, *The History of Men's Underwear* (Los Angeles: Added Dimensions, 1991).

Middle-class women in Western cultures began to wear drawers between 1790 and 1820. Previously, women wore only a chemise, or long shift, closest to the skin. Costume historians credit Catherine de Medici with introducing Italian drawers to France after her sixteenth-century marriage to Henry II. Catherine's fashion inspiration was likely men's breeches and/or the drawers worn since the Middle Ages by peasant women, who did not observe the upper-class practice of wearing a chemise. Cunnington and Cunnington, *History of Underclothes,* p. 70; Elizabeth Ewing, *Dress and Undress: A History of Women's Underwear* (New York: Drama Book Specialists, 1978), pp. 40, 56, 61; Ludmilla K. Kybalová, Olga H. Herbenná, and Milena L. Lavnarová, *The Pictorial Encyclopedia of Fashion* (London: Paul Hamlyn, 1968), p. 462; Cecil Saint-Laurent, *The Great Book of Lingerie* (Singapore: Vendome Press, 1986), pp. 62–63; Alison Carter, *Underwear: The Fashion History* (New York: Drama Book Publishers, 1992), pp. 14, 30. From the early modern period, prostitutes also wore drawers on occasion. See Rudolf M. Dekker and Lotte C. van de Pol, *The Tradition of Female Transvestism in Early Modern Europe* (London: Macmillan Press, 1989).

In France, the use of drawers by other than peasant women or prostitutes did not become widespread until several centuries later. A royal decree by Louis XV in 1775 dictated that dancers wear drawers, part of his efforts to promote the respectability of this art form. Saint-Laurent, p. 96, notes that dancers liked wearing drawers because the undergarments allowed them to wear shorter skirts that provided greater freedom of movement and enhanced their ability to display their art form. However, actresses, who were also mandated to wear drawers, quite often refused to obey this law. See also Francois Boucher, *20,000 Years of Fashion: The History of Costume and Personal Adornment* (New York: Harry Abrams, 1987), p. 65. During the French Revolution, republican women donned trousers as outerwear briefly, in concert with the fleeting trend of gender equity at the time. This practice ended in 1793, when legislators outlawed women's republican societies, justifying their action as a means of maintaining the separate spheres made necessary by women's purported domestic, anti-intellectual nature. Scott Lytle, "The Second Sex (September, 1793)," *Journal of Modern History* 27, no. 1 (March 1955): 14–26. A January 1797 decree outlawed the wearing of "clothes of another sex than one's own." Lynn Hunt, *Politics, Culture and Class in the French Revolution* (Berkeley: University of California Press, 1984), pp. 66–67. Though Hunt discusses this decree in reference to the suppression of traditional cross-dressing Carnival practices, the decree also curtailed the potential ordinary use of trousers by women.

Englishwomen did not wear drawers during this period, though they would be the first to don them in the early nineteenth century as part of Victorian dress. Perrot, *Fashioning the Bourgeoisie*, p. 146; Cunnington and Cunnington, *History of Underclothes*, 72. The meager clothing styled on an impoverished model of European customs that slave owners supplied to African American women meant that most of these women did not wear drawers at this time. See Christine Stansell, *City of Women* (Urbana: University of Illinois Press, 1982), pp. 4–5. Kybalová, Herbenná, and Lavnarová, *Pictorial Encyclopedia*, p. 450; Barbara M. Starke, "Nineteenth-Century African-American Dress," in *Dress in American Culture*, ed. Patricia A. Cunningham and Susan Voso (Bowling Green, OH: Bowling Green State University Popular Press, 1993), pp. 66–79. Helen Bradley Foster, *New Raiments of Self: African American Clothing in the Antebellum South* (Oxford: Berg, 1997), pp. 147–49, reports that some African American women fashioned drawers for themselves from burlap sacks, or from men's drawers or other clothing cast off by slave owners; others received cotton or woolen cloth or yarn for making undergarments. Enslaved women who worked in the fields "reefed up" their dresses around their hips to allow greater freedom of movement and to protect outerwear from dirt. Drawers would thus also protect the women's modesty. Deborah Gray White, *Ar'n't I a Woman?: Female Slaves in the Plantation South* (New York: W. W. Norton, 1985, 1991), pp. 32–33.

3. For a discussion of other films of this era that explore contending notions of women's sexuality, see Molly Haskell, *From Reverence to Rape: The Treatment of Women in the Movies* (New York: Holt, Rinehart and Winston, 1973); Marjorie Rosen, *Popcorn Venus: Women, Movies & the American Dream* (New York: Coward, McCann & Geoghegan, 1973); Lary May, *Screening Out the Past* (New York: Oxford University Press, 1980); Mary Ryan, "The Projection of a New Womanhood: The Movie Moderns in the 1920's," in *Decades of Discontent: The Women's Movement, 1920–1940,* ed. Lois Scharf and Joan M. Jensen (Westport, CT: Greenwood Press, 1983), pp. 113–30.

4. The rivalry between Ann and Diana is also coded by class. Class difference explains Ann's financial ambitions but also sets aside working women from the debate on new standards of female propriety. The compassionate scrubwomen who wear plain and unfashionable work dresses are neither Anns, Beas, nor Dianas. These older women do not question class boundaries; they accept their fate of hard and dreary work, which places them outside the bounds of middle-class femininity. The only other working women in the film are domestic servants and some dancing girls—scantily dressed in silk shorts and midriff-baring tops—who appear briefly in a scene at a yacht party.

5. The opening sequence of the film and the scene in which Joan Crawford dances without her skirt were cut by the censors in several states and Canadian provinces. The film was banned entirely in Ontario and by the mayor of Lynn, Massachusetts. Florence Clarendon, chair of the Better Films Committee, in a December 7, 1928, letter to the Motion Picture Producers Association (MPPA), complained about the "good deal of girls undressing" depicted in the film, claiming the audience "is not interested in viewing various articles from a lingerie shop." She was wrong. One review noted that "displaying undies and much stocking, Beaumont [was] evidently desiring to make sure that no one would leave this effort early." *Our Dancing Daughters* MPPA file, Herrick Library.

6. See Alison Carter's helpful glossary in *Underwear*, pp. 150–53. The initial defeat of a 1994 bill in the California state legislature to end the prohibition on trousers for women in the workplace shows that uneasiness persisted about undoing this fundamental distinction of dress. Public outcry forced the reintroduction of this legislation, which passed and became law the following month. *Los Angeles Times,* August 26 and 27, 1994. Sociologist Fred Davis notes that "whereas most items of male attire adopted by women have been viewed with indulgence or amusement after their initial shock value has worn off, the same cannot be said of trousers. . . . Following their mass adoption by women in the wake of the women's movement of the late 1960s numerous fashionable hotels, restaurants, and other public accommodations barred entrance to women wearing them." *Fashion, Culture and Identity* (Chicago: University of Chicago Press, 1992), p. 34, n. 2.

A note on terminology: In the United States, the term *pants* can refer to both outerwear (trousers) and underwear (underpants), whereas in the United Kingdom, Northerners use the word in both senses, underpants and trousers, but Southerners use it to refer only to underpants, also known as knickers. A class distinction may be at work here. (Personal correspondence with English resident Deborah Sazer and Liverpudlian John Anderson, August 5, 2001.) The colloquial questioning in the United States of "who wears the pants in the family" speaks to the conventional association of pants with masculine authority and power. Interestingly, the British *The New Shorter Oxford English Dictionary* (1993) defines pants via an extended list of expressions, such as "scare the pants off," "bore the pants off," "charm the pants off," and "by the seat of one's pants," but the list does not include the only such phrase in the American *Random House Unabridged Dictionary* (2nd ed., 1993) definition, "I guess we know who wears the pants in that family."

7. *Godey's Lady's Book,* January 1872, July 1872; *Women's Wear Daily,* May 7, 1917, p. 5; May 22, 1917, p. 5; Cunnington and Cunnington, *History of Underclothes,* pp. 124, 137, 147.

8. Jill Fields, "Three Sides to Every Story: The Material Culture of Intimate Apparel," *Dress* 23 (1996): 75–81; this discussion also draws on personal conversations and correspondence with costume historians who responded to this and subsequent presentations of my argument. Farid Chenoune, *Beneath It All: A Century of French Lingerie* (New York: Rizzoli, 1999), appeared while I was revising this chapter for publication in *Gender & History;* Chenoune cites my work in ch. 1, n. 11 (see also pp. 22, 25). J. C. Flugel, *The Psychology of Clothes* (London: Hogarth Press and the Institute of Psychoanalysis, 1930); and James Laver, *A Concise History of Costume and Fashion* (New York: Scribner's, 1969). Valerie Steele, *Fashion and Eroticism: Ideals of Feminine Beauty from the Victorian Era to the Jazz Age* (New York: Oxford University Press, 1985), pp. 198–99, mentions the open crotch of nineteenth-century drawers but does not consider the sexual meaning of this feature. See Fred Davis, "Ambivalences of Sexuality, the Dialectic of the Erotic and the Chaste," ch. 2 in *Fashion, Culture,* for a thorough analysis of Flugel's so-called Theory of the Shifting Erogenous Zones and its application by Laver and Steele. While I was completing this book, Lois Banner alerted me to Richard Wortley, *Pin-Up's Progress: An Illustrated History of the Immodest Art, 1870–1970* (London: Panther, 1971), the only source prior to my work that I have found that links open drawers with eroticism (p. 18).

9. Ellen Ross and Rayna Rapp ask us to consider how society specifically shapes sexuality and to move beyond abstract understandings of how sexuality is socially structured. Ross and Rapp, "Sex and Society: A Research Note from Social History and Anthropology," in *Powers of Desire: The Politics of Sexuality,* ed. Ann Snitow, Christine Stansell, and Sharon Thompson (New York: Monthly Review Press, 1983), pp. 51, 52, 63, 68. A vast literature addresses the many facets of their question. Of special relevance are Nancy Cott, "Passionlessness: An Interpretation of Victorian Sexual Ideology, 1790–1850," *Signs* 4 (1978): 219–36; Carroll Smith-Rosenberg, "The Female World of Love and Ritual," *Disorderly Conduct: Visions of Gender in Victorian America* (New York: Oxford University Press, 1985); C. J. Barker-Benfield, *The Horrors of the Half-Known Life: Male Attitudes toward Women and Sexuality in Nineteenth-*

Century America (New York: Harper & Row, 1976); and the widely influential Michel Foucault, *The History of Sexuality* (New York: Pantheon Books, 1978). Karen Lystra analyzes evidence contrary to female passionless ideology in *Searching the Heart: Women, Men and Romantic Love in Nineteenth-Century America* (New York: Oxford University Press, 1989), as does Lillian Faderman, *To Believe in Women: What Lesbians Have Done for America—A History* (New York: Houghton Mifflin, 1999). *Passion and Power: Sexuality in History* (Philadelphia: Temple University Press, 1989), Kathy Peiss and Christina Simmons, eds., analyzes a wide range of sexual practices through the lenses of race and class. Studies that investigate changing sexual attitudes and practices include Kathy Peiss, *Cheap Amusements: Working Women and Leisure in Turn-of-the Century New York* (Philadelphia: Temple University Press, 1986); Beth Bailey, *From Front Porch to Back Seat: Courtship in Twentieth-Century America* (Baltimore: Johns Hopkins University Press, 1988); Mary Odem, *Delinquent Daughters: Protecting and Policing Adolescent Female Sexuality in the United States, 1885–1920* (Chapel Hill: University of North Carolina Press, 1995); and Peter Laipson, " 'Kiss Without Shame, for She Desires It': Sexual Foreplay in American Marital Advice Literature, 1900–1925," *Journal of Social History* 29, no. 4 (1996): 507–26. On the topic of nineteenth-century fashion and sexuality in particular, see Lois Banner, *American Beauty* (Chicago: University of Chicago Press, 1983); Steele, *Fashion and Eroticism;* and David Kunzle, *Fashion and Fetishism: A Social History of the Corset, Tight-Lacing and Other Forms of Body Sculpture in the West* (Totowa, NJ: Rowman and Littlefield, 1982).

　　10. Individuals making open drawers produced variations in crotch construction. See, for example, 64.24C, 43.35B, 54.16 (Met); 982.183.1 (ROM); 81.121.7 (ΓΙΤ); 58909. 243178.4 (Smith).

　　11. Flugel, *Psychology of Clothes;* Vern Bullough and Bonnie Bullough, *Cross Dressing, Sex and Gender* (Philadelphia: University of Pennsylvania Press, 1993), p. 175; Banner, *American Beauty,* p. 234; Steele, *Fashion and Eroticism,* p. 52; Davis, *Fashion, Culture,* pp. 33–34; James Laver, *Taste and Fashion, from the French Revolution until Today* (London: George G. Harrap, 1937), pp. 168–70. Men of the rising middle classes generally eschewed the flamboyant styles available to elite men in the past and assumed a more uniform and darker appearance, representative of the new sober business ethic. As John Harvey and Christopher Breward have recently demonstrated, some men resisted conforming to the new strictures of masculine attire. Yet though both historians offer a more nuanced portrait, neither fully refutes the dominance of the trend in male dress that Flugel famously termed the "Great Masculine Renunciation" nor does either contest the gendered nature of consumption in industrializing society generally. John Harvey, *Men in Black* (Chicago: University of Chicago Press, 1995); Christopher Breward, *The Hidden Consumer: Masculinities, Fashion and City Life, 1860–1914* (Manchester: Manchester University Press, 1999). See also Diana de Marly, *Fashion for Men: An Illustrated History* (New York: Holmes & Meier, 1985); and Farid Chenoune, *A History of Men's Fashion* (Paris: Flammarion, 1993).

12. Thorstein Veblen, *Theory of the Leisure Class* (New York: Macmillan, 1899); Karen Halttunen, *Confidence Men and Painted Ladies: A Study of Middle Class Culture in America, 1830–1870* (New Haven, CT: Yale University Press, 1982); Sally Helvenston, "Popular Advice for the Well Dressed Woman in the 19th Century," *Dress* 5 (1980): 31–46; John Kasson, *Rudeness & Civility: Manners in Nineteenth-Century Urban America* (New York: Hill and Wang, 1990); Lawrence Levine, *Highbrow/Lowbrow: The Emergence of Cultural Hierarchy in the United States* (Cambridge, MA: Harvard University Press, 1988).

13. Steele, *Fashion and Eroticism*, 6–8; Joan Severa, *Dressed for the Photographer: Ordinary Americans and Fashion, 1840–1900* (Kent, OH: Kent State University Press, 1995), pp. 25, 185, 292, 300, and photographs on pp. 243, 260, 263, 285, 325, 451, 478, 494, 497, 507. See also Erna Olafson Hellerstein, Leslie Parker Hume, and Karen M. Offen, eds., and Estelle B. Freedman, Barbara Charlesworth Gelpi, and Marilyn Yalom, associate eds., *Victorian Women: A Documentary Account of Women's Lives in Nineteenth-Century England, France, and the United States* (Stanford, CA: Stanford University Press, 1981); Bonnie G. Smith, *Ladies of the Leisure Class: The Bourgeoises of Northern France in the Nineteenth Century* (Princeton, NJ: Princeton University Press, 1981); Leora Auslander, *Taste and Power: Furnishing Modern France* (Berkeley: University of California Press, 1996); and Nancy L. Green, *Ready-to-Wear and Ready-to-Work: A Century of Industry and Immigrants in Paris and New York* (Durham, NC: Duke University Press, 1997).

14. Lee Hall, *Common Threads* (Boston: Little, Brown, 1992), pp. 188–99, text and photographs; Jo B. Paoletti and Carol L. Kregloh, "The Children's Department," in *Men and Women: Dressing the Part*, ed. Claudia Brush Kidwell and Valerie Steele (Washington, DC: Smithsonian Institution Press, 1989), pp. 22–41; Boucher, *20,000 Years*, p. 304; *Godey's Lady's Book*, April 1857, p. 362, and July 1857, p. 78; Robert Holliday, *Unmentionables from Figleaves to Scanties* (New York: Ray Long & Richard Smith, 1933), pp. 172–73, 179; Anne Buck, *Victorian Costume & Costume Accessories* (Bedford, UK: Ruth Bean, 1984/1961), pp. 202, 209–10, 214, ch. 20, "Children's Costume"; Severa, *Dressed for the Photographer*, pp. 23–24, 107–108, 122–23, 129, 133, 134, 144, 146, 156, 181, 210–11, 220, 255, 281, 315–16, 363–64, 428–29, 431, 447, 483; Stella Blum, ed., *Victorian Fashions and Costumes from Harper's Bazar, 1867–1898* (New York: Dover, 1974), pp. 116–17, 131, 143, 154–57, 168–69, 184–85, 214–15, 222–23, 251; Michelle Perrot, ed., *A History of Private Life: From the Fires of Revolution to the Great War* (Cambridge, MA: Harvard University Press, 1990), pp. 196–219.

15. Saint-Laurent, *Great Book*, pp. 104–15; Perrot, *Fashioning the Bourgeoisie*, pp. 146–48; Cunnington and Cunnington, *History of Underclothes*, p. 82, includes a line drawing of a pair of 1834 pantalettes at the Victoria and Albert Museum. *Godey's Lady's Book*, July 1855, p. 96, and July 1857, p. 554, describe girls' pantalettes. For examples of girls' nineteenth-century closed drawers, see 945.50.3, 970.30.4, and 976.199.1.A-B (ROM). Some girls wore open drawers in the early to mid-nineteenth century, but girls' use of closed drawers

increased as the century progressed. See, for example, 64.06.05 in the University of Rhode Island Textile and Costume Collection. Further research is clearly needed on this topic. During menstruation, another underresearched topic, nineteenth-century women made washable pads and attached them to undergarments or belts. Some used nothing at all, according to anecdotal evidence collected by the Museum of Menstruation at www.mum.org/whatwore.htm. By the 1880s, girls and women could purchase manufactured pads and belts at pharmacies. Kotex, a disposable napkin, was first sold in 1919. Jane Farrell-Beck and Laura Klosterman Kid, "The Roles of Health Professionals in the Development and Dissemination of Women's Sanitary Products, 1880–1940," *Journal of the History of Medicine and Allied Sciences* 51, no. 3 (July 1996): 325–52; Thomas Heinrich and Bob Batchelor, *Kotex, Kleenex, Huggies: Kimberly-Clark and the Consumer Revolution in American Business* (Columbus: Ohio State University Press, 2004), pp. 49–50. The impropriety of speaking about drawers also indicates their close association with sexuality and the female body. Holliday, *Unmentionables*, pp. 136, 153–54, 162–64, 172.

16. Ewing, *Dress and Undress*, p. 56; *Glenbervie Journals* (1811), edited by F. Bickley (1928), cited by Cunnington and Cunnington, *History of Underclothes*, p. 70.

17. Ewing, *Dress and Undress*, p. 57; Richard Martin and Harold Koda, *Infra-Apparel* (New York: Metropolitan Museum of Art, 1993), p. 62.

18. Hall, *Common Threads*, p. 43; Ewing, *Dress and Undress*, p. 61. Cunnington and Cunnington, *History of Underclothes*, p. 82, find that open drawers by the 1830s in England were an important component in middle-class women's construction of their privileged status.

19. Horseback riding was the primary sport for which some women wore trousers. Laver notes these multiple sources of fashion innovation in *Taste and Fashion*, as do many other costume historians. See, for example, Severa, *Dressed for the Photographer*, p. 197; de Marly, *Fashion for Men*, p. 97; Saint-Laurent, *Great Book*, pp. 100, 113, 145; Ewing, *Dress and Undress*, p. 166; and Blum, *Victorian Fashions*, p. 77.

20. Saint-Laurent, *Great Book*, p. 222; and Steele, *Fashion and Eroticism*, p. 199, who quotes an 1890 French memoir cited by Pierre Dufay, *Le Pantalon Féminin. Un Chapitre Inedit de L'histoire du Costume* (Paris: Charles Carrington, 1906). Cunnington and Cunnington, *History of Underclothes*, p. 99, cite an 1858 unnamed magazine editor's advice that young women who are suffering unduly from vulgar comments should remain indoors; Perrot, *Fashioning the Bourgeoisie*, p. 148; Steele, *Fashion and Eroticism*, p. 86, cites an 1862 letter written by a married man who allowed that "girls of our time like to show their legs . . . it pleases them, and does no harm to us." See Roland Barthes, *Mythologies* (New York: The Noonday Press, 1990), pp. 41–42, for more on the cultural functions of "inoculation."

21. James Laver, *Costume and Fashion: A Concise History*, 2nd ed. (New York: Thames and Hudson, 1982), pp. 162–72.

22. *The Handbook of the Toilet*, cited by Cunnington and Cunnington, *His-*

tory of Underclothes, p. 94. The authors provide no specific date for this English publication, but two subsequent citations in this chronologically organized section on drawers date from 1847 and 1851. Matilda Kitchens, *When Underwear Counted, Being the Evolution of Underclothes* (Talladega, AL: Brannon Printing Co., 1931), p. 51. The nineteenth-century promotion of open drawers as healthful in exposing female genitals to air seems contrary to Valerie Steele's claim that the chemise worn underneath the corset always fully shielded "the thighs," and presumably the crotch, "from view." *Fashion and Eroticism,* p. 198.

23. Sally Helvenston, "Popular Advice for the Well Dressed Woman in the 19th Century," *Dress* 5 (1980): 31–47; Jeanette C. Lauer and Robert H. Lauer, "The Battle of the Sexes Fashion in 19th Century America," *Journal of Popular Culture* 13, no. 4 (Spring 1980): 581–89; Shelley Foote, "Challenging Gender Symbols," in Kidwell and Steele, eds., *Men and Women,* pp. 144–57; "Bloomers," *Dress* 5 (1980): 1–12. See also "The First of the Flappers," *Literary Digest* (May 13, 1922): 44–45.

24. Lauer and Lauer, "Battle of the Sexes," p. 582.

25. Foote, "Challenging Gender Symbols," pp. 149–50; Ewing, "Dress and Undress," p. 64; Lauer and Lauer, "Battle of the Sexes"; Laver, *Costume and Fashion,* pp. 180–83.

26. Foote, "Challenging Gender Symbols," p. 148. For analysis of the shifting and complex meanings of gender, race, and nation evinced by Western women's wearing of "Turkish trousers," see Reina Lewis, *Gendering Orientalism: Race, Femininity and Representation* (New York: Routledge, 1996); and Dianne Sachko Macleod, "Cross-Cultural Cross-Dressing: Class, Gender and Modernist Sexual Identity," in *Orientalism Transposed: The Impact of the Colonies on British Culture,* ed. Julie Codell and Dianne Sachko Macleod (Hants, UK: Ashgate, 1998), pp. 63–85. Chilla Bulbeck further notes that "when western women were 'civilised' Victorians because they covered up, exposure was deemed barbaric. Today, the covered veiled woman has replaced the exposed woman as the signifier of the 'other' indicating western woman's superiority." Chilla Bulbeck, *Re-Orienting Western Feminisms: Women's Diversity in a Postcolonial World* (Cambridge: Cambridge University Press, 1998), p. 30.

27. Patricia Cunningham, *Reforming Women's Fashion, 1850–1920: Politics, Health, and Art* (Kent, OH: Kent State University Press, 2003), p. 53. Banner, *American Beauty,* pp. 147–50, notes the difficulties faced by post-Bloomer dress-reform advocates. Severa, *Dressed for the Photographer,* pp. 205, 239, 250, 257, 274, 403. English dress reformers promoted a "Travelling Costume" that included "Turkish trousers" at the International Health Exhibition in 1884 and advocated the divided skirt the following year. Elizabeth Wilson and Lou Taylor, *Through the Looking Glass: A History of Dress from 1860 to the Present Day* (London: BBC Books, 1989), p. 52. In the United States, widespread interest in bicycling in the 1890s popularized bifurcated garments (see below) and enabled reformers in England also to foreground divided attire for women (pp. 54–59).

28. Lauer and Lauer, "The Battle of the Sexes," p. 583. See Foucault, *History*

of Sexuality, and Smith-Rosenberg, *Disorderly Conduct*, for more on the workings of such discourses.

29. *Godey's Lady's Book*, May 1858, p. 454. Stansell, *City of Women*, p. 164, notes an 1855 report of Irish immigrant women's desires for hoop skirts upon arrival in the United States. Ewing, *Dress & Undress*, p. 72, describes English factory and agricultural workers in crinolines; Steele, *Fashion and Eroticism*, p. 75, notes that an English factory instituted a rule in 1860 requesting "our hands at all Factories to leave Hoop and Crinoline at Home." Deborah Gray White, *Ar'n't I a Woman?: Female Slaves in the Plantation South* (New York: W. W. Norton, 1999), p. 95. See also Severa, *Dressed for the Photographer*, pp. 87–88, 98, 201–2, 205, 239, 278–79, 310; and Hall, *Common Threads*, p. 98.

30. Ewing, *Dress & Undress*, pp. 69–76, 85; Perrot, *Fashioning the Bourgeoisie*, pp. 147–48; Steele, *Fashion and Eroticism*, p. 114.

31. I am grateful to Patricia Cline Cohen for sharing with me the *Weekly Rake* drawings of July 9, 1842, pp. 1, 3, that she found in the American Antiquarian Society archives.

32. Carter, *Underwear*, p. 55; Chenoune, *Beneath It All*, p. 22; Perrot, *Fashioning the Bourgeoisie*, pp. 108–9.

33. Cunnington and Cunnington, *History of Underclothes*, p. 94, note an 1851 advertisement for "richly trimmed" drawers. "Plain" drawers were also available at a lower cost.

34. Cunnington and Cunnington, *History of Underclothes*, p. 106, illustrate the trim of the era with a line drawing reproducing a pair of drawers, ca. 1860–70, held at the Gallery of English Costume, Platt Hall, Manchester, and on p. 98 note the exasperated comment in an 1866 issue of *Englishwoman's Domestic Magazine* that "the amount of embroidery put upon underclothing nowadays is sinful."

35. Cunnington and Cunnington, *History of Underclothes*, pp. 98–99; Martin and Koda, *Infra-Apparel*, p. 64. Perrot, *Fashioning the Bourgeoisie*, p. 101. In 1856, eighteen-year-old Englishman William Perkin accidentally invented the first aniline dye while searching for a method of producing quinine. Instead of creating aniline, he produced the color he named mauve as well as a means of developing chemically synthesized dyes that freed manufacturers from the greater expense and time required to derive dyes from plants. Simon Garfield, *Mauve: How One Man Invented a Color That Changed the World* (New York: W. W. Norton, 2001).

36. Ewing, *Dress and Undress*, p. 101; Christina Probert, *Lingerie in Vogue since 1910* (New York: Abbeville Press, 1981), p. 7; Carter, *Underwear*, p. 50. Holliday, *Unmentionables*, p. 208. Ewing, *Dress and Undress*, p. 85. Valerie Twelves, "An Investigation of the Impact of the Dress Reform Movement: A Case Study of Reform Movements in the Years 1890 to 1920" (master's thesis, Cornell University, 1969); Cunningham, *Reforming Women's Fashion*.

37. Ellen Garvey, *The Adman in the Parlor* (New York: Oxford, 1996), ch. 4; Ewing, *Dress and Undress*, p. 64; Saint-Laurent, *Great Book*, p. 140; Banner, *American Beauty*, p. 149; *Harper's Bazar*, April 14, 1894, cover, reproduced in

Blum, *Victorian Fashions*, p. 266. A May 13, 1894, *San Francisco Chronicle* report, "New Dress of Los Angeles Wheelwomen," noted in the headline the "Unconventional but Very Sensible Turkish Trousers, Leggings and Eton Jackets" the women wore.

38. Edward Van Every, *Sins of America as "Exposed" by the Police Gazette* (New York: Frederick A. Stokes Company, 1931), p. 180; *The Police Gazette*, edited by Gene Smith and Jayne Barry Smith (New York: Simon and Schuster, 1972), pp. 198, 201, 202. See also Margaret Finnegan, *Selling Suffrage: Consumer Culture and Votes for Women* (New York: Columbia University Press, 1999), for later promotions of women's rights that incorporated female spectacle.

39. Ewing, *Dress and Undress*, p. 112; Wilson and Taylor, *Through the Looking Glass*, p. 57; Banner, *American Beauty*, p. 149. Patricia Campbell Warner, "Public and Private: Men's Influence on American Women's Dress for Sport and Physical Education," *Dress* (1988): 48–55, finds evidence of exercise dresses with pantaloons as early as 1832.

40. Cunnington and Cunnington, *History of Underclothes*, pp. 128–29, describe Edwardian fashion for men and women. In this period, English speakers widely began using the French term *lingerie* to describe the new turn in undergarments, superseding the previous and more specific meaning of lingerie as articles made of linen. The newer definition drew on the nineteenth-century practice of making expensive undergarments of fine linen. Thus, the new specialized meaning of the term *lingerie* carried the connotation of luxury, elegance, wealth, and privilege. In 1901, an English women's magazine noted, "Among the lower-class Englishwoman there still lingers a desire for heavy durable longcloth, but we do not call that *lingerie*. A wish for dainty underwear is generally actuated by a desire for cleanliness. The lingerie of the moment is as luxurious as ever, in fact, even more so" (p. 133). See Alison Gernsheim, *Victorian and Edwardian Fashion: A Photographic Survey* (New York: Dover Publications, 1981), for distinctions between the Victorian and Edwardian eras of fashion. She dates the origins of Edwardian fashion from Queen Victoria's Diamond Jubilee in 1897, pp. 83–86. See also de Marly, *Fashion for Men*, pp. 97–98, 109–14. Alma Whitaker, *Trousers and Skirts* (Los Angeles: Times-Mirror Press, 1923), p. 108.

41. Ewing, *Dress and Undress*, p. 112, notes the parallel development of "frou-frou" and "practical" undergarments; for example, "Shall it be pretty or practical? Fray-Pruf Lingerie insists on being both." *Vogue*, July 1944, p. 12; Gary Abrams, "Lore Caulfield: Sexy Lingerie the Antidote for Career Dressing," *Los Angeles Times*, April 29, 1983.

42. Probert, *Lingerie in Vogue*, p. 9. A peignoir is a long dressing gown; a matinée is a shorter bed jacket. Costume historian Linda Welters clarified this distinction for me.

43. Cunnington and Cunnington, *History of Underclothes*, pp. 108, 124; Saint Laurent, *Great Book*, p. 115; Carter, *Underwear*, p. 152; *The Barnhardt Dictionary of Etymology* (1988), p. 568; *The Dressmaker: A Complete Book on*

all matters connected with Sewing and Dressmaking from the simplest stitches to the cutting, making, altering, mending and caring for the clothes (New York: Butterick Publishing Company, 1911, 1916), pp. 42–44.

44. Cunnington and Cunnington, *History of Underclothes*, p. 137.

45. *Eaton's Spring & Summer Catalogue* 46 (1901), pp. 54–55. Eaton's was Canada's largest department store and mail-order company at the time. See also the Sears, Roebuck and Co. catalog, 1897, p. 308, for illustrations with subtle visual cues denoting crotch construction. Carter, *Underwear*, p. 64, describes commercial representation of ready-made drawers as "shyly drawn—folded with just parts of the embroidery or lace showing."

46. I examined all relevant drawers and corset covers in the costume collections of the Royal Ontario Museum, New York Metropolitan Museum, and Smithsonian Institution. *Eaton's Fall & Winter Catalogue* 47 (1901–02), p. 96.

47. See, for example, artifacts 954.73.1.A and 954.73.1.B, 1904; 963.123.D and 963.123.E, 1906 (ROM); 243178.4 & 243178.7, 1902; 237724.2a & 237724.5, 1906; 58909 & 58907, 1910 (Smith); 54.51ab, 1916 (Met).

48. See, for example, the following early twentieth-century closed-drawer sets: 967.175.16A and 967.175.16B; 942.27.14 and 942.27.13, 1908; 964.153A and 964.153B, 1912 (ROM); 243102.2 and 243102.3, 1902; 212884.024 and 212884.025, 1905–10; 273774.1 and 273774.2, 1913. (Smith).

49. Cunnington and Cunnington, *History of Underclothes*, p. 38.

50. Lisa See, *On Gold Mountain: The One-Hundred-Year Odyssey of My Chinese American Family* (New York: Vintage Books, 1996), pp. xix, 39–40, 57.

51. Marguérite d'Aincourt, *Études sur le costume féminin* (Paris, 1883), pp. 14–15, quoted in Perrot, *Fashioning the Bourgeoisie*, p. 166. Roland Barthes, *The Pleasure of the Text* (Oxford: Oxford University Press, 1990), pp. 9–10.

52. Steele, *Fashion and Eroticism*, pp. 13–17, summarizes the long history and biblical origins of this assertion; Perrot, *Fashioning the Bourgeoisie*, p. 12; Flugel, *Psychology of Clothes*, p. 16, sees decoration, modesty, and protection as the three purposes of clothing and finds the opposition between decoration and modesty fundamental to the psychology of clothing; Kathleen Canning, "The Body as Method? Reflections on the Place of the Body in Gender History," *Gender and History* 11, no. 3 (1999): 499–513. The question of the female body as marked by and marking gender difference (or as unmarked) has been addressed by feminist theorists such as Simone de Beauvoir, Monique Wittig, and Luce Irigaray. For an analysis of their perspectives, see Judith Butler, *Gender Trouble: Feminist Theory and the Subversion of Identity* (New York: Routledge, 1990).

53. Peiss, *Cheap Amusement*, pp. 134–35. See also David Nasaw, *Going Out: The Rise and Fall of Public Amusements* (New York: Basic Books, 1993). Perrot, *Fashioning the Bourgeoisie*, p. 100; Chenoune, *Beneath It All*, p. 25.

54. 966.17.4 and 958.41 (ROM); Cunnington and Cunnington, *History of Underclothes*, pp. 133, 137; Wilson and Taylor, *Through the Looking Glass*, p. 52.

55. Laver, *Costume and Fashion*, p. 224.

56. Cunnington and Cunnington, *History of Underclothes*, p. 140.

57. Hall, *Common Threads*, pp. 217–18; Sara Evans, *Born for Liberty: A History of Women in America* (New York: Free Press, 1989), pp. 161, 176; Ryan, "Projection of a New Womanhood," p. 120, cites a 1920 *Ladies' Home Journal* article, "Flapper Is Dead."

58. Cunnington and Cunnington, *History of Underclothes*, p. 147, includes a 1913 description of tango knickers from *The Lady* and a photograph of tango knickers, ca. 1914.

59. *Women's Wear Daily*, May 22, 1917, p. 5.

60. Ibid., May 7, 1917, p. 5; May 22, 1917, p. 5.

61. In the twentieth century, the "woman's rights movement" of the previous century changed to the "women's rights movement."

62. See Nancy Cott, *The Grounding of Modern Feminism* (New Haven: Yale University Press, 1987); Eleanor Flexner, *Century of Struggle: The Woman's Rights Movement in the United States* (Cambridge, MA: Harvard University Press, 1959, 1975); and Linda Gordon, *Woman's Body, Woman's Right: A Social History of Birth Control in America* (New York: Penguin, 1977).

63. Gordon, *Woman's Body*, ch. 7.

64. Maurine Greenwald, *Women, War, and Work: The Impact of World War I on Women Workers in the United States* (Westport, CT: Greenwood Press, 1980), pp. 121, 31, 48. Concerns about women in overalls resurfaced during World War II, despite government efforts to feminize women's defense work. In a letter to the editor, "Two Overall Gals" wrote about the disdain and insults they received from "society girls" and "soldiers" when wearing their work clothes in town. *Fresno Bee*, July 7, 1944.

65. Saint-Laurent, *Great Book*, p. 152; *Women's Wear Daily*, May 25, 1917, p. 19.

66. On 1920s pajamas, see Saint-Laurent, *Great Book*, p. 88; Probert, *Lingerie in Vogue*, pp. 19, 24.

67. *Women's Wear Daily*, September 19, 1924, p. 24; Bettina Berch, *Radical by Design: The Life & Style of Elizabeth Hawes* (New York: E. P. Dutton, 1988), pp. 61, 69.

68. Cunnington and Cunnington, *History of Underclothes*, pp. 111, 123. Page 111 notes that an 1874 edition of the *Young Ladies' Journal* includes patterns for a combination of "chemise and drawers" and reports an 1878 reference to the wide availability of combinations in *Cassell's Family Magazine*.

69. Carter, *Underwear*, p. 49.

70. Ewing, *Dress and Undress*, p. 129.

71. Envelope chemise: *Women's Wear Daily*, May 7, 1917, p. 5; teddy-bear drawers: ibid., May 28, 1917, p. 5; teddy: Carter, *Underwear*, p. 153. The teddy bear owes its origins to a 1902 cartoon depicting Theodore Roosevelt's refusal to shoot a cub while hunting. National Museum of American History, 1992.

72. Cunnington and Cunnington, *History of Underclothes*, p. 141; artifact 971.250.2 (ROM); Marybelle Bigelow, *Fashion in History: Apparel in the Western World* (Minneapolis: Burgess Publishing Co., 1970), p. 247.

73. *Women's Wear Daily*, September 11, 1924, p. 15.

74. Artifacts 989.60.8, 979.225.25, 973.272 (ROM).

75. Artifact 971.259.13 (ROM).

76. Flugel, *Psychology of Clothes*, pp. 172–73.

77. Mary Louise Roberts, "Samson and Delilah Revisited: The Politics of Women's Fashion in 1920s France," *American Historical Review* (June 1993): 658; Kitchens, *When Underwear Counted*, pp. 9, 16, 51, 55.

78. Cunningham, *Reforming Women's Fashion*, pp. 78–80. As Christina Simmons notes, "For women to abandon their modesty and follow men's lascivious behavior was to threaten the very basis of civilization." Christina Simmons, "Modern Sexuality and the Myth of Victorian Repression," in Peiss and Simmons, eds., *Passion and Power*, p. 171.

79. *Women's Wear Daily*, September 23, 1924, p. 9.

80. Simmons, "Modern Sexuality," pp. 158, 167–70.

81. *Topper*, directed by Norman Z. McLeod (MGM, 1937).

82. The film includes a spontaneous trip to a lingerie shop by Marion Kirby and Cosmo Topper, who doesn't realize that a pair of step-ins are in his coat pocket until Mrs. Topper discovers them. Cosmo claims he bought them for her; these are the step-ins she wears at the end of the film. Film-industry censors decided that some references to step-ins violated the Production Code, ordered the word *pants* deleted from dialogue, and curtailed scenes in which the undergarment was visible. Letters Joseph Breen to Mat O'Brien, March 18 and 20, 1937; Joseph Breen to Hal Roach, March 19 and June 24, 1937; memorandum for *Topper* files by E. R. O'Neil, March 19, 1937. Herrick Library.

CHAPTER 2. CORSETS AND GIRDLES

This chapter previously appeared as " 'Fighting the Corsetless Evil': Shaping Corsets & Culture, 1900–1930," *Journal of Social History* 33, no. 2 (Winter 1999): 355–84; and in *Beauty & Business: Commerce, Gender, and Culture in Modern America*, ed. Philip Scranton (New York: Routledge, 2001), 109–41.

Epigraph: Betty Hicks, "Babe Didrikson Zaharias: 'Stand back! This ain't no kid hittin'," *Women Sports* (November 1975), pp. 24, 28. Mary Biggs, ed., *Women's Words: Columbia Book of Quotations by Women* (New York: Columbia University Press, 1996), p. 381, suggests that the comment dates from the 1930s.

1. G. B. Pulfer, "Fighting the Corsetless Evil," *Corsets & Lingerie*, November 1921, p. 30.

2. The following trade journal articles reveal manufacturers' panic about corsetlessness: "The Evils of the No-Corset Fad," *Corsets & Lingerie*, November 1921, pp. 24–25; "Flappers Are Responsible for the Corsetless Craze," *Corsets & Lingerie*, November 1922, p. 33; "Eminent Surgeons Endorse the Corset," *Corsets & Lingerie*, December 1921, pp. 32–35.

3. Helene E. Roberts, "The Exquisite Slave: The Role of Clothes in the Making of the Victorian Woman," *Signs: Journal of Women in Culture and Society* (Spring 1977): 564–69; David Kunzle, "Dress Reform as Antifeminism: A Re-

sponse to Helene E. Roberts's 'The Exquisite Slave: The Role of Clothes in the Making of the Victorian Woman,'" *Signs* (Spring 1977): 570–79; Helene Roberts, "Reply to David Kunzle's 'Dress Reform as Antifeminism: A Response to Helene E. Roberts's 'The Exquisite Slave,'" *Signs* (Winter 1977): 518–19; Joanna Russ, "Comment on Helene Roberts' 'The Exquisite Slave: The Role of Clothes in the Making of the Victorian Woman,' and David Kunzle's 'Dress Reform as Antifeminism,'" *Signs* (Winter 1977): 520–21; David Kunzle, *Fashion and Fetishism: A Social History of the Corset, Tight-Lacing and Other Forms of Body-Sculpture in the West* (Totowa, NJ: Rowman and Littlefield, 1982); Lois Banner, *American Beauty* (Chicago: University of Chicago Press, 1983); Valerie Steele, *Fashion and Eroticism: Ideals of Feminine Beauty from the Victorian Era to the Jazz Age* (New York: Oxford University Press, 1985).

4. Elizabeth Ewing, *Dress and Undress: A History of Women's Underwear* (New York: Drama Book Specialists, 1978), pp. 110–13.

5. Havelock Ellis, "An Anatomical Vindication of the Straight Front Corset," *Current Literature*, February 1910, pp. 172–74.

6. "How Prehistoric Woman Solved the Problem of Her Waist Line," *Current Opinion*, March 1914, pp. 201–2.

7. Paul Poiret, *My First 50 Years* (London: Victor Gollancz, Ltd., 1931), pp. 72–73.

8. Ewing, *Dress and Undress*, pp. 89–91, 93, 108–110; C. Willett and Phillis Cunnington, *The History of Underclothes* (London: Faber and Faber, 1981, 1951), pp. 87, 114, 125–26; Norah Waugh, *Corsets and Crinolines* (London: B. T. Batsford, Ltd., 1954), p. 87. On the influence of the Russian ballet and the rational dress movement on Poiret's designs, see Peter Wollen, "Out of the Past: Fashion/Orientalism/The Body," in his *Raiding the Icebox: Reflections on Twentieth-Century Culture* (Bloomington: Indiana University Press, 1993), pp. 1–34. Fashion layouts and advertisements, such as "New Low Bust Flexible Model" and "New Supple Figure Corsets," *Women's & Infants' Furnisher*, January 1914, pp. 42–43, and "The Athletic Girl's Experience," Bon Ton Corset advertisement, *Vogue*, May 1914, p. 93, displayed the more flexible and sports corsets. *Women's & Infants' Furnisher*, first published in 1895, changed its name to *Corsets & Lingerie* in July 1921 and then again to *Corsets & Brassieres* in March 1926. Its publication continues today under the name *Intimate Fashion News*.

9. Ewing, *Dress and Undress*, p. 120; Mitchel Gray and Mary Kennedy, *The Lingerie Book* (New York: St. Martin's Press, 1980), p. 15; "A Graceful Dancing Corset," *Women's & Infants' Furnisher*, February 1914, p. 31. Banner, *American Beauty*, p. 176, offers evidence of the flapper's emergence in the mid-1910s. "Where Efficiency and Economy Meet," *Vogue*, April 1914, pp. 54–55; "Corseting the Corsetless Figure," *Vogue*, January 1914, p. 58.

10. "Woman Decides to Support Herself," *Vogue*, August 1917, pp. 67, 80.

11. See Eleanor Flexner, *Century of Struggle: The Woman's Rights Movement in the United States* (Cambridge, MA: Harvard University Press, 1959, 1975); and Linda Gordon, *Woman's Body, Woman's Right: A Social History of*

Birth Control in America (New York: Penguin, 1977), on the suffrage and birth control movements, respectively. The *New York Times* reported extensively on the fashion debates. For example, see August 30, 1922, p. 17, on the skirt-length controversy; see January 17, 1919, p. 5; February 16, 1921, p. 15; February 17, 1921, p. 6; May 22, 1919, p. 9; May 23, 1921, p. 15; June 15, 1921, p. 7; and June 21, 1921, p. 19, on modesty and morality; and see February 26, 1922, p. 12, on college dress codes.

12. Howard Zinn, *A People's History of the United States* (New York: HarperCollins, 1980), pp. 366–72.

13. My grandmother Mildred Rosenstein Schwartz (born 1902) on many occasions provided me with historical data drawn from her life experience; "The Renaissance of the C-rs-t," *The Independent*, July 25, 1925, p. 88.

14. James Laver, *Clothes* (New York: Horizon Press, 1953), pp. 40–47; Paul Nystrom, *Economics of Fashion* (New York: The Ronald Press Company, 1928), pp. 28, 145; Davis, *Fashion, Culture & Identity* (Chicago: University of Chicago Press, 1992), pp. 58–59; Pearl Binder, *Muffs and Morals* (New York: William Morrow & Company, 1954), ch. 7; Lynn Hunt, *Politics, Culture and Class in the French Revolution* (Berkeley: University of California Press, 1984), pp. 52–53, 74–85.

15. Elizabeth Lapovsky and Madeline D. Davis, *Boots of Leather, Slippers of Gold: The History of a Lesbian Community* (New York: Penguin Books, 1994), p. 180; George Chauncey, *Gay New York: Gender, Urban Culture, and the Making of the Gay Male World, 1890–1940* (New York: Basic Books, 1994), pp. 249–50; "Bifurcation," *Independent* (March 16, 1911), pp. 581–82.

16. *New York Times* June 3, 1922.

17. Ibid., June 21, 1921.

18. "The Problem of the Wardrobe: Dressing Smartly on a Modest Income," *Good Housekeeping*, October 1922, p. 136.

19. "The Well Groomed Woman—by the Perfection of Detail and Appropriateness of Costume You Will Know Her," *Good Housekeeping*, October 1922, pp. 46–47, 173.

20. *Women's & Infants' Furnisher*, January 1910, p. 44. For more on the development and expansion of the ready-to-wear industry, see Jessica Daves, *Ready-Made Miracle: The American Story of Fashion for the Millions* (New York: G. P. Putnam's Sons, 1967).

21. *New York Times* August 30, 1922. Women also organized in support of longer skirts. Society women in Washington, DC, condemned short skirts on moral grounds and called upon their cohort nationally to "band together to condemn such vulgar fashions of women's apparel that do not tend to cultivate innate modesty, good taste or good morals." "A New Crusade for Longer Skirts," *Literary Digest*, January 16, 1926, pp. 31–32.

22. *Corsets & Lingerie* first identified corsetlessness as dangerous in "Buyers Against Corsetless Fad: New York Department Store Buyers All Against Fad and Say It Is on the Wane," *Corsets & Lingerie*, September 1921, pp. 27, 29. The first assertion that it was also evil is in "The Evils of the No-Corset Fad," *Corsets*

& Lingerie, November 1921, pp. 24–25. *Corsets & Lingerie,* January 1924, p. 31, and *Women's Wear Daily,* September 24, 1924, p. 28, identify the fad's beginning date. Nicole Thornton, *Poiret* (New York: Rizzoli International Publications, 1979), p. 1; Paul Poiret, *My First Fifty Years,* pp. 72–73; Julian Robinson, *Body Packaging: A Guide to Human Sexual Display* (Los Angeles: Elysium Growth Press), 1988, p. 78; "Corseting the Corsetless Figure," *Vogue,* January 1, 1914, p. 58; "Tango Popularizes Corsetless Figure," *Women's & Infants' Furnisher,* January 1914, p. 68; Anderman Form Company advertisement, *Women's & Infants' Furnisher,* February 1915, p. 20.

23. G. B. Pulfer, "Fighting the Corsetless Evil," *Corsets & Lingerie,* November 1921, p. 30.

24. "The Evils of the No-Corset Fad," *Corsets & Lingerie,* November 1921, pp. 24–25; "Flappers Are Responsible for the Corsetless Craze," *Corsets & Lingerie,* November 1922, p. 33; "Eminent Surgeons Endorse the Corset," *Corsets & Lingerie,* December 1921, pp. 32–35.

25. "Woman's Friend, the Corset," *Literary Digest,* November 5, 1921, p. 20.

26. "The Depression of 1920–1922 in the Women's Clothing Industry," Research Department, International Ladies Garment Workers Union (ILGWU). Report included with letter from Mitchell to Dubinsky, May 11, 1945. ILGWU Collection, Labor-Management Documentation Center, Cornell University, David Dubinsky Box 160, Folder 2B. "Table 1—Corsets and Allied Garments— Summary for the United States: 1899–1929," 1930 Census of Manufacturers, M1930.2, p. 385; *Profits of Underwear Manufacturers, 1918–1942: A Survey Made for Underwear Institute,* Research & Statistical Division (New York: Dun & Bradstreet, Inc., 1943); Joseph Swanson and Samuel Williamson, "Estimates of National Product and Income for the United States Economy, 1919–1941," *Explorations in Economic History* (Fall 1972): 53–74. I am grateful to Kathleen Barrett for providing the Swanson and Williamson citation and for sharing her expertise in business history with me.

27. 1930 Census of Manufacturers, p. 385; "The Corset," *Fortune,* March 1938, pp. 95ff.

28. "Corsets Still in Vogue," *Corsets & Lingerie,* July 1921, pp. 37, 52. "New Novelties for Fall," *Corsets & Lingerie,* p. 32. "Elastic Girdles and Novelties" first appeared as a new department in *Corsets & Lingerie* in June 1922, p. 43. *Corsets & Lingerie,* October 1922, p. 4. A discussion of the girdle as merely a corset with a new name appears in *Corsets & Lingerie,* April 1924, p. 32. *Corset and Underwear Review,* December 1924, p. 89, blames the older corset for figure problems.

29. "Parisian Women Wear Corsets," *Corsets & Lingerie,* August 1921, p. 31; "Paris on the Corset Question," *Corsets & Lingerie,* December 1921, pp. 25–26.

30. Gertrude L. Nickerson, "The American Woman and Her Corset," *Corset and Underwear Review,* November 1924, pp. 83–84.

31. "The Evils of the No-Corset Fad," *Corsets & Lingerie,* November 1921, pp. 24–25.

32. "Eminent Surgeons Endorse the Corset," *Corsets & Lingerie,* December 1921, pp. 32–35.

33. Ibid., p. 33.

34. Ibid., pp. 33–34. See Steven J. Ross, "Struggles for the Screen: Workers, Radicals and the Political Uses of Silent Film," *American Historical Review* 96 (April 1991): 333–68, for more on the public media's mocking of radical women as failed men.

35. Royal Worcester Corset Company advertisement, *Corsets & Lingerie,* November 1922, p. 7; 1930 Census of Manufacturers, p. 385; Helen Walser, "The Renaissance of the Corset," *Corsets & Brassieres,* February 1930, p. 55; "Corset Show Big Help," *Corsets & Brassieres,* December 1930, p. 33; "Joel Alexander Looks at 1935," *Corsets & Brassieres,* January 1935, p. 45.

36. Ethel Allen authored the following articles in the series for *Women's & Infants' Furnisher:* "Corset Fitting the Young Girl Figure," April 1921, p. 28; "Corset Fitting the Top-Heavy Figure," May 1921, p. 28; "Corset Fitting the Curved Back Figure," p. 32. The series continued when the magazine changed its name to *Corsets & Lingerie:* "Corset Fitting the Full Proportioned Figure," July 1921, p. 34; "Corset Fitting the Thigh Figure," August 1921, p. 30; "Corset Fitting the Maternity Figure," September 1921, p. 34. In 1921, Ethel Allen was the supervisor of instruction at the Kabo School of Corsetry.

37. *Women's & Infants' Furnisher,* January 1921, p. 64.

38. Ibid., January 1921, p. 44; "Corsets of Distinct Types," September 1906, p. 35. *The Principles of Scientific Corset Fitting,* preface by Bertha A. Strickler (New York: Modart Corset Co., 1925).

39. For other sources on the movement of scientific rationalization into the domestic sphere, see Dolores Hayden, *The Grand Domestic Revolution: A History of Feminist Designs for American Homes, Neighborhoods, and Cities* (Cambridge, MA: MIT Press, 1981); and Ruth Schwartz Cowan, *More Work for Mother: The Ironies of Household Technology from the Open Hearth to the Microwave* (London: Free Association Books, 1989).

40. *Corsets & Lingerie,* July 1921, p. 15; January 1925, p. 23; *The Principles of Scientific Corset Fitting* (New York: Modart, 1925); *Women's & Infants' Furnisher,* March 1921, p. 49; *Corsets & Brassieres,* July 1928, p. 41.

41. *Corsets & Lingerie,* January 1925, p. 23.

42. *Principles of Scientific Corset Fitting,* p. 12; "Woman's Friend, the Corset," *Literary Digest,* November 5, 1921, p. 20; Modart's use of ptosis to sell corsets was similar to other companies' use of medicalized conditions for advertising purposes in the 1920s, such as Listerine's promotion of its product to combat halitosis. See Stephen Fox, *The Mirror Makers: A History of American Advertising and Its Creators* (New York: William Morrow, 1984), pp. 97–98, and Roland Marchand, *Advertising the American Dream: Making Way for Modernity, 1920 to 1940* (Berkeley: University of California Press, 1985), pp. 18–20, 218–19.

43. "The corset stock is one of the safest of all the stocks in the dry goods store." *Women's & Infants' Furnisher,* 1896, quoted in its twenty-fifth-

anniversary issue, January 1921, p. 61; "Corset Departments Lead in Store Prof-
its!" Warner Brothers ad, *Corsets & Brassieres,* January 1933, p. 3; *Corsets &
Brassieres,* February 1938, p. 25; *Corset Preview: The Bulletin of the National
Retail Dry Goods Association,* July 1941, p. 13; *Corset & Underwear Review,*
Sales Training Manual Issue, August 1942, p. 122; "Corset Selling Is an Art,"
Corsets & Brassieres, February 1946, p. 34.

44. *Women's & Infants' Furnisher,* April 1921, p. 2. Gossard also encouraged
buyers to reduce the number of lines their corset departments carried. Its 1921
analysis of the current economic depression suggested that stores could resolve
the problem of "stock liquidation" by carrying complete lines by fewer companies. The point of view expressed by Warner's and Gossard obviously favored
larger companies that widely advertised their products. *Women's & Infants'
Furnisher,* January 1921, p. 3.

45. Modart Corset Company used these category names in *The Principles of
Scientific Corset Fitting.*

46. "How to Choose the Right Corset," *Good Housekeeping,* September
1921, pp. 52–53; "Modern Styles Do Not Cater to One Type of Silhouette But
to Several," *Corsets & Brassieres,* May 1933, pp. 26–27; *Corsets & Lingerie,* January 1921, p. 43; "A Matter of Opinion," *Corsets & Lingerie,* February 1925,
p. 35.

47. Ewing, *Dress and Undress,* pp. 136, 137; *Corsets & Lingerie,* July 1921,
p. 43.

48. "A Significant New Development in Modern Merchandising," Bon Ton
Corsets advertisement, *Corsets & Brassieres,* 1929, p. 14; *Corset & Underwear
Review,* Sales Training Manual Issue, August 1942, p. 54.

49. *Time,* December 25, 1939, p. 13. The survey is also discussed in Jean Gordon's *The Good Corsetiere* (Strouse, Adler Company, 1947, p. 21), a widely circulated instruction booklet for new employees of corset departments. The booklet and information about Gordon are in Corsets Box 3, Folder 44, and Corsets
Box 5, Folder 10, Warshaw Collection, Smithsonian Institution. See also *Corsets
& Underwear Review,* Sales Training Manual Issue, August 1942, p. 21.

50. "Curriculum for the Corset Salesgirl," *Corsets & Brassieres,* July 1941,
pp. 34–35; *Corset & Underwear Review,* Sales Training Manual Issue, August
1942, pp. 26–27.

51. "Adjustment and Care of the Corset: A Corset Right Laced and Rightly
Worn Insures Poise and Grace to the Figure," *Good Housekeeping,* October
1921, pp. 45, 121.

52. Allen, "Corseting the Curved Back Figure," p. 32.

53. *Women's Wear Daily,* May 19, 1917, p. 15; November 14, 1940, p. 31.

54. Allen, "Corset-Fitting the Full Proportioned Figure," p. 30; and "Corset-
Fitting the Top-Heavy Figure," p. 28. *Corset & Underwear Review,* Sales Training Manual Issue, August 1942.

55. "Curriculum for the Corset Salesgirl," *Corsets & Brassieres,* July 1941,
pp. 34–35. For a fuller discussion of the tensions between department store
saleswomen, customers, and managers, see Susan Porter Benson, *Counter Cul-*

tures: Saleswomen, Managers and Customers in American Department Stores, 1890–1940 (Chicago: University of Illinois Press, 1986).

56. Allen, "Corseting the Curved Back Figure," p. 32.

57. *Women's & Infants' Furnisher,* April 1918, p. 38; Gordon, *The Good Corsetiere,* p. 9.

58. "Training the New Salesgirl," *Corsets & Brassieres,* September 1946, p. 48–49; Allen, "Corset Fitting the Curved Back Figure," p. 32. On corset selling as an art, see *Women's & Infants' Furnisher,* May 1925, p. 27, and "Corset Selling Is an Art," *Corsets & Brassieres,* February 1946, p. 34.

59. Allen, "Corset Fitting the Young Girl Figure," p. 28; *Corsets & Brassieres,* January 1933, p. 35.

60. "New Interest in Junior Garments," *Corsets & Brassieres,* January 1929, p. 28; "Warner Opening Well Attended," *Corsets & Brassieres,* March 1930, p. 41.

61. The retailer B. Altman & Company, for example, focused on this commercial rite of passage in advertisements announcing "that a young girl's first corset is an important event." *Women's Wear Daily,* April 2, 1931; *Women's Wear Daily,* April 30, 1931, sec. 2, p. 4; *Corsets & Brassieres,* August 1946, p. 16.

62. *Women's & Infants' Furnisher,* February 1915, p. 49.

63. "The Junior Department," *Corsets & Brassieres,* April 1930, pp. 34–35.

64. "The Junior Corset Department," *Corsets & Brassieres,* January 1930, p. 41; "A Prosperous Outlook—Corset Buyers and Manufacturers Are All Very Optimistic," *Corsets & Brassieres,* February 1930, p. 25; *Corsets & Brassieres,* March 1930, p. 41.

65. *Corsets & Brassieres,* July 1930, p. 43; October 1930, p. 27.

66. *Corsets & Lingerie,* January 1924, pp. 31–32.

67. This point is also made in *Corsets & Brassieres,* January 1933, p. 35.

68. "Junior Week Arouses Interest," *Corsets & Brassieres,* July 1930, p. 43; "Junior Corset Week a Success," *Corsets & Brassieres,* October 1930, p. 27; *Corsets & Brassieres,* January 1933, p. 35.

69. *Corsets & Lingerie,* September 1921, n.p., October 1922, p. 34; July 1921, p. 37; June 1922, p. 43; *Women's & Infants' Furnisher,* January 1914, p. 39; *Corsets & Lingerie,* April 1924, p. 29; *Women's Wear Daily,* September 3, 1924, p. 32.

70. *Corsets & Lingerie,* June 1924, p. 49; *Women's Wear Daily,* September 3, 1924, p. 32; September 24, 1924, p. 28; *Corsets & Lingerie,* February 1925, p. 9; "What Others Say about Rubber Goods," *Corsets & Lingerie,* February 1925, pp. 40–41; "Do Corsets Further Femininity?" *Corsets & Lingerie,* April 1925, p. 29. The Madame X name carried a suggestion of illicit sexuality. See "The Meaning of Black Lingerie," chapter 4 of this book.

71. See chapter 3 for more on "boyshform."

72. "Flappers Are Responsible for the Corsetless Craze," *Corsets & Lingerie,* November 1922, p. 33; February 1925, p. 42. On the decreasing emphasis on the diaphragm, see, for example, *Corsets & Brassieres,* January 1937, p. 41; October 1937, p. 41; January 1938, pp. 11, 40, 49.

73. Designers and manufacturers attempted to bring back boned corsets and cinched waists as early as 1939. "The Revolution in Corsets," *Look*, October 10, 1939. For more on the New Look from 1947 to 1952, see chapter 7 of this book.

74. Michel Foucault, *Language, Counter-Memory, Practice: Selected Essays and Interviews*, ed. Donald F. Bouchard (Ithaca, NY: Cornell University Press, 1977), p. 150.

CHAPTER 3. BRASSIERES

1. Lou Valentino, *The Films of Lana Turner* (Seacaucus, NJ: Citadel Press, 1976), pp. 55–56; *They Won't Forget*, directed by Mervyn LeRoy (First National Pictures, 1937); Steve Oney, *And the Dead Shall Rise: The Murder of Mary Phagan and the Lynching of Leo Frank* (New York: Pantheon, 2003).

2. Valentino, *Films of Lana Turner*, pp. 7, 57. The importance of the costume in the film is clear in a dramatic courtroom moment when the ambitious district attorney (Claude Rains) holds up the dead girl's skirt and sweater as a surrogate for her body.

3. Valentino, *Films of Lana Turner*, p. 20.

4. Lana Turner clippings file, Herrick Library.

5. *Los Angeles Times*, June 30, 1995; Marjorie Rosen, *Popcorn Venus: Women, Movies and the American Dream* (New York: Avon Books, 1973), p. 315. Rosen comments that Turner's "image was founded on a beauty ideal rather than on any strength of character."

6. *Newsweek*, February 28, 1994, p. 41. In claiming the brassiere as a twentieth-century garment, I do not deny the existence of earlier nineteenth-century bust improvers, but seek to point out that twentieth-century brassieres were a distinct phenomenon that focused attention on the breasts in new ways.

7. François Boucher, *20,000 Years of Fashion: The History of Costume and Personal Adornment* (New York: Harry N. Abrams, 1987), p. 400; James Laver, *Costume and Fashion: A Concise History* (London: Thames and Hudson, 1982), pp. 217–25; Elizabeth Ewing, *Dress and Undress: A History of Women's Underwear* (New York: Drama Book Specialists, 1978), pp. 86–87; Philippe Perrot, *Fashioning the Bourgeoisie: A History of Clothing in the Nineteenth Century* (Princeton, NJ: Princeton University Press, 1994), pp. 93, 96–98.

8. Claudia Glenn Dowling, "Ooh-La-La! The Bra," *Life*, June 1989, p. 88; Lady Duff Gordon, *Discretions & Indiscretions* (London: Jarrolds Publishers, 1932), p. 66. Poiret states, "In the name of Liberty . . . I proclaimed the fall of the corset and the adoption of the brassière, which, since then, has won the day." Paul Poiret, *My First Fifty Years* (London: Victor Gollancz, Ltd., 1931), pp. 72–73.

9. Caresse Crosby, *The Passionate Years* (New York: Dial Press, 1953), p. 10. A cleverly written 1971 book, which is taken to be legitimate in some circles but which appears to me to be a parody, claims that Otto Titzling invented the brassiere in 1912 but that Phillippe de Brassiere appropriated the unpatented design in the late 1920s. Wallace Reyburn, *Bust-Up: The Uplifting Tale of Otto Titzling and the Development of the Bra* (London: Macdonald & Co. Ltd., 1971).

10. *Larousse's French-English/English-French Dictionary* (New York: Pocket Books, 1971), pp. 58, 150, 251; Ewing, *Dress and Undress*, p. 115.

11. *Women's & Infants' Furnisher*, June 1915, p. 45; December 1915, p. 37; February 1916, p. 37; May 1914, p. 39; and December 1916, p. 41. *Woman's Home Companion*, March 1914, p. 85; *Vogue*, August 15, 1919, p. 66. See Lois Banner, *American Beauty* (Chicago: University of Chicago Press, 1983), p. 148, on the introduction of the shirtwaist.

12. *Women's & Infants' Furnisher*, January 1921, pp. 55, 57; June 1905, p. 17; January 1910, inside front cover; and September 1906, p. 16; *Women's Wear Daily*, September 4, 1947, p. 14.

13. *Women's & Infants' Furnisher*, January 1921, p. 61.

14. Ibid., pp. 50–52.

15. *Women's Wear Daily*, September 4, 1947, p. 14; *Women's & Infants' Furnisher*, January 1914, pp. 40–41; *Women's Wear Daily*, May 31, 1919, p. 90; *Women's & Infants' Furnisher*, January 1921, p. 57; Ewing, *Dress and Undress*, p. 127.

16. *Women's & Infants' Furnisher*, June 1910, pp. 88, 94; May 1913, pp. 31–35; and May 1914, p. 39; *Vogue*, August 15, 1919, p. 66. Ewing, *Dress and Undress*, p. 142; *Women's & Infants' Furnisher*, December 1916, p. 31. My grandmother Mildred Rosenstein Schwartz (1902–98) told me that in the late 1910s, she wore her first brassiere over her undershirt until her girlfriends told her it was to be worn underneath.

17. *Women's & Infants' Furnisher*, May 1914, p. 39.

18. Ibid., January 1914, pp. 38, 11; November 1915, p. 37. Rubber reducing brassieres continued to be featured in the Montgomery Ward's mail-order catalog in the mid-1920s and in the Sears, Roebuck catalog in the late 1930s. *Montgomery Ward Catalog*, 1925, p. 66; 1925–26, p. 77; *Sears, Roebuck and Co. Catalogue*, 1936–37, p. 153. *Women's & Infants' Furnisher*, November 1915, p. 37. For examples of 1910s brassieres, see artifacts 43.44.18, 1978.477.42, 1978.385.2 (Met); 960.40, 981.146.2 (ROM).

19. *Women's & Infants' Furnisher*, January 1914, pp. 40–41; *Women's Wear Daily*, June 11, 1919, p. 16. Ribbon bandeau, 1914: 982.104.5 (ROM).

20. *Corsets & Lingerie*, October 1922, p. 47; De Bevoise brassieres, 1917: 1979.346.149 and 1979.346.151 (Met); *Women's & Infants' Furnisher*, December 1916, p. 41; and January 1910, inside front cover; *Women's Wear Daily*, May 25, 1917, p. 17; *Women's & Infants' Furnisher*, November 1915, p. 37. The Lucille Somarco Company claimed to be the first firm to produce the bandeaux. Ibid., January 1921, p. 43.

21. *Women's & Infants' Furnisher*, January 1914, p. 60. Lucille Somarco claimed to be the originator of the strapless; *Women's & Infants' Furnisher*, January 1921, p. 8. Ewing, *Dress and Undress*, p. 162.

22. *Women's & Infants' Furnisher*, December 1916, p. 31; January 1918, p. 31; and October 1921, p. 15; *Corsets & Brassieres*, March 1938, p. 53. The disappearance of sports brassieres until the revival of feminism may relate to wider attitudes toward female participation in sports. Sara Evans notes that although

female athletes gained fame in the 1920s, colleges also disbanded some women's athletics programs at that time due to concerns about their defeminizing effects. *Born for Liberty: A History of Women in America* (New York: Free Press, 1989), p. 178. However, Susan Cahn reports a steady increase in women's sports throughout the 1930s in *Coming on Strong: Gender and Sexuality in Twentieth-Century Women's Sport* (New York: Free Press, 1994). See also Janet Phillips and Peter Phillips, "History from Below: Women's Underwear and the Rise of Women's Sport," *Journal of Popular Culture* 27 (Fall 1993): 129–48.

23. *Women's & Infants' Furnisher,* February 1921, p. 47; *Women's Wear Daily,* February 13, 1919, p. 34; *Corsets & Lingerie,* August 1922, p. 27; April 1924, p. 18; February 1921, p. 47. *Women's & Infants' Furnisher,* October 1922, p. 49.

24. *Women's & Infants' Furnisher,* June 1915, p. 45; January 1916, p. 37. Boucher, *20,000 Years of Fashion,* pp. 405–7. *Women's & Infants' Furnisher,* February 1921, p. 47; January 1921, p. 50. *Montgomery Ward Catalog,* 1920, p. 110; 1922, p. 111.

25. *Women's & Infants' Furnisher,* December 1915, p. 37; July 1916, p. 31; December 1916, p. 41; May 1918, pp. 39–40. Ewing, *Dress and Undress,* p. 127. See also TR 7758.517, CR 187.61.11 (LACMA).

26. Ewing, *Dress and Undress,* p. 128; *Montgomery Ward Catalog,* 1922, p. 108; 1925–26, p. 77; *Corsets & Lingerie,* November 1924, p. 37.

27. Ewing, *Dress and Undress,* p. 126; Michael Colmer, *Whalebone to See-Through: A History of Body Packaging* (South Brunswick, NJ: A. S. Barnes & Co., 1980), n.p.

28. Girlish Form brassiere, artifact 976.221.1 (ROM); *Corset & Underwear Review,* October 1924, p. 124.

29. *Corsets & Lingerie,* December 1921, p. 29; *Women's & Infants' Furnisher,* January 1921, p. 48; *Corsets & Lingerie,* November 1922, p. 36.

30. *Montgomery Ward Catalog,* 1925–26, p. 76; *Corsets & Lingerie,* May 1925, p. 41.

31. Harry Braverman, *Labor and Monopoly Capital: The Degradation of Work in the Twentieth Century* (New York: Monthly Review Press, 1974); David Montgomery, *Workers Control in America: Studies in the History of Work, Technology, and Labor Struggles* (New York: Cambridge University Press, 1979).

32. *Corsets & Lingerie,* October 1922, p. 47, November 1922, p. 42. *Vogue,* September 15, 1924; *Corsets & Brassieres,* March 1926, p. 33; *Corset & Underwear Review,* December 1924, p. 99. See also CR-15 1-60-7a (LACMA).

33. Artifact 303278.1 (Smith); *Body Fashions/Intimate Apparel* 2 (1993): 18–19; "Maidenform and You May Be Looking for Each Other" (company publication), n.d., n.p. The company registered the trade name Maiden Form in 1925 and joined the two words together (Maidenform) after World War II; *Corsets & Lingerie,* November 1922, p. 42.

34. Ewing, *Dress and Undress,* p. 130; Christina Probert, *Lingerie in Vogue* (New York: Abbeville Press Publishers, 1981), p. 19; *Sears, Roebuck and Co. Catalogue,* 1931, p. 127.

35. *Corsets & Lingerie,* November 1924, p. 37; *Corset & Underwear Review,* October 1927, pp. 85, 35. The brassiere was still advertised for its health benefits in the 1936–37 *Sears, Roebuck and Co. Catalogue,* p. 152 (italics original). *Corsets & Brassieres,* February 1930, p. 35.

36. *Corsets & Brassieres,* March 1930, p. 39.

37. *Women's & Infants' Furnisher,* March 1930, p. 41. The same point is made in *Corset & Underwear Review,* January 1928, p. 90.

38. *Corset & Underwear Review,* November 1924, p. 96; December 1924, p. 99; February 1925, p. 98. *Women's & Infants' Furnisher,* January 1914, p. 6; *Corset & Underwear Review,* February 1925, p. 98; *Maiden Form Mirror,* January 1934, p. 1; *Corset & Underwear Review,* February 1925, p. 98.

39. *Women's & Infants' Furnisher,* November 1915, p. 37; January 1918, p. 31.

40. *Corsets & Lingerie,* November 1924, p. 37; *Maiden Form Mirror,* February 1932, p. 7; *Corsets & Brassieres,* October 1927, p. 33; March 1926, p. 33; March 1930, p. 39; August 1930, p. 41; May 1935, p. 53. *Maiden Form Mirror,* November 1939, p. 5; *Corset & Underwear Review,* October 1927, pp. 80, 85; *Corsets & Brassieres,* February 1930, p. 35; March 1930, p. 39.

41. *Corsets & Brassieres,* January 1930, p. 42; *Corsets & Lingerie,* October 1925, p. 35.

42. *Corsets & Brassieres,* November 1935, p. 29; January 1933, p. 41; May 1933, p. 29.

43. Ibid., October 1930, pp. 35, 67; January 1933, p. 41.

44. Ibid., January 1933, p. 41.

45. Ibid., December 1933, p. 29; January 1933, p. 41.

46. Ibid., January 1933, pp. 8–9; *Maiden Form Mirror,* May 1932, p. 3; February 1933, p. 3 (italics original). The term *glorification* stems from the Ziegfeld Follies. See chapter 4 of this book.

47. *Corsets & Brassieres,* May 1933, p. 32; March 1935, pp. 46–47; December 1933, p. 29; September 1935, pp. 36, 60; February 1935, p. 23.

48. *Maiden Form Mirror,* September 1933, p. 3; January 1934, p. 1 (italics original).

49. *Corsets & Brassieres,* October 1930, p. 35; February 1938, pp. 48–49; October 1946, p. 43.

50. Ibid., March 1935, pp. 16, 28; January 1938, inside front cover and p. 51.

51. Ibid., April 1930, p. 31; November 1935, p. 29; January 1930, p. 42. *Maiden Form Mirror,* March 1931, p. 2; August 1931, p. 2; January 1932, p. 2; May 1932, p. 1. *Corsets & Brassieres,* August 1937, p. 3; February 1930, p. 35.

52. *Corsets & Brassieres,* April 1944, p. 7; January 1938, p. 43. *Maiden Form Mirror,* November 1937, p. 3. The Variation was the first Maiden Form brassiere to sell one million units. *Maiden Form Mirror,* February 1941, p. 7; *Corsets & Brassieres,* January 1937, p. 41; January 1938, pp. 67–69.

53. *Corsets & Brassieres,* January 1938, p. 46; November 1946, p. 60.

54. Kathy Peiss, "Making Faces: The Cosmetics Industry and the Cultural Construction of Gender," *Genders* 7 (March 1990): 143–69. For an example of

a personality test, see Doris Webster and Mary Alden Hopkins, "Charm—or What Have You?" *Ladies' Home Journal*, April 1928, pp. 32, 126, 129–30.

55. *Movie Mirror*, August 1939, pp. 44–45, 68; Rosen, *Popcorn Venus*, ch. 9; *Movie Mirror*, October 1939, pp. 36–37, 65; *The Women*, directed by George Cukor (MGM, 1939), screenplay by Clare Boothe Luce.

56. The 1930 marketing of the Actress brassiere by a small company is an early example. *Corsets & Brassieres*, March 1930, p. 39; Charles Eckert, "The Carole Lombard in Macy's Window," in *Fabrications: Costume and the Female Body*, ed. Jane Gaines and Charlotte Herzog (New York: Routledge, 1990), pp. 100–121; *Sears, Roebuck and Co. Catalogue*, 1928–29, pp. 80–81; and 1940, p. 334; *Corsets & Brassieres*, March 1935, p. 53.

57. *Corsets & Brassieres*, March 1935, pp. 65, 28, 62; March 1930, p. 39; July 1937, pp. 8–9. *Women's Wear Daily*, August 21, 1947, sect. 2, p. 48. Maiden Form, for example, advertised heavily in the Fawcett Group publications, which included *True Confessions, Screen Book, Hollywood Magazine,* and *Screen Play Magazine. Maiden Form Mirror*, September 1934, p. 1.

58. Theodor Adorno with the assistance of George Simpson, "On Popular Music," *Studies in Philosophy and Social Science* 9 (1941): 24–26. Women today still consider their brassiere size extremely personal information, which they are not likely to share with anyone but a few intimate friends and perhaps a brassiere saleswoman. This need for secrecy indicates the power of brassiere size in defining female subjectivity.

59. *Corsets & Brassieres*, January 1937, p. 41.

60. *Maiden Form Mirror*, June 1943, p. 5; November 1948, p. 3; June 1949, p. 2; June–July 1955, p. 3. *Sears, Roebuck and Co. Catalogue*, 1948, pp. 388–89, 392–93.

61. *Corsets & Brassieres*, July 1941, p. 12 (italics original).

62. Artifact 972.53.20 (ROM); *Corsets & Brassieres*, March 1935, pp. 19, 46–47, 66, 41; *Sears, Roebuck and Co. Catalogue*, 1940, p. 154.

63. Sara Nickel, " 'The Awful Truth': Screwball Comedy and the Disruption of Male Identity in the Great Depression," OAH Conference Paper, April 1995; *Corsets & Brassieres*, May 1933, p. 32. See also Barbara Melosh, *Engendering Culture: Manhood and Womanhood in the New Deal Public Art and Theater* (Washington, DC: Smithsonian, 1991). For more about the construction of gender in the 1940s, see Maureen Honey, *Creating Rosie the Riveter: Class, Gender and Propaganda during World War II* (Amherst: University of Massachusetts Press, 1984); and Susan M. Hartmann, *The Home Front and Beyond: American Women in the 1940s* (Boston: Twayne Publishers, 1982).

64. *Corsets & Brassieres*, March 1935, p. 62; January 1938, pp. 67–69. Ewing, *Dress and Undress*, p. 134; *Maiden Form Mirror*, February 1940, p. 1; April 1940, p. 7; July 1940, p. 7; August 1940, p. 5.

65. *Maiden Form Mirror*, May 1942, p. 5; August 1942, p. 1; December 1942, pp. 4–5. *Corsets & Brassieres*, October 1941, pp. 24–25; *Maiden Form Mirror*, August 1940, p. 5.

66. Mark Gabor, *The Pin-Up: A Modest History* (New York: Bell Publish-

ing Company, 1972); Tom Robotham, *Varga* (San Diego: Thunder Bay Press, 1994). An 1868 newspaper article on Lydia Thompson's popular troupe British Blondes was entitled "Busts and Legs." See Robert C. Allen, *Horrible Prettiness: Burlesque and American Culture* (Chapel Hill: University of North Carolina Press, 1991), p. 148.

67. *The Maiden Forum*, April 1945, p. 1; May 1945, p. 1.

68. Ibid., May 1945, pp. 3–6; June 1945, p. 1.

69. Ibid., July 1945, p. 3.

70. Ibid., May 1945, p. 4; July 1945, p. 3.

71. Ibid., December 1945, p. 1.

72. See *The Maiden Forum*, "Staff Profiles," November and December 1944; and January, February, April, June, July, and August 1945; as well as the "Our Pin-Up" features for April and June 1946. The "Pin-Up for March" 1947 (p. 3) showed a male mechanic seated at his workbench, looking away from the camera. Commercial pinup photos adorn his wall. See also *Corsets & Brassieres*, January 1946, p. 68, for a report on the Maiden Form pinup contests.

73. Valentino, *Films of Lana Turner*, pp. 22, 27, 28, 31, 36. Rosen, *Popcorn Venus*, p. 315. The headline of the June 30, 1995, *Los Angeles Times* obituary on p. 1 read "Lana Turner, Glamorous Star of 50 Films, Dies at 75," whereas the subheadline was " 'Sweater Girl' was a favorite GI pinup." See also Jeanine Basinger, *Lana Turner* (New York: Pyramid Publications, 1976), for numerous references to Turner as the embodiment of glamour.

74. All of the following periodical references are from the Jane Russell clippings file at the Academy of Motion Picture Arts & Sciences Library. Ashton Reid, "Jane Does a Movie," *Collier's*, January 13, 1945, n.p. Jane Russell, *My Paths and My Detours* (New York: Franklin Watts, Inc., 1985), pp. 59–60.

75. *Citizen-News*, July 12, 1944; Russell, *My Paths*, pp. 18–19; *Boxoffice*, June 13, 1942, n.p.; *Collier's*, January 13, 1945, n.p.; *Life*, July 29, 1945, n.p.; *Look*, October 21, 1941, n.p.; *Los Angeles Times*, May 6, 1945.

76. *Look*, October 21, 1941, n.p.; *Los Angeles Times*, September 23, 1949.

77. *Quick*, April 9, 1951, n.p.; *Chicago Tribune*, November 1, 1953, pp. 22–24.

78. Marilyn Monroe had a more ambivalent relationship to her objectified body. "That's the trouble, a sex symbol becomes a thing. I just hate being a thing. . . . But if I'm going to be a symbol of something, I'd rather have it sex than some of the other things they've got symbols of." *Life* magazine interview, quoted in Richard Wortley, *Pin-Up's Progress* (London: Panther, 1971), p. 91.

CHAPTER 4. THE MEANING OF BLACK LINGERIE

Epigraph: I thank Ellen Garvey for alerting me to *Clotheslines* and award-winning documentary filmmaker Roberta Cantwell for sending me a copy of the film.

1. A 1905 women's magazine notes that "white reigns supreme." C. Willett and Phillis Cunnington, *The History of Underclothes* (London: Faber and Faber,

1981), p. 133; Harry Lang, *"62": Biography of a Union* (New York: Undergarment & Negligee Workers' Union Local 62, ILGWU, 1940), p. 55. There is a growing body of scholarship on whiteness, race, and gender. See, for example, Richard Dyer, "White," *Screen* 29, no. 4 (1988): 44–65; Jane Gaines, "White Privilege and Looking Relations: Race and Gender in Feminist Film Theory," *Screen* 29, no. 4 (1988): 12–27; Toni Morrison, *Playing in the Dark: Whiteness and the Literary Imagination* (Cambridge, MA: Harvard University Press, 1992); Ware Vron, *Beyond the Pale: White Women, Racism and History* (London: Verso, 1992); Ruth Frankenberg, *White Women, Race Matters: The Social Construction of Whiteness* (Minneapolis: University of Minnesota Press, 1993); Mike Hill, ed., *Whiteness: A Critical Reader* (New York: New York University Press, 1997); Grace Hale, *Making Whiteness: The Culture of Segregation in the South, 1890–1940* (New York: Shocken Books, 1998); Mason Stokes, *The Color of Sex: Whiteness, Heterosexuality and the Fictions of White Supremacy* (Durham, NC: Duke University Press, 2001).

2. *The Women's Muslin-Underwear Industry,* Department of Commerce Miscellaneous Series No. 29 (Washington, DC: Government Printing Office), p. 7. Numerous examples of undergarments made of bleached white and unbleached fabrics in this period are in the costume collections I viewed at the Los Angeles County Museum of Art, New York Metropolitan Museum of Art, Smithsonian Institution, and Royal Ontario Museum. Mrs. Eric Pritchard, *The Cult of Chiffon* (London: Grant Richards, 1902).

3. Eric Lott, *Love and Theft: Blackface Minstrelsy and the American Working Class* (New York: Oxford University Press, 1995). See also, for example, Susan Gubar, *White Skin, Black Face in American Culture* (New York: Oxford University Press, 1997); Alice Echols, "White Faces, Black Masks," in *Shaky Ground: The '60s and Its Aftershocks* (New York: Columbia University Press, 2002); Wini Breines, "Postwar White Girls' Dark Others," in *The Other Fifties: Interrogating Midcentury American Icons*, ed. Joel Foreman (Chicago: University of Illinois Press, 1997), pp. 53–77.

4. Lou Taylor, *Mourning Dress: A Costume and Social History* (London: George Allen and Unwin, 1983), pp. 251–52. Taylor notes also that Christian meanings did not fully undermine European peasants' uses of black, including for wedding dresses. John Harvey, *Men in Black* (Chicago: University of Chicago Press, 1995); Christopher Breward, *The Hidden Consumer* (Manchester: Manchester University Press, 1999); Valerie Mendes, *Dressed in Black* (London: V&A Publications, 1999), pp. 9, 29; Amy Holman Edelman, *The Little Black Dress* (New York: Simon & Schuster, 1997), ch. 1; Henry James, *Wings of the Dove* (1902), cited by Mendes, *Dressed in Black*, pp. 9–11; Ruth Carson, "Black Market," *Collier's*, March 4, 1944, pp. 18–19. I am grateful to Hanna Griff for the reference "Black Lace Bra Kind of Woman," in Sandra Cisneros, *Loose Women: Poems* (New York: Vintage, 1995), p. 78.

5. Pritchard, *Cult of Chiffon*, pp. 44–45; Mrs. Forrester, *Success through Dress* (1925), cited in Mendes, *Dressed in Black*, p. 15; *Women's Wear Daily*, September 11, 1952, p. 6; Pritchard, *Cult of Chiffon*, p. 114; Leigh Summers,

Bound to Please: A History of the Victorian Corset (Oxford: Berg, 2001), pp. 57, 199; Taylor, *Mourning Dress,* p. 204; "Mourning Glory: Fashion's Untimely Demise," an exhibition at the Fashion Institute of Design & Merchandising (Los Angeles, California), July 17–December 31, 2003, found black corsets unavailable until the 1880s. See also c. 1905 black satin corset (CI 50.109.2, Met). In 1880, experts also warned against wearing black for health reasons. "If white is the best color for summer, it does not follow that black is the best for winter. . . . A black garment robs the body of a larger amount of heat than white, and consequently the latter color is the best for winter garments. It is the best color for both summer and winter." C. H. Fowler, DD, LLD, and W. H. DePuy, AM, DD, *Home and Health and Home Economics: A Cyclopedia of Facts and Hints for All Departments of Home Life, Health and Domestic Economy* (Cincinnati: Hitchcock and Walden, 1879; New York: Phillips & Hunt, 1880), p. 188.

6. Thinking about race and gender as interrelated categories of analysis is also important for understanding this dynamic. For more on the concept of "racialized gender," see Tessie Liu, "Teaching the Differences among Women from a Historical Perspective: Rethinking Race and Gender as Social Categories," in *Unequal Sisters: A Multicultural Reader in U.S. Women's History,* 3rd ed., ed. Vicki Ruiz and Carol DuBois (New York: Routledge, 2000), pp. 627–38; Eileen Boris, " 'You Wouldn't Want One of 'Em Dancing with Your Wife': Racialized Bodies on the Job in World War II," *American Studies Quarterly* 50, no. 1 (1998): 77–108; Eileen Boris and Angelique Janssens, "Complicating Categories: An Introduction," in *Complicating Categories,* ed. Boris and Janssens (Cambridge: Cambridge University Press, 2000), pp. 1–13. See also Shirley J. Carlson, "Black Ideals of Womanhood in the Late Victorian Era," *Journal of Negro History* 77, no. 2 (Spring 1992): 61–73, for a discussion of African American interpretations of Victorian respectability; and Hazel Carby, "Policing the Black Woman's Body in an Urban Context," in her *Cultures in Babylon: Black Britain and African America* (New York: Verso, 1999), pp. 22–39, for more on twentieth-century characterizations of black women's bodies as pathological.

7. Winthrop Jordan, *White over Black: American Attitudes toward the Negro, 1550–1812* (Chapel Hill: University of North Carolina Press, 1968), pp. 7–8, 15, 24, 30–43, 94–97, 143, 219–39, 458, 482–511.

8. Ibid., pp. 30–43, 94–97, 219–39, 482–511; Linda Schiebinger, *Gender in the Making of Modern Science* (Boston: Beacon Press, 1993), p. 159; Hazel Carby, " 'On the Threshold of Woman's Era,' Lynching, Empire and Sexuality in Black Feminist Theory," in *Dangerous Liaisons: Gender, Nation & Postcolonial Perspectives,* ed. Anne McClintock, Aamir Mufti, and Ella Shohat (Minneapolis: University of Minnesota Press, 1997), pp. 330–43; Jacqueline Dowd Hall, "The Mind That Burns in Each Body: Women, Rape and Racial Violence," in *Powers of Desire: The Politics of Sexuality,* ed. Ann Smitow, Christine Stansell, and Sharon Thompson (New York: Monthly Review Press), pp. 328–49.

9. Schiebinger, *Gender,* pp. 161–63; Sander Gilman, *Difference and Pathol-*

ogy: Stereotypes of Sexuality, Race and Madness (Ithaca, NY: Cornell University Press, 1985); Anne Fausto-Sterling, "Gender, Race and Nation: The Comparative Anatomy of 'Hottentot' Women in Europe, 1815–1817," in *Deviant Bodies: Critical Perspectives on Difference in Science & Popular Culture,* ed. Jennifer Terry and Jacqueline Urla (Bloomington: Indiana University Press, 1995), p. 21.

10. Fausto-Sterling, "Gender, Race and Nation," pp. 20, 22, 29; T. Denean Sharpley-Whiting, *Sexualized Savages, Primal Fears, and Primitive Narratives in French* (Durham, NC: Duke University Press, 1999), pp. 17–18; Schiebinger, *Gender,* p. 168; Robert Rydall, *All The World's a Fair: Visions of Empire at American International Exhibitions, 1876–1916* (Chicago: University of Chicago Press, 1984). In "Gender, Race and Nation" (p. 22), Fausto-Sterling notes that "Hottentot" is a Dutch name, often used interchangeably with "Bushman" by Europeans in the eighteenth and nineteenth centuries. Khoikhoi did not exist as an independent culture sixty years after the Dutch colony was established in 1652, due to disease and "encroachment." Variant spellings of Saartjie Baartman's name can be found in print from her era through the present. In this book, I have chosen to use the spelling most commonly found today.

11. Deborah Gray White, *Ar'n't I a Woman?: Female Slaves in the Plantation South* (New York: Norton, 1999).

12. Gilman, *Difference and Pathology,* p. 85; Stephen Jay Gould, "The Hottentot Venus," in his *The Flamingo's Smile: Reflections in Natural History* (New York: W. W. Norton & Co., 1985), p. 293; Schiebinger, *Gender,* p. 169; Fausto-Sterling, "Gender, Race and Nation," p. 31. During an 1810 trial that questioned Baartman's status (slavery was illegal in England), a contract produced as evidence and Baartman's testimony raised questions about whether she was paid. The case was dismissed. For a discussion of the trial's usefulness as legal precedent, see Clement Vallandigham, *The Trial of Hon. Clement L. Vallandigham* (Cincinnati: Ricky & Carroll, 1863), p. 193.

13. Sander Gilman, "Black Bodies, White Bodies: Toward an Iconography of Female Sexuality in Late Nineteenth-Century Art, Medicine, and Literature," *Critical Inquiry* 12 (Autumn 1985): 213; Schiebinger, *Gender,* p. 169; Fausto-Sterling, "Gender, Race and Nation," pp. 28–29, 32; Sharpley-Whiting, *Sexualized Savages,* pp. 23–24.

14. Gilman, "Black Bodies," p. 294; Sharpley-Whiting, *Sexualized Savages,* pp. 18, 32–33; Fausto-Sterling, "Gender, Race and Nation," pp. 31, 34.

15. Fausto-Sterling, "Gender, Race and Nation," pp. 20, 23, 29, 33–34; Schiebinger, *Gender,* pp. 169–70; Gilman, "Black Bodies," p. 213.

16. Gould, "Hottentot Venus," p. 297; Schiebinger, *Gender,* pp. 163–65, 171; Fausto-Sterling, "Gender, Race and Nation," pp. 23, 32, 35.

17. Gould, "Hottentot Venus," p. 294; Schiebinger, *Gender,* p. 170; Fausto-Sterling, "Gender, Race and Nation," p. 37.

18. Fausto-Sterling, "Gender, Race and Nation," p. 29; Sharpley-Whiting, *Sexualized Savages,* p. 23. Fausto-Sterling cites Georges Cuvier's 1817 published report on p. 35.

19. Fausto-Sterling, "Gender, Race and Nation," pp. 36–37; Schiebinger, *Gender*, p. 171; Sharpley-Whiting, *Sexualized Savages*, pp. 24–25, 27–28. Fausto-Sterling, p. 37, says that Cuvier's measurement was "more than four inches," whereas Sharpley-Whiting, p. 28, cites his measurement as "two and a half inches."

20. Sharpley-Whiting, *Sexualized Savages*, pp. 32, 168 (endnote 1). *Los Angeles Times* and *New York Times* (May 4, 2002, and August 10, 2002). See also Janell Hobson, *Venus in the Dark: Blackness and Beauty in Popular Culture* (New York: Routledge, 2005).

21. Josiah Clark, *Types of Mankind: or, Ethnological Researches, Based upon the Ancient Monuments, Paintings, Sculptures, and Crania of the Races, and upon Their Natural, Geographical, Philological and Biblical History* (Philadelphia: Lippincott, Grambo & Co., 1855), p. 183. A grotesque illustration of the Hottentot Venus is on p. 431. Gilman, *Difference and Pathology*, p. 88. See also Thomas Huxley, *Evidence as to Man's Place in Nature* (New York: D. Appleton & Co., 1873), p. 167, on the Hottentot Venus's "apelike" brain structure. For commentary on the Hottentot Venus as an icon of ugliness and vulgarity, see Judge Harper, "Memoir of Slavery," *Southern Literary Messenger* 4, no. 10 (October 1838): 635; "Are We a Good-Looking People?" *Putnam's Monthly Magazine of American Literature, Science & Art* 1, no. 3 (March 1853): 309; Victor Cousin, *Lectures on the True, the Beautiful and the Good* (New York: D. Appleton & Co., 1854 and 1871), p. 129; "Ambrosia—A Nose Offering," *Harper's New Monthly Magazine*, June 1856, p. 59; "Saccharissa Mellasys," *Atlantic Monthly*, September 1861, pp. 293, 294; Cuthbert Bede, *The Adventures of Mr. Verdant Green* (New York: Carleton Publishers, 1870), p. 106; Robert Tomes, *The Bazar Book of Decorum* (New York: Harper & Brothers, 1873), p. 36.

22. Gilman, *Difference and Pathology*, p. 95, describes Darwin's ear as "simplification of the convolutions of the ear shell and the absence of a lobe." See also Ruth Rosen, *The Lost Sisterhood: Prostitution in America, 1900–1918* (Baltimore: Johns Hopkins University Press, 1983); Timothy Gilfoyle, *City of Eros: New York City, Prostitution, and the Commercialization of Sex, 1790–1920* (New York: W. W. Norton, 1992); Patricia Cline Cohen, *The Murder of Helen Jewitt: The Life and Death of a Prostitute in Nineteenth-Century New York* (New York: W. W. Norton, 1998).

23. Gilman, "Black Bodies," pp. 204–42; Gilman, *Difference and Pathology*, ch. 3 and 4; see also Jan Nederveen Pieterse, *White on Black: Images of Africa and Blacks in Western Popular Culture* (New Haven, CT: Yale University Press, 1992). Models Victorine Meurent and Laura posed as Olympia and the maid, respectively. Lorraine O'Grady, "Olympia's Maid: Reclaiming Black Female Subjectivity," in *New Feminist Criticism: Art, Identity, Action*, ed. Joanna Frueh, Cassandra Langer, and Arlene Raven (New York: HarperCollins, 1991), pp. 152–70. Mary Ann Doane, *Femmes Fatales: Feminism, Film Theory, Psychoanalysis* (New York: Routledge, 1991), pp. 214–15. Doane observes, "When Marlene Dietrich emerges from the ape costume in the 'Hot Voodoo' number, blackness is transformed . . . into a disguise which can be easily shed."

24. Linda Williams, *Playing the Race Card: Melodramas of Black and White from Uncle Tom to O. J. Simpson* (Princeton, NJ: Princeton University Press, 2001). Williams notes Henry James's use of the metaphor of "a wonderful 'leaping' fish" to describe the movement of *Uncle Tom's Cabin* into multiple media depictions that suffused American culture, making the novel a "state of vision, of feeling and consciousness" (p. 6). She draws on the metaphor to explain her own thesis that racial melodrama in general made this type of leap. Here, I add dress to Williams's extensive list of cultural media in which such leaping takes place. Eric Lott, *Love and Theft*, also cites James's phrase (p. 215). Baudelaire commented on the close association of women's bodies and clothing in Western culture in 1863: "Everything that adorns woman, everything that serves to show off her beauty, is part of herself; and those artists who have made a particular study of this enigmatic being dote no less on all the details of the *mundus muliebris* than on Woman herself." Cited in Aileen Ribeiro, *Ingres in Fashion: Representations of Dress and Appearance in Ingres's Images of Women* (New Haven, CT: Yale University Press, 1999), p. 31.

25. Sharpley-Whiting, *Sexualized Savages*, p. 132.

26. Ibid., pp. 134, 138.

27. Ibid., pp. 37–38, 143, 149, 157–58.

28. Ibid., pp. 153, 160–64.

29. Ibid., p. 40.

30. Richard Sheil, *Sketches of the Irish Bar* (New York: Redfield, 1854), p. 27; George Sala, *A Journey Due North* (Boston: Ticknor & Fields, 1858), p. 152.

31. "Gatherings of the Month," *Ladies Repository: A Monthly Periodical, Devoted to Literature, Arts and Religion* 10, no. 3 (September 1872): 228. A tun is a large cask.

32. Sharpley-Whiting, *Sexualized Savages*, p. 65; Anne McClintock, *Imperial Leather: Race, Gender and Sexuality in the Colonial Contest* (New York: Routledge, 1995), p. 85; Pieterse, *White on Black*. For statistical tables on female domestics and other wage earners in the United States from 1880 to 1920, see David Katzman, *Seven Days a Week: Women and Domestic Service in Industrializing America* (New York: Oxford University Press, 1978), pp. 282–97, particularly p. 287. Katzman analyzes these statistics throughout his book. See also Faye Dudden, *Serving Women: Household Service in Nineteenth-Century America* (Middletown, CT: Wesleyan University Press, 1983), pp. 77–78, 108; and Phyllis Palmer, *Domesticity and Dirt: Housewives and Domestic Servants in the United States, 1920–1945* (Philadelphia: Temple University Press, 1989).

33. Hawthorne, cited in Cline Cohen, *Murder of Helen Jewitt*, pp. 206–7; McClintock, *Imperial Leather*, pp. 84–87.

34. Sharpley-Whiting, *Sexualized Savages*, p. 64; McClintock, *Imperial Leather*, pp. 86–87; Gilfoyle, *City of Eros*, pp. 61–62. In addition to references cited above, see Cline Cohen, *Murder of Helen Jewitt*, and Gray White, *Ar'n't I a Woman?* for more on race, class, and domestic service in America. DuBois is quoted in Daniel E. Sutherland, *Americans and Their Servants: Domestic Ser-*

vice in the United States from 1800 to 1920 (Baton Rouge: Louisiana State University Press, 1981), pp. 4–7.

35. Sharpley-Whiting, *Sexualized Savages,* pp. 64, 66–67; Pieterse, *White on Black,* p. 160. See also "Sunday in the Park with George," episode of *Desperate Housewives* (2005).

36. Lott, *Love and Theft,* pp. 90, 119, 140, 267 (endnote 47). Lott emphasizes the homoerotic subtexts of love scenes played out between cross-dressed female impersonators and actors dressed in masculine attire, both in blackface, pp. 27, 147, 159, 165. See also William J. Mahar, *Behind the Burnt Cork Mask: Early Blackface Minstrelsy and Antebellum American Popular Culture* (Urbana: University of Illinois Press, 1999), p. 283.

37. Mahar, *Behind,* pp. 276–77; Lott, *Love and Theft,* p. 89. See also Susan Gillman, "The Mulatto, Tragic or Triumphant? The Nineteenth-Century American Race Melodrama," in *The Culture of Sentiment,* ed. Shirley Samuels (Oxford: Oxford University Press, 1992), pp. 221–43; Christine Palumbo-DeSimone, "Race, Womanhood, and the Tragic Mulatta: An Issue of Ambiguity," in *Multiculturalism: Roots and Realities,* ed. C. James Trotman (Bloomington: Indiana University Press, 2002), pp. 125–36; Elizabeth Fox-Genovese, "Slavery, Race and the Figure of the Tragic Mulatta; or, The Ghost of Southern History in the Writing of African American Women," in *Haunted Bodies: Gender and Southern Texts,* ed. Anne Goodwyn Jones and Susan V. Donaldson (Charlottesville: University Press of Virginia), pp. 464–91. The references to the Hottentot Venus's complexion are from William Thackeray, *Vanity Fair* (New York: Harper & Brothers, 185?), p. 103; and Josiah Nott, *Types of Mankind* (Philadelphia: Lippincott, Grambo & Co., 1855), p. 183.

38. Peggy Pascoe, "Miscegenation Law, Court Cases and Ideologies of 'Race' in Twentieth-Century America," *Journal of American History* 83, no. 1 (June 1996): 44–89; Martha Hodes, *White Women, Black Men: Illicit Sex in the 19th-Century South* (New Haven, CT: Yale University Press, 1997). Robert Allen, *Horrible Prettiness: Burlesque and American Culture* (Chapel Hill: University of North Carolina Press, 1991); M. Alison Kibler, *Rank Ladies: Gender and Cultural Hierarchy in American Vaudeville* (Chapel Hill: University of North Carolina Press, 1999); Linda Mizejewski, *Ziegfeld Girl: Image and Icon in Culture and Cinema* (Durham, NC: Duke University Press, 1999), pp. 120–21.

39. Donald Bogle, *Brown Sugar: Eighty Years of America's Black Female Superstars* (New York: Da Capo Press, 1980), p. 38; Mizejewski, *Ziegfeld Girl,* pp. 11, 122, 131.

40. Mizejewski, *Ziegfeld Girl,* pp. 124, 128; Bogle, *Brown Sugar,* p. 36.

41. Mizejewski, *Ziegfeld Girl,* pp. 124–25, 129. See also Lewis Erenberg, *Steppin' Out: New York Nightlife and the Transformation of American Culture, 1890–1930* (Westport, CT: Greenwood Press, 1981). Gilfoyle, *City of Eros,* pp. 41–43, 209, 231, discusses the term *black and tan* in reference to interracial prostitution and nineteenth-century concert saloons.

42. Mizejewski, *Ziegfeld Girl,* pp. 56–57, 124; Susan Glenn, *Female Specta-*

cle: The Theatrical Roots of Modern Feminism (Cambridge, MA: Harvard University Press, 2000), pp. 112–13.

43. Glenn, *Female Spectacle*, pp. 52–33. See also June Sochen, *From Mae to Madonna: Women Entertainers in Twentieth-Century America* (Lexington: University Press of Kentucky, 1999), ch. 1 and 2. On Mae West, see Marybeth Hamilton, *When I'm Bad, I'm Better: Mae West, Sex, and American Entertainment* (New York: HarperCollins, 1995); Pamela Robertson, *Guilty Pleasures: Feminist Camp from Mae West to Madonna* (Durham, NC: Duke University Press, 1996), ch. 1; Ramona Curry, *Too Much of a Good Thing: Mae West as Cultural Icon* (Minneapolis: University of Minnesota Press, 1996); Jill Watts, *Mae West: An Icon in Black and White* (Oxford: Oxford University Press, 2001); and Gwendolyn Foster, *Performing Whiteness: Postmodern Re/Constructions in the Cinema* (Albany: SUNY Press, 2003), pp. 34–41. On blues women, see Shirley Ann Moore, " 'Her Husband Didn't Have a Word to Say': Black Women and Blues Clubs in Richmond, California, during World War II," in *American Labor in the Era of World War II*, ed. Sally Miller and Daniel Cornford (Westport, CT: Praeger, 1995), pp. 147–64; Hazel Carby, " 'It Just Bes Dat Way Some Times': The Sexual Politics of Women's Blues," in *Unequal Sisters: A Multicultural Reader in U.S. Women's History*, 2nd ed., ed. Vicki L. Ruiz and Ellen Carol DuBois (New York: Routledge, 1994), pp. 330–41; and Angela Davis, *Blues Legacies and Black Feminism: Gertrude "Ma" Rainey, Bessie Smith, and Billie Holiday* (New York: Pantheon Books, 1998). Judy Garland's first cinematic appearance in blackface was in the 1939 musical *Babes in Arms*. See Mizejewski, *Ziegfeld Girl*, pp. 176–77.

44. Gail Bederman, *Manliness & Civilization: A Cultural History of Gender and Race in the United States, 1880–1917* (Chicago: University of Chicago Press, 1995); Marianna Torgovnick, *Gone Primitive: Savage Intellects, Modern Lives* (Chicago: University of Chicago Press, 1990); Louise Newman, *White Women's Rights: The Racial Origins of Feminism in the United States* (Oxford: Oxford University Press, 1999); Hal Foster, "The 'Primitive' Unconscious of Modern Art, or White Skin Black Masks," in his *Recodings: Art, Spectacle, Cultural Politics* (Seattle: Bay Press, 1985), pp. 181–210; Abigail Solomon-Godeau, "Going Native: Paul Gauguin and the Invention of Primitivist Modernism," *Art in America* 77 (July 1989): 118–29.

45. Torgovnick, *Gone Primitive*, ch. 2; John Kasson, *Houdini, Tarzan and the Perfect Man: The White Male Body and the Challenge of Modernity in America* (New York: Hill and Wang, 2001); Gabe Essoe, *Tarzan of the Movies: A Pictorial History of More Than Fifty Years of Edgar Rice Burroughs' Legendary Hero* (Secaucus, NJ: Citadel Press, 1978); Richard McGhee, " 'There's Something Sad about Retracing': Jane Parker in the *Tarzan* Films of the Thirties," *Kansas Quarterly* 16, no. 3 (1984): 101–23; Barbara Creed, "Me Jane: You Tarzan!—A Case of Mistaken Identity in Paradise," *Continuum: An Australian Journal of the Media* 1, no. 1 (1987): 159–74.

46. Walter Benn Michaels, "The Souls of White Folk," in *Literature and the Body: Essays on Populations and Persons*, ed. Elaine Scarry (Baltimore: Johns

Hopkins University Press, 1988), pp. 185–209; Jacquelyn Dowd Hall, " 'The Mind That Burns in Each Body': Women, Rape, and Racial Violence," in *Powers of Desire: The Politics of Sexuality*, ed. Ann Snitow, Christine Stansell, and Sharon Thompson (New York: Monthly Review Press, 1983), pp. 328–49; Valerie Smith, "Split Affinities: The Case of Interracial Rape," in *Conflicts in Feminism*, ed. Marianne Hirsch and Evelyn Fox Keller (New York: Routledge, 1990), pp. 271–87.

47. Williams, *Playing the Race Card*, p. 6. See note 24.

48. Karen Halttunen, *Confidence Men and Painted Women: A Study of Middle Class Culture in America, 1830–1870* (New Haven, CT: Yale University Press, 1982), p. 124. The concern about public displays of emotion was great. Middle-class women were not allowed to attend burials because they might become inappropriately emotional. Pat Jalland, *Death in the Victorian Family* (Oxford: Oxford University Press, 1996), p. 221.

49. Beecher, quoted in James J. Farrell, *Inventing the American Way of Death, 1830–1920* (Philadelphia: Temple University Press, 1980), pp. 81, 93–94, 181. On reform of funerals, see Jalland, *Death in the Victorian Family*, pp. 199–202. See also Taylor, *Mourning Dress*, p. 36, on the professionalization of undertaking in the United States from 1830 to 1860; Ann Douglas, "Heaven Our Home: Consolation Literature in the Northern United States, 1830–1880," in *Death in America*, ed. David Stannard (Philadelphia: University of Pennsylvania Press, 1975), pp. 49–68; Halttunen, *Confidence Men*, p. 127, ch. 5.

50. *Harper's Bazar*, April 17, 1886, p. 249; Jalland, *Death in the Victorian Family*, p. 301; Nugent Robinson, compiler, *Collier's Cyclopedia of Commercial and Social Information and Treasury of Useful and Entertaining Knowledge on Art, Science, Pastimes, Belles-Lettres, and Many Other Subjects of Interest in the American Home Circle* (New York: P. F. Fenelon, 1882), p. 630.

51. Jalland, *Death in the Victorian Family*, pp. 252–54, 301; Taylor, *Mourning Dress*, pp. 61, 134–36, 303; John Morley, *Death, Heaven and the Victorians* (Pittsburgh: University of Pittsburgh Press, 1971), p. 63; *Harper's Bazar*, April 17, 1886, p. 249. Social and cultural historians wrestle with determining the differences, if any, between prescriptive literature like etiquette manuals and actual practices. Changes in mourning-dress rituals over time, variations in advice, and other factors, such as adjustments to accommodate budgets, make it difficult to avoid generalizations.

52. Morley, *Death, Heaven*, p. 68; Jalland, *Death in the Victorian Family*, p. 300; Taylor, *Mourning Dress*, pp. 56–57, 128, 136, 141, 146, 148. Halttunen, *Confidence Men*, pp. 136–37, 143, concurs about the design of mourning dress but finds widows' mourning period to be two years; *Harper's Bazar*, April 17, 1886, p. 249. *Colliers Cyclopedia*, 1882, pp. 627–30. The latter two sources reported that bombazine was being replaced by "Henrietta cloth." Bombazine is mentioned by diarist Lucy Breckinridge, in Mary Robertson, ed., *Lucy Breckinridge of Grove Hill: The Journal of a Virginia Girl, 1862–1864* (Kent, OH: Kent State University Press, 1979), p. 93 (entry for January 2, 1863).

53. Mrs. John Sherwood, *Manners and Social Usages* (New York, 1884),

quoted in Jalland, *Death in the Victorian Family,* p. 302. Morley, *Death, Heaven,* pp. 68–69; Jalland, pp. 301, 305–6; Taylor, *Mourning Dress,* pp. 56, 61, 302–4; Halttunen, *Confidence Men,* pp. 137–38.

54. Taylor, *Mourning Dress,* p. 66; *Harper's Bazar,* April 17, 1886, p. 249.

55. Jalland, *Death in the Victorian Family,* pp. 230–31. Though some widows remained single because they appreciated the greater independence that life without a husband brought, others who suffered economic, social, and emotional deprivations might have remarried if they had had more opportunities to do so. According to Cheryl Elman and Andrew S. London, in the late nineteenth and early twentieth centuries, African American women were more likely to remarry than white women were, though all women, especially those over forty, remarried at lower rates than men. Elman and London, "Sociohistorical and Demographic Perspectives on U.S. Remarriage in 1910," *Social Science History* 26, no. 1 (Spring 2002): 199–241. Among other sources showing lower remarriage rates for widows are Barbara Todd, "The Remarrying Widow: A Stereotype Reconsidered," in *Women in English Society,* ed. Mary Prior (New York: Methuen, 1985), pp. 54–92; Olwen Hufton, "Women Without Men: Widows and Spinsters in Britain and France in the 18th Century," in *Between Poverty and the Pyre: Moments in the History of Widowhood,* ed. Jan Bremmer and Lourens van den Bosch (New York: Routledge, 1995), pp. 122–51; and Bettina Bradbury, "Surviving as a Widow in 19th-Century Montreal," *Urban History Review* 17, no. 3 (1989): 148–60. See also Helena Lopata, *Women as Widows* (New York: Elsevier, 1979); Arlene Scadron, ed., *On Their Own: Widows and Widowhood in the American Southwest, 1848–1939* (Urbana: University of Illinois Press, 1988). Many scholars of widowhood maintain that the topic remains understudied. Remarriage rates in Europe from the early modern era through the nineteenth century have been more widely assayed than those for the United States after the colonial period.

56. Philippe Aries, "The Reversal of Death: Changes in Attitudes toward Death in Western Societies," *American Quarterly* 26, no. 5 (special issue, Death in America, December 1974): 536–60; Cornel Reinhart, Margaret Tacardon, and Philip Hardy, "The Sexual Politics of Widowhood: The Virgin Rebirth in the Social Construction of Nineteenth- and Early-Twentieth-Century Feminine Reality," *Journal of Family History* 23, no. 1 (January 1998): 28–46.

57. Christiane Klapisch-Zuber, "The 'Cruel Mother': Maternity, Widowhood, and Dowry in Florence in the Fourteenth and Fifteenth Centuries," in her *Women, Family and Ritual in Renaissance Italy* (Chicago: University of Chicago Press, 1985), pp. 117–31; Nicole Pellegrin, "The Gender of Crape: Widows' Weeds in *Ancien Régime* France," and Allison Levy, "The Widow's Cleavage and Other Compromising Pictures," papers presented at the "The Widows' Might" conference, Rutgers Center for Historical Analysis, April 2004.

58. Taylor, *Mourning Dress,* p. 136. Prohibitions against widows remarrying occurred across cultures. See Taylor, ch. 2. Amy Hofman Edelman, *The Little Black Dress* (New York: Simon & Schuster, 1997), p. 35.

59. Sigmund Freud, *Civilization and Its Discontents* (New York: W. W.

Norton, 1961/1930), pp. 76–77; Sigmund Freud, *The Ego and the Id* (New York: W. W. Norton, 1960/1923), pp. 38–39; Sigmund Freud, *Beyond the Pleasure Principle* (New York: W. W. Norton, 1959/1920), pp. 45–46 (italics original); Ellie Ragland, *Essays on the Pleasures of Death from Freud to Lacan* (New York: Routledge, 1995), p. 88 (italics original).

60. Freud, *Ego*, pp. 39, 46–47. Freud problematically, and perhaps typically, does not account here for the female experience of *taking in* "sexual substances." Though women may also be said to eject substances such as fluids and ovum, their experience of both expulsion and ingestion is left unanalyzed here.

61. Freud, *Civilization*, pp. 78–79, 81.

62. Ragland, *Essays*, p. 87. Lacan suggests that the sketchiness of Freud's ideas about the death drive may have resulted from his colleagues' opposition to it. Ragland says that "no one except Freud throughout his career and Lacan throughout his fifty years of teaching claim that humans are actually driven by a death principle" (pp. 84–85); Elizabeth Bronfen, *Over Her Dead Body: Death, Femininity and the Aesthetic* (Manchester: Manchester University Press, 1992), p. 200.

63. Ragland, *Essays*, p. 85; Bronfen, *Over Her Dead Body* (p. 27), notes that replacement can also be vindictive.

64. Bronfen, *Over Her Dead Body*, pp. 25–26; Ragland, *Essays*, p. 87. Both Ragland (p. 97) and Bronfen (p. 96) explain that desire is impossible to satisfy because it relates to a fantasy, not a real object. Bronfen further explains, "The social order is a form of violence, given that it kills substance to make it signify"; in other words, "the symbol is the murder of the thing."

65. Georges Bataille, *Death and Sensuality: A Study of Eroticism and the Taboo* (Salem, NH: Ayer Company, 1992/1962), pp. 13–15.

66. Ibid., pp. 15–17, 100, 105–7.

67. Ibid., pp. 36, 107–8; Fred Botting and Scott Wilson, eds., *The Bataille Reader* (Oxford: Blackwell Publishers, 1997), p. 223.

68. Bataille, *Death and Sensuality*, p. 11; Botting and Wilson, *Bataille Reader*, pp. 244, 246. Bataille writes, "The multiplication of beings goes hand in hand with death. The parents survive the birth of their offspring but the reprieve is only temporary. . . . The appearance of the newcomers guarantees the disappearance of their predecessors. Death follows reproduction . . . even if not immediately" (Bataille, *Death and Sensuality*, pp. 100–101).

69. Patrick Bade, *Femme Fatale: Images of Evil and Fascinating Women* (New York: Mayflower Books, 1979); Mary Ann Doane, *Femmes Fatales*; Bram Dijkstra, *Evil Sisters: The Threat of Female Sexuality in Twentieth-Century Culture* (New York: Henry Holt, 1996), pp. 86–88; Caroline Evans, *Fashion at the Edge: Spectacle, Modernity & Deathliness* (New Haven, CT: Yale University Press, 2003); G. J. Barker-Benfield, *The Horrors of the Half-Known Life: Male Attitudes toward Women and Sexuality in Nineteenth-Century America* (New York: Routledge, 1999/1976).

70. Dijkstra, *Evil Sisters*, p. 87; Bram Dijkstra, *Idols of Perversity: Fantasies of Feminine Evil in Fin-de-Siecle Culture* (Oxford: Oxford University Press,

1996); Martha Banta, *Imaging American Women: Idea and Ideals in Cultural History* (New York: Columbia University Press, 1987), pp. 487–98.

71. Bronfen, *Over Her Dead Body*, pp. 19, 33, 211, 213, 217. Bronfen similarly cites Prosper Mérimée's novella *Carmen* (1845), which begins with a Greek motto from Palladas: "Every woman is as bitter as gall; but she has two good moments, one in bed, the other at her death."

72. Ibid., pp. 62–63, 65, 121, 189. Bronfen explores many other subtle points of correspondence between women and death in this book.

73. Ibid., p. 183. See also Banta, pp. 198–99, 311–16, 623, 667, for more on images of dark, deadly, and drowning women; and Lorna Duffin, "The Conspicuous Consumptive: Woman as an Invalid," in *The Nineteenth Century Woman: Her Cultural and Physical World*, ed. Sara Delamont and Lorna Duffin (New York: Barnes & Noble Books, 1978), pp. 26–56, for more analysis of the Victorian idealization of female invalids.

74. Leslie Fishbein, "The Demise of the Cult of True Womanhood in Early American Film, 1900–1930: Two Modes of Subversion," *Journal of Popular Film and Television* 12, no. 2 (1984): 66–72.

75. Ribeiro, *Ingres in Fashion*, pp. 44, 120; Aileen Ribeiro, "Fashion and Whistler," in *Whistler, Women, & Fashion*, ed. Margaret MacDonald, Susan Galassi, and Aileen Ribeiro (New Haven, CT: Yale University Press, 2003), pp. 22, 26, 35; Stella Blum, ed., *Fashions and Costumes from Godey's Lady's Book, 1837–1869* (New York: Dover, 1985): dresses, pp. 40, 73 (light mourning), 80 (mourning); 1863 corsage (bodice), p. 56; 1864 corselet, p. 60. Stella Blum, ed., *Victorian Fashions & Costumes from Harper's Bazar: 1867–1898* (New York: Dover, 1974): dresses, pp. 13, 28–29, 52–53, 61, 72, 75, 217, 219 (velvet), 229, 291 (mourning); corsets, pp. 20, 135; *1897 Sears, Roebuck and Co. Catalog* (New York: Chelsea House, 1968), p. 300; Taylor, *Mourning Dress*, p. 132. Ribeiro, "Fashion and Whistler," p. 26, and *Ingres*, p. 102, notes that the rising popularity of black for evening dress had to contend with the predilection for white by Worth, the most influential couturier of his era.

76. Taylor, *Mourning Dress*, pp. 132–33, 220; *Colliers Cyclopedia*, 1882, p. 628; *Harper's Bazar*, April 17, 1886, p. 249.

77. Morley, *Death, Heaven*, p. 65; Jalland, *Death in the Victorian Family*, p. 371; *Woman's Home Companion*, July 1898.

78. Maureen Montgomery, *Displaying Women: Spectacles of Leisure in Edith Wharton's New York* (New York: Routledge, 1998), pp. 34, 126–35, 137–38, 189 (endnote 46); Anne Hollander, *Seeing through Clothes* (Berkeley: University of California Press, 1993), p. 373; Blum, *Harper's Bazaar*, p. 219.

79. Blum, *Harper's Bazaar*, p. 132, reports, for example, that black Spanish lace was featured in *Harper's Bazaar*. An example of severe black is John Singer Sargent, *Mrs. Adrian Iselin* (1888), in Richard Ormand, *John Singer Sargent Complete Paintings*, vol. 1: *Early Portraits* (New Haven, CT: Yale University Press, 1998), pp. 216–17; of ordinary black, William Chase, *Lady in Black* (1888), in Kathleen Luhrs, *American Paintings in the Metropolitan Museum of Art*, vol. 3 (New York: Metropolitan Museum of Art in association with Prince-

ton University Press, 1980), p. 111; of fashionable black, James McNeill Whistler, *Arrangement in Brown and Black: Portrait of Miss Rosa Corder* (1876–78), in MacDonald, Galassi, and Ribeiro, *Whistler, Women, and Fashion,* plate 111; and of risqué black, Giovanni Boldini, *Gertrude Elizabeth, Lady Colin Campbell* (1897), in ibid., plate 36. For a history of widow portraiture, see Allison Levy, ed., *Widowhood and Visual Culture in Early Modern Europe* (Aldershot, UK: Ashgate Publishing, 2003).

80. Marc Simpson, *Uncanny Spectacle: The Public Career of the Young John Singer Sargent* (New Haven, CT: Yale University Press, 1997), p. 118.

81. Ibid., p. 120; Susan Siklauskas, "Painting Skin: John Singer Sargent's *Madame X*," *American Art* 15, no. 3 (Fall 2001): 18; Ribeiro, *Ingres*, p. 43. Conflicting accounts exist about the substance Gautreau used on her skin. Siklauskas believes she used chemical cosmetic powder, whereas Sargent biographer Stanley Olsen and Gautreau biographer Deborah Davis believe she used rice powder. Miranda Seymour, "White Shoulders," *New York Times Book Review*, September 28, 2003; Deborah Davis, *Strapless: John Singer Sargent and the Fall of Madame X* (New York: Penguin, 2003), pp. 50–53, 56. See also Ribeiro, *Ingres*, p. 43, on face powder.

82. Siklauskas, "Painting Skin," pp. 12, 23, 27; Ormand, *John Singer Sargent*, p. 113.

83. Hollander, *Seeing through Clothes*, p. 376. Significantly, both painter and subject moved from black to white after their scandalous collaboration. After the 1884 Salon, Sargent completed a few previously commissioned portraits and some interior studies. His reputation was restored in full force by his painting *Carnation, Lily, Lily, Rose* (1885–87), exhibited to great acclaim at the Royal Academy in England in 1887 and quickly purchased and installed in the academy's permanent collection. In the impressionist-influenced image, two English children dressed in white hold white lanterns in an imaginative garden in which they play fully surrounded by green grass and white flowers. The next year, Sargent painted his best-known post–*Madame X* painting of a woman in black, his 1888 portrait of Bostonian Isabella Stewart Gardner. Gardner reputedly desired a portrait of some notoriety, and the painting caused a bit of a stir upon its display in Boston. However, though unusual in its presentation of its subject, and despite public comments about Gardner's posture—she leans forward to display her fashionable yet far-from-extreme décolleté neckline—the portrait is a much more modest depiction than *Madame X* is. In 1891, Gautreau commissioned a portrait from Gustave Courtois, which exhibited at that year's Paris Salon. In the painting, she wears a low-cut white gown with layers of gauzy fabric and net. In a seemingly deliberate reference to her earlier presence at the Salon, the left strap of the sleeveless dress bodice has slipped off her shoulder and down her arm. Gautreau's alabaster-white skin and proud bearing—her head in profile, her expression pleasing and confident, and her body in a three-quarters stance—give her torso the feeling of a statue. The painting was warmly received. See Trevor Fairbrother, *John Singer Sargent* (New York: Harry Abrams, 1994), p. 64; Trevor Fairbrother, "The Shock of John Singer Sar-

gent's 'Madame Gautreau,'" *Arts Magazine* 55 (January 1981): 96; Davis, *Strapless*, p. 224.

84. Siklauskas, "Painting Skin," p. 28. The portrait likely also draws upon bohemian use of black as resistance to conformity, as well as the bourgeois man's black suit of authority. Both of these meanings were apt to offend bourgeois sensibilities when exhibited by a society woman of fashion. Sargent originally painted Gautreau's left strap fallen away from her shoulder and stretched across her upper arm, a provocative gesture that nonetheless visually balances the subject's turn to her right. After the Salon, Sargent repositioned the strap on Gautreau's shoulder. The painting's reception marred Sargent's otherwise stellar and rising reputation in Paris. With his potential for commissions in France drastically reduced, Sargent moved soon after to London, never to live in Paris again. Fairbrother, "Shock," pp. 90–97.

85. Henry James, "John S. Sargent," *Harper's New Monthly Magazine* 75, no. 449 (October 1887): 683–92; Fairbrother, *John Singer Sargent*, p. 44; Simpson, *Uncanny Spectacle*, pp. 59, 135, 164 (endnote 143). *Lady with a Rose* clearly does not also violate conventions of female bodily representation, either in terms of sensuality or in possibilities for visual possession by the spectator.

86. MacDonald, Galassi, and Ribeiro, *Whistler, Women and Fashion*, pp. 119, 165, 170.

87. John Kobal, *Rita Hayworth: The Time, the Place and the Woman* (New York: W. W. Norton & Co., 1978), p. 198; David Chierichetti, "Star Style: Hollywood's Legendary Fashion Firsts," *Los Angeles Times*, October 27, 1978, "Fashion 78," p. H6. A more recent reincarnation of *Madame X* is a 1999 *Vogue* photo simulation with actress Nicole Kidman, though her black dress is much more modest than Gautreau's. Gautreau's image was also featured in an elaborate pop-up card sold in conjunction with a 1999 Sargent retrospective at the Boston Museum of Fine Arts. See Siklauskas, "Painting Skin," pp. 9, 12–13. Kidman later appeared in a fashion photograph in *Vogue* (May 2004, p. 262) that referenced Rita Hayworth as Gilda. While not directly related to the portrait or Gautreau's reputation, a play that shares the title and theme of female dishonor was staged in New York City in 1910. *Madame X*, an English version of the 1908 French play *La Femme X* by Alexandre Bisson, spawned at least nine film versions in English between 1916 and 1981, the best known of which starred Lana Turner (1966); it also was filmed in Spanish (1931), Turkish (1955), and Portuguese (Brazil, 1966). In the play, a woman marries into a wealthy, respected family but is forced to leave her home to protect the reputation of her son after her respectability is compromised. While she drifts through a life of disappointment and dissolution, her son becomes an attorney who ends up defending his mother, unknowingly, against a murder charge. In the Lana Turner version, the woman wears black in the fateful scene in which her lover accidentally falls down a staircase to his death, the event that also marks the death of her life as she has known it. See the Internet Movie Database (www.imdb.com) for more information about these films.

88. "Black Goods at a Premium in London Following King Edward's Death,"

Women's & Infants' Furnisher, May 1910, p. 75; Charles Dana Gibson, *The Widow and Her Friends* (New York: R. H. Russell, 1901).

89. The high-profile American films include the 1925 silent directed by Erich von Stroheim and starring Mae Murray and John Gilbert, the 1934 version directed by Ernest Lubitsch and starring Jeannette MacDonald and Maurice Chevalier, and the 1952 film directed by Curtis Bernhardt and starring Lana Turner and Fernando Lamas; www.metopera.org/synopses/widow.html and www.operetta.org/merrywidowtext.html; Merry Widow ad, *Vogue,* August 1, 1954.

90. Charles Dana Gibson, *The Gibson Book* (New York: Charles Scribner's Sons, 1907); John Cecil Clay and Oliver Herford, *Cupid's Cyclopedia* (New York: Charles Scribner's Sons, 1910). Allison Levy, "Widow's Peek: Looking at Ritual Representation," in Levy, *Widowhood and Visual Culture,* p. 4.

91. Pritchard, *Cult of Chiffon,* pp. 100–101, 126, 179, 184.

92. Ibid., p. 19. Pritchard's remark about the "washing bill" is another indication that women would not necessarily choose black simply because it didn't show dirt and would require less frequent washing than white would.

93. *Women's & Infants' Furnisher,* January 1910, p. 40; *Gimbels Illustrated 1915 Fashion Catalog* (New York: Dover, 1994), p. 95. For more examples of reporting on black without comment, see *Women's & Infants' Furnisher,* September 1916, p. 1; *Gimbels,* pp. 54, 104; *Women's and Children's Fashions of 1917: The Complete Perry, Dame & Co. Catalog* (New York: Dover, 1992), p. 119; *Corsets & Lingerie,* November 1924, p. 37. Trade journal references to the need for black undergarments in current black fashions include *Women's & Infants' Furnisher,* November 1915, p. 37; *Women's Wear Daily,* February 25, 1920, p. 19c; *Corset and Underwear Review,* January 1928, p. 90c.

94. *Women's Wear Daily,* November 13, 1919, p. 36; May 3, 1917, p. 1; October 16, 1919, p. 28; June 30, 1920, p. 9. *Corsets & Lingerie,* September 1921, p. 27; December 1921, p. 29.

95. *Women's and Children's Fashions,* p. 143, features twelve corset covers and brassieres in muslin, white, and flesh pink, and one in black; London *Vogue,* September 1, 1937, p. 78; *Corsets & Lingerie,* December 1921, p. 2; *Women's & Infants' Furnisher,* January 1914, pp. 40–41; *Corsets & Lingerie,* September 1921, p. 30. Thanks to Lois Banner for providing this *Vogue* reference as well as Derek and Julia Parker's *The Natural History of the Chorus Girl* (New York: Bobbs-Merrill, 1975), pp. 36–37.

96. *New York Times,* June 1921, p. 7. See also Anny Latour, *Kings of Fashion* (New York: Coward-McCann, 1956), p. 189, on the popularity of black in the early 1920s.

97. *Women's Wear Daily,* September 1, 1921, pp. 2, 6. See also artifacts such as 1920 corset of black taffeta ribbon. 80.113.1–47 (FIT); early 1920s black silk and satin slip, 964.144.2.B (ROM); late 1920s black silk slip trimmed in floral-pattern lace, 1987.433.1 (Met); 1929 black bandeau with ribbon straps, M678311 (LACMA), and black silk and satin slip, 964.200.1.B (ROM).

98. *Women's Wear Daily,* October 3, 1921, p. 2. *Vogue,* November 15, 1921,

334 / NOTES TO PAGES 158–159

p. 54; December 1, 1921, p. 62; January 1922, n.p. (thanks to Lois Banner for this source); July 15, 1926, p. 62. Alice Mackrell, *Coco Chanel* (New York: Holmes & Meier, 1992), pp. 22–23, 31. On p. 30, Mackrell notes the much-repeated speculation that Chanel embraced black to mourn a lover lost in World War I. The terrible casualties of World War I are also seen as a reason for dispensing with Victorian mourning-costume rituals and making black fashionable. These theories do not take into account the evidence I present here about black's rise to fashion and Victorian culture's decline before World War I. Mackrell, pp. 25–27, and Valerie Steele note Chanel's use of men's outerwear as inspiration for women's clothing designs and black color. Valerie Steele, *Women of Fashion: Twentieth-Century Designers* (New York: Rizzoli, 1991), pp. 41–44. In this sense, the wearing of sophisticated black dresses also carried a hint of the transgression of cross-dressing. Another indication that black could express urbane sophistication is Pritchard's remark that black doesn't wear well in the countryside. "The black frock which is so delightful in town loses some of its charm where all is fresh and green." Pritchard, *Cult of Chiffon*, p. 101. In 1941, *Vogue* underscored the urban meaning of fashionable black dress as well as its role in American women's coming-of-age rituals in an examination of black sweaters, "the most sophisticated" items in the wardrobe of an "urbane woman—perhaps New York—who lives a gay, active life." Not a "college-girl idea," these black sweaters are adult," and can be worn with "a wicked little cocktail suit." The urbane woman "thinks the black-sweater idea is such a good one . . . [that it will be] the wedding present she intends to give a young friend" (October 14, 1941, p. 39).

99. Richard Wortley, *Pin-Ups Progress* (New York: Panther, 1971), pp. 14–15; Howard Greer, *Designing Male* (New York: G. P. Putnam & Sons, 1949), p. 158. Whistler made a similar comment about the dress of white muslin or cambric he painted in *Symphony in White, No. 3* (1865–67): "The body, the legs, etc., are seen perfectly through the dress." Ribeiro, "Fashion and Whistler," pp. 90–91. E. J. Bellocq, *Storyville Portraits: Photographs from the New Orleans Red-Light District, circa 1912* (New York: Museum of Modern Art, 1970), plates 5, 7, 14, 27, 33, also in E. J. Bellocq, *Bellocq: Photographs from Storyville, the Red-Light District of New Orleans* (New York: Random House, 1996).

100. Betty Smith, *A Tree Grows in Brooklyn* (New York: HarperCollins, 1998/1943), pp. 386, 389. Carol Siri Johnson, "The Life and Work of Betty Smith, Author of *A Tree Grows in Brooklyn*" (PhD dissertation, City University of New York, 1995), at www.atreegrowsinbrooklyn.org. See a 1916 black chemise and open drawers of black lace and net, CI 54.51ab (Met). According to the accession card, Costume Institute curators affirmed the dating of this set, donated in 1954 by Diana Vreeland, by referencing the Sears Roebuck catalog for 1916–17. See also ca. 1910–15 black brassiere, 1977.0320.1 (Smith), and 1915 black silk knit "party" brassiere ornamented with black cotton lace and black silk ribbon straps, 981.146.2 (ROM). On Charmion, see Charles S. Angoff, ed., *The World of George Jean Nathan: Essays, Reviews & Commentary* (New York: Applause Books, 1998), pp. 442–43.

101. Bell hooks, *Bone Black: Memories of Girlhood* (New York: Owl Books, 1996), p. 32. I am grateful to Tania Modleski for alerting me to this reference.

102. Ibid., p. 33.

103. Ellen Melinkoff, *An Offbeat Social History of Women's Clothing, 1950 to 1980* (New York: William Morrow, 1984), pp. 33, 34–39, 85.

104. Jay Gertzman, *Bootleggers and Smuthounds: The Trade in Erotica, 1920–1940* (Philadelphia: University of Pennsylvania Press, 1999), pp. 8–10, 65, 67, 86, 189. See also Gilfoyle, *City of Eros,* pp. 130–32; Steven Marcus, *The Other Victorians: A Study of Sexuality and Pornography in Mid-Nineteenth-Century England* (New York: Basic Books, 1966); and Walter Kendrik, *The Secret Museum: Pornography in Modern Culture* (New York: Viking, 1987). Nigel Cawthorne, *Key Moments in Fashion: The Evolution of Style* (London: Hamlyn Publishers, 1999), p. 69.

105. *Double Whoopee,* directed by Lewis Foster (Hal Roach Studios, 1929). Available on DVD. A still of Laurel, Hardy, and Harlow that is not in the film is reprinted in Michael Conway and Mark Ricci, *The Films of Jean Harlow* (New York: Citadel Press, 1965), p. 26, and in Eve Golden, *Platinum Girl: The Life and Legends of Jean Harlow* (New York: Abbeville Press, 1991), p. 41. In a possibly apocryphal yet widely circulated tale, Harlow reportedly convinced producer Hal Roach to release her from her contract with him after her grandfather back home in the Midwest saw *Double Whoopee.* Her grandfather so objected to her scanty attire that he demanded she end her film career. However, according to biographer David Stern, Harlow almost revealed even more of her body. Asked before shooting the taxi scene "whether she was 'underdressed,'" Harlow replied that she was, not knowing the term referred to "the flesh-colored tights worn in so-called 'nude' scenes. . . . As a result, she had appeared on camera in a truly transparent slip." After a quick trip to the dressing room, Harlow returned to the "set in real underdress and reshot the scene." David Stern, *Bombshell: The Life & Death of Jean Harlow* (New York: Doubleday, 1993), pp. 31–32; Golden, *Platinum Girl,* pp. 38, 40–43; Curtis Brown, *Jean Harlow* (New York: Pyramid, 1977), p. 31; Dentner Davies, *Jean Harlow: Hollywood Comet* (London: Constable, 1937), pp. 94–97, 103.

106. The high cost resulted from the extensive and still-spectacular air-war sequences and also because the silent era ended before the original version's release, and Hughes decided to reshoot *Hell's Angels* as a talkie. *Los Angeles Evening Herald,* May 28, 1930, cited in G. D. Hamann, ed., *Jean Harlow in the 30s* (Hollywood, CA: Filming Today Press, 1996), p. 5.

107. *Los Angeles Record,* July 2, 1932, cited in Hamann, *Jean Harlow in the 30s,* p. 37. On May 28, 1930, the *Los Angeles Evening Herald* reported that $25,000 "was spent alone on the final three days' preparations for this premiere," and the Hollywood *Daily Citizen* reported, "75,000 persons clogged Hollywood Boulevard from Vine to La Brea to watch the audience of 2500 celebrities arrive at the Chinese Theater. . . ." Cited in Hamann, p. 6. The Garrick Theater poster is on microfilm at the Herrick Library.

108. Mary Ryan, "The Projection of a New Womanhood: The Movie Mod-

erns of the 1920s," in *Decades of Discontent: The Women's Movement, 1920 to 1940*, ed. Lois Scharf and Joan Jensen (Westport, CT: Greenwood Press, 1983), pp. 113–30; Conway and Ricci, *Films of Jean Harlow,* pp. 20–21, 26; Sidney Skolsky, *Don't Get Me Wrong: I Love Hollywood* (New York: G. P. Putnam's Sons, 1975), p. 81. News clips edited by Hamann document Harlow's erotic persona, for example by describing her hair color as "Sexquisite," p. 82; reporting jokes written for Harlow about her lack of brassiere wear, p. 82; and describing the origins and repetition of the "platinum blonde" moniker. *Red-Headed Woman* (1932), directed by Jack Conway.

109. Nancy Pryor, "No More Nighties for Jeanette," *Motion Picture,* February 1933, pp. 27, 97.

110. "A Movie 'Undie' Parade," *Photoplay,* August 1930, pp. 36–37. The increasing presence of black-and-white photographs and moving pictures in U.S. visual culture may also explain the black dress's rise in popularity in the early twentieth century. Edward Steichen moved from softer-focused fashion photography to sharper black-and-white photographs when he began working for *Vogue* in 1923. Mackrell, *Coco Chanel,* pp. 30–31. See also 1930 black silk slip, 64.200.2.B (ROM); 1932 black rayon crape slip, 971.259.5.C (ROM); 1934 black satin slip, 969.241.5.B (ROM); and a very sheer and delicate 1930s black chiffon step-in combination ornamented with chantilly lace, 1976.37.21 (Met).

111. Mary McCarthy, *The Group* (New York: Harcourt, 1989/1963), pp. 164–65. See also 1930s black chiffon and chantilly-type lace step-ins, 1976.37.22 (Met); 1935 black chiffon panties trimmed with black lace and appliqued pink chiffon hearts, 69.160.65 (FIT); and 1930 black silk crape de chine underpants, 971.259.13 (ROM); advertisement in *Vogue,* August 1, 1954.

112. Leslie Cabarga, *The Fleischer Story* (New York: Nostalgia Press, 1976), pp. 27–58, 85–86, 106; Eric Smoodin, *Animating Culture: Hollywood Cartoons from the Sound Era* (New Brunswick, NJ: Rutgers University Press, 1993), pp. 30–39; Karl Cohen, *Forbidden Animation: Censored Cartoons and Blacklisted Animators in America* (Jefferson, NC: McFarland Publishers, 1997), pp. 5, 10, 16–25, 30; Norman Klein, *Seven Minutes: The Life and Death of the American Animated Cartoon* (New York: Verso, 1993), pp. 59–90; Stefan Kanfer, *Serious Business: The Art and Commerce of Animation in America from Betty Boop to Toy Story* (New York: Scribner, 1997), ch. 3. Patricia Simmons interviewed Mae Questel, the voice of Betty Boop, in 1978, in "Betty Boop, aka Aunt Bluebell, Wears Her Age Well," *San Jose Mercury News,* October 15, 1978, section L, p. 3. See also Gertzman, *Bootleggers,* p. 79, on "eight-pagers."

113. Cabarga, *Fleischer Story,* pp. 51–52; Robert G. O'Meally, "Checking Our Balances: Ellison on Armstrong's Humor," *boundary 2* 30, no. 2 (2003): 115–36.

114. Richard Lamparski, *Whatever Became of . . . ?* (New York: Crown, 1968), pp. 140–41; *New York Times,* February 14, 1941. Film review in Special Collections, Herrick Library; Ruth Carson, "Black Market," *Collier's,* March 4, 1944, pp. 18–19.

115. *Maiden Form Mirror,* December 1937, p. 7.

116. Carson, "Black Market"; *Maiden Form Mirror*, December 1942, p. 7; *Women's Wear Daily*, March 16, 1944, p. 16; "Black lace spins its wiles . . . ," *Vogue*, October 1, 1941, p. 61; "Black Magic for the New 1940s Fashion," *Sears, Roebuck and Co. Catalogue*, 1939, p. 149, in Stella Blum, ed., *Everyday Fashions of the Thirties as Pictured in Sears Catalog* (New York: Dover, 1986), p. 123; "The Witchery of Black Lingerie," *Women's Wear Daily*, September 11, 1947, section 2; September 4, 1952. See also 1940s black lace and satin bra, 86.39.10 (FIT); 1942 black half slip, 70.107.2 (FIT); 1947 black satin panier, 81.69.24 (FIT); 1948 Hattie Carnegie black nylon net and taffeta petticoat, 1980.485.9 (Met); 1950 black taffeta Dior petticoat, 53.40.16d (Met); 1950 black net bustier, Hearst-K-22 (FIT); 1950 black silk slip, 974.318.C (ROM); 1950s black waist cincher, X61.7 (Met); 1950s black lace and satin strapless décolleté bustier, 1987.304 (Met); 1950s black net waist-cincher long-line bra, 75-109-1-72.22 (FIT); 1955 black elasticized satin and lace lingerie bra and girdle set, 1982.401.10ab (Met); 1955 black net slip, 964.152.1.D (ROM); 1956 black nylon lace corselette, 82.155.8 (FIT); late-1950s black nylon tricot and organza petticoat trimmed with lace and ribbon bows, 1975.4.3 (Met); late-1950s silk strapless bra, 967.199.24 (ROM); late-1950s black net crinoline, 970.358.7.B (ROM); black Merry Widow trimmed with red satin ribbon, M.85.201 (LACMA).

117. "Abracadabra" lyrics reprinted here by the kind permission of Steve Miller. I am grateful to Gerry Ronning for alerting me to the song, a track on the Steve Miller album of the same name. See also Jonathan Schroeder and Janet Borgerson, "Dark Desires: Fetishism, Ontology, and Representation in Contemporary Advertising," in *Sex in Advertising: Perspectives on the Erotic Appeal*, ed. Tom Reichert and Jacqueline Lambiase (London: Lawrence Erlbaum, 2003), pp. 65–87.

118. *10 Things I Hate about You* (1999), directed by Gil Junger. I thank Lani Hall for providing this film source. *Welcome to Mooseport* (2004), directed by Donald Petrie, incorporates a similar meaning of black lingerie for middle-aged Americans.

119. Shadee Malaklou, "Words from the Black Book"; for responses to Malaklou's column, see *The Chronicle Online: The Independent Daily at Duke University*, www.chronicle.duke.edu.

120. Author interview with Mabel Durham Fuller, July 19, 1993, Kingston, New York. African American women continued to have difficulties getting work as sewing-machine operators in the 1930s and 1940s. Author interview with Vetha Coward, December 13, 1993, New York City; author interview with Flora Travers, December 13, 1993, New York City.

121. Author interview with Mabel Durham Fuller, November 23, 1993, Kingston, New York; *New York Herald Tribune*, January 27, 1946.

122. Author interview with Mabel Durham Fuller, July 19, 1993, Kingston, New York; *New York Herald Tribune*, January 27, 1946.

123. Author interview with Mabel Durham Fuller, November 23, 1993, Kingston, New York. For evidence of racial conflict and cooperation in south-

eastern organizing drives, see ILGWU archive files, such as David Dubinsky Collection, Box 93, files 2A-B and 3A, Kheel Center.

124. Author interview with Willie Mae Foxworth, December 15, 1993, Bay-onne, New Jersey; author interview with Miriam Baratz, December 12, 1993, New York City. Baratz also noted that "sometimes everybody in the plant would work on [black] at the same time just to get it out of the way."

125. Michaels, "Souls of White Folks"; Toni Morrison, *Playing in the Dark: Whiteness and the Literary Imagination* (New York: Random House, 1993); Lois Banner, *American Beauty* (Chicago: University of Chicago Press, 1983), p. 234; Gilman, "Black Bodies." See bell hooks for a discussion of the links among blackness, pleasure, and death: *Black Looks: Race and Representation* (Boston: South End Press, 1992), pp. 26–27, 35–36. Mary Ann Doane, *Femmes Fatale*; Patrice Petro, *Aftershocks of the New: Feminism and Film History* (New Brunswick, NJ: Rutgers University Press, 2002), pp. 136–56. I am grateful to Lois Banner for alerting me to Rowland Barber, *The Night They Raided Min-sky's: A Fanciful Expedition to the Lost Atlantis of Show Business* (New York: Simon and Schuster, 1960), p. 310.

CHAPTER 5. THE INVISIBLE WOMAN

Epigraph: Alexander Woollcott, "Our Mrs. Parker," *While Rome Burns* (New York: Viking Press, 1934), p. 146.

1. *Corsets & Brassieres*, November 1941, p. 39; *Corsets & Brassieres*, September 1937, pp. 16–17. S. H. Camp & Company, among others, promoted the concept of "prescription" corsets for postoperative and pregnant women and women with back problems or hernias, making doctors' offices important loca-tions for corset advocacy, with health professionals essentially acting as sales-people. The Camp Transparent Woman was used to champion the medicalized corset. *Corsets & Brassieres*, September 1937, p. 17. Michael Schudson, *Adver-tising: The Uneasy Persuasion* (New York: Basic Books, Inc., 1984), p. 97.

2. Ludmilla K. Kybalová, Olga H. Herbenná, and Milena L. Larnarová, *Pic-torial Encyclopedia of Fashion* (London: Paul Hamlyn, 1968), p. 450.

3. See Laura Mulvey, "Visual Pleasure and Narrative Cinema," in *Issues in Feminist Film Criticism*, ed. Patricia Ehrens (Bloomington: Indiana University Press, 1990), pp. 28–40, for more on the male gaze, particularly the section en-titled "Woman as Image, Man as Bearer of the Look."

4. *Vogue*, March 15, 1915, p. 93; November 15, 1919, p. 1.

5. In addition, though close analysis of words and images may seem to per-vert advertising "intentions," it is important to remember that my scrutiny of these ads may still not equal that of the admen and their clients. Erving Goff-man discusses the detailed attention given to the production of ads in *Gender Advertisements* (New York: Harper and Row, 1979).

6. Betty Friedan, *The Feminine Mystique* (New York: Dell Publishing, 1963), pp. 197–223; Rosalind Coward, *Female Desires: How They Are Sought,*

Bought, and Packaged (New York: Grove Weidenfeld, 1985); Ellen McCracken, *Decoding Women's Magazines: From Mademoiselle to Ms.* (New York: St. Martin's Press, 1993).

7. Roland Marchand, *Advertising the American Dream: Making Way for Modernity, 1920–1940* (Berkeley: University of California Press, 1985), and Jackson Lears, *Fables of Abundance: A Cultural History of Advertising in America* (New York: Basic Books, 1994), provide more nuanced gender analysis than previous works on advertising history. Earlier studies could not neglect women altogether because of their dominance as consumers in American families. In some respects, these works responded to the advertising industry's cognizance of the need to address a wide range of ads to women. Michael Schudson (*Advertising*, p. 40), for example, rightly discusses Clairol's wildly successful 1960s hair-dye campaign, but he provides no gender analysis of its meanings. See also Daniel Pope, *The Making of Modern Advertising* (New York: Basic Books, 1983), and Stephen Fox, *The Mirror Makers: A History of American Advertising and Its Creators* (New York: William Morrow, 1984). Recent works by Jennifer Scanlon and Ellen Gruber Garvey provide new information and perspectives on women and advertising. Scanlon's work widens the scope by focusing on women working in advertising as well as on advertising directed to women, whereas Garvey's deepens our understanding of the ways advertising entered into private life in the early twentieth century. Jennifer Scanlon, *Inarticulate Longings: The Ladies' Home Journal, Gender and the Promises of Consumer Culture* (New York: Routledge, 1995); Ellen Gruber Garvey, *The Adman in the Parlor: Magazines and the Gendering of Consumer Culture, 1880s to 1910s* (New York: Oxford University Press, 1996). Richard Martin's research analyzes constructions of masculinity in advertising. Richard Martin, "Gay Blades: Homoerotic Content in J. C. Leyendecker's Gillette Advertising Images," *Journal of American Culture* 18, no. 2 (Summer 1995): 75–82; and " 'Feel Like a Million!': The Propitious Epoch in Men's Underwear Imagery, 1939–1952," *Journal of American Culture* 18, no. 4 (Winter 1995): 51–58.

8. Linda Nochlin and Thomas Hess, eds., *Woman as Sex Object: Studies in Erotic Art, 1730–1970* (New York: Newsweek, 1972); Abigail Solomon-Godeau, "The Legs of the Countess," *October* 39 (Winter 1986): 65–108; Marcia Pointon, *Naked Authority: The Body in Western Painting, 1830–1908* (Cambridge: Cambridge University Press, 1990); Lynda Nead, *The Female Nude: Art, Obscenity and Sexuality* (London: Routledge, 1992); Tania Modleski, *The Women Who Knew Too Much: Hitchcock and Feminist Theory* (New York: Routledge, 1989); Mary Ann Doane, *The Desire to Desire: The Woman's Film of the 1940s* (Bloomington: Indiana University Press, 1987); and Jane Gaines and Charlotte Herzog, eds., *Fabrications: Costume and the Female Body* (New York: Routledge, 1990). See also Nancy Vickers, "Preface to the *Blasons Anatomiques:* The Poetic and Philosophical Contexts of Descriptions of the Female Body in the Renaissance," (PhD diss., Yale University, 1976), for an interesting account of the lyric appreciation for the textually dismembered female body in sixteenth-century poetry. Steven Marcus, *The Other Victorians: A Study of Sexuality and*

Pornography in Mid-Nineteenth-Century England (New York: Basic Books, 1964), pp. 278–79. Marchand, *Advertising the American Dream*, p. 62.

9. When advertising work became increasingly lucrative in the 1920s, the upper ranks of admen solidified their positions among the elites of society. By the 1930s, even the middling ranks of admen lived lives far more affluent than those of the mass of American consumers they sought to influence. Lears, *Fables of Abundance*, pp. 196–97.

10. Fox, *Mirror Makers*, pp. 17–19, 50–51, 61, 65, 67, 74–75, 187–88; Lears, *Fables of Abundance*, p. 261, ch. 9.

11. Elizabeth Ewing, *Dress and Undress: A History of Women's Underwear* (New York: Drama Book Specialists, 1978), p. 48; Garvey, *Adman in the Parlor*, pp. 9–13. The relationship between wholesale and retail promotion is evident in numerous issues of the *Women's & Infants' Furnisher*, and in its successive incarnations as *Corsets & Lingerie* and *Corsets & Brassieres*.

12. Arthur W. Pearce, *The Future out of the Past: An Illustrated History of the Warner Brothers Company on Its 90th Anniversary with the Histories of the Corporate Family, CF Hathaway, Puritan Sportswear and Warners' Packaging* (Bridgeport, CT: Warner Brothers Company, 1964), p. 26. The book notes censorship by *Vogue* and *The Boston Transcript*, but the image appears fully drawn in *Vogue*, April 1914, p. 33.

13. Pearce, *Future out of the Past*, p. 26.

14. Ibid. See also chapters 2 and 3 for more about women's growing public presence in the early twentieth century.

15. Fox, *Mirror Makers*, p. 49. *Vogue*, February 15, 1915, p. 9. Front-lace corsets were an innovation that allowed the wearer to put on and adjust her corset without the assistance required by back-lace corsets.

16. *Vogue*, November 1, 1919, p. 28; November 15, 1924, p. 19; June 15, 1931, p. 94; October 15, 1947, p. 197. *Ebony*, December 1951, p. 44.

17. *Vogue*, February 15, 1915, p. 69; May 15, 1914, p. 93.

18. Ibid., February 15, 1915, p. 69; October 15, 1919, p. 1.

19. *Woman's Home Companion*, October 1921, p. 69; October 1923, p. 51. A similar example is "Wear Gossard Corsets and Brassieres [to] keep the figure youthful without imposing stiffness and restriction. . . . Combined with absolute freedom of breathing and body movement, Gossard gives support against fatigue and insurance against unbeautiful lines." *Woman's Home Companion*, October 1923, p. 88. Additional ads that express the relationship between fashion and restraint include "Frolaset Front Lacing Corsets will give you as much as you demand in fashion—more than you expect in freedom of movement and comfort" (*Vogue*, May 1, 1921, p. 12); "Model corset-brassiere . . . defines the figure fashionably, but it does not confine it rigidly" (ibid., August 15, 1921, n.p.); and "Athena . . . fits with glove-like smoothness, yet gives perfect freedom" (ibid., April 1, 1921, p. 8).

20. *Vogue*, October 15, 1923, p. 18; September 15, 1924, p. 150. The phrase "New Freedom" was the name given to the progressive reforms that President Woodrow Wilson proposed in the 1910s.

21. *Vogue,* April 15, 1937, p. 125; May 15, 1947, p. 116. *California Apparel News,* October 10, 1947, p. 7. *Vogue,* April 15, 1937, p. 125; November 15, 1941, p. 99; February 1, 1943, p. 16L; August 15, 1950, p. 6; February 1942, p. 6; October 1, 1947, p. 153; October 1, 1952, p. 46; November 1, 1952, p. 87; October 15, 1941, p. 99; November 1, 1952, p. 66; May 1, 1947, p. 86. *Ebony,* May 1952, p. 96.

22. A 1915 ad claimed it was "Madame['s] . . . duty to be beautiful!" to avoid the "tragedies" of "superfluous flesh, bumps and protuberances" (*Vogue,* January 15, 1915, p. 67). Additional examples of ads with a beauty emphasis appeared in subsequent decades, including "La Resista Corsets . . . Made for stylish women who appreciate the value of a beautiful figure" (Ibid., April 15, 1921, p. 7); "America's Venus wears and endorses La Camille Front Lace Corsets" (Ibid., May 1, 1921, p. 15); "Beauty alone is not sufficient" (*Women's Wear Daily,* March 16, 1944, p. 13); "Beautiful in itself" (*Vogue,* September 15, 1952, p. 72).

23. *Vogue,* March 21, pp. 88, 98; April 15, 1921, p. 9; June 15, 1931, p. 21. *Women's Wear Daily,* March 16, 1944, p. 13. See also *Vogue,* November 15, 1947, p. 187, for a Kabo brassiere ad in which a woman's torso adorned with the K-bra emerges, genielike, from a steaming test tube; and "Just be yourself . . . with some improvements" (*Vogue,* May 15, 1931, p. 25).

24. *Vogue,* August 25, 1950, p. 81. Joan Riviere, "Womanliness as a Masquerade," in *Formations of Fantasy,* ed. V. Burgin, James Donald, and Cora Kaplan (London: McMillan, 1986), pp. 35–61. Written in 1929, this article is foundational to feminist criticism of gendered culture and femininity as socially constructed.

25. *Women's Wear Daily,* November 6, 1952, sect. 2, p. 35. Revealing this masquerade is subversive because it removes cultural limits on the behavior of women (and men).

26. *Vogue,* November 1, 1947, p. 199; *Women's Wear Daily,* November 11, 1952, sect. 2, p. 7. Raymond Williams identifies magic as the central concept that explains modern advertising: "a highly organized and professional system of magical inducements and satisfactions, functionally very similar to magical systems in simpler societies, but rather strangely coexistent with a highly developed scientific technology" (p. 185). Williams suggests that twentieth-century advertising serves ruling-class needs for market control. Beyond creating demand for particular products, advertising obscures the inability of consumption to satisfy human needs and keeps choice at the level of selecting commodities rather than at the level of determining how commodities are produced and distributed. The fantasy validated by advertising does so "at the cost of preserving the general unreality which it obscures: the real failures of the society" (p. 189). Though my focus is on gender analysis of intimate apparel ads, certainly many of the themes that appear in these ads uphold Williams's views. Raymond Williams, "Advertising: The Magic System," in his *Problems in Materialism and Culture: Selected Essays* (London: New Left Books, 1980), pp. 170–95. See also Lears, *Fables of Abundance,* on advertising and magic.

27. *Woman's Home Companion,* October 1923, p. 145; *Vogue,* November 1, 1952, p. 86; November 15, 1947, p. 66. *Good Housekeeping,* November 1950, p. 19; *Vogue,* August 15, 1952, p. 174.

28. *Vogue,* November 15, 1924, p. 19; February 15, 1933, p. 84; December 1952, p. 174; October 1, 1952, p. 71; May 1, 1952, p. 74; April 1, 1952, p. 74; August 15, 1950, p. 174.

29. *Harper's Bazaar,* November 1956, p. 89; January 1951, p. 156. *Vogue,* April 1, 1952, p. 53; September 15, 1952, p. 52.

30. *Ladies' Home Journal,* September 1930, p. 91; *Vogue,* May 15, 1931, p. 139. March 15, 1933, p. 20. *Women's Wear Daily,* September 11, 1952, p. 20.

31. *Vogue,* November 1, 1941, p. 118; October 1, 1952, p. 68. See chapter 3 in this book on brassieres. One rare countervailing sentiment amid the myriad appeals and references to glamour in *Ebony* ads and articles is "Being a Glamour Girl isn't all it's cracked up to be, according to Lena Horne," *Ebony,* November 1947, p. 11. In addition to its numerous intimate apparel ads, *Ebony* featured pro-glamour ads for makeup (December 1947, p. 18), blouses (February 1948, p. 46), hair products (March 1948, p. 41), skin-lightening cream (December 1951), and bathing suits (June 1953, p. 87).

32. *Vogue,* February 1, 1943, p. 31. See also similar ads touting "glorification" in *Lingerie Merchandising,* July 1947, p. 133; and *California Stylist,* January 1945, p. 137. Submission to discipline—a "light but wise restraint"—is also required to achieve "glamorous curves ahead," as a Lastex ad notes in *Vogue,* March 15, 1938, p. 24.

33. *Vogue,* November 1, 1919, p. 42. Gossard advertised corsets using a series of such ads in the 1920s. See *Vogue,* February 15, 1921, p. 6, and November 1, 1921, p. 6. Other Gossard ads with similar layouts approximated the style of magazine nonfiction articles. See *Vogue,* March 1, 1915, p. 36; March 15, 1921, p. 4; September 15, 1921, p. 6; October 15, 1921, p. 4; September 15, 1922, p. 8. Garvey discusses the use of magazine-style fiction in ads in chapter 3 of *Adman in the Parlor.*

34. *Vogue,* February 15, 1933, p. 73; January 15, 1938, p. 27. *Women's Wear Daily,* August 21, 1947, p. 35; *Vogue,* September 15, 1952, p. 53.

35. Rosalind Williams, "The Dream World of Mass Consumption," in *Rethinking Popular Culture: Contemporary Perspectives in Cultural Studies,* ed. Chandra Mukerji and Michael Schudson (Berkeley: University of California Press, 1991), p. 203.

36. *Vogue,* November 1, 1952, pp. 63, 31; September 15, 1952, p. 53. See also Warner's ad in *Vogue,* June 1942, p. 44; August 1, 1952, p. 113.

37. *Maiden Form Mirror,* August 1949, p. 1; List of "Dream Ads" (Smith); *Maiden Form Mirror,* February 1950, p. 3; May 1950, p. 1; October 1950, pp. 4–5; April 1951, p. 3; August 1950, p. 1; Maidenform Museum display; *Maiden Form Mirror,* June 1951, p. 10.

38. Maidenform "Dream Ads"; *Harper's Bazaar,* March 1951, p. 89; *Vogue,* April 1, 1952, p. 20; August 1, 1952, p. 33; November 1, 1952, p. 161. For more on gendered domesticity in the 1950s, see Friedan, *The Feminine Mystique;* and

Elaine Tyler May, *Homeward Bound: American Families in the Cold War Era* (New York: Basic Books, 1988). See Eugenia Kaledin, *Mothers and More: American Women in the 1950s* (Boston: Twayne Publishers, 1984); and Joanne Meyerowitz, ed., *Not June Cleaver: Women and Gender in Postwar America, 1945–1960* (Philadelphia: Temple University Press, 1994), for critical reappraisals of Friedan's and May's studies and for evidence of women at work during the 1950s.

39. James Still, "The Maidenform Campaigns: Reaffirming the Feminine Ideal," *Connecticut Review* 16 (Spring 1992): 1–7.

40. *Vogue*, March 1, 1915, p. 125; April 1, 1921, p. 109; October 1, 1924, p. 137; October 15, 1924, p. 112; April 1, 1921, p. 109; November 15, 1924, p. 19.

41. Ibid., February 1, 1933, p. 79; October 15, 1937, p. 39.

42. Ibid., October 15, 1947, p. 100; October 1, 1947, p. 124; November 1, 1947, p. 197; May 1, 1952, p. 74; April 1, 1952, p. 53; April 15, 1952, p. 2.

43. Ibid., September 15, 1923, p. 33; July 1, 1926, p. 103; October 1, 1941, p. 23; September 15, 1923, p. 123. For examples of garments worn by invisible women, see *Vogue*, September 1, 1941, p. 103; March 1, 1943, p. 103; May 15, 1947, n.p; June 1948, pp. 145–47.

44. Ibid., February 15, 1915, p. 11; March 1, 1915, p. 9. For additional examples of transparency in ads, see *Vogue*, January 15, 1933, p. 73; March 1, 1943, p. 71.

45. Ibid., October 15, 1921, p. 22; *Woman's Home Companion*, November 1921, p. 63. See also *Vogue*, March 15, 1935, p. 19, for a disappearing panther that leaps across a Carter's bra and pantie girdle. *Vogue*, April 1, 1935, p. 117; October 15, 1947, pp. 176, 78.

46. *Vogue*, September 15, 1923, inside front cover; March 1, 1921, p. 13; November 1, 1924, p. 29; March 1, 1933, p. 22; April 1, 1935, p. 24e; April 15, 1935, p. 15; May 1, 1935, pp. 114–15; May 14, 1935, p. 102; October 15, 1937, pp. 40, 43; November 1, 1937, p. 44; November 15, 1937, pp. 23, 25; November 1, 1947, pp. 89, 188; November 15, 1947, p. 202; October 15, 1924, p. 133.

47. Ibid., May 1, 1921, p. 12; November 1, 1924, p. 29; October 1, 1937, p. 155; August 15, 1950, p. 69; October 15, 1947, p. 176.

48. Models with hands in front of their faces appear in "positive" images as well. See, for example, *Vogue*, November 15, 1941, p. 96.

49. Ibid., October 15, 1923, p. 86; April 15, 1931, pp. 94–95, 120; May 1, 1931, p. 14; June 1, 1931, p. 105; April 1, 1935, pp. 80–83; April 15, 1935, p. 30; October 15, 1947, pp. 190, 196; September 15, 1952, p. 103.

50. Ibid., February 1, 1942, pp. 9–10d; October 15, 1947, p. 160; April 15, 1952, pp. 104–5, 120–21; August 15, 1952, pp. 176–77.

51. McCracken extensively discusses the relationship between paid advertisements and editorials, which she terms "covert advertisements" in *Decoding Women's Magazines*. See also Garvey, *Adman in the Parlor*, pp. 12, 150, 211 n4. A recent newspaper article also commented on this long-held relationship. *Los Angeles Times*, September 12, 1996.

52. Stuart Ewen, *Captains of Consciousness: Advertising and the Social*

Roots of the Consumer Culture (New York: McGraw Hill, 1976), p. 177. Hand-held mirrors appear in numerous ads from the 1910s to the 1950s, including in *Vogue*, March 1, 1915, pp. 36, 84; March 15, 1915, p. 3; November 1, 1919, p. 28; March 1, 1921, p. 13; May 1, 1921, p. 130; October 1, 1921, p. 20; September 15, 1922, p. 17; September 15, 1923, p. 25; February 15, 1931, p. 116; March 15, 1943, p. 110; October 1, 1947, pp. 101, 128; November 1, 1947, p. 194; December 1952, p. 169; and in *Women's Wear Daily*, August 7, 1947, p. 24.

53. Mirrors with no reflection appear in *Vogue*, May 11, 1929, p. 39; May 1, 1935, p. 126. See also *Vogue*, April 1, 1931, p. 110, for a reflected image that extends beyond the bounds of the mirror. An invitation to see oneself in the magazine page occurs in a Talon Slide Fastener ad. In bold type next to an illustration of a "fashion editor" standing behind her desk, the ad's headline reads, "but you CAN look like the Fashion Ads!" *Vogue*, October 15, 1937, p. 40.

54. *Vogue*, November 1, 1921, inside front cover. Ads in which women show no concern about the mirror's presence appear in *Vogue*, November 1, 1919, p. 43; April 15, 1921, p. 6; May 1, 1921, pp. 13, 14; November 15, 1921, p. 4; April 1, 1952, p. 53, September 1, 1952, p. 124; September 15, 1952, p. 55; December 1952, p. 71. Mirrors with no image appear in *Vogue*, November 15, 1916, p. 16; October 1, 1919, p. 34; December 1, 1919, p. 10; September 15, 1921, p. 17; October 15, 1921, p. 4; September 15, 1924, p. 35; November 15, 1924, p. 14. For a woman with a rose, see *Vogue*, February 15, 1915, p. 89.

55. For ads showing self-touching during self-viewing, see *Vogue*, October 15, 1919, p. 98; March 1, 1921, p. 13; May 1, 1921, p. 130; September 15, 1922, pp. 17, 118; February 15, 1931, p. 166; March 15, 1943, p. 110; October 1, 1947, p. 128; December 1952, p. 169. *Women's Wear Daily*, August 7, 1947, p. 24; *Good Housekeeping*, November 1950, p. 19. For images of a woman caressing the mirror, see *Vogue*, March 1, 1915, p. 109; May 1, 1921, 15.

56. *Vogue*, October 15, 1941, p. 24e. Women appear in front of windows and doorways in *Vogue*, October 1, 1919, pp. 167, 160, 179; October 15, 1919, p. 18; May 15, 1921, p. 5; July 15, 1921, p. 61; September 15, 1921, p. 17; September 15, 1923, p. 94; October 15, 1924, p. 112; May 15, 1931, p. 8; October 1, 1947, p. 101; November 1, 1952, p. 43.

57. "In a world ordered by sexual imbalance, pleasure in looking has been split between active/male and passive/female. The determining male gaze projects its fantasy onto the female figure, which is styled accordingly. In their traditional exhibitionist role women are simultaneously looked at and displayed, with their appearance coded for strong visual and erotic impact so that they can be said to connote *to-be-looked-at-ness*. Woman displayed as sexual object is the leitmotif of erotic spectacle: from pin-ups to strip-tease, from Ziegfeld to Busby Berkeley, she holds the look, plays to and signifies male desire." Laura Mulvey, "Visual Pleasure," p. 33. Mulvey's article was originally published in 1975, and the concept of "to-be-looked-at-ness" became critically important to the feminist film criticism that followed.

58. "Mrs. Brown" appears in Claudia Kidwell and Valerie Steele, eds., *Men and Women: Dressing the Part* (Washington, DC: Smithsonian Institution

Press, 1989), p. 53. *Vogue*, November 1, 1952, p. 43. *Ebony*, June 1953, p. 86, contains a similar ad.

59. *Vogue*, September 15, 1923, p. 4. Similar use of frames occurs in *Vogue*, January 15, 1915, p. 105; March 1, 1915, pp. 14, 120; October 1, 1919, pp. 5, 131; November 1, 1919, p. 157; November 15, 1919, p. 107; October 15, 1919, p. 20; November 1, 1919, p. 134; December 1, 1919, p. 143; March 15, 1921, pp. 7, 88, 98; May 1, 1921, p. 4; October 15, 1921, p. 107; September 15, 1922, p. 14; July 15, 1923, p. 85; September 15, 1923, p. 33; October 15, 1924, p. 4; October 1, 1947, p. 87.

60. Ibid., February 1, 1915, p. 69.

61. Spotlights and/or stage effects occur in *Vogue*, April 15, 1921, p. 7; October 15, 1921, p. 121; September 15, 1923, inside front cover, pp. 122, 137; May 15, 1929, p. 24; June 15, 1931, p. 94; September 15, 1952, p. 31. Drapery and fan appear in *Vogue*, August 1, 1922, p. 19; September 15, 1923, p. 26; May 1, 1952, p. 51; October 1, 1952, p. 46. Self-conscious poseurs appear in ads in *Vogue*, November 15, 1919, p. 1; October 15, 1921, p. 6; September 15, 1926, p. 164; October 1, 1947, pp. 101, 228. Exhibitionist ads include Maidenform dream ads such as those in *Vogue*, April 1, 1952, p. 20; August 1, 1952, p. 33; November 1, 1952, p. 161. *Ebony*, March and April 1949, pp. 7, 3.

62. Pointon, *Naked Authority*, pp. 14, 23–27. The "Degas" ad is in *Vogue*, November 1, 1947, p. 195. Painterly ads include those in *Vogue*, March 1, 1921, p. 15; April 1, 1921, p. 9; May 1, 1921, p. 110; July 1, 1926, p. 34; March 15, 1943, p. 17. A female figure is shown with an art object in *Vogue*, September 1, 1921, p. 104; October 1, 1921, p. 123; October 15, 1921, p. 22; October 15, 1923, p. 19; March 1, 1943, p. 90; September 15, 1952, p. 71. The Artist Model style name used by the American Lady Corset Co. also evokes this genre (*Vogue*, April 15, 1935, p. 132), as do the many evocations of the "three graces" (*Vogue*, October 15, 1941, p. 94e; October 15, 1947, p. 68).

63. *Vogue*, September 15, 1923, p. 122; April 1, 1952, p. 41; June 1952, p. 44; October 1952, p. 46.

64. The model in the ad in *Vogue*, October 15, 1921, p. 6, adopts a posture similar to that of a woman on a "saucy" French postcard reproduced in Cecil St. Laurent, *The Great Book of Lingerie* (London: The Vendome Press, 1986), p. 12. "Calendar" poses appear in *Vogue*, October 1, 1947, p. 153; April 15, 1935, p. 15.

65. *Vogue*, September 15, 1923, p. 147; March 1, 1933, p. 78; March 15, 1943, p. 28; August 15, 1952, p. 75.

66. Pinup ad images appear in *Vogue*, December 1, 1919, p. 147; October 1, 1921, p. 138; November 1, 1937, p. 41; January 15, 1938, pp. 31, 26; October 15, 1941, pp. 94, 112; February 15, 1943, pp. 78, 83; March 15, 1943, p. 100; November 15, 1947, pp. 184, 199; November 1, 1947, pp. 41, 188; June 1952, p. 18; August 15, 1952, p. 170; September 15, 1952, p. 2; October 1, 1952, p. 71; November 1, 1952, p. 63.

67. *Woman's Home Companion*, September 1911, p. 40; *Vogue*, October 1, 1952, p. 168; April 15, 1952, p. 32; August 15, 1952, p. 174. See also *Vogue*, October 15, 1947, p. 80, for an ad in which a man in pajamas peers from behind a

mirror to engage the gaze of a woman whose reflection looks at her. Only the man's head and one shoulder and arm are visible. Whole-bodied men do appear occasionally in ads in which the female figure is fully clothed. Captioned "when a slip becomes a social error," a series of 1940s ads for Mary Barron slips depicted women unwittingly exhibiting their undergarments to male companions or male professionals such as dentists and policemen. See *Vogue,* March 1, 1943, p. 16; October 1, 1947, p. 128.

68. Goffman, *Gender Advertisements,* p. 51; Roland Barthes, *Mythologies* (New York: Farrar, Straus and Giroux, 1972/1957), p. 51.

69. Laura Mulvey, "Visual Pleasure and Narrative Cinema," *Screen* 16 (Autumn 1975), reprinted in Bill Nichols, ed., *Movies and Methods,* vol. 2 (Berkeley: University of California Press, 1985); Mary Ann Doane, "Film and the Masquerade: Theorizing the Female Spectator," *Screen* 23 (September–October 1982), reprinted in Ehrens, *Issues in Feminist Film Criticism,* pp. 41–57; Tania Modleski, "Hitchcock, Feminism, and the Patriarchal Unconscious," excerpt from *The Women Who Knew Too Much: Hitchcock and Feminist Theory* (New York: Methuen, 1988), reprinted in Erens, pp. 58–74; Linda Williams, "When the Woman Looks," in *Re-Vision: Essays in Feminist Film Criticism,* ed. Mary Doane, Patricia Mellencamp, and Linda Williams (Frederick, MD: University Publications of America, 1984), pp. 83–99. Diana Fuss, "Fashion and the Homospectatorial Look," *Critical Inquiry* 18 (Summer 1992): 713–37.

70. I base my conclusions on a survey of ads in *Vogue* and *Harper's Bazaar* magazines (1910s–50s), Sears, Roebuck catalogs (1902–61), and Frederick's of Hollywood catalogs (1947–60). Current issues of the *Los Angeles Times* provide almost daily evidence of the continuing importance of these evasive postures in ads. See *Vogue,* February 1, 1915, p. 73; March 1, 1915, p. 19; November 15, 1919, p. 16; July 15, 1921, p. 61; June 1, 1931, p. 108; January 1, 1943, p. 80; February 1, 1943, p. 15; March 15, 1943, p. 24; July 1952, p. 4. *Harper's Bazaar,* March 1951, p. 98. See also "White is back, summer light," *Vogue,* May 1, 1947, p. 174, for an example of invisible women wearing bras and girdles.

71. See the following Sears, Roebuck and Co. catalogs: "Sears Lead in Corsetry Styles . . . and Values!" 1931, p. 80; "Answering Fashion's Edict," 1931, p. 86 ("Co-ed" Corsetry); 1931, p. 128; "You'll feel lovelier, wearing Luxurious Lace-Trimmed Slips," 1947, p. 348; "Sears scientifically designed Maternity Supports," 1947–48, p. 387; "Nationally Famous Maiden Form Bras," 1951, p. 331.

72. For example, see "Uplifts Are a Girl's Best Friend," *Frederick's of Hollywood Catalog,* Fall 1956, p. 29; "Frederick's Padded Push Up Sweater Girl Bras," *Frederick's of Hollywood Catalog,* Fall 1957, pp. 2–3; Laura and Janusz Gottwald, eds., *Frederick's of Hollywood 1947–1973: 26 Years of Mail Order Seduction* (New York: Drake Publishers, 1973).

73. For examples of *Ebony's* evocation of Frenchness, see December 1951, p. 75; February 1952, p. 76; March 1952, pp. 13, 96; October 1952, p. 116; June 1953, p. 90. For ads that are similar to those in *Frederick's,* see *Ebony,* July 1947, p. 4; July 1948, p. 39; September 1948, p. 30; November 1948, p. 46; November 1951,

p. 116; February 1952, p. 49; March 1952, p. 13; October 1952, p. 116. For ads similar to those in *Vogue*, see *Ebony*, September 1947, p. 8; March 1948, p. 3; January 1952, p. 76; March 1952, p. 47; November 1952, p. 105; June 1953, p. 86. For ads similar to those in the Sears catalog, see *Ebony*, February 1952, pp. 50, 69, 76, 92; April 1952, p. 76; May 1953, p. 63. For hybrid ads, see *Ebony*, October 1947, p. 4; April 1949, p. 3; September 1953, p. 90.

74. Numerous advertisements acknowledge and encourage fetishism of intimate apparel—for example, by conferring the abilities of "caressing," "flattering," and being "in love" on these undergarments. *Vogue*, September 1, 1952, p. 54; December 1952, p. 71; May 1, 1952, p. 50.

75. Christian Dior, *Christian Dior's Little Dictionary of Fashion* (London: Cassell & Company, Ltd., 1954), p. 54.

CHAPTER 6. THE PRODUCTION OF GLAMOUR

1. William Leach, in *Land of Desire: Merchants, Power, and the Rise of a New American Culture* (New York: Vintage, 1993), pp. 146–49, dates the split between production and consumption in the 1880s and sees the domination of the corporate structure in both spheres firmly in place by the 1890s. He also notes some effects of this change, including difficulties for consumers, particularly women, who were newly distanced from production, in determining the value and quality of goods for sale. He finds the role of service to be central in developing consumer society.

2. Nan Enstad, *Ladies of Labor, Girls of Adventure: Working Women, Popular Culture, and Labor Politics at the Turn of the Twentieth Century* (New York: Columbia University Press, 1999), was published after this chapter was completed, as were Margaret Finnegan, *Selling Suffrage: Consumer Culture and Votes for Women* (New York: Columbia University Press, 1999), and Lizabeth Cohen, *A Consumer's Republic: The Politics of Mass Consumption in Postwar America* (New York: Vintage Books, 2003). For more on consumer strategies, see Nancy Schrom Dye, *As Equals and as Sisters: Feminism, the Labor Movement, and the Women's Trade Union League of New York* (Columbia: University of Missouri Press, 1980); Paula Hyman, "Immigrant Women and Consumer Protest: The New York City Kosher Meat Boycott of 1902," *American Jewish History* 70, no. 1 (1980): 91–105; Dana Frank, *Purchasing Power: Consumer Organizing, Gender and the Seattle Labor Movement, 1919–1929* (New York: Cambridge University Press, 1994); Kathryn Kish Sklar, *Florence Kelley and the Nation's Work* (New Haven, CT: Yale University Press, 1995); Meg Jacobs, " 'How about Some Meat?': The Office of Price Administration, Consumption Politics, and State Building from the Bottom Up, 1941–1946," *Journal of American History* 84, no. 3 (1997): 910–41; and Daniel Bender, *Sweated Work, Weak Bodies: Anti-Sweatshop Campaigns and Languages of Labor* (New Brunswick, NJ: Rutgers University Press, 2004).

3. Ann Schofield, "The Uprising of the 20,000: The Making of a Labor Legend," in *A Needle, A Bobbin, A Strike: Women Needleworkers in America*, ed.

Joan Jensen and Sue Davidson (Philadelphia: Temple University Press, 1984), pp. 167–82; Gus Tyler, *Look for the Union Label: A History of the International Ladies' Garment Workers' Union* (London: M. E. Sharpe, 1995), p. 44; Philip Foner, *Women and the American Labor Movement from Colonial Time to the Eve of World War I* (New York: Free Press, 1977), pp. 368–69; *The Women's Muslin-Underwear Industry*, Department of Commerce Miscellaneous Series No. 29 (Washington, DC: Government Printing Office, 1915), p. 7. A white goods local affiliated with the Women's Trade Union League (WTUL) in 1907 with Schneiderman's help, but its ranks were decimated by the 1908 depression. Dye, *As Equals and as Sisters*, p. 71. The average age of white goods workers in this period was nineteen. "The Stress of the Seasons," *Survey* 29 (March 8, 1913): 806.

4. *Women's Muslin-Underwear Industry*, p. 7. The 1816 invention of the tubular knitting machine may have enabled some factory production of knitted undergarments before the development of the women's muslin-undergarment industry later in the nineteenth century. Census and industry statistics treat knitted undergarments as a separate trade. Pennsylvania Department of Labor and Industry, "The Undergarment Industry in Pennsylvania," *Statistical Information Bulletin No. 83* (1951), pp. 2–8.

5. Roy Helfgott, "Women's and Children's Apparel," in *Made in New York: Case Studies in Metropolitan Manufacturing*, ed. Max Hall (Cambridge, MA: Harvard University Press, 1959), pp. 47–54; Claudia Brush Kidwell, *Suiting Everyone: The Democratization of Clothing in America* (Washington, DC: Smithsonian Institution Press, 1974), pp. 87–101.

6. Dye points out that undergarment shops were also a point of entry for workers because of the relatively unskilled nature of undergarment production. Dye, *As Equals and as Sisters*, p. 71.

7. *Women's Muslin-Underwear Industry*, p. 9.

8. Foner, *Women*, p. 243; *Women's Muslin-Underwear Industry*, pp. 8, 27; "The Corset," *Fortune*, March 1938, pp. 95–99; 1920 *Census of Manufacturers*; Helfgott, "Women's and Children's Apparel," p. 36; Bernard Smith, "Market Development, Industrial Development: The Case of the American Corset Trade, 1860–1920," *Business History Review* 65 (Spring 1991): 91–129. Louis Levine, *The Women's Garment Workers* (New York: B. W. Huebsch, Inc., 1924), p. 219.

9. Foner, *Women*, 368–69; Gus Tyler, *Look for the Union Label*, 84; Levine, *Women's Garment Workers*, pp. 226–27; Dye, *As Equals and as Sisters*, pp. 99–100; Harry Lang, *"62": Biography of a Union* (New York: Undergarment & Negligee Workers' Union Local 62, ILGWU, 1940), pp. 97–99; Annelise Orleck, *Common Sense & a Little Fire: Women and Working-Class Politics in the United States, 1900–1964* (Chapel Hill: University of North Carolina Press, 1995), pp. 76–79.

10. Foner, *Women*, pp. 369–70; Mary Goff Papers, Box 1, ILGWU Collection Kheel Center; Lang, *"62,"* pp. 102–106.

11. Lang, *"62,"* pp. 110–11; Levine, *Women's Garment Workers*, p. 227; Foner, *Women*, p. 371.

12. Foner, *Women*, pp. 368–72; Levine, *Women's Garment Workers*, pp. 228–30; Lang, *"62,"* p. 131; "The White Goods Workers Protocol," *Survey* 29 (March 8, 1913): 807.

13. Boris Emmet, "Trade Agreements in the Women's Clothing Industries in New York City," *Monthly Review* 5 (December 1917): 36. In 1915, 13,517 factory workers were in the trade in New York City, of whom 11,762 were women. *Women's Muslin-Underwear Industry*, p. 8.

14. *Women's Muslin-Underwear Industry*, p. 7.

15. Foner, *Women*, p. 387; Wilfred Carel, *A History of the Chicago Ladies' Garment Workers' Union* (Chicago: Normandie House, 1940), pp. 58–59, 87–101; Orleck, *Common Sense*, p. 79; Benjamin Schlesinger Collection, Box 4, Files 2, 7–8, Kheel Center.

16. *Women's Muslin-Underwear Industry*, pp. 27, 115–17; Foner, *Women*, p. 387.

17. "The Corset," pp. 95–99; *1920 Census of Manufacturers*; Helfgott, "Women's and Children's Apparel," p. 36. However, white goods shops were still on average larger than waist and dress shops. Levine, *Women's Garment Workers*, p. 219.

18. Foner, *Women*, p. 314. Clubwomen's support for corset workers was not unequivocal. When the Illinois State Federation of Women's Clubs voted to allow the WTUL to affiliate at its convention after the Kabo strike, one clubwoman was heard to say, "Isn't it dreadful! I suppose next year we'll have those corset workers here as members!" Robin Miller Jacoby, "The Women's Trade Union League and American Feminism," in *Class, Sex, and the Woman Worker*, ed. Milton Cantor and Bruce Laurie (Westport, CT: Greenwood Press, 1977), p. 218.

19. Karen M. Mason, "Feeling the Pinch: The Kalamazoo Corsetmakers' Strike of 1912," in *"To Toil the Livelong Day": America's Women at Work, 1780–1980*, ed. Carol Groneman and Mary Beth Norton (Ithaca, NY: Cornell University Press, 1987), pp. 141–60.

20. Mason, "Feeling the Pinch," pp. 144–52; Tyler, *Look for the Union Label*, p. 81; Foner, *Women*, pp. 357–58.

21. Mason, "Feeling the Pinch," pp. 152–56, 159–60; Levine, *Women's Garment Workers*, pp. 221–22.

22. "The Corset," p. 113; *New York Times*, July 18, 20, 22, 24, 26, 27, 1919; Tyler, *Look for the Union Label*, p. 135; Levine, *Women's Garment Workers*, pp. 292, 330–31.

23. Nancy Green, *Ready-to-Wear and Ready-to-Work: A Century of Industry and Immigrants in Paris and New York* (Durham, NC: Duke University Press, 1997), p. 56; Tyler, *Look for the Union Label*, p. 151; Levine, *Women's Garment Workers*, p. 351; John Laslett and Mary Tyler, *The ILGWU in Los Angeles, 1907–1988* (Inglewood, CA: Ten Star Press, 1989), pp. 24, 119.

24. Levine, *Women's Garment Workers*, p. 351; Green, *Ready-to-Wear*, p. 57; Helfgott, "Women's and Children's Apparel," p. 26.

25. Helfgott, "Women's and Children's Apparel," pp. 36–37.

26. Ibid., pp. 37, 81–82; Kidwell, *Suiting Everyone*, pp. 45–53, 63–64, 93–95, 108–9, 137–51.

27. Lang, *"62,"* p. 211; Helfgott, "Women's and Children's Apparel," pp. 21, 60–63, 114.

28. Kidwell, *Suiting Everyone*, pp. 175–77.

29. Dye, *As Equals and as Sisters*, pp. 162–66. For a detailed analysis of the declining effectiveness of organized labor's use of consumer boycotts in the 1920s, see Frank, *Purchasing Power.*

30. *1930 Census of Manufacturers*; Lang, *"62,"* pp. 188–92, 195, 211.

31. Lang, *"62,"* pp. 195–96, 199–201.

32. Ibid., pp. 202–3; Green, *Ready-to-Wear*, pp. 63–64.

33. Lang, pp. 206–7.

34. Ibid., pp. 203, 211–14, 217; David Dubinsky Collection, Box 111, File 1B, Kheel Center; Green, *Ready-to-Wear*, ch. 5.

35. *Our Union* began publishing in 1933 and detailed Local 62's activities throughout the 1930s and 1940s.

36. ILGWU Research Department, File ICBN (L): 07; Green, *Ready-to-Wear*, pp. 64–65; *Women's Wear Daily*, December 5, 1935. Some shop owners also moved south to Miami for health reasons.

37. Local 62 Collection, Box 2, File 8, Kheel Center; Dubinsky Collection, Box 92, Files 3A-3B and Box 93, File 2B.

38. In the 1920s New York was the largest garment center in the United States, and Los Angeles ranked fifth. By 1944, Los Angeles moved to third place, largely because of the growth of the sportswear trade and the promotion of a "California Look" by California manufacturers organizations capitalizing on the allure of Hollywood fashions worn by film stars both on- and offscreen. Thus, in women's clothing production, Los Angeles ranked second. *1929 Census of Manufacturers*, Reel M-1, vol. 2, p. 377; ibid., vol. 3, p. 77; Laslett and Tyler, *ILGWU in Los Angeles*, pp. 14–15; "Los Angeles' Little Cutters," *Fortune*, May 1945, p. 134; Julian C. Riley with the assistance of Hal Berggren, *Apparel Manufacturing in California: A Report Requested by Assembly Resolution No. 84 Fifty-fifth (Fourth Extraordinary) Session California Legislature* (Sacramento: State Reconstruction and Reemployment Commission, 1945), pp. 1–2, 8–10, 54–56; Edward Lassiter, "An Analysis of Garment Manufacturing in the Los Angeles Area" (MBA thesis, University of Southern California, 1953), pp. 81, 98.

39. The Job Analysis and Information Section, Divisions of Standards and Research, *Job Descriptions for the Garment Manufacturing Industry* (Washington, DC: United States Government Printing Office, 1941), pp. xxix–xxx; Laslett and Tyler, *ILGWU in Los Angeles*, p. 31; Clementina Durón, "Mexican Women and Labor Conflict in Los Angeles: The ILGWU Dressmakers' Strike of 1933," *Aztlán* 15, no. 1 (Spring 1984): 149–50; Tyler, *Look for the Union Label*, pp. 42, 142–43, 177–78; author interview with Iris Gonzalez, December 13, 1993, New York City; author interview with Nona Evans and Sylvia Jacobs, December 13, 1993, New York City. Labor agreements between manufacturers'

associations and the union included stipulations for piece price committees. Committees were commonly composed of three to five employees selected by their coworkers. If the committee and the shop owner could not agree on a new piece rate, the employer and the committee selected a worker with a minimum of two months' experience to do a test run of the disputed sewing operation. Officials of the union and the manufacturer's association could be present at the test. Union contracts forbade shop owners to subcontract disputed sewing operations. See, for example, 1921 agreement form, Local 62 Collection, Box 14, File 8; Cotton Garment Manufacturers of New York, Inc., agreement with White Goods Workers Union Local 62 and Cutters' Union Local 10, ILGWU, March 8, 1927, Local 62 Collection, Box 14, File 8; Lingerie Manufacturers Association of New York agreement with White Goods Workers Union Local 62 and Cutters' Union Local 10, ILGWU, October 28, 1931, Local 62 Collection, Box 14, File 8; Nagler Underwear agreement with Local 62 and Local 10, ILGWU, October 1934, Local 62 Collection, Box 14, File 8; 1950–1953 Lingerie Manufacturers Association of New York agreement with Local 62 and Local 10, ILGWU, September 15, 1950, New York Public Library; 1953–1956 Lingerie Manufacturers agreement with Local 62 and Local 10, September 23, 1953, New York Public Library. An interesting examination of the relative merits of piece versus week work (set payment by hour) appears in the transcript of a 1935 arbitration hearing on a negligee manufacturer's proposal to switch his shop from piece to week work. Local 62 manager Samuel Shore notes that in the production of higher-quality garments, such as the ones made in this shop, a prohibitive number of style changes make piece work untenable. "The settling of prices would be a constant source of trouble causing less earnings for the workers" due to the production stoppages necessary to negotiate rates. He also points out "that price fixing is not as simple as Mr. Rossant makes it out to be, for there are bodies and bodies in which the work is more complicated and difficult." B. Cohen & Company versus Local 62, ILGWU, July 10, 1935, Local 62 Collection, Box 1, File 19.

40. Author interviews with retired undergarment workers: Mabel Durham Fuller, July 19, 1993, Kingston, New York; Miriam Baratz, December 13, 1993, New York City; Dorothy Morris, December 13, 1993, New York City; Mary B. Allen, December 13, 1993, New York City; Alice Knox, December 13, 1993, New York City.

41. Harry Goldman, "When Social Significance Came to Broadway: 'Pins and Needles' in Production," *Theatre Quarterly* 7, no. 28 (Winter 1977–78): 27; "Twenty-Fifth Anniversary Album," liner notes; *Herald Tribune*, December 1, 1938, Dubinsky Collection, Box 79, File 8; clipping, *Philadelphia Record*, Dubinsky Collection, Box 80, File 2; Gary Smith, "The International Ladies Garment Workers' Union's Labor Stage, A Propagandistic Venture" (PhD diss., Kent State University, 1975), pp. 108–9.

42. Harold Rome, "Sing Me a Song with Social Significance" (New York: Mills Music, Inc., 1937); and *Pins and Needles: Musical Program* (New York: Florence Music Company, Inc., 1968); "The Twenty-Fifth Anniversary Album."

Goldman, "When Social Significance," contains song lyrics and photographs of the show that are not available in other sources.

43. *Vogue*, February 1, 1938, pp. 162–63, Dubinsky Collection, Box 79, File 8. *Pins & Needles: 25th Anniversary Edition of the Hit Musical Revue* (Columbia, 1962).

44. Macy's instituted intelligence tests in 1925, adding psychological tests in 1927. Leach, *Land of Desire*, p. 333. It was the first store to do so.

45. Newspaper clippings, BSAU *Ledger*, Dubinsky Collection, Box 79, File 8.

46. Kansas City *Journal-Post*, September 30, 1938, Dubinsky Collection, Box 80, File 1.

47. *New York Times*, March 13, 1938, Dubinsky Collection, Box 79, File 8; *New Yorker*, January 8, 1938, p. 21, Dubinsky Collection, Box 79, File 8.

48. *Philadelphia Record*, n.d., Dubinsky Collection, Box 80, File 2; *Cleveland Press*, November 15, 1938, Dubinsky Collection, Box 80, File 1; Chicago newspaper clipping, Dubinsky Collection, Box 80, File 1; ibid; *Philadelphia Record*, Dubinsky Collection, Box 80, File 2.

49. *Manchester Guardian*, February 10, 1939, Dubinsky Collection, Box 80, File 1.

50. *Minneapolis Star*, October 7, 1938, Dubinsky Collection, Box 80, File 2.

51. *Kansas City Journal-Post*, September 30, 1938, Dubinsky Collection, Box 80, File 1.

52. *Mirror*, February 2, 1938, Dubinsky Collection, Box 79, File 8.

53. *Cleveland Press*, November 15, 1938, Dubinsky Collection, Box 80, File 1.

54. *New York Post*, September 7, 1938, Dubinsky Collection, Box 79, File 8.

55. *Philadelphia Record*, n.d., Dubinsky Collection, Box 80, File 2.

56. *Chicago Defender*, November 5, 1938, Dubinsky Collection, Box 80, File 4; Harry Goldman, " 'Pins and Needles': An Oral History" (PhD diss., New York University, 1977), pp. 191–99.

57. San Francisco newspaper clipping, n.d., Dubinsky Collection, Box 80, File 4.

58. *Mirror*, February 2, 1938, Dubinsky Collection, Box 79, File 8. *Nu* is a Yiddish word of multiple meanings, including "So-o" and "Well, then." Leo Rosten, *The Joys of Yiddish* (New York: McGraw-Hill, 1968), pp. 267–69; Uriel Weinreich, *Modern English-Yiddish Yiddish-English Dictionary* (New York: McGraw-Hill, 1968), p. 262.

59. In addition to the events I describe here, Pesotta organized an elaborate style-show float for the 1940 Labor Day parade. The float was also the only one that carried political banners. Its combination of forthright statements, model of a garment factory, and models depicting the evolution of fashion and "simple and glamorous modern attire" brought the ILGWU more press attention than other unions participating in the parade. Pesotta also included children's fashion so that union members who would otherwise be tempted to take the family on vacation over the holiday weekend would instead proudly watch their "offspring ride in a parade." Rose Pesotta, *Bread Upon the Waters* (New York: Dodd,

Mead and Co., 1944; reprint, Ithaca, NY: Cornell University Press, 1987), p. 359; *Los Angeles Times*, September 3, 1940. For more on how organized labor celebrated Labor Day in the 1930s and 1940s, see Steven J. Ross and Michael Kazin, "America's Labor Day: The Dilemma of a Workers' Celebration," *Journal of American History* 78 (March 1992): 1294–1323. In the fall of 1941, the State Federation of Labor convention-arrangements committee asked Pesotta to display Los Angeles–produced garments by staging a style show at a dance. Pesotta notes in *Bread Upon the Waters*, p. 360, that "the style show went off with flying colors. The delegates and guests made it clear that we would have their whole-hearted support in any conflict with the employers."

60. Pesotta's first experience in Los Angeles was in 1933, when she worked briefly in a dress shop and was fired "for union activities." After losing her job and telling her employer she would return some day "to help organize Los Angeles," she hitchhiked to New York. "Part of Address Delivered by Rose Pesotta at a Testimonial Dinner Tendered Her by Locals 266 7 384," February 27, 1942, Dubinsky Collection, Box 114, File 1F. Elaine Leeder, *The Gentle General: Rose Pesotta, Anarchist and Labor Organizer* (Albany: State University of New York Press, 1993), pp. 53–103; Pesotta, *Bread Upon the Waters*. See chapters 2 and 30 on Pesotta's activities in Los Angeles, as well as Durón, "Mexican Women and Labor Conflict." In 1940, Pesotta proposed to buy radio time during the day to gain support for the union among "housewives, mothers, etc., who buy garments." She particularly hoped to appeal to "women in this city who belong to various women's clubs and auxiliaries, and may be of help in the event we decide to strike." Dubinsky did not see the value of Pesotta's proposal, because he saw it as "appealing to a limited number of women" and "housewives [who] will be of very little help in your organization drive." However, he was willing to let her have a month's trial. Although one cannot easily gauge the effect of this radio campaign, when undergarment and sportswear workers did strike in July 1941, a number of community leaders and ministers supported the union and even joined picket lines. Rose Pesotta to David Dubinsky, September 4, 1940, and David Dubinsky to Rose Pesotta, September 14, 1940, Dubinsky Collection, Box 60, File 4C. See also Douglas Monroy, *Rebirth: Mexican Los Angeles from the Great Migration to the Great Depression* (Berkeley: University of California Press, 1999), pp. 122–23, 234–41; Irene Ledesma, "Texas Newspapers and Chicana Workers' Activism, 1919–1974," *Western Historical Quarterly* 26 (Autumn 1995): 309–31; Jill Fields, "La Costura: A Social History of Mexicanas in the Los Angeles Garment Industry, 1930–1950," unpublished paper, 1992.

61. Leeder, *Gentle General*, pp. 65–86; Laslett and Tyler, *ILGWU in Los Angeles*, p. 119; Orleck, *Common Sense*, pp. 79, 191.

62. Riley and Berggren, "Apparel Manufacturing in California," pp. 8–10; Pesotta, *Bread Upon the Waters*, p. 333; Charles Eckert, "The Carole Lombard in Macy's Window," in *Fabrications: Costume and the Female Body*, ed. Jane Gaines and Charlotte Herzog (New York: Routledge, 1990), pp. 100–121.

63. Laslett and Tyler, *ILGWU in Los Angeles*, p. 47; Pesotta, *Bread Upon the Waters*, pp. 332–33.

64. Pesotta, *Bread Upon the Waters*, pp. 333–34; Leeder, *Gentle General*, p. 87. See also Ross and Kazin, "America's Labor Day."

65. Pesotta, *Bread Upon the Waters*, p. 40. See also ILGWU Photograph Collection, Box 33, Files 1, 8, 9, 11, and 13; Box 34, Files 4 and 11; Box 37, File 18, Kheel Center. "American Lady Corset workers on strike," ILGWU Photograph Collection, Box 37, File 12. For additional evidence of women's use of fashionable clothing on the picket line, see Jacquelyn Dowd Hall, "Disorderly Women: Gender and Labor Militancy in the Appalachian South," in *Unequal Sisters: A Multi-Cultural Reader in U.S. Women's History*, ed. Ellen DuBois and Vicki Ruiz (New York: Routledge, 1990), pp. 298–321.

66. *Los Angeles Citizen*, February 28 and March 7, 1941; Pesotta, *Bread Upon the Waters*, p. 360.

67. *Los Angeles Citizen*, March 7, 1941.

68. Ibid.

69. Quoted in the *Los Angeles Citizen*, March 21, 1941.

70. Ibid., March 7 and May 23, 1941.

71. Pesotta, *Bread Upon the Waters*, pp. 364, 367; Leeder, *Gentle General*, pp. 87–89; Laslett and Tyler, *ILGWU in Los Angeles*, pp. 48–49, 137. For evidence of Levy's ongoing conflicts with union staff, see the following items in the Dubinsky Collection: Rebecca Holland (Local 266 Business Agent) to David Dubinsky, May 21, 1942, Box 98, File 1; Louis Levy to David Dubinsky, June 11, 1942, Box 98, File 1; memo on telephone call from Louis Taback, Los Angeles garment manufacturer, regarding how dispute between Holland and Levy is hampering negotiations, July 16, 1942, Box 98, File 1; George Wishnak to David Dubinsky, July 11 and 17, 1942, Box 98, File 1; Margaret Corwin (Local 266 member) to David Dubinsky, July 29, 1942, Box 98, File 1; J. L. Goldberg (Local 266 Business Agent) to David Dubinsky, August 6, 1942, Box 98, File 1; Margie Lewis (Local 266 Vice-President), Billie Duff (Local 266 Treasurer), and Lillian Lauchlan (Local 266 member) to David Dubinsky, August 11, 1942, Box 97, File 10; David Dubinsky to Louis Levy, August 14 and August 26, 1942, Box 97, File 10; Louis Levy to David Dubinsky, August 28, 1942, Box 97, File 10; Margie Lewis to David Dubinsky, September 12, 1942, Box 97, File 10; David Dubinsky to Margie Lewis, September 17, 1942, Box 97, File 10; Memo in regard to dispute between Luther Eggertsen, Local 266 manager, and Louis Levy, April 28, 1945–August 30, 1946, Box 97, File 9B; transcript of telephone conversation between David Dubinsky and Joseph Springer and Fannie Borax of the Los Angeles Dress Joint Board, March 25, 1948, Box 319, File 17B; David Dubinsky to Louis Levy, October 6, 1950, Local 62, Box 2, File 1. Levy resigned from the General Executive Board (GEB) in 1947, and Dubinsky asked him also to relinquish the position of Pacific Coast director in 1950. Levy was expected to do so upon his resignation from the GEB but announced publicly at the national convention that he intended to retain the post. Though surprised, Dubinsky allowed him to continue as Pacific Coast director until 1950.

72. Laslett and Tyler, *ILGWU in Los Angeles*, p. 141; Leeder, *Gentle General*, pp. 90–97. In the Dubinsky Collection, Grace Blancett (Local 384 member) to

David Dubinsky, February 26, 1942, Box 114, File 1F; Freda Rosas (Local 384 Lingerie Department chairlady) to David Dubinsky, March 2, 1942, Box 114, File 1F; Freda Rosas to David Dubinsky, March 9, 1942, Box 114, File 1E; Freda Rosas and members of the Lingerie Department to David Dubinsky, June 12, 1942, Box 114, File 1D; "Statement by Rose Pesotta," 25th Convention, ILGWU, June 1944, Box 134, File 2.

73. Leeder, *Gentle General,* pp. 93–95; report from Local 384 officers, members, and business agent to General Executive Board, August 18, 1947; Dubinsky Collection, Box 370, File 2B. This fifty-five-page report chronicles in great detail the chartering, victories, conflicts, and decline of the local. The Lingerie Department at Mode O'Day was the last to remain in the union.

74. Pesotta, *Bread Upon the Waters,* p. 334.

75. For more on the problems faced by women activists in the ILGWU, see Alice Kessler Harris, "Organizing the Unorganizable: Three Jewish Women and Their Union," *Labor History* 7 (Winter 1976): 5–23. The concept of "to-be-looked-at-ness" was developed by Laura Mulvey in "Visual Pleasure and Narrative Cinema," *Screen* 16 (Autumn 1975), reprinted in Bill Nichols, ed., *Movies and Methods,* vol. 2 (Berkeley: University of California Press, 1985).

76. Tyler, *Look for the Union Label,* pp. 291–92; Pamela Ulrich, " 'Look for the Label'—The International Ladies Garment Workers' Union Label Campaign," *Clothing and Textile Research Journal* 13 (1995): 50. For more on the ongoing effort to adopt a union label, see "Report of the General Executive Board Quarterly meeting," February 1942, p. 3, ILGWU Collection, Southern California Research Library.

77. Tyler, *Look for the Union Label,* p. 293; Ulrich, " 'Look for the Label,' " pp. 50–51.

78. Ledesma, "Texas Newspapers"; Vicki Ruiz, "Tex-Son Strike, 1959–1962," in *Latinas in the United States: A Historical Encyclopedia,* ed. Vicki Ruiz and Virginia Sanchez Korrol (Bloomington: Indiana University Press, 2006).

79. Ulrich, " 'Look for the Label,' " p. 49.

80. Ibid., p. 51.

81. Ibid. The fashion booklets are in Joint Board Collection, Box 5, Files 28 and 29, Kheel Center. Amy Fine Collins, "The Lady, the List, the Legacy," *Vanity Fair,* April 2004.

82. *How to Be Well-Dressed,* pp. 3–7; *Your Trousseau and How to Plan It,* p. 2; *College Wardrobe: A Guide to the Right Clothes for Women's Colleges, Coed Schools, Big Universities,* p. 3; *Your Dream Wardrobe,* pp. 10–11.

83. *Your Dream Wardrobe,* p. 1.

84. *How to Be Well-Dressed,* pp. 1–2; *Your Dream Wardrobe,* p. 2. Cohen, *A Consumer's Republic,* part 1.

85. The fashion films that the ILGWU produced for its union-label campaign are part of the ILGWU Collection at the Kheel Center.

86. Ulrich, " 'Look for the Label,' " pp. 54, 52.

87. *Los Angeles Times,* December 24, 1996.

CHAPTER 7. RETURN OF THE REPRESSED (WAIST),
1947–1952

Epigraph: Simone de Beauvoir, *The Second Sex* (New York: Knopf, 1953), p. 379 (italics original).

1. Richard Martin and Harold Koda, *Christian Dior*, catalog for the 1996 Costume Institute Dior exhibition (New York: Metropolitan Museum of Art, 1996), pp. 10–14; Françoise Giroud, *Dior* (New York: Rizzoli, 1987), pp. 9–15; Elizabeth Ewing, *Dress and Undress: A History of Women's Underwear* (New York: Drama Book Specialists, 1978), ch. 15. Lou Taylor, "Paris Couture, 1940–1944," in *Chic Thrills: A Fashion Reader*, ed. Juliet Ash and Elizabeth Wilson (Berkeley: University of California Press, 1993), pp. 127–44; Ewing, *Dress and Undress*, pp. 153–56. See also Christopher Sladen, *The Conscription of Fashion: Utility Cloth, Clothing and Footwear, 1941–1952* (Aldershot, UK: Scolar Press, 1995). During World War II, corsetry also became a matter for U.S. federal consideration when the U.S. Army determined what undergarments to include in enlisted women's uniforms. *Women's Wear Daily*, June 17, 1942; *The American Magazine*, November 1942, n.p.; *Time*, May 25, 1942, p. 72; *New York Times*, July 19, 1942 (Hagley Museum and Library).

2. Giroud, *Dior*, pp. 9, 11, 15, 304.

3. Taylor, "Paris Couture." See also Irene Guenther, *Nazi Chic?: Fashioning Women in the Third Reich* (London: Berg, 2004).

4. Ibid.

5. Ibid.; Ewing, *Dress and Undress*, pp. 153–56. *Time*, March 4, 1957, pp. 30–34; Anna Rothe and Constance Ellis, *Current Biography: Who's News and Why, 1948* (New York: H. W. Wilson, 1949), pp. 147–48. A debate on skirt length aired on the CBS network television program *We the People* and included members of the "Little Below the Knee" Club of Dallas. *Women's Wear Daily*, August 25, 1947.

6. Ewing, *Dress and Undress*, p. 156; *Women's Wear Daily*, September 23, 1947; Angela Partington, "Popular Fashion and Working-Class Affluence," in *Chic Thrills*, p. 154; Sladen, *Conscription of Fashion*, pp. 77–79, 89, 91.

7. *California Apparel News*, September 18, 1959; ILGWU Archives, David Dubinsky Collection, Box 97, File 9B, Kheel Center. For examples of Adrian's designs, search the LACMA website: http://collectionsonline.lacma.org.

8. *California Apparel News*, August 29, 1947.

9. *Women's Wear Daily*, September 3, September 4, and September 23, 1947; *Current Biography 1948*, p. 148; Giroud, *Dior*, p. 10; "Resistance," *Time*, September 1, 1947, p. 14; "Counter-Revolution," *Time*, September 15, 1947, pp. 87ff.

10. *Women's Wear Daily*, September 2, 1947.

11. *California Apparel News*, November 7, 1947.

12. For examples of Adrian's and Dior's designs, see 60.7ab, 1979.432.7ab, x62.6.1ab, 1981.264.11ab, and 1974.177.2 (Adrian), and 57.55ab, 1974.312.1abc, 53.40.16d (Dior) at the Costume Institute (Met). See also Martin and Koda,

Christian Dior; and *Adrian: The Couture Years, 1942–52,* the brochure for the LACMA Adrian exhibition, August 1995 to January 1996.

13. Betty Friedan, "The Gal Who Defied Dior," *Town Journal,* October 1955, pp. 32–33, 97–98. For an example of McCardell's Monastic design, search http://collectionsonline.lacma.org.

14. Claire McCardell, *What Shall I Wear?: The What, Where, When and How Much of Fashion* (New York: Simon and Schuster, 1956), pp. vii–xii.

15. Ibid., p. xii.

16. *Harper's Bazaar,* October 1947, p. 100, and August 1948, n.p.

17. United Press newspaper clipping, dateline San Francisco, September 17, 1949, Dior file, Costume Institute (Met).

18. Partington, "Popular Fashion," pp. 145–61.

19. ILGWU Archives, Local 62 Collection, Box 6, File 4, and Box 9, File 17, Kheel Center, contains a number of documents that refer to the importance of the slips and petticoats revival for union members' employment.

20. Stanley Aronowitz, *False Promises: The Shaping of American Working-Class Consciousness* (New York: McGraw-Hill, 1973), pp. 253, 259, 333, 341, 349, 364.

21. *The Future out of the Past* (Bridgeport, CT: Warner Brothers Co., 1964), p. 47.

22. *The Merry Widow* clippings file, Herrick Library. See chapter 3, "Brassieres," for more on Lana Turner.

23. *The Merry Widow,* directed by Curtis Bernhardt (MGM, 1952).

24. Playtex has issued a one-page history of the company. "Playtex Apparel, Inc." (Stamford, CT: Playtex Apparel, Inc., 1993). See also *Women's Wear Daily,* August 1947.

25. *Women's Wear Daily,* July 17, 1947, p. 3; "Slackees," 966.12.13 (ROM).

EPILOGUE

1. Underwear as outerwear long predates the 1980s. In the fifteenth century, when elite women at court began to wear linen rather than wool chemises, they slit their skirts to reveal the linen underneath. Elizabeth Sage, *A Study of Costume from the Days of the Egyptians to Modern Times* (New York: Charles Scribner's Sons, 1926), p. 78. The visible corset covers and drawers worn in the nineteenth century had a similar intent, as did the slips women wore underneath sheer and loosely woven outer dresses in the early twentieth century. See the costume collections of ROM and the Met for examples of such dresses and slips. The trend continued in the 1930s, when, as with the recent popularity of the "slip dress," many bias dresses were indistinguishable from slips. Moreover, the bouffant petticoats worn in the neo-Victorian fashion of the 1950s mimicked their progenitors in establishing their presence both visually and aurally.

2. Feminist artists have also imaged gender reversals to reveal the absurdity of the historic positioning of women as objects of the male painter's gaze. See, for example, Linda Nochlin, *Buy My Bananas* (1972), in Norma Broude and

Mary Garrard, *The Power of Feminist Art: The American Movement of the 1970s, History and Impact* (New York: Harry Abrams, 1994), p. 136; "Front Range" (1884), photograph by Meridel Rubenstein, in Broude and Garrard, *Power of Feminist Art;* Faith Ringgold, *#3 The Picnic at Giverny* (1991), in Amelia Jones, ed., *Sexual Politics: Judy Chicago's Dinner Party in Feminist Art History* (Berkeley: University of California Press, 1996), p. 231. These works also make clear the vulnerability of female bodies when viewed as culturally authorized nudes.

3. For reproductions of many of the images I cite here, see Broude and Garrard, *Power of Feminist Art;* and Jones, *Sexual Politics.* Their excellent essays inform my brief summary of the themes of feminist art. See, for example, Judy Chicago et al., *Birth Project,* 1980–1985; Hannah Wilke, *Intra-Venus,* 1992–93; Sue Williams, *A Funny Thing Happened,* 1992.

4. See, for example, the collaborative installations of *Womanhouse* (1972); Gaza Bowen, *Shoes for the Little Woman* (1986); and Annette Messager, *Histoires des Robes* (1990).

5. Broude and Garrard, *Power of Feminist Art,* p. 45.

6. See, for example, Harmony Hammond, *Floorpiece VI* (1973); Faith Ringgold, *Mrs. Jones and Family* (1973, PFA 143) and *Woman Painting the Bay Bridge* (1988). Miriam Schapiro incorporated fabric and images of clothing in her work during and after the *Womanhouse* project. She coined the term *femmage* to describe her method of collage and assemblage that self-consciously incorporates materials culturally defined as feminine. See Thalia Gouma-Peterson, *Miriam Schapiro* (New York: Harry Abrams, 1999), especially ch. 4. Ch. 1, footnote 14, defines *femmage* as "woman-centered fabric collage" (p. 146).

7. Both these works also qualify as soft sculpture, an art form that many women artists embraced and that developed in tandem with the feminist art movement. Legitimized by established pop artist Claes Oldenberg's soft sculptures of artifacts of everyday life, such as *Ice Cream Cone* (1962), *Soft Typewriter* (1963), and *Soft Toilet* (1966), women weavers and artists who worked with fiber and textiles began to find venues for exhibition in craft museums and fiber-themed exhibits in New York City, Los Angeles, and other major cultural centers between 1969 and 1973. Dona Z. Meilach, *Soft Sculpture and Other Soft Art Forms* (New York: Crown Publishers, 1974), ch. 1. Meilach's book does not draw connections between the emergence of soft sculpture and the rising feminist movement, though the artists in her book are almost all women. Mimi Smith is a soft-sculpture artist who began working from a feminist perspective as early as the mid-1960s. See the catalog introduction by Judith Tannenbaum, *Steel Wool Politics* (Philadelphia: Institute of Contemporary Art, University of Pennsylvania, 1994). One example of a feminist soft-sculpture work that depicts intimate apparel is Nancy Youdelman's *Stuffed Sculpture* (1972), a pink torso with neck, arm, and leg stumps dressed in white bra and underpants.

8. Griselda Pollock, "Feminism and Modernism," in *Framing Feminism: Art and the Women's Movement 1970–85,* ed. Rozsika Parker and Griselda Pollock (London: Pandora, 1987), p. 94.

9. For more on Erika Rothenberg, see Paul Von Blum, *Other Visions, Other Voices: Women Political Artists in Greater Los Angeles* (Lanham, MD: University Press of America, 1994), ch. 14.

10. Maidenform's first Dream Campaign lasted from 1949 to 1969. In 1980, the company began a new series of ads that drew on the same concept. Using the slogan "The Maidenform woman: you never know where she'll turn up," these ads often showed a woman in public dressed only in a fur coat and undergarments, a typical pornographic scenario. Similar ads that depicted incompletely dressed female doctors, lawyers, or stockbrokers drew the most criticism. The ads received a Zap Award from Women Against Pornography and the Badvertising Award from *Adweek East,* a trade publication. *Business Week,* November 4, 1991, p. 90; *New York Times,* March 30, 1983. See also Ellen Goodman's commentary, *Boston Globe,* December 12, 1985.

11. Lucy Lippard, *The Pink Glass Swan: Selected Essays on Feminist Art* (New York: New Press, 1995), p. 19. Edward Kienholz also used steel wool in a number of works in the 1960s, including *Bunny, Bunny, You're So Funny* (1962), a sculpture of a partial female body, from waist to thighs, encased in a metal garter belt and chain-link fishnet hose and with steel-wool pubic hair. From the side, the viewer can see a baby suspended inside the hollow piece, and the baby can be turned by a small handle on top of the torso. Although the sculpture notes the harshness and danger of erotic undergarments, the steel-wool pubic hair implies that the deception also originates within the female body itself.

12. *Heresies #6* 2, no. 2 (1978): 36. Smith wrote the commentary when she completed the piece in 1966.

13. Ironically, a March 1996 *Glamour* ad for Lovable brassieres used an image of a bra made of hanger wire, barbs, razor blades, and screws to assert that its new design was far more comfortable than the average underwire design. The ad is not unlike the early twentieth-century corset ads that asserted that corsets were not inherently uncomfortable but that women were not buying the proper model for their figure. This ad fits into the genre of corporate feminism begun much earlier by Virginia Slims and embraced by Maidenform in the 1990s, in which companies sought to project a "pro-woman" corporate image in the wake of criticism. I heard Willy Scholten speak about her work at the Western Region Costume Society of America program, "Costume as Art as Costume," March 1, 1997, San Jose, California.

14. *Ob/De+Con(Struction),* Valie Export exhibition catalog, Santa Monica Museum of Art (March 9–April 28, 2001), p. 16.

15. Materials provided by artist, July 25, 2000. Another piece that presents underwear as text is a mixed-media work by Sharon Gilbert, *Etymography,* published in *Heresies* 18 (1985): 51. Gilbert constructed a girdle-shaped garment and imprinted words on it that commonly identify women and feminize particular concepts, including *daughter, grandmother, she, feminist, womanize, mama, motherland, motherlode, spinster, coquette, lady,* and *women's rights.*

16. Lynn Cothern, "Inside Miriam Schaer's Girdle Books," *Fiberarts*

(March/April 2001): 50–53. To view examples of Schaer's work, go to www.colophon.com/gallery/mschaer. Schaer's work speaks to intimate apparel and the body as vessels of meaning, and presents the dual significations of containing as holding and restricting. Marcia Cooper's 1997 *Specimens* also addresses this theme. Her work consists of ten white net bikini underpants sewn by the artist and filled with sets of white objects, such as cotton balls, string, pom-poms, plastic golf balls, and feathers.

17. Leslie Shapiro, *Bra vs. Bra* (1989), n.p.

18. The BraBall was completed in November 2003 with 18,085 bras. Duffy's website, www.braball.com, includes photographs, a revised version of the original e-mail, and links to press coverage of her story. The site also excerpts letters that accompanied donations. Many letter writers expressed relief at getting rid of bras that did not fit well and caused discomfort. Duffy's intimate apparel art includes a 1995 sculpture, *Mammolith,* a nine-foot-high white bustier the artist built to counter the phallic imagery of the Washington Monument.

Index

ideology and, 103; marketing innovations and, 87; mass production of, 83–85; merchandizing of, 90–92; 1930s design innovations in, 95–99; origin of, 81–82; padding in, 103–4, 104, 106, 189, 214; "pointed lines" of, 95–96; standardized cup sizing of, 99–104; as term, 82; underwires in, 98; uplift trend in, 92–95, 103, 104–5, 106

Bra vs. Bra (Sharpe), 17, 285–86

breasts: changes in fashionable shape of, 80–81, 92–95, 96–99, 104–8; fetishism of, 108–12; surgical alteration of, 80, 94, 105

Breward, Christopher, 299n11

bridal trousseau, 33–37

Bridgeport (CT), 223–24. *See also* Warner Brothers Corset Company

Broadway shows: advertising images and, 208; all-black revues, 128–29; *Pins and Needles*, 16, 231–39

Brody, Sherry, 17, 275

Bronfen, Elizabeth, 139, 142–43

Broude, Norma, 274

Brown, Anne, 238

Burckhardt, Charlotte Louise, 148

Burke, Billie, 44, 45

Burnham, Linda, 275

Burroughs, Edgar Rice, 130

Butler, Judith, 9

Cadolle, Herminie, 81

cage crinoline, 27–28

"California couture," 260

California Institute of the Arts, Feminist Art Program, 275

Calloway, Cab, 166

camisoles, 33, 83, 89

Camp, S. H., 174

Campion, John, 107

Camp Transparent Woman, 174, 198, 338n1

Candy Bra (Smith), 281

Casey, Josephine, 223

Cassatt, Mary, 145

Catherine de Medici, 295n2

CGMA. *See* Cotton Garment Manufacturers Association

"Chain Store Daisy" (song), 233, 234, 238

Chambre Syndicale de la Couture Parisienne, 258

Chanel, Coco, 114, 158, 259, 334n98

Charma Brassiere Company, 83

Charmion (striptease artist), 159

Chase, Edna Woolman, 259

Chevalier, Maurice, 267–68

Chicago (IL), Local 59 in, 221–22

Chicago, Judy, 274

Cisneros, Sandra, 115

Civil War, 144–45

Clark, Josiah, 120

class-based constructions: of beauty, 16; birth control movement and, 39; ILGWU fashion strategy and, 255; of sexual identity, 22

closed-crotch drawers: Bloomer Costume and, 25–27; cycling bloomers and, 30–31; girls and, 22; knickers and, 32–33; sets of undergarments and, 34, 36; *Topper* (film) and, 43–45, 44; transition to, 19–22, 21

Cohen, Lizabeth, 218, 251

Cohn, Fannia, 221, 240

college girls: corsets and, 71, 74; New Look and, 264

Collier's (magazine), 109, 115

Collier's Cyclopedia, 144

colored underwear: drawers, 28, 30, 37; dye stability and, 115–16; in early twentieth century, 154–55, 156. *See also* black lingerie

combination undergarments: in 1920s, 41–42, 91–92. *See also* "all-in-one" garments

commerce in fashion, emergence of, 9–11, 219

Coney Island, 37

Consumer's League, 218

contractor system, 224, 225

"coon singers," 129–30

Douglas, Melvyn, 244

drawers, 18–46; age distinctions and, 23–24; combination undergarments and, 40–42; in early twentieth century, 36–45; 1850s dress reform and, 25–30; gendered meanings of, 14, 18–23; in late nineteenth century, 30–36; length of, 24, 25; open- vs. closed-crotch, 14, 18–23, *20, 21,* 32, 33–36, *35,* 37–39, *38,* 41–42, *44;* as term, 14, 37; undergarment sets and, 33–36; women's first use of, 295n2; women's rights movement and, 38–40

Drebing, Charlotte, 68–69

dress codes, 9, 53, 54–55

dress reform: in 1850s, 25–30; in 1890s, 30–31

Dubinsky, David, 226, 228, 239, 246, 353n60

Dubois, W. E. B., 125

Duff Gordon, Lady, 81, 83, 158

Duffy, Emily, 286–88, 360n18

Durham Fuller, Mabel, 168–70, *170*

dyes, 303n35; for black clothing, 144; for colored underwear, 115–16

Eaton's catalog, 37, *38,* 305n45

Ebony (magazine), *96,* 186, *187, 192,* 207, 214, 216

Edward VII (king of England), 11, 31–32

Eisenberg, Emanuel, 232

Elastowear Manufacturing Company, 59

Ellis, Havelock, 49

Elvissa (Davidson), 277

Enstad, Nan, 218

"envelope chemises," 41

eroticism. *See* black lingerie; eroticism of undergarments; glamour; homoeroticism and advertising; invisible woman in advertising; pornography; sex and death, relationship between

eroticism of undergarments, 11–12; advertising images and, 16, 181, 183; bridal trousseaux and, 34–36; open-crotch drawers and, 45–46. *See also* modesty and eroticism

Evans, Sara, 315n22

Ewen, Stuart, 202

Ewing, Elizabeth, 5, 82, 89

exhibitionism in advertising, 207–9

Export, Valie, 282

fashion changes, 15, 56, 76; garment workers and, 230–31; industry intervention in, 75–78; legal statutes and, 54; mourning dress and, 144–45

fashion-industrial complex, 10, 256, 271, 277

fashion industry vs. garment industry, 12–13, 217–18, 225–26, 235–39

The Fashion Picture (ILGWU film), 252–54

fashion press, 10, 55, 225–26. *See also* trade journals; women's magazines

fashion silhouette: acceptance of body constriction and, 271; early-twentieth-century, 37, 50, *51,* 67, *70,* 75, 85; late-nineteenth-century, 30; mid-nineteenth-century, 25–28; mid-twentieth-century, 75–76, 256, *257,* 262, *263;* 1930s "womanly" figure and, 75, 77, 93, 95; role of brassiere in, 81

female body, display of: advertising representations and, 175 (*see also* invisible woman in advertising); black women and, 117; ILGWU fashion strategy and, 247–48; mirrors and, *157,* 201–4, *203;* as partitioned, 199, *201, 202,* 216; servants and, 124–26; "to-be-looked-at-ness" and, 344n57

The Female Body (Hamoy), 282

female impersonators, 126–27

female spectatorship, 16, 209–11

femininity: death and, 141–43; straight silhouette and, 89–90; whiteness and, 113–14, 116–17, 120, 122–23

Gibson, Charles Dana, 150, *151*, 153
Gibson Girls, 49
Gilda (film), 149
Gilfoyle, Timothy, 125
Gilman, Sander, 120
Gimbel's Department Store (New York City), 74
Girdle (Smith), 281
girdle books (Schaer), 282–85
"girdle pants," 195
girdles: elastic, 74; feminist art and, 281, 282–85; transition from corsets to, 15, 59, 60, 74, 75, 76
glamour: advertising and, 188–93, *192*; large breasts and, 109–12; magical power of, 6–7; *Pins and Needles* revue and, 235–39; as social mechanism, 16–17; union activities and, 235–39, 245
Glamour (magazine), 6–7, 359n13
G. M. Poix., Inc. (company), 103
Goddard, Paulette, 166
Godey's Lady's Book (magazine), 27
Goffman, Erving, 210
The Good Corsetiere (Gordon), 70
Good Housekeeping (magazine), 55, 65, 67–68
Gordon, Jean, 70
Gossard Corsets (company), 99, 183–84, 193, 198; figure types and, 66; sales strategies and, 312n44, 340n19
Gramsci, Antonio, 8
Gray, Gilda, 129

Hall, Alexander, 166
Hall, Jacquelyn Dowd, 132
Halttunen, Karen, 133–34
Hamoy, Carol, 282, *283*
Harlow, Jean, 80, 161–62, *163*, 335n105
Harper's Bazar (magazine; later *Harper's Bazaar*): cycling bloomers and, 30–31; fashionable black and, 145; mourning requirements and, 134, 144; New Look and, 256, 264
Harper's Weekly (magazine), 181

Harrison, Margaret, 275–76
Harvey, John, 299n11
Hawthorne, Nathaniel, 124
Hayworth, Rita, 149–50
health concerns: advertising and, 184, 197; brassieres and, 89, 92–93, 94; corsetless trend in 1900s and, 50, 89; corsets and, 63, 64, 65, 76, 184; 1840s silhouette and, 25; wool undergarments and, 30, 41
Held, Anna, 129
Hell's Angels (film), 161–62
Hepburn, Audrey, 160
Heresies (journal), 276, 281
Herford, Oliver, 181, 183
He's Only a Bunny Boy but He's Quite Nice Really (Harrison), 275–76
high culture: advertising images and, 207–8; black women, eroticism, and, 120–21, 127; fashionable black and, 145–49, *147*; ILGWU label campaign and, 253–54. *See also* theater
Hill, J. Leubrie, 128
"hobble skirts," 37, 50
Hochman, Julius, 248, 250
Hollander, Anne, 146
Hollywood: brassiere manufacturers and, 99–101; fashion industry and, 240; New Look and, 17, 259–60
Hollywood Maxwell (company), 98, 101, 103
homoeroticism and advertising, 16, 210–11, *212*
hooks, bell, 159–60
hoop skirts (cage crinolines), 27–28
Hopper, Hedda, 110
"Hottentot apron," 118, 124–26
Hottentot Venus (Saartjie Baartman), 117–20, *119*, 122–24, 132, 173
Housekeeping (Schaer), 283, 284
Houssaye, Henri, 146
How Do You Compare? (Schaer), 283, 284–85
Hughes, Howard, 109, 161
H&W Company, 71, 83, 85

Text: 10/13 Aldus
Display: Franklin Gothic
Compositor: Binghamton Valley Composition, LLC
Printer and Binder: Maple-Vail Manufacturing Group